ON THE LINE

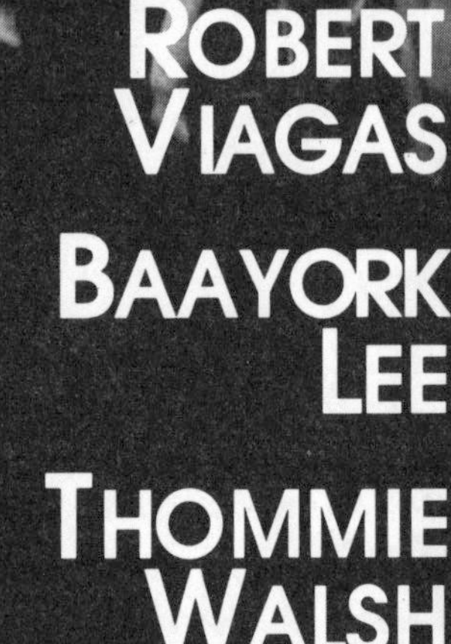

ROBERT VIAGAS

BAAYORK LEE

THOMMIE WALSH

with the entire original cast

ON THE LINE

THE CREATION OF *A CHORUS LINE*

William Morrow and Company, Inc.   New York

Title page photograph by Martha Swope

Recognizing the importance of preserving what has been written, it is the policy of William Morrow and Company, Inc., and its imprints and affiliates to have the books it publishes printed on acid-free paper, and we exert our best efforts to that end.

Library of Congress Cataloging-in-Publication Data

Viagas, Robert.
On the line : the creation of a Chorus Line / Robert Viagas,
Baayork Lee, Thommie Walsh.
p. cm.
ISBN 0-688-08429-X
1. Hamlisch, Marvin. Chorus Line. I. Lee, Baayork. II. Walsh, Thommie. III. Chorus Line. IV. Title.
ML410.H1745V5 1990
792.6'42—dc20 89-13493
CIP

Printed in the United States of America

First Edition

1 2 3 4 5 6 7 8 9 10

BOOK DESIGN BY JAYE ZIMET

There were many slips twixt cup and lip on this project. Without the following people, readers would not have this chance to sip:

Mothers, fathers, sisters, brothers, friends, lovers—those still at our sides and those passed away.

Our agent Mitch Douglas, our lawyer Chandler Warren, our financial adviser Edward Greenberg, our friends the Original Company . . . and Michael Bennett.
With thanks

—Baayork Lee and Thommie Walsh

For Catherine Ryan who is a daily inspiration; the cornucopias Anthony and Lillian Viagas; Mitch Douglas who godfathered this book; David Spencer who arranged the ticket; and Murray.

—Robert Viagas

AUTHORS' NOTE

Aside from critics, only the nineteen dancers whose stories form the primary action of *A Chorus Line* are quoted in this book. This is their memoir exclusively.

Tennessee Williams wrote that in memory everything seems to happen to music. That's particularly so for the nineteen original cast members, for whom the familiar music of rehearsal and the new music being written to accompany their life stories formed a daily matrix for their memories. Those who read this book while listening to the original cast recording will come closest to sharing that experience.

CONTENTS

THE ORIGINAL PRODUCTION OF *A CHORUS LINE*

Presented by the New York Shakespeare Festival in association with Plum Productions
Conceived, choreographed and directed by Michael Bennett
Book by Nicholas Dante and James Kirkwood
Music by Marvin Hamlisch
Lyrics by Edward Kleban
Co-choreographer Bob Avian

Members of "The Line"

Renee Baughman as Kristine DeLuca
Carole (Kelly) Bishop as Sheila Bryant
Pamela Blair as Valerie Clark
Wayne Cilento as Mike Costa
Clive Clerk (Wilson) as Larry
Kay Cole as Maggie Winslow
Ronald Dennis as Richie Walters
Patricia Garland as Judy Turner
Ron Kuhlman as Don Kerr
Nancy Lane as Bebe Benzenheimer
Baayork Lee as Connie Wong
Priscilla Lopez as Diana Morales
Robert LuPone as Zach
Cameron (Rick) Mason as Mark Tabori
Donna McKechnie as Cassie Ferguson
Don Percassi as Alan DeLuca
Michel Stuart as Gregory Gardner

Thomas J. (Thommie) Walsh as Robert Charles Joseph Henry Mills III
Sammy Williams as Paul San Marco

*Understudies**

Scott Allen as Roy
Chuck Cissel as Butch Burton
Donna Drake as Tricia
Brandt Edwards as Tom
Carolyn Kirsch as Lois
Carole Schweid as Barbara
Michael Serrecchia as Frank D'Leo
Crissy Wilzak as Vicki
*also appearing in the opening number

Settings by Robin Wagner
Costumes by Theoni V. Aldredge
Lighting by Tharon Musser
Orchestrations by Bill Byers, Hershy Kay, and Jonathan Tunick
Music coordinator Robert Thomas
Music direction and vocal arrangements by Don Pippin
Associate producer Bernard Gersten
Rehearsal pianist Fran Liebergall

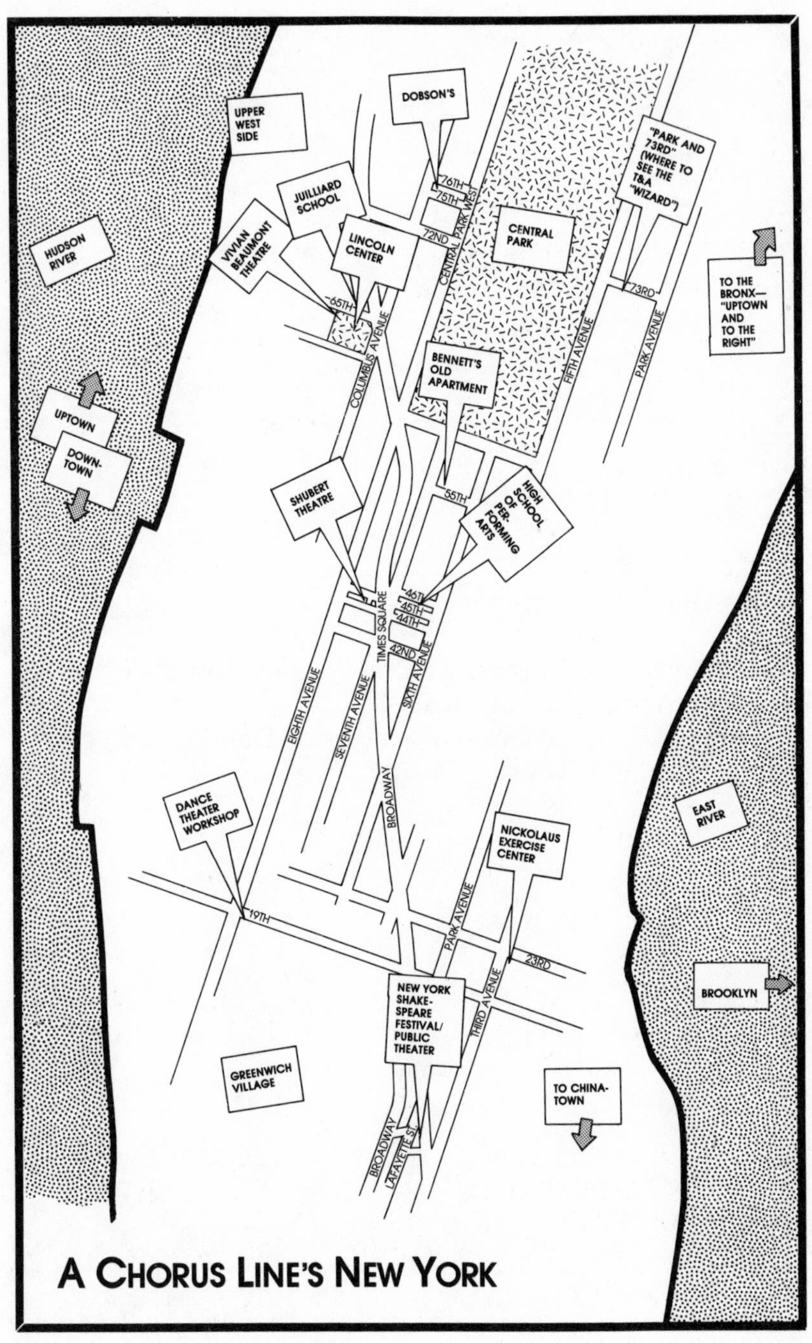

A CHORUS LINE'S NEW YORK

Perched in the balcony of Broadway's Shubert Theatre and surveying the stage, you'll see a white line painted from wing to wing. The edge of the stage is numbered, indicating dance positions.

The rest is black.

ON THE LINE

1.

REMEMBERING

If you glance at the logo of *A Chorus Line* you see a uniform line of faceless dancers.

But wait, no they're not.

Each one holds himself or herself a little differently. It's there if you look. The slim, strawberry-blond Trish Garland stands pony-ish and shy with one knocked knee. There's a very personal flair about Thommie Walsh's scarf, and a proud challenge in Ron Dennis's black chest. Statuesque Kelly Bishop stands with the sensuality of a fallen Miss America. Sammy Williams, the one with the moustache, seems to be asking for something. It's in the way he holds his head.

Before they speak, before they move, before they even appear on the stage, the dancers on that logo are telling who they are. They may be just another chorus line, but each is special.

Most reunions stir mixed feelings, but the ones taking place in apartments in Manhattan and Los Angeles among the original cast members of *A Chorus Line* had a special claim on ambivalence. They were getting together to try to piece together the story behind the making of their musical. Their memories became this book.

As of June 1989, *A Chorus Line* had been running for more than fourteen years, the longest run in Broadway history. It has played more than fifty-eight hundred performances, and grossed more than a quarter-billion dollars. It won the Pulitzer Prize and Drama Desk Award for best musical, and earned a total of nine Tony Awards.

None of those statistical riches begin to touch the spiritual payout to the more than five million people who have seen the show on Broadway, plus the millions more across the United States and in fourteen foreign countries who have seen one of the many touring companies or stock productions.

In telling the backstage story of a choreographer and his assistant who are auditioning seventeen dancers for eight roles in an unnamed Broadway musical, *A Chorus Line* "has a common thread for people," said Garland, who created the role of Judy. "Even though we're different in appearance, shapes, sizes, we all need and want the same things. *Chorus Line* allowed you to feel human lives, all different lives, in a situation where they all had the same need. Everybody can put themselves on the line. Everybody in life has to audition, no matter what it's for."

The musical's great strength is the way it gets inside the private and emotion-fraught world of professional dancers, and makes their lives universal.

"The core was a very personal expression," said Donna McKechnie, who originated "Cassie," "and the more personal your communication is, whether it's the written word or an actor's interpretation, the more clearly it will be communicated. Emotions understand emotions. That was the heart of *A Chorus Line:* It's a brilliantly constructed show, very theatrical and very precise. But it's also very personal. It's about anyone who every grew up."

Dancers are particularly good subjects for this treatment. Perhaps because dancers make their art with nothing but their bodies and souls—with no canvas, marble, strings, or reeds to serve as intermediary—they tend to be even more intensely directed inward to their spirits and outward to the audience than painters, sculptors, or musicians.

Priscilla Lopez, the show's "Morales," said, "People talk about how powerful the childhood stories are, but what registers with me is how it *looks*. You're in blackness, in a black hole standing on a very narrow white line talking into nothingness, to this anonymous voice. There's nothing to hold on to. How much more vulnerable can one be? The show hits the vulnerability in everyone."

Backstage musicals are perennially popular because they are an environment where passions ignite easily. The reasons for that are no secret: collaboration and pressure. Perhaps more than any other art form, theater depends on collaboration. The greatest choreographer in the world is nothing without a dancer. With collaboration comes inspiration, conflict, compromise, and synthesis—along with broken hearts and bruised egos. There's pain even at the birth of a success.

A Chorus Line was even more collaborative than most, owing to its unique genesis. Two dancers, Michon Peacock and Tony Stevens, had the idea for a project that would create work for some of New York City's top dancers. Choreographer Michael Bennett came aboard as the "muscle," and eventually attracted writers Nicholas Dante and James Kirkwood, composer Marvin Hamlisch, lyricist Ed Kleban, cochoreographer Bob Avian, and producer Joseph Papp of the New York Shakespeare Festival.

But the heart of the project was the dancers, the unbilled and almost completely unacknowledged collaborators in the writing of a Pulitzer Prize-winning drama. Their life stories are the basis of all songs and monologues. All dance steps were created for the way they moved, or created by them. From the first tape session in January 1974 until the morning of the first off-Broadway preview, April 16, 1975, the dancers worked with the writers to shape the hours of tapes into a workable stage show. *A Chorus Line* was forged in two workshops, one five weeks long in the autumn, the other fifteen weeks in late winter and early spring.

When it became apparent that the resulting show was a phenomenon, the original cast members began talking about making a permanent record of their collaboration. They wanted to tell their story in their own words. *A Chorus Line* shows a day in the creation of an unspecified musical. The *Chorus Line* dancers wanted to take that idea and expand on it, showing the months of hurly-burly it took to assemble and polish their show. They wanted to leave an oral history of what life was like backstage at the backstage musical.

Burgeoning careers postponed the project, but the spark was provided eight years later on September 29, 1983, by the massive celebration marking *A Chorus Line*'s 3,389th performance, surpassing *Grease* to become "Broadway's Longest Running Musical. Ever.," as it has been promoted by the New York Shakespeare Festival. Everyone who had ever appeared in the show professionally was invited to appear onstage at the Shubert Theatre in a special expanded version of the show. Among the approximately

350 dancers who appeared were the original cast members, some of whom had their first chance to see one another since the original run. Talk of the book was revived, and meeting dates set.

As they had in the beginning, the dancers were asked to talk on tape about their experiences. Out came a lot of happy memories, but also stories of rivalries, power plays, politics, anger over money and artistic differences, the press, and preferential treatment by one or another of the show's credited creators.

One thing that emerged intact was the dancers' feelings of cohesion, of having pulled together in a mighty endeavor. Rick Mason said, "When we were downtown there would be our bickering and our complaining and tempers would flare because we were in this vacuum for so long. But one day Trish Garland said to me one of the most beautiful things ever said about the company: 'We're like a family. We may bicker and fight in this company, but if anyone ever said anything about any of you, I'll fight to the nth degree to come to your defense.' We hated each other at times and we adored each other. It was so true, it was a very tight unit. What we went through bound us tight and no one could ever take that away."

A lot of myth grows up around a flop. Even more around a hit. Possibly because they are so appealing, such myths are almost impossible to uproot.

Thommie Walsh said, "I think this book will give the original people of *A Chorus Line* the last say—not even the last say, *their voice* of how they saw it unfold. I think we're all going to be totally different in the way we saw it. Because everybody went through different things. I saw everybody go through changes, divorces left and right, things with Michael, things with one another, things with friends. A lot of changing happened here."

Like any adventure, any journey, there are certain goals, but the sojourners never can be certain what they'll find along the way, whether they'll get to their destination, or whether they really wanted to go there at all. Each of the nineteen Originals started out looking for a job, and wound up meeting that fascinating stranger who turned out to be themselves. In making *On the Line* they hoped to meet that stranger again.

But there was more. A static of unresolved emotion needed to be organized, clarified, and amplified into a clear signal. Those who felt slighted wanted to stake out a larger piece of the property. By playing it all out one more time, they hoped to exorcise some of the scarier ghosts, clear out the cobwebs, and to share the actual experience with the audiences who had poured out so much love to them.

Baayork Lee said, "It's important they realize that those people onstage are portraying *real lives*—that most of the original people were speaking about themselves. Most people think they're just seeing a play, and don't get it. They just see pure entertainment, and of course there's nothing wrong with that. But we gave so much of ourselves that we are a part of that show, and that show is a part of us. I'd love for people to see that. I would love for people to say, 'Oh my God, that person was talking about their father. This stuff isn't made up.' So that's why I'm here today. I want to let people know through this book that those stories are true, that all those ingredients were put in by *all of us:* the choreography, the lyrics, costumes, everything. As for a title for this book—'Nineteen Rashomon.' "

Lee and the others said those things into the microphone of a tape recorder. They were comfortable with that method. It had worked once before.

2.

The First Taping Session (January 1974)

A lot of people think *A Chorus Line* is about "kids" trying to break into show business. That's misconception number one. *A Chorus Line* is about veterans of the limelight. Call them hoofers, call them gypsies—or just dancers, which they prefer. *A Chorus Line* is about Broadway dancers who have *been there,* and want more than anything to be there again and again, as long as they can. That is the way the musical that has won the Tony, Drama Critics Circle, Obie, and Drama Desk awards, and the Pulitzer Prize, was born.

A great number of people also think *A Chorus Line* is fiction. Misconception number two. Everything in the show is either adapted from or based on the details of someone's life story. In most cases, the details are taken directly from someone's life story.

Lastly, there is a general impression that *A Chorus Line* sprung fully formed from the forehead of director-choreographer Michael Bennett. Misconception number three. Though Donna McKechnie and Baayork Lee recall discussing the idea of a "dancers' musical" some years before *A Chorus Line,* the actual project was born in the minds of two dancers whose names rarely are brought up in connection with *A Chorus Line:* Tony Stevens and Michon Peacock, hardworking vets you might have seen tapping, strutting, and pirouetting in shows throughout the 1960s and early 1970s.

Their idea was not the result of divine inspiration. It was very practical. Stevens and Peacock wanted to drum up some work for themselves and for their friends. It started out as simply as that. Ed Kleban's lyric in *A Chorus Line*'s opening number "I Hope I Get It" is very careful not to say, "I want this job"; it says, "Oh God, I *need* this job. I've got to *get* this job." Kleban and everyone else involved with *A Chorus Line* heard the plaint often. It provides the dramatic engine that drives the show, and it was the brass-tacks motivation for Peacock and Stevens when they invited their colleagues to a special meeting on January 26, 1974.

Statistics had them spooked. Broadway production pace had hit a high in the 1926–27 season when there were 264 new shows. The number had been declining gently ever since. In the 1973–74 season that had just ended the previous year (theater seasons traditionally run June 1 to May 31) there had been just 54 shows, the same number as the year before, which had been a new low. Just seven seasons earlier the number had been 84.

With less dancing work, the dancers also wanted to create a means for themselves to branch out. So-called triple-threat performers—those who can sing, dance, and act—are almost standard on Broadway today, partly owing to economics that discourage separate singing and dancing choruses. But triple-threats were unusual or overlooked in 1974. Peacock and Stevens invited dancers who wanted to show off or develop their other two threats. The desire to evolve into acting or singing is endemic among dancers, who know they really are athletes whose careers are unmercifully brief.

Trish Garland had worked with Peacock and Stevens before, and had chewed over the problem again and again, as had the previous two generations of Broadway dancers. Garland, who created the role of the bubbly Judy Turner in *A Chorus Line,* had appeared in a short-lived 1973 musical, *Smith,* with Nicholas Dante, a dancer who had a desire to write. She wasn't surprised when Peacock called and invited her to the taping. "We had been talking for a long time about how many dancers are multitalented. Like Nicholas they could write, or they could act or be costumers and set designers. We discussed the feasibility of getting them all together in a company."

Kelly Bishop (then using the first name Carole), who created the role of the sultry Sheila, said that the original idea, as Stevens explained it to her, "was trying to get professional dancer-actor people together to be able to do productions as a resident company. That was very appealing to me, as an actress: getting a wonderful little group of people together who were really professionals who'd been around for a long time, to put on minimusicals or miniplays."

There it is, the original idea. Its building blocks were practical needs, but its foundation was sunk in old magic. Resident repertory companies of that sort are a recurring dream for theater people. In such companies everyone shares in the myriad tasks of putting on a play. Though appealing, the process rarely has worked in America, where star quality is quickly developed and encouraged, and where the gravitational draw of movies and TV tend to pull talented actors out of the orbit of a repertory company.

Still, Peacock and Stevens weren't naive. They knew their idea not only had value. It had a chance. The theater community in New York City is almost impossibly demanding, but it recognizes and appreciates professionalism. As in any closely knit village, its rivalries are intense, but it protects its own. Like the Alvin Ailey American Dance Theater, the Merce Cunningham Dance Company, the Martha Graham Dance Company, Maurice Bejart's Ballet of the Twentieth Century, George Balanchine's New York City Ballet, American Dance Machine, and others, this new resident company consisting of the cream of Broadway dancers could find an audience—but only if its programs offered some specialty, were of impeccably high quality and stood on sound financial ground.

In this case, the new troupe's specialty would be its ability to capture the essence of the show dancer. How it would do that, Stevens and Peacock weren't sure, but they figured that the best way to decide would be to get everyone together to relate their common experiences and to decide how the project would proceed and what form it would take. But also like those other dance companies, it needed one crucial ingredient to lure dancers and financing of the correct caliber. It needed a star—a dancer, a choreographer, or a financial "angel."

Less than a year earlier Peacock and Stevens had appeared in the original cast of the Cy Coleman musical *Seesaw,* and knew that the director of that musical, Michael Bennett, was an unusually gifted choreographer with a bankable track record. More important, he was one of those gurus to whom dancers seem irresistably drawn.

From Bennett's point of view, the call from Stevens and Peacock couldn't have been more perfectly timed. Long ago a dancer in the London production of *West Side Story,* a show regarded as something like nirvana by dancers, he had dreamed for some years of topping it. However, instead of doing another dancing show about teen gang members, he wanted to do a dancing show about dancers. Bennett had a tentative title and a vague concept; but he lacked a story, characters, and a reason for them to dance.

Without those things there wasn't much chance of a show coming about. Musicals were getting more expensive all the time. *Seesaw* in 1973 had cost a then unimaginable $1.25 million. By comparison, 1988's *Phantom of the Opera* reportedly cost $10 million. Nevertheless, there had been a time not too long before when a musical could come to Broadway for less than $100,000, and a single entrepreneur with a vision could produce one. In January 1974, that was a thing of the past. The dancers knew it and so did Bennett, so that even Bennett came to Peacock and Stevens's meeting unsure of what would come out of it. He hoped to encounter an idea. And he was in a position to exert an unusual degree of control over its outcome.

Though *Seesaw* had not been a great success, dancers loved it because of its stylish and flamboyant dance numbers. Among other *Seesaw* alumni invited to the first meeting were Wayne Cilento, Mitzi Hamilton, Crissy Wilzak, Thomas J. (later "Thommie") Walsh, Steve Anthony, and Baayork Lee.

A childhood friend and former dance partner of Bennett's who had launched her career as Yul Brynner's youngest princess in the original *The King and I,* Lee had helped stage the national company of *Seesaw* at the end of 1973 and was about to start work on the more modest bus-and-truck company. But she remembers Bennett telling her to wait.

"I didn't understand because I'd done all the auditions," recalled the woman who would create the role of the feisty Asian dancer, Connie Wong. "But he said, 'Don't worry, we're going to be doing something else, Baayork.'

"I remember getting a phone call from Michon Peacock saying, 'We're going to have this session, a marathon all night.' I can't remember the phrasing of it."

The phone in Thommie Walsh's apartment rang, too.

"Tony called and said, 'We're doing this workshop next week and we're going to talk about being dancers. Michael Bennett is going to be there and we're going to dance. It's going to be a marathon. We're going to try to stay up all night, talk about life, and what it's like to be a dancer.' "

Walsh, memorable as the exuberantly extroverted Bobby, who breaks into people's houses not to steal anything—just to rearrange their furniture—remembers how, in that career-altering phone call, "I asked him a thousand questions because it sounded so fascinating. It was the kind of thing I felt I would be a fool to turn down. I might not have been thinking it would turn into a job, but I felt I was being invited to something I knew would be special, something very select."

Sammy Williams remembers that call well, because he was with Walsh when it came. Williams's first step on the road to his Tony Award for playing the conflict-filled gay dancer Paul was a casual one. "Thommie mentioned that I was in town and Tony said to ask me if I wanted to come along, too. I agreed and that's how I got invited. Talk about being in the right place at the right time!"

By various accounts, fifteen to twenty-two dancers were there the night *A Chorus Line* was born. Aside from hosts Tony Stevens and Michon Peacock there were eight of the nineteen dancers who eventually wound up in the show: Renee Baughman, Kelly Bishop, Wayne Cilento, Patricia Garland, Priscilla Lopez, Donna McKechnie, Thommie Walsh, and Sammy Williams. That number includes all three who later were to win the show's three Tony Awards for acting: McKechnie (Best Actress in a Musical), Williams (Best Featured Actor in a Musical), and Bishop (Best Featured Actress in a Musical).

One of those invited, Crissy Wilzak, would understudy the original cast. Another, Nicholas Dante, would cowrite the libretto with James Kirkwood.

Those whose voices appear on that tape and subsequent tapes include Mitzi Hamilton, Jane Robertson, Candy Brown, Jacki Garland, Steve Anthony, Steve Boockvor, Denise Pence (a.k.a. Denise

Boockvor), Andy Bew, Christopher Chadman—names that recur in Playbills of the period.

Most of them had either worked together before, or knew of one another. Like *Seesaw,* several shows of the late 1960s and early 1970s were prime sources for people at the tape session: *Promises, Promises* (Bennett, McKechnie, Lee, Bishop), *Rachael Lily Rosenbloom and Don't You Ever Forget It* (Bishop, Cilento, Robertson, Peacock, Walsh, Stevens), *Smith* (Garland, Baughman, Dante) plus *Sugar, Irene, Music! Music!,* and others.

One person who didn't make it to that first meeting was Baayork Lee. She was upset that Bennett hadn't invited her himself. "One night," she recalls, after a performance of *Henry, Sweet Henry* in Philadelphia, "Michael and I were sitting on the stairs talking about our future and what we wanted out of life. He turned to me and said, 'Baayork, do you want me to make you a star?' And I looked him square in the eye and said, 'No Michael, I just want to work.' And he said, 'You'll never have to worry about anything. I'll always take care of you, Baayork.' He always signed his cards to me, 'For life.' Michael always dealt with me on a one-to-one level. I had a misconception: I thought Michael had organized this meeting and asked Michon to make his phone calls for him. Also, I didn't want to talk about my private self to people I still considered strangers even though I had worked with many of them."

Her attitude would change, but in the meantime the rest were coming to quite different decisions.

"All I knew is that we'd dance and we'd talk and that Michael Bennett would be there," Garland said. "I went because my sister Jacki was going." The two Garland girls had helped and encouraged each other since they had come to New York to be dancers. "I trusted Michon, I respected Michael Bennett's work, and I knew it was a sure thing. I knew everyone who was going and I respected all these dancers who were being asked. It also piqued my interest."

The chosen time was midnight Saturday night, to give the folks working in shows a chance to shower and change. The chosen place was the Nickolaus Exercise Center on Third Avenue in the East Thirties that would be empty for the rest of the weekend. The idea was a combination group encounter session and pajama party. Participants were told no specifics beforehand, the idea being that they could make up the rules as they went along. However, the unstructured nature of the meeting made everyone as nervous as anything else. No one knew what they were getting into.

"Thommie and I had major phone conversations but we didn't want to go," said Cilento, whose character, Mike Costa, would introduce the song "I Can Do That." "We decided that if one went, the other would. There was nothing certain that it was going to turn into anything. We held hands and we all went. I was scared to death."

"I wasn't working," said Renee Baughman, whose character, Kristine, would protest "I could never really sing." That January night, her protest was, "I was what I considered fat. I had not met Michael Bennett before, or rather I had not worked for him. I had auditioned for him. I was very much in awe of his work and I certainly didn't want to go to that rap session fat. Nicholas actually had to come to my apartment and take me by the hand."

Williams recalled, "I went over to Thommie's house beforehand and we all got stoned. It was Thommie and, I believe, Kelly and Priscilla. There were more but I don't remember who they were. It was snowing that night. I remember all of us huddling together in the cab, we were all so scared. You could feel the tension in the cab."

Bishop remembers the entrance to the dance studio, "up a steep and very narrow staircase."

"Every step was like going to your doom," Williams said. "I think being stoned helped make it even more scary."

At the top of the stairs was a door that opened on a rehearsal room with a barre. As cohost, Stevens was leading an exercise session. There were four lines of some of Broadway's firmest, healthiest, most graceful bodies. They worked out for twenty to forty minutes, allowing for stragglers.

"We were having fun," Williams recalled, "it was about midnight by then. Then, in the middle of this class, in walked Mr. Bennett in a hooded fur coat. Here was a man I could have died for."

Bennett was accompanied by Donna McKechnie, for whom he had created featured dances in *Promises, Promises* and *Company*. McKechnie, who would create the role of Cassie in *A Chorus Line,* said she came as an encouragement to Bennett, who was trying to sort out his plans for the dancers' show. Though she speaks of how excited and hopeful Bennett was that night, she also remembers how he clutched her hand in the taxi on the way over. She was wrestling with other demons as well. "I was facing my own personal crossroads," she said. "I'd had a taste of what success can be like and it's too good not to go for it."

She had been in therapy following the breakup of her first marriage, and she hoped that this new project would help her "to put the fragments back, to be a whole person. Even when I had problems with low self-esteen, I always respected the work and music and dancing."

McKechnie was attracted by the prospect of plunging into the unknown. "It was something very different and I was ready for something to stir me up, to get me going again."

After Bennett's arrival, Walsh said, the mood of the meeting changed. "All of a sudden it became a dance *audition,* and we were all showing off in a fierce competition to be teacher's pet. It wasn't a party anymore. People who were friends suddenly were at each others' throats."

Priscilla Lopez was appearing in the Bob Fosse musical *Pippin* at the time. As Diana Morales, she would introduce "Nothing" and *A Chorus Line*'s hit song, "What I Did for Love." But on that snowy midnight, all she remembers was "Michael walked in and I got terrified. I didn't know what was going to happen. I just wanted to be good and I wanted him to like me."

Bishop's relationship with Bennett extended back to *Promises, Promises* in 1968. She recalls, "There was always a tremendous attraction between us. And a tremendous battle of wills, very much what 'Zach' [the director] and 'Sheila' have in the show. He was used to telling people what to do, and most people would do exactly what he said. I wouldn't. It was more my stubbornness than anything else, because very often he was right. Some part of me knew that, but I didn't want him to get away with just telling me what to do like I had no mind of my own."

Bennett and Bishop had often confided in one another. Their friendship had had its ups and downs, and was in a downswing on the night of the first tape session.

Looking around at the group Peacock and Stevens had assembled, Bishop saw that they had picked consummate professional Broadway dancers with respectable resumes. There was no one there who'd never had a job before. "I think maybe the youngest, newest one was Steve Anthony," she said. "But he was an incredibly talented dancer, a wonderful dancer. There certainly were a good number of people in the dance community who were excluded who were excellent dancers, but they were people who were maybe not terribly special or interesting."

When Bennett arrived, he took a place next to Bishop "and sort of started stretching with me and made some comment about 'Oh God, I'm so stiff and so sore.' And I thought, 'This is interesting, he's making an effort to relate to me.' We then continued to dance for maybe twenty to twenty-five minutes, maybe not that long, and I was more than ready to quit. A few of the other people were out of shape. That's when Michael said, 'Now we're going to talk.' "

Adjoining the rehearsal hall was a dressing room or office from which the desks and tables had been removed. There were pillows, however, and Bennett sat on one, inviting the dancers to gather in a circle.

"There was a rush to Michael's side," Bishop recalled. "I picked the opposite end and I was surrounded by my small entourage, my buddies: Thommie, Sammy, Wayne, and Steve Anthony."

"I was shaking but it was exciting, thrilling," Williams said. "The anticipation of what was about to happen was so incredible. For the first time in my whole career I felt part of a group."

There was some thin carpeting, but even with the pillows it was uncomfortable. Yet no one left. Bennett brought out a big old reel-to-reel tape recorder and asked whether anyone objected if he taped the proceedings.

Clearly having taken over as chairman, Bennett turned on the tape and told everyone to relax. Walsh heard Bennett say "something like, 'Look, I don't know what this is, if this is a movie or a book or a musical, but I know that dancers have a lot to say. I've always wanted to do something about dancers.' "

Williams recalled, "He said we might have an idea for a book or a movie or a musical or a play—or nothing. He would ask us a series of questions and all he asked was that we answer honestly. We weren't being forced to answer anything we didn't want to. If we didn't answer we shouldn't feel that we weren't going to get a job or that anyone was going to hate us."

According to Bishop, "Then Michael went through basically what Zach says. He wanted to start with your name, your real name if it's different, where you were born and when. He went through a speech about being very honest and very open and then he said something to the effect of, 'Oh, the women don't have to give their age.'

"I said, 'Wait a minute, you just went through a speech about being honest and being open, and if we're being honest and open, I don't see why the women can't give their age, too.' That made a couple of the women squirm.

"So he said, 'Okay, then it will be everybody's age.' And I said, 'And astrological sign,' because I always want to know. So he said, 'Okay, and your sign.' "

"Michael was real smart," Cilento said. "He said to us, 'Okay, I'll start with my life.' He broke the ice by talking about himself and then we all started talking, too. I thought Michael was great that night. I didn't really know him so there was nothing pretentious, nothing evil, nothing superficial. If he was acting or not, who knows? It was good that he put himself in the beginning of it, set it up.

"Basically he told a lot of heartbreaks and a lot of situations that he was in that were not perfect and ideal. . . . He talked about having relationships with men and not knowing if he was straight. He said he had had a relationship with a girl in *West Side Story* and she got pregnant by him. I think he set the precedent for us all to be very honest and very open."

Lopez agreed, "When I saw that he was being honest and open I figured I could do it."

Many of the first things said in the tape session made their way into the final text of *A Chorus Line*.

"When it came to my turn I said, 'My name is Kelly Bishop, my real name is Carole Jane Bishop, which I really hate. I was born February twenty-eighth, 1944, in Colorado Springs, Colorado. And I'm going to be thirty real soon. And I'm real glad.' Which is exactly what Sheila says, except that the name is different. We changed the date of Sheila's birth in order to make her a Leo."

Not everyone had Bishop's bravado.

"I was dreadfully scared at the tape sessions," Williams said. "They said all we want you to do is talk about yourself. I realized I couldn't talk about myself. I'm embarrassed about myself, how could I talk? I made Walsh promise to sit next to me the whole time, which he did, I think. It was painful, difficult, scary. I didn't even know how to talk to people in those days, I couldn't even carry on a decent conversation with anyone."

But right away something happened that opened the dancers' hearts. People started hearing their own stories coming from other people's mouths.

"We just started talking about dancing school and it seemed that so many people said things I could relate to," Baughman said. "I told my story very early on. I felt so free that night, I don't know why. People really listened and they didn't interrupt a lot."

"Oh my God, I'm not as special as I think I am," is Thommie Walsh's memory of his reaction to hearing the other stories. "I thought I was the only person who had a father who drank, a mother who thought she was Auntie Mame, and a sister who beat me up—all that stuff. I thought these were great problems, but I was hearing things even more staggering in that room."

Bishop said, "It was odd that in the first few minutes as we started around with our names, ages and such, I realized how little I knew about these people that I had worked with over and over and over again. I knew their current problems with a specific show, maybe, but I didn't know how old they were and I didn't know where they came from or whether they had brothers and sisters or their parents were dead. I was ready to talk. Once I decided I was going to go there I was fearless."

Natural performers in front of an audience of peers, they loosened up very quickly. "Kelly made us laugh," Baughman said. "It was so easy talking. I had never experienced so many of my emotions as I did that night. I was so fascinated by everybody's story. And the time went so quickly. I had never heard all of Nicholas's [Dante] story before, even though I had known him since I was fifteen. I had even met his parents. I knew Trish but I was always intimidated by her. She was so beautiful and talented. Who needed that in a girlfriend? I had worked with Steve Boockvor on *The Ed Sullivan Show*. He scared me to death, he was such a macho guy."

As the only married couple in the room, Boockvor and Pence talked about what it was like auditioning together and how they managed when one got a job and the other didn't. The other dancers were struck by the way Boockvor's assertive personality dovetailed with Pence's delicate one.

Priscilla Lopez recounted her horror stories about being humiliated by two teachers at the High School of the Performing Arts. Kelly Bishop described how she escaped from an unhappy childhood into a ballet world where everything was beautiful. McKechnie told what it was like to grow up with a father away in the military, and how she would fantasize that he was like an Indian chief, and he would invite her to dance.

Knowing what she knew about Bennett's own agenda—"he wanted to get behind what their lives were like, their experiences," McKechnie said—the session was paying off in gold. "Everybody realized how similar their lives were; growing up is growing up," she said. "If there was a theme to the session, it would have to be 'growing up.' That prevailed more than talking about dancing. It was the relationships you had as you grew up and went to dance school. Wayne [Cilento] had hilarious recollections of when he and Cathy got married. Those stories were just wildly funny and very moving."

The questions seemed to have the power to unlock all kinds of memories and feelings.

"My sister Jacki and I were the only ones there who had a childhood together," Garland said. "Not knowing where these questions were going or what it meant to anyone, I was worried that some were going to be detrimental to my relationship with my sister. She had no idea about how I felt about a lot of things or the hurts. I wasn't the kind of person who spewed them out. A lot of the questions were very personal so I didn't express myself openly for fear that I would hurt her. She had no idea of the pains that I felt and how deep the resentment I had for her went. And yet I loved her so much and she was older and she was talented. I always thought she was much more talented than I was and much prettier and all of those things.

"Jacki was much more open than I was. She didn't have that problem. She couldn't have hurt me in these sessions because when we talked about our childhoods she was the special one, the one who always went first. Ultimately I guess I really did want to get rid of some of this stuff, and here I was being given the opportunity. But I couldn't do it. Some of the people were so open, going on and on, that I wanted to scream.

"Otherwise," Garland continued, "the tape sessions were very warm for me, It was womblike in some ways. I never feel comfortable talking about private things in front of a large group of people. I can razzle-dazzle you with a superficial answer, but when you come down to the basics . . . and we were talking about very raw emotions."

The questions and replies went around the room, more or less the way they do in the show, but not telescoped or intercut for pacing.

"When we finished that round," Walsh recalls, "then he [Bennett] said, 'We've gotten through the beginnings. Let's talk about ever since you remember dancing and why you wanted to dance up to the first time you kissed a guy or a girl.'

"I found it real hard to express myself," Walsh said, "because I had heard a lot of heavy stuff. Part of my sense of humor said, 'We need to change the mood of this room. Make it light, Thommie.' Another part of me also worried whether I should reveal myself like this in front of some people I barely knew. 'In my house I remember dishes flying'—stuff like that. But other people were saying things like that. I saw two sisters, Trish Garland and Jacki Garland, experiencing things for the first time in front of a lot of people. Well, that totally blew me away. I didn't have that kind of freedom. A few people had been in therapy, so maybe that was one reason some of them were so fluid and so free. Mine was relatively documentary. I did get into the twisted kid that I was, that I was this little demented villager."

But soon the intimate mood infected Walsh as well. "I remember getting up and just hugging Renee Baughman. She was my first dance partner in New York. We had done *The Ed Sullivan Show*. I think I did the same thing with Candy Brown because of all the people there, Candy was weeping. She had been class president and her shoes were always polished and her father made a good living and her mother always went to church and made her dresses and she was on the honor roll. . . . Her life was so perfect that she started crying when it got to her because everyone else had such painful childhoods and she was raised like Ozzie and Harriet raised Ricky and David. Candy was the exception. Otherwise there was a common denominator of pain in that room."

As the characters do in the show, the dancers worried what they were going to say when they were called upon. "Everyone else's life was so much more interesting," Cilento said. "I just thought my life was so boring. I listened to Nick Dante before me and I thought, what could I say that could be anywhere up to what he talked about? You got so devastated just listening, everything was so interesting. When it got to you would it be as good, as interesting? Should you lie? Should you tell the truth? How could you spice it up?

"When it was my turn I just told my story," Cilento said. "I didn't beef it up. People were laughing—that was great. I think it was a real good experience. In the back of my mind I went in thinking, 'It's a job.' But then, being in that situation, I just couldn't even imagine how that could be a job. I couldn't imagine how any of us could make a show or a job out of it. It was just being in his company that was probably important at that time. And being among the dancers who were called—that was special."

Thommie Walsh said, "I listened to everybody's buzz. Michon, Tony, and Michael laid out huge sandwiches from the Stage Deli for us, we smoked grass or at least our little group did. People took catnaps which made me furious. *Who could sleep?*"

As dawn approached and passed, the dancers stretched out on the floor, propping their heads up on arms or pillows, listening to one another bare their souls. Lubricating the talk was the desire to please and impress Bennett. It helped the adrenaline.

Lopez recalls, "Since I was sitting at ten o'clock in the circle, I had to listen to all these other people. By then I'm dying to talk. Michael knew that I could dance and sing but he didn't know *me,* and this was my chance to let him know about me. So even though I related to the group, I was really talking to him. After all these years I felt I was telling Michael Bennett who I was, and he heard me."

Moreover, the others heard her, too. "I seemed to be entertaining because people were laughing," she said. "I cried only once, when I talked about the High School of the Performing Arts, about when that woman, Gertrude Scher, told me I wasn't good, and I believed her. I was totally honest.

"The only time I felt a little inhibited was when people got into their sexual experiences. I hadn't had a lot of boyfriends and I felt kind of inadequate. The fact that these people were being so open blew my mind in a good way because I felt as if I had suddenly acquired all these friends. We all did have something in common: We all were dancers and we all wanted the same things. No matter how alone you had felt before, now you knew that other people felt as alone as you did. I had gotten to a point in my life where I was blocking out people I felt I had no time for. I figured they weren't really important anyway. But by the time the tape sessions were over, I was amazed that I had thought of crossing anyone off my list, thinking that they weren't good enough to relate to. I just fell in love with everybody."

Williams, who had been so anxious when he came in, drew courage from the frankness of those around him. "I remembered what had happened during my parents' divorce," he said, "and how the focus switched from being a son to being a replacement for my father for my mother. How at age seventeen that was a very big burden for me to carry and I couldn't cope with it. My mother kept saying to me, 'Why, why, why did he leave me?' And I kept saying, 'I don't know why. Don't ask me.' It was the first time that I had ever really talked about it to anyone. I answered all of the other questions, too."

Between the camaraderie, the wine, the smoke, the lateness of the hour, and the revolving questions and answers, the room was spinning in more than one sense. It became a pinwheel of bright eyes, long muscular legs in tights or dance pants, the perfume of sweat, high voices, a sense of intimacy . . . almost a lovers' intimacy.

3.

"CHILDHOOD"

In dancers' parlance, "childhood" is that period, innocent or not, from birth to one's first show. In this instance, "childhood" will extend to mean each dancer's history until they were hired for *A Chorus Line*.

The dancers were born between the early 1940s and the early 1950s, putting most of them in the first wave of the Baby Boom. They grew up in the years following World War II, in some ways a golden age for Broadway dancers. They came from New York City, upstate New York, New Jersey, Kansas, Michigan, Missouri, Vermont, Ohio, California, Florida, Arizona, Canada—even Trinidad. They made their Broadway debuts between the mid 1950s and the early 1970s.

They often were loners, usually smarter, more self-reliant, and more sensitive than the kids around them. But many of them got poor grades, born of an impatience with schoolwork. They wanted to dance. As is reflected in the show's song, "Hello Twelve, Hello Thirteen, Hello Love," childhood is a crucial and often painful time for dancers. Unlike most other professions, which can be chosen in late high school, college, or almost any time in adulthood, dancing is a career that often must be chosen before puberty. As a result, some of these dancers had established national and international reputations before they could legally obtain driver's licenses.

The key to their success was their ability to make themselves a part of a web of professional relationships centering on the major choreographers of the day: George Balanchine, Bob Fosse, Jerome Robbins, Ron Field, Michael Kidd, Peter Gennaro, Gower Champion, and others. The dancers' involvement with *A Chorus Line* was determined by their having established such a relationship with Michael Bennett, Michon Peacock, Tony Stevens, or all three.

Three asterisks next to their names indicate that they were at the taping sessions in winter and spring 1974, and took part in both workshops. Two asterisks indicate that they joined the project in summer 1974 and took part in both workshops. One asterisk indicates that they came aboard in January or early February 1975 and took part in the second workshop.

CLIVE WILSON (CLERK)*

Wilson was born in Port of Spain, Trinidad, on October 17, 1945. His parents owned a private hospital there, and at his mother's urging, Wilson would put on shows at Christmas to entertain the doctors and their families.

Wilson's parents divorced when he was four, and his mother remarried when he was six. Wilson was one of four white children among eight hundred black students at the local school, and he was further isolated by being relatively affluent. He remembers being delivered to school each morning by a chauffeur, which did not endear him to his classmates, who regularly beat him up. Dancing offered a way to escape inside himself.

His mom, a movie buff, encouraged his dancing ability and sent him for dancing lessons at age eight. To further his studies, his mother sent him at age ten to live for a time with relatives in Oakland, California.

At home, Trinidad began undergoing a series of upheavals that would lead to independence. Wilson's parents wanted to resettle in the United States, but the waiting list for immigration was too long. Instead, they moved to Toronto, Canada.

During the course of these moves, Wilson got to see his first Broadway shows, *My Fair Lady, Bells Are Ringing,* and *West Side Story.* He sat in the fifth row center for the last-named and remembers, "I just got goose bumps. Everything on that stage came rushing out at me and I really wanted to be a part of it. At that point I decided I wanted to be on the stage." He was twelve.

He got his first professional dancing job the same year, for the TV show *Junior Magazine* on the CBC in Toronto, then worked his way through high school, appearing in countless weekly variety shows and specials. One of these was a musical special featuring American performers Chita Rivera and Carol Lawrence. Lee Becker was choreographer, and Wilson worked with her assistant, Michael Bennett, who was in his mid teens at the time.

That was 1960, a pivotal year for Wilson. He got his first speaking role in a musical, a production of *The Most Happy Fella* choreographed by Ron Field at the O'Keefe Center in Toronto. But Wilson and his mother didn't always wait for musicals to come to them. Together, they made regular pilgrimages to Broadway. During one of these trips, Wilson saw a notice in the trade newspaper *Variety* that Bob Fosse was casting dancers for the new Cy Coleman musical *Little Me.* Just for the experience, the fifteen-year-old went to the audition and was chosen "from among what seemed like four hundred thousand gypsies."

Unfortunately, he couldn't take the job. "I thought I could lie and be in deep trouble later," he said, "or tell the truth. I'd been raised to tell the truth. So I had to turn down Bob Fosse. I told him I was fifteen years old and I can't work here because I live in Toronto. He told me to come back when I grew up."

Fired up by the realization that he had been accepted in the big time, he auditioned for Canadian productions of *Bye Bye Birdie* and *Flower Drum Song* with actress Juanita Hall. Hall's manager scouted him and sent him to Hollywood. Now seventeen going on eighteen, Wilson was able to get a work permit in the United States, and almost immediately was cast in the Doris Day movie *Send Me No Flowers,* in which he did a three-minute dance with the star and had his first screen kiss. He also did stints in the TV soap opera *The Days of Our Lives* and a Patty Duke film *Billy,* on which he met dancer Donna McKechnie.

Between acting assignments in *The Mod Squad, I Spy,* and other shows, he went to UCLA and the Arts Center College of Design studying art and design.

Wilson's status as a wunderkind, plus his style and good looks, made such an impression on Michael Bennett that he remembered Wilson when they ran into each other at a New York party in the early part of 1975, when Bennett was casting dancers for the second workshop of *A Chorus Line*.

RON KUHLMAN**

Kuhlman's career is unusual in that he did not begin dancing professionally until college. His dancing career grew from his acting career, which runs counter to the usual path.

Kuhlman was born in Cleveland, Ohio, and was introduced to the arts by playing in his high school band and orchestra. His father, a delivery man, had a lung removed when Kuhlman was nine, and his mother, a drill press operator, was severely injured on the way to the hospital to visit him. With both his parents invalids, Kuhlman grew up in near poverty. He remembers getting charity packages of food and clothing from the neighborhood church.

As a consequence, Kuhlman was raised by a great-aunt and spent much of his after-school time sweating over a variety of odd jobs, mowing lawns, delivering newspapers, and working as a stock boy in his uncle's shoe store. In this way he earned enough to pay for tap dance lessons with Dave Morgenstern and to put himself through college.

Kuhlman's innate dancing skill first manifested itself at school dances. He won dance contests at the local YMCA. His high school did not present musicals, but Kuhlman did find time to appear in *The Diary of Anne Frank* and *I Remember Mama*.

The high school's theater director steered him to the community summer theater, where he danced in his first musical, *Irma La Douce,* and acted in straight plays, *Gaslight* and *Summer and Smoke*.

His parents wanted him to be an engineer so he entered Ohio University, majoring in biochemistry. But his career came to a crossroads in his freshman year when he took a course in Afro-Cuban dancing. That got him interested in performing, and soon he changed his major, studying theater and dance. One of his dance teachers was Martha Graham protégée Shirley Wimmer, and she loaned him enough money to travel to California and take part in a dance program in Long Beach. Just dancing did not satisfy him, however. "I felt I wasn't communicating enough with just my body, I wanted to communicate verbally."

After college he began his professional acting career doing summer stock productions of *Much Ado About Nothing* and *Joe Egg* in Cape Cod, Massachusetts.

Using a friend's apartment in the East Village section of Manhattan as a base, he got a job dancing in *Once upon a Mattress* at Club Bene, a dinner theater-style club in South Amboy, New Jersey, and then got his Equity card playing Biff in a national tour of *Death of a Salesman.* In the next few seasons his employment was eclectic but steady. He helped launch a new Actors Equity theater company in Old Forge, New York, performed in commercials, did stock productions of *Hello, Dolly!* and *Funny Face,* and worked off-Broadway at the Equity Library Theatre.

In 1974, Kuhlman was hired as a dancer for "The Milliken Breakfast Show," a lavish fashion show in the style of a Broadway musical. New York City is home to many such "industrials," which traditionally have provided a showcase for theater dancers, and helped them keep food on the table. But "Milliken," produced by Milliken & Co., a textile firm, was the granddaddy of all industrials and it was a coup for Kuhlman to land it.

The coup was compounded by the fact that Michael Bennett spotted Kuhlman in that "Milliken" and invited him to audition for the first workshop of *A Chorus Line.*

KAY COLE*

Kay Cole appeared in a Los Angeles production of *Me Candido* at age six, she said, and remembers the distinct feeling as the lights went down on opening night, of having found a home. "It sounds like a fantasy a writer would put in a script, because it sounds great. But it really did happen to me."

Born in Florida and resettled to Los Angeles, Cole started taking ballet lessons when she was five. A director scouted her from that class and began her in a career as a child actress. Her father worked for Lockheed and her mother was a nurse. She said her parents did not push her into a dance career; she wanted it and her parents acquiesced. For the next five years she did theater and television in Los Angeles, appearing on *Playhouse 90, The Loretta Young Hour,* and *Bachelor Father,* among others.

She took part in a national tour of *The Music Man* when she was ten, her mother traveling with her as chaperone and nurse for the children. Cole continued her education through tutors, and strove to take dance classes.

Always on the move, Cole got used to making herself feel at home wherever she happened to be. That adaptation helped her thrive in touring companies and on location shoots. "My life has been very focused without my doing anything about it," she said.

When she was twelve she was offered a scholarship to join a local ballet company in Canada, but she passed up the chance to put down roots in favor of continuing her gypsy existence.

That changed when she joined the Broadway production *Bye Bye Birdie* at age thirteen and matriculated at a professional school for young working people. Before she graduated at age fifteen she had appeared in concerts and on soap operas, but her career hit a slough because there are relatively few roles for teenagers.

Cole returned to Broadway at age sixteen as half of a pair of twins (with actress Jill Choder) in the Anthony Newley musical *Stop the World—I Want to Get Off.* She said, "I always thought of myself as an actress. I think the expression of everything to the fullest comes from an acting point of view, whether you are singing a song or dancing a dance step. It's like the root of a tree with many different branches."

After appearing in the original cast of Newley's next musical, *The Roar of the Greasepaint—The Smell of the Crowd,* Cole moved back to California and appeared there in West Coast versions of 1960s musicals including *Hair* and *Salvation.* In the early 1970s, *Hair* director Tom O'Horgan asked Cole to return to New York and take her place in the Broadway version of that musical. She appeared in the original cast of Leonard Bernstein's *Mass,* after which O'Horgan cast her in his next two major musicals, *Jesus*

Christ Superstar and *Sgt. Pepper's Lonely Hearts Club Band,* a musical based on the Beatles album of the same name.

Sgt. Pepper's opened in November 1974 and had a disappointingly short run. It closed on January 5, 1975, sending Cole back into the audition circuit. Cole is unusual among the dancers of *A Chorus Line* in that she had no previous connection with Michael Bennett until the show's open-call audition later that January.

WAYNE CILENTO***

Born and raised in the Bronx, later moving to suburban Westchester County, Cilento decided to make his career as a dancer after he was taken to the original production of *Cabaret* when he was a junior in high school. "I couldn't believe those people were doing that for a living," he said. "I was about seventeen and I thought 'I really *could* do that.' "

He had attended one dance class when he was seven or eight, and the teacher zeroed in on him and he panicked. *Cabaret* cured that, and when his high school did *Oklahoma!* he was cast as the lead dancer, even though he had never danced before. He began taking modern dance and jazz classes twice a week and the following year when his school did *Li'l Abner,* he was again cast as the lead dancer.

Cilento had a family precedent. His grandmother's brother had been a ballroom dancer. An only child, he remembers dancing around the house to Dionne Warwick and Johnny Mathis records. He worried that his high school dancing would bring taunts of "sissy" from his classmates, a common complaint of male dancers, but Cilento said that never happened to him.

Cilento entered Westchester Community College as a liberal arts major, then transferred to State University of New York College at Brockport in upstate New York to study dance, with a physical education minor. Among his teachers was Bill Glassman of American Ballet Theatre. Cilento said, "He was short and straight—someone I could use as a role model."

Cilento had maintained contact with a high school classmate named Cathy Colety, who had appeared with him in the two high school musicals, and who was studying physical education in Texas. He worked his last two nonshowbiz jobs—coating pills at his uncle's pharmaceutical company and waiting tables—in order to save up enough money for an engagement ring. Cilento was working in his first summer stock production, *Hello Dolly!,* when she accepted. He left the show two weeks early to marry her. "I don't think I would have survived in this business if I didn't have another relationship," he said. "There aren't many people who have that support system." She became a teacher and they had their first child while Cilento was appearing in *A Chorus Line.*

After their marriage, Cilento auditioned for two incoming shows, *Irene* and *Seesaw,* and was hired for *Seesaw* just before Michael Bennett was engaged as replacement director, and began making major changes. "I watched Michael clean house and revamp the show," he said. "It was the first time I'd seen something like that happen, a transformation from a piece of junk into something very successful, very commercial. That was my first experience with Michael."

Broadway assignments came quickly after that. After quitting *Seesaw,* he understudied "everyone" in *Rachael Lily Rosenbloom and Don't You Ever Forget It,* which closed in previews on Broadway. Choreographed by Tony Stevens, the musical employed many members of the original cast of *A Chorus Line.* Cilento then found steady work as a replacement dancer in *Irene.* Cilento was one of the first dancers they considered when drawing up a list of people to invite to the first taping session.

BAAYORK LEE***

In the mid 1980s, Lee staged *A Broadway Baby* for Goodspeed Opera House. That could serve as the title of her autobiography. Born of an Indian mother and a Chinese father in Manhattan's Chinatown, she made her Broadway debut at age five as one of Yul Brynner's brood in the original cast of Rodgers and Hammerstein's *The King and I.* She was Princess Ying Yawolak, the tiniest of the princesses introduced in "The March of the Siamese Children."

She had been introduced to dance by Claude Marchant, a member of the Katharine Dunham Dance Troupe who lived in her apartment building. Lee still remembers the first day her mother took her to Dunham's school: "I couldn't reach the barre, but I remember the mirrors, the smell, the sun shining in the window. I just loved it." Dancing became a Saturday ritual for her until Marchant saw an audition notice seeking oriental children. Not yet able to read, she learned the audition lines by rote with her mom's help, and landed the role.

Lee has vivid memories of the St. James Theatre, which she likens to a temple. "I would watch the dancers warming up in their dressing rooms, and I decided then and there that's what I wanted to do: I wanted to do what the big girls were doing." Her dressing room was on the theater's seventh floor, and sometimes the dancers would carry their tiny colleague upstairs. Lee would come directly to the theater after school and do her homework while listening to Gertrude Lawrence warming up for that evening's performance.

Over the two years she spent with the show, she established a close relationship with Brynner, whom the children called "Father" offstage and on. "He loved the original children like his own," she said. "The resonance in his voice, his command, the way he walked . . . It was the first time I was aware of a Man. That was what a man should be. He became my father because the theater became my life."

Lee outgrew the part and was let go. At age eight she was collecting unemployment. Her mother told her the children had gotten the parts because they were oriental, not because they could sing or dance, and that fired her to become proficient at those things and make sure she was hired for her abilities. She studied Afro-Cuban and modern dance techniques with Syvilla Fort and later enrolled in the School of American Ballet, Balanchine's school, where Jerome Robbins was one of the teachers. She made her debut with the company in Balanchine's original *Nutcracker Suite,* featuring American Indian ballerina Maria Tallchief as the Sugarplum Fairy. Lee took her as a role model.

When she was old enough, she was accepted at the High School of the Performing Arts (subject of the film *Fame*), and was hired by Rodgers and Hammerstein for their musical *Flower Drum Song,* for which choreographer Carol Haney taught Lee to walk in high heels. A photo of her with Rodgers was published in *Life* magazine. She was dancing with the big girls now, although she had already topped out at four foot ten. She recalls the day she got the job, running back to dancing school and crowing about it, making several of her classmates jealous, including a skinny kid named Michael Bennett. But he couldn't be too mad at her; she had been his first friend in New York.

Unfortunately, the High School of the Performing Arts, or "PA," didn't allow students to work commercially during school hours. She had to make a choice, and she chose PA, where she eventually graduated with honors in dance. Lee then was faced with another tough choice: a scholarship to Juilliard or a dancing role in Haney's next musical, *Bravo Giovanni.* This time she went for the show, which had a very short run. She was quickly hired by Peter Gennaro to play an Eskimo and a Thai diplomat in what turned out to be Irving Berlin's last musical, *Mr. President.* On closing night, producer Norman Jewison sent her a note inviting her to appear in his next show, *Here's Love,* a musical version of *The Miracle on 34th Street,* choreographed by Michael Kidd.

Dancing in that show reunited her with her friend from Syvilla Fort's, Michael Bennett. She stayed in contact with Bennett through her next show, *Golden Boy,* and took dance lessons from him until 1967 when he hired her for *A Joyful Noise,* the first musical for which Bennett did his own choreography. It closed quickly, but Lee and Bennett moved together directly into *Henry, Sweet Henry,* which also had a short run. Nevertheless, she said, "you could smell his success. He was just radiating success and creativity and artistry."

Lee was hired for the London company of *Golden Boy,* but she returned to the United States when Bennett promised her a speaking role in his next show, *Promises, Promises.* The speaking part never materialized, but Lee was one of three featured dancers, along with Donna McKechnie and Margo Sappington. Lee got her first chance to be dance captain during that show, and Bennett agreed to let her re-create his choreography for subsequent touring versions of the show.

Jewison next hired her for the film version of the rock musical *Jesus Christ Superstar*. While location filming in Israel she met several dancers who later became close friends, including future *Chorus Line* dancers Thommie Walsh and Robert LuPone.

Upon her return to the States in 1973, she was invited to Detroit where Bennett was doctoring the musical *Seesaw,* which employed several more future *ACL* alumni.

If Bob Avian was Bennett's right hand, Lee had become his left. The only reason Lee did not attend the first taping session is she felt hurt at not being asked by Bennett personally. She later made auxiliary tapes for the show at Bennett's apartment.

MICHEL STUART*

Stuart was born Michel Joseph Kleinman in the Washington Heights section of Manhattan, and took his brother's surname when he created a stage name for himself. "Dancing was my escape world," he said. He discovered that world at age seven when he started taking classes at a neighborhood dance school.

Stuart's parents had come to America in 1939, fleeing Nazism. His mother was the only survivor in her family; his father escaped with several other siblings. When Stuart was growing up, his mother was president of the PTA at the local synagogue where they did plays, which he agreed to help stage. His other after-school job was making deliveries for his furrier father.

Stuart was the only boy in a dance class conducted by Estelle Field, aunt of Ron Field. One of Stuart's closest childhood friends was another future choreographer, Eliot Feld, who lived in Stuart's neighborhood. The two became friends through their common interest in dance. Estelle Field drilled Stuart in ballet and, seeing his promise, encouraged him to audition for the High School of the Performing Arts.

Stuart attended PA for "two of the best years of my life." The first live ballet he saw was the New York City Ballet's *Firebird.* During this period he also saw the original Broadway production of *West Side Story,* a show that would figure prominently in his career.

After Stuart began studying jazz dancing with Peter Gennaro at the Dance Center on Eighth Avenue and Forty-fifth Street, Gennaro invited him to appear in a film he was making in the Bronx, a rock and roll movie called *Let's Rock.* At age thirteen, Stuart made his film debut.

During the summer of 1958 he worked for a non-Equity theater in Beach Haven, New Jersey, performing in fifteen shows in fifteen weeks—revues, book musicals, comedies, and dramas. At age fourteen he played an eighty-year-old Oriental in *Teahouse of the August Moon.* He made fifteen dollars a week, plus food, and was called upon to choreograph and design the sets and costumes.

Stuart appeared before Robbins early in the summer to audition as a replacement dancer in *West Side Story.* During the summer at Beach Haven he got a telegram saying that he had been hired for the London cast. Not quite fifteen yet, Stuart made his West End debut in *West Side Story.* He did have one regret. "I had no teenage life," he said, "I went right from childhood to adulthood." While in London, Stuart studied at the London Academy of Music and Dramatic Arts while continuing correspondence courses with Professional Children's School.

Shortly after his return, Stuart was hired for a musical, *Beg, Borrow, and Steal,* which ran seven performances. During rehearsals and previews, Stuart said he found himself rewriting the obviously flawed show in the back of his head. He also had strong opinions on ways to improve the sets, the costumes, and the casting. It gave him the idea that someday he'd like to be a producer.

The next summer, 1961, Robbins allowed Stuart to adapt the *West Side Story* choreography for summer stock productions in the round, along with Jerry Friedman and Lee Becker. Among their casting choices, they picked Michael Bennett to play Baby John. The show opened in Cleveland, and the sixteen-year-old Stuart remembers taking his SATs in his hotel room. Outside the window was a cinema marquee advertising *Let's Rock,* which Stuart said he was too busy to go to see.

Stuart and Bennett subsequently toured together with the international company of *West Side Story,* visiting Israel, France, Italy, the Netherlands, and West Germany. Stuart left the company to appear in a short-lived musical, *The Gay Life* based on Arthur Schnitzler's *The Loves of Anatol.*

When Stuart was seventeen he was hired as resident choreographer in Cape Cod, Massachusetts, staging grand musicals like *The New Moon, Gypsy,* and *Fiorello!,* for which he hired Bennett as his assistant.

Stuart and choreographer Ron Field had staged casino shows in France and the Middle East in the mid 1960s, so when Field got the job of choreographer of the original Broadway *Cabaret* in 1966, he took Stuart on as associate choreographer.

In addition to these choreographic assignments during the 1960s, Stuart went out to California and danced on many of the era's TV variety shows, including those hosted by Judy Garland, Dinah Shore, Danny Kaye, and Carol Burnett.

Having had some experience producing nightclub shows in Florida, Stuart was trying to get involved with producing off-off- and off-Broadway when Bennett invited him to audition for the second workshop in January 1975. Looking for an "older" veteran, Bennett turned to Stuart.

DONNA McKECHNIE***

Born Donna Ruth McKechnie in Pontiac, Michigan, on November 16, 1941, McKechnie said, "I saw *The Red Shoes* when I was seven and it changed my life drastically that night."

She begged her mother for classes and soon was installed at the side of a local ballet teacher who used a line of folding chairs as a barre. When McKechnie outgrew that school, her mother moved her to Roth and Berdon, a school in Detroit that boasted Joan Leslie, a home-town girl who had starred in Hollywood films. The school offered classes in ballet, tap, baton twirling, and elocution.

"Going to ballet class made me feel like I was living," she said. She considered academic schooling a waste of time, and was slow to make friends, but she fell in love with her dance teacher, Pam Dunworth, as little girls tend to do.

Her father was self-employed and suffered chronic business problems, moving his family frequently. To help make the family's ends meet, the thirteen-year-old Donna began teaching dance to the younger students, and soon had a roster of seventy-five pupils. "I tried to help out financially, really to earn his approval, but I only got his resentment," she said. "I didn't realize how it made him feel: like he couldn't support his family."

While McKechnie didn't graduate from high school, she did serve as one of the founding members of the Detroit City Ballet with American Ballet Theatre choreographer William Dollar, bringing it together with a new ballet commissioned by the company. Though still only thirteen, she had eighteen-year-old Paul Sutherland as her first dance partner in the company.

She earned her Actors Equity membership (after her first audition) in a New York-originated company that did four musicals in repertory at Detroit's Cass Theater.

She endured several notable blowups with her father. One of them was prompted by her decision, at age fifteen, to join a dance company that was touring the South in a station wagon and a U-Haul truck for seventy-five dollars a week. The tour was a revelation, bringing McKechnie to parts of the country where there still existed separate accommodations and facilities for blacks and whites. When she returned to New York she unwillingly took up residence in a series of fleabag hotels while hunting for work.

She went to American Ballet Theatre's auditions for a tour of Russia, and survived several rounds of winnowing until she was one of the finalists. But when the director, Lucia Chase, pulled her over and inquired about her age (fifteen) and ABT academy experience (none) the picture changed abruptly. They told her that if she studied for a year at the school, they would consider her for the following year's tour. "I took it as a total rejection," McKechnie said. "It broke my heart. As a result, I didn't take another ballet class for years. I went straight to jazz."

It worked. She was hired to play a Jet girl in a New England tent tour of *West Side Story*.

After that, the pace of her professional career picked up markedly. She appeared in an industrial show, which led to her Broadway debut in *How to Succeed in Business Without Really Trying,* the first of two Pulitzer Prize-winning musicals with which she was involved. Bob Fosse choreographed the show, which had a big influence on the seventeen-year-old McKechnie, as did working with dance captain Gwen Verdon.

McKechnie said her parents began to feel more sanguine about her dance career after *How to Succeed.* Following that show, she was hired to play Philia in the first national tour of Stephen Sondheim's *A Funny Thing Happened on the Way to the Forum,* then left on a national tour that stopped in forty cities over fifty-two weeks. After that McKechnie got a job as a dancer in the TV show *Hullabaloo.* There she met her future husband, Michael Bennett, then a full-time dancer. "He told me he wanted to be a choreographer. I remember thinking 'It's good to have a dream.' "

The dream came true quickly, when the show's directors offered the four full-time dancers a chance to design some of their own steps. Bennett complied eagerly, creating some of his first choreography expressly for her. The bond was forged and they worked together often after that.

McKechnie worked on the film *Billy,* where she met dancer Clive Clerk, and made appearances on *The Tonight Show, The Ed Sullivan Show, The Steve Lawrence Show,* and in some industrial shows. She also was married, briefly.

She returned to Broadway in 1967 with Bennett's *A Joyful Noise,* playing the leading lady opposite John Raitt. Though her option was dropped before the show reached Broadway, McKechnie worked again with Bennett on *Promises, Promises* and *Company,* both of which helped her shake the notion that dancers were inferior to actors. "It started connecting something for me," she said, "that my dancing was indeed important to me, I could be more than just a dancer, the dance could be integrated with the text."

Though now identified as a "Michael Bennett dancer," she worked with Fosse once more, on the film *The Little Prince.*

McKechnie said she and Bennett were not romantically involved at that point, but she said they often discussed the state of theater and fantasized about running away together to New Zealand. Bennett also shared his ideas about an all-dancer show that would have no scenery, just mirrors and perhaps a barre. But he hadn't figured out a way to go about developing that very general idea into a musical. The next thing McKechnie heard, she was invited to take part in a tape session hosted by two of Bennett's dancer friends.

KELLY (CAROLE) BISHOP***

Bishop was born in Colorado Springs in 1945, and raised in Denver. She spent her high school years in northern California. "My mother was just as 'Sheila' describes her," said Bishop. "She was determined that I'd dance, from the moment she saw she had a girl."

Bishop's mother had studied ballet, but had stopped when she married. Bishop got lessons from her mother when she was a child, then found a ballet school. She immersed herself in ballet and fell in love with the film *The Red Shoes.*

Fate intervened at this point. The American Ballet Theatre opened a branch in Denver and at age nine or ten, Bishop enrolled. Her primary teacher, Francesca Romanoff, encouraged her lavishly. Romanoff's husband Dmitri, regisseur of ABT, taught there and served as Bishop's mentor. The branch school closed when Bishop was fourteen. Bishop's mother made the decision to move with the Romanoffs to San Jose, California, so that she could continue her training.

Bishop trained with them throughout her high school years, and when she graduated she went East to New York, having been promised a spot in the corps of the American Ballet Theatre. A political rivalry between the Romanoffs and ABT major-domo Lucia Chase prevented her from moving directly into the company, but Bishop did get a scholarship to the theater's school, where she continued to train for a time. But needing to support herself, she got a job in the Radio City Music Hall corps de ballet, and later discovered the world of Broadway gypsies. "I wanted to be in that world," she said, "so I moved in a completely different direction," from where her ballet training was leading.

She moved into the orbit of influential choreographer Ron Lewis, a protégé of the legendary Jack Cole who had trained Fosse, along with dance world demigods Chita Rivera and Gwen Verdon. From 1964 to 1966, Bishop became a Ron Lewis Dancer in nightclubs in Las Vegas and Lake Tahoe. In 1966 she decided to return to legitimate theater and worked in summer stock before passing an audition for her first Broadway musical, *Golden Rainbow,* in 1967. She appeared in several editions of "The Milliken Breakfast Show," and in 1968 was back on Broadway in *Promises, Promises,* choreographed by Michael Bennett.

Bishop was another of the *Rachael Lily Rosenbloom* alumni on Stevens's, Peacock's, and Bennett's minds when it came time to invite dance veterans to the tape session.

THOMMIE (THOMAS J.) WALSH***

Thomas Joseph Walsh III was born March 15, 1950, into a home filled with music. His paternal grandfather leased out cash registers, cigarette machines, and jukeboxes in the region of their home in upstate Auburn, New York. So as new hits climbed the charts, older 45s climbed out of the jukeboxes and onto Walsh's record player. Walsh learned how to work the machine early, and would dance around the house to the music.

Walsh described his father as "the Steve Rubell of Auburn." Instead of Studio 54, he operated Jitch's, a notorious bar and grill on the shore of Lake Owasco, one of the Finger Lakes. During the summer the place, a glorified hot dog stand with a Wurlitzer jukebox, would bring the little town some Mardi Gras atmosphere, but mostly it attracted the wrath of the local clergy and constabulary for allegedly serving alcohol to underage patrons. Walsh's father was the owner and bartender.

Repeatedly catching Walsh dancing in front of the mirror, his parents enrolled him in dance classes before he was five years old, and he soon was practicing tap, jazz, acrobatics, and ballet. He stayed with the same teacher, Irma Baker, for twelve years, with only one interruption.

His parents separated when he was six, and Walsh relocated for a time to Florida with his mother and maternal grandparents.

A confessed "pyro" and a lover of pranks, Walsh left his mark on the Sunshine State by breaking into a local theater, trying on the wigs and costumes, and then setting the building on fire for entertainment. "It was the first time my grandfather ever laid hands on me," he said, contritely. "Those poor actors." No one was hurt.

His parents reconciled the next year and they moved back to Auburn, but the local authorities finally shut down Jitch's and money became tight. When Walsh was twelve he started getting harassed and called a sissy for dancing. His mother wanted to take him out of dance class, but his father urged her to let him stay, since it was the thing he did best.

Walsh remembers watching *The Ed Sullivan Show* religiously and collecting Broadway show albums. He also watched what he calls "normal families" on TV sitcoms. He began flunking high school classes because he wanted only to dance. For two years he took a bus to nearby Syracuse to study dance on a higher level, and he remembers being enthralled when American Ballet Theatre did a performance in Syracuse. He auditioned for the Juilliard School and was so depressed about being rejected that he nearly joined the army.

Instead, he entered the Boston Conservatory of Music, an arts college, with the idea of someday becoming a member of the New York City Ballet. On the same trip to Manhattan during which he had his Juilliard audition, he saw his first Broadway shows: *Mame* with Angela Lansbury and *Hello, Dolly!* with Pearl Bailey.

Walsh worked briefly as assistant to the director of a musical theater camp in New Hampshire for $100 a week, and got his Equity card by appearing in a summer stock production of *Mame*. Unhappy at college, he tried hitchhiking back to Auburn during his junior year, but made it only as far as Albany, where he stayed with a friend who was preparing to go on tour with *Disney on Parade*. Walsh quit school and joined the tour, making $300 a week playing thirty cities in thirty weeks.

Becoming bored with *Disney,* Walsh quit to do a summer stock production of *Hello, Dolly!* starring Jane Morgan. Now twenty, he returned to the *Disney* show as a swing dancer for three weeks in Mexico.

His next job was the national tour of the Lauren Bacall musical *Applause,* directed by Ron Field, one of his idols. He was hired as understudy to Sammy Williams, and the two struck up a friendship. Walsh left the tour when he was hired as an apostle for the movie of *Jesus Christ Superstar,* being filmed in Israel. He sent his $1,000 weekly checks home to his parents and lived on his per diem pay. More valuable still were the friendships he made there with Baayork Lee and Robert LuPone.

Back in the United States, Walsh was invited by Ron Field to dance on *The Ed Sullivan Show,* which had been Walsh's career goal. He got called by Bob Avian via Baayork Lee, inviting him to join the cast of the musical *Seesaw,* directed by Michael Bennett. Also in the company were Anita Morris, Michon Peacock, Wayne Cilento, Mitzi Hamilton, and Tommy Tune, with whom he would do his most productive work for the next decade.

Walsh moved from there to the infamous *Rachael Lily Rosenbloom,* a short-lived musical that put him in touch again with choreographer Tony Stevens and dancer Michon Peacock.

Walsh's last pre-*Chorus Line* job was sashaying around the stage as "escort" to female impersonators in *Manhattan Follies,* a drag revue. Walsh passed up the national tour of *Seesaw* to stay in the show. Thus he was in town when Stevens called to invite him to the first tape session.

NANCY LANE*

Nancy Lane, which is her real name, felt handicapped by her looks when she was growing up in Clifton, New Jersey, where she was born in 1951. Her body was too thin, she thought, and her nose too big. Believing that she was too typed by her features to get a variety of acting roles, she began to dance.

"I was always funny and making people laugh," she said. "I wanted to be wanted. I felt I had to do that, so I was always entertaining people. It wasn't until I left *ACL* that I realized I didn't have to do that."

Lane began taking ballet lessons at age nine as therapy for bad feet, but her inborn dancing talent soon rose to the surface and she advanced quickly. In the euphoria at being named top of her class, she auditioned for the New York City Ballet, but was rebuffed. Discouraged, she avoided ballet until she got out of college.

The afternoon she was rejected by the NYCB, her mother saw an audition notice in the local paper. The community theater at the YMHA was seeking a Barbra Streisand type for a play it was doing. Lane had been taking singing lessons since she was seven and landed the part. To buttress her experience, she began studying at the Jarvis Dance Studio in New Jersey, where a teacher who became her mentor helped her get scholarships for three summers at the School for Creative Arts in Martha's Vineyard. She won studio awards in ballet when she was ages eleven, twelve, and thirteen, which hooked her on show business.

Lane had a close brush with Broadway at age 9 when one of her teachers, who was then appearing in the Jerry Herman musical *Milk and Honey,* arranged for Lane to audition for a child part in the show. Unfortunately, her mother feared a New York job would disrupt her life, and vetoed the audition.

Having tasted Broadway, Lane would sing and dance for hours to the five original cast albums they had in the house: *Funny Girl, Fiddler on the Roof, Hello, Dolly!, Oklahoma!,* and *South Pacific.* Though she was a mediocre student academically, she became involved at school in performing groups, the choir, the music department, the sports department, and cheerleading.

Funny Girl was the first Broadway show she saw. "I just fell in love with it," she said. "I loved everything about the theater, even just holding the tickets."

Lane finally made it to New York at age seventeen, when she began attending the Academy of Dramatic Arts. She would buy two-dollar standing-room tickets to whatever she could get into, and remembers seeing *Man of La Mancha* "about a million times."

Nevertheless, she said her parents didn't take her interest in show business seriously until she was in *A Chorus Line.* They pushed her to go to college, and despite low marks on her board exams, she was accepted at a college in Richmond, Virginia. Though she matriculated as a recreational leadership major, thinking that if all else failed she could become a camp counselor or a social director on a cruise ship, she wound up fast-talking the chairman of the theater department into admitting her as a theater major. She remembers flunking almost everything except theater, in which she got A's.

She did a season of non-Equity summer stock, then took an apartment in New York with her friend Gary in the middle of the theater district. She supported her studies by performing in dinner theater and stock productions, and one Equity season finally earned her a union card.

Lane was aware that she bore a resemblance to a New York dancer named Michon Peacock, then appearing in Michael Bennett's *Seesaw* on Broadway. So when she heard that Peacock was not going to take part in the national tour of the show, Lane hurried down to audition. She got the job, and in the ensuing tour made many of the contacts that prepared her for the *Chorus Line* audition. She met Baayork Lee, Sammy Williams, Crissy Wilzak—and Bennett.

PATRICIA GARLAND***

Born Patricia Sue Garland in Flint, Michigan, she adopted Trish as her stage name when she was appearing in the musical *Follies*. Her family moved to Lawrence, Kansas, when she was very young and she was raised there by a mother who had been discouraged in her own ambition to be a nurse. Garland said, "So she promised herself that when she had children she would help them fulfill their dreams."

Garland was very close to her older sister, Jacki, when she was growing up, though there was some sibling rivalry as well. Their traveling salesman father did not earn enough money to allow both sisters to take dance classes, so Garland would sit and watch as her sister took tap and ballet. Garland says she learned to dance by watching her sister in those classes, then trying to imitate the steps.

To pay for lessons, their mother did laundry and the girls cleaned the dance studio. Soon, Garland was taking classes of her own. "We couldn't have done it without her," Garland said. "She fed our interest."

To help earn money, the sisters danced at county fair contests.

Garland would dance in her tutu and Jacki would do acrobatics on boxes. They frequently won cash prizes in these amateur contests, eventually signing a guaranteed contract to perform at the fairs. "There I was," she said, "ten years old, dancing away on these truck beds full of holes, and I'm tripping and falling on my little ballet routine."

During winter she went to school and became a cheerleader and joined her school's pep club. She and her sister would fantasize about being movie stars. "I was always Kim Novak," Garland said, "and Jacki was Debbie Reynolds. We had different stars as our boyfriends." Because her ballet teacher was allied with the New York City Ballet, however, the Garland sisters were encouraged to shift their sights to New York, where they traveled by bus to audition.

But disappointment awaited Garland. She was eleven, and the age cutoff for NYCB summer courses was twelve. "We had come all this way and spent all this money and now I couldn't be a part of the classes but Jacki could." Instead, Garland studied with Madame Nevelska who had been with the Bolshoi Ballet. Garland then joined a regional dance company in Kansas City, and spent her summers dancing in Chicago on scholarship for Stone-Camryn, a school affiliated with the Ruth Page Ballet Company.

At age fifteen she auditioned for a summer with the San Francisco Ballet, and paid for her tuition with a Ford Foundation scholarship. A brother in the service, stationed in Oakland, helped her get set up in a boarding house. Garland danced all summer and ushered for the performances.

Garland came to New York at age seventeen hoping to restart her ballet career. Several companies wanted her to apprentice but she wanted a full membership in a corps. She joined a regional company with several former members of the San Francisco Ballet. To help support herself she baby-sat and borrowed money from her older sister.

Her luck changed one day as she was returning from a babysitting gig and glimpsed an audition notice in *Backstage* magazine seeking dancers five foot eight and over. That's how Ron Field came to hire her for her first musical comedy job, a national tour of *Cabaret* starting in Los Angeles. By the time she was nineteen, Garland had worked in several shows, including her first Broadway musical, *Georgie,* where she met Tony Stevens and Michael Shawn.

Garland was trying to pursue careers in both theater and television, and a time came in 1972 when she was hired by Michael Bennett to appear on Broadway in *Follies,* and by Bob Fosse to dance in the TV special "Liza with a Z." She also danced on *The Ed Sullivan Show.* Both Garland sisters were invited to the first tape session for *A Chorus Line.*

RONALD DENNIS*

Dennis's real name is Ronald Dennis Watson, though he dropped the "Watson" in 1966 when he got his first Equity show, the *Show Boat* revival at Lincoln Center.

Born in Dayton, Ohio, Dennis said he grew up in a town where the whites not only looked down on the blacks, but the blacks from one side of town looked down on those from the other side—his side.

"Dance class was the first place I felt free and accepted," he said. "The teachers and the students didn't put you down."

He started taking lessons at the neighborhood recreational center when he was five or six. A lady named Bessie Grady who ran the arts programs encouraged him to take classes. Dennis studied modern dance and then tap. He remembers putting taps on his regular shoes because he couldn't afford a separate pair of tap shoes. It made no difference to his innate ability, which blossomed. When he was still in junior high school Dennis was asked to take over teaching the younger children. In junior and senior high school he studied ballet, paying for classes by cleaning mirrors and mopping the floor.

Because both of Dennis's parents worked, they urged him to pursue something more practical. But he would get inspired by borrowing books and magazines on dance from the library, or by watching Garry Moore's and Red Skelton's variety shows on TV. Dennis then would dance for hours to the record player in front of a mirror.

Dennis said, "I always had a vision of the New York skyline in my head, New York or Hollywood. I had no fantasies about being a star, just being a dancer." At the school he met more people who shared his interest in the arts, many of whom happened to be white.

Dennis applied to Butler University in Indianapolis not far from Dayton. He won a half scholarship and worked for a year to earn money for tuition. One of his jobs was in summer stock theater, which he repeated after his junior and senior high school years. Among the shows he did were *Wildcat* with Martha Raye and Don Potter, and *Show Boat.*

On a less glamorous level, he got a job with the supermarket promotion company Plaid Stamps, which allowed him to transfer to its New York stamp redemption center after a year. Dennis therefore arrived in Manhattan with a steady source of income, which allowed him to study at the Joffrey Ballet School. When it became apparent that the company wouldn't accept him, he quit and began studying jazz dancing, and auditioning for Broadway shows.

In 1966 he was hired for the *Show Boat* revival, which had a cast that also included Garrett Morris. It ran six months, then went on tour. After that, his career took off. Dennis danced in the national tour of *Hallelujah, Baby!* He played Stanley and understudied Barnaby in the last six months of the Broadway run of *Hello, Dolly!* starring Pearl Bailey, and then went with it on tour. Barnaby was played by Winston DeWitt Hemsley, who later replaced Dennis as "Richie" in *A Chorus Line.* Dennis appeared in a summer stock package of *Sweet Charity* and developed his singing voice and his comedic skills with the Prince Street Players. Among his other jobs in the late 1960s was a nightclub stint in Florida, where he worked with Michel Stuart and Priscilla Lopez. He also began doing commercials.

When Dennis came back to New York he got a job in the long-running musical revue *Don't Bother Me, I Can't Cope,* which he held for a year and a half before he heard about the workshop of Bennett's "Dancer Project." Dennis is another of the dancers whom Bennett hired for the second workshop of *A Chorus Line* without a previous collaboration.

DON PERCASSI*

Donaldo Ricardo Michaele Umberto Percassi was born in Amsterdam, New York. His mother sang in nightclubs with her two brothers who played in the band and acted as her escorts. His father was a handsome marathon dancer who nearly made it to Hollywood.

Inspired by Fred Astaire, Gene Kelly and other dancing movie stars, and stimulated by all kinds of music, young Percassi literally would dance on the desks at school, prompting many notes home. He didn't hesitate to commandeer the other children to help put on shows any time, anywhere, including a children's playhouse where he attempted to stage a combination of *Kiss Me Kate, Brigadoon,* and *Good News.*

To channel his energy (and to help cure his flat feet), his parents sent him to dance school where he began studying tap at age five. While still in grade school he absorbed all he could of dance in Amsterdam, so his mother started driving him 60 miles to take classes in Albany, the state capital.

"I always had a lot of energy," he said, "To me, dancing felt natural. I picked up new steps as if somehow I had done them before. Still, I couldn't figure out what I was going to do with dance, until I met this English nun who had been a dancer. She's the one who advised me, 'If you're going to be loud, jump around and drive everybody crazy, why not get paid for it?' "

By the time he was thirteen the ritual was established: every Friday he would be driven to Manhattan where he had been admitted to the Joffrey School. He would stay with relatives and use the commuting time to memorize the great musicals instead of doing his homework. He eventually performed many of those same shows in New Jersey summer stock theaters where he earned his union card.

Immediately upon graduation from the High School of Commerce, Percassi was hired for the first London company of *West*

Side Story. "Imagine me working with—or even being in the same room with—theater greats Jerome Robbins, Leonard Bernstein, Chita Rivera . . . It was better than my wildest imaginings." Bob Avian and Michael Bennett were in the Paris company of *West Side Story,* and Percassi recalls sitting next to the two of them at a dinner Jerry Robbins gave for both companies. It was their first meeting.

Percassi made his Broadway debut in *High Spirits,* a musical based on Noël Coward's *Blithe Spirit.* Choreographed by Danny Daniels and directed by Coward himself, it starred Tammy Grimes and Bea Lillie. Percassi's part called for some flying on cables above the stage. One night in New Haven, he crashed into Grimes, knocking himself unconscious.

Many Broadway shows and TV stints later, he did the musical *Coco* with Katharine Hepburn, which he recalls as one of the most exciting moments of his career. But it was that show's choreographer, Bennett, who would have the most profound impact on Percassi's career when, five years later, he was auditioning dancers for the second workshop of *A Chorus Line.*

RENEE BAUGHMAN***

The sight of the wandlike and serenely magical Fred Astaire gliding through his elegant films made Charlene Renee Baughman, born July 27, 1949, in St. Louis, decide at age seven that she had to dance. "It was a great way to express myself and it pleased my parents," she said. "I was good at it and I didn't have to talk."

Though shy and quick to tears, she was ready to fall for a salesman's pitch (just as her *Chorus Line* character describes) when he came to her house selling dance lessons, touched her toe to the back of her head, and proclaimed her a natural dancer. Also like her onstage alter ego, she could never really sing. But that didn't stop her.

Baughman's brothers promised to take her to and from her lessons, but soon the task fell to her parents, who wound up ferrying her to classes almost nightly until she was 16 and old enough to drive a car. She picked up tap and ballet, both of which she executed for the entertainment of her movie buff father. She became so competitive and engrossed in her dancing, constantly improving her costumes and adding bits of business to her assigned dance routines, that her jealous classmates couldn't stand it. She finally was asked to leave her dance school, but moved to a better one in East St. Louis, requiring a trip across the Mississippi.

Jealousy pushed her out of her second school as well, when she had the temerity to beat the daughter of the school's owner in a competition for the junior company of the St. Louis Civic Ballet.

Continuing her precocity in her early teens, she was chosen a year early for the Civic's senior company, and got her first chorus line job when she was still underage, dancing at a chain of nightclubs in the St. Louis Gaslight Square area.

At age fourteen she auditioned for the local summer stock company, the St. Louis Municipal Opera, hoping to impress choreographer Ron Field. The Muny enforced a minimum age of sixteen for the adult chorus, sending her home disappointed. But she returned the following year, when Buddy Schwab was doing the dances, and managed to slip onto the line. It was an Equity production, and at age fifteen she was in the union. The Muny did a show a week, and her first was *My Fair Lady* with Douglas Fairbanks, Jr. She returned the following two years as well, practicing her dances on the wooden back porch of her house.

Baughman met Bennett in St. Louis when she was seventeen. Directing a company of *West Side Story,* he hired her for a walk-on part. "We were just supposed to fill in around the gym," she said, referring to the "Dance at the Gym" number, "but we were all in awe of him. It was a great company of dancers, incredibly choreographed. We had never seen anything like that."

She had gone to see the Radio City Music Hall Rockettes when she was ten. She also auditioned for the *Ted Mack Amateur Hour* doing a stair tap dance with a cane. She dropped the cane at the audition, however, "and needless to say, that was that. No Ted Mack for me."

Baughman's break came at the Muny the year Larry Fuller choreographed *The Wizard of Oz.* He told her that if she ever came to New York to call him for an audition. She did, and was cast in *Li'l Abner* at New Jersey's Papermill Playhouse.

In 1969 Baughman's mother helped her get settled in an apartment on West Fifty-first Street. To pay rent, Baughman had to start trudging to open chorus calls, which became a source of terror: She'd ace the dancing part, but would "wreck" the singing part. It didn't stop her from dancing on *The Ed Sullivan Show* for Peter Gennaro, or from being hired by Ron Field for her first Broadway musical, *Applause,* which gave her a steady job for two years. While dancing in a series of TV variety shows in the early 1970s, she resumed classes in Manhattan.

Baughman returned to the stage in 1973 for *Smith,* where she met Nicholas Dante and Trish Garland. The next she heard, Stevens was phoning to invite her to the tape session for *A Chorus Line*.

RICK (CAMERON) MASON**

Richard Maurice Mason was born December 8, 1949, in Denver, later taking the stage name Cameron Mason. Old movie musicals on TV made him want to dance. "I could escape into it," he said. "I was quiet and shy, and dancing was an outlet."

His family moved to Phoenix when he was very young, and he had a normal childhood there, growing up among the citrus groves. He was closer to his mother than he was to his father, a contractor who often was away from home. When Mason was in the seventh grade his mother got him a present: tap lessons with former Rockette Gerry Johnson. His mom took the lessons with him, twice a week. Mason was the only male at his level, and he took some razzing, including some from his father, who said he didn't want his son in tights. It wasn't until after *A Chorus Line* that Mason and his father established a relationship of mutual respect.

In the meantime, Mason was singing, dancing, and choreographing for neighborhood kids, at his church, and at his school. One of his leading ladies at school was Judy Kaye, who later won a Tony Award for *The Phantom of the Opera*. Though he was voted

"Most Congenial Senior," Mason was not an outstanding student. His thoughts were fixed on Broadway.

In Phoenix in the early 1960s his contact with professional theater was limited mostly to touring companies, of *Bye Bye Birdie* and other such contemporary musicals, though he did travel to Las Vegas to see *Hello, Dolly!,* with Bob Avian in the chorus.

To start a dancing career, he knew he had to leave Phoenix. So, one summer, Mason and a half-dozen other aspiring dancers traveled to Dallas to audition for Dallas Summer Music Theatre, a professional stock company operating there. Mason was the only one of the group to be hired. His first paying job was in a production of *Irma La Douce* starring Chita Rivera.

Mason did a half-dozen musicals in Dallas that summer, and though he remembers people telling him he should go to New York, he balked at doing so, not knowing anyone there. Instead, he headed West to Los Angeles where he had friends. He got a job as a messenger with a law firm, while taking classes at the Eugene Loring School and auditioning. His parents urged him to go to college and offered to pay his tuition, so he enrolled at University of California/Irvine, where Loring was a department head.

His grades were low but because of his talent the deal allowed him to continue. Mason studied ballet and jazz, and he shone in the next year's school musical, *Kiss Me, Kate,* but failed the written final exam. Now out on his own, he began auditioning, which led to his TV debut, splashing out of the ocean in a frog suit in a Julie Andrews special.

Mason was hired for a nightclub act in Paris, which catapulted him out of the Southwest where he had spent all his life. On his return to the United States he stopped in New York to visit a college friend, who took Mason to his first Broadway show, *Pippin.* Mason recalls, "I was bowled over. Bob Fosse became my idol."

Mason saw several other musicals, plays, and dance recitals, all of which made him resolve to relocate to New York. He arrived January 17, 1973, and was hired on his second audition, for a Florida production of *Promises, Promises,* which introduced him to Bennett's choreography.

In his brief, intense career in the two years before *A Chorus*

Line, Mason appeared in a revival of *The Pajama Game* on Broadway, in *The Most Happy Fella* at Wolftrap Farm Park, a theater in Vienna, Virginia, and in "The Milliken Breakfast Show" with Chita Rivera. Wayne Cilento also was in that "Milliken," as was Baayork Lee, who told Mason that Bennett had seen him in a rehearsal and wanted his name for future jobs.

The next time Mason heard from them, it was inviting him to audition for the first workshop of *A Chorus Line.*

PAMELA BLAIR**

John Lennon's assassination was a special blow to Blair, born in Bennington, Vermont. She said her two teenage ambitions were to escape the "normal and boring" life of Bennington, and to meet the Beatles. "He's the reason I'm in this business," she said, "and I never got to meet the guy."

Her life was laid out before her like a smooth, familiar path when she was a child—but then she heard the Beatles. "They told me through their music that there was a whole exciting world out there," she said.

Her family lived on a farm with horses, and she reports that from ages nine to eleven her horse was her best friend. When she was fifteen years old she first heard the Beatles, and "I started taking ballet lessons to be different as the Beatles were different." She studied tap and ballet and dreamed of becoming a Rockette.

Soon she lost interest in horses and became leader of the pack at her school. An athlete who played basketball and field hockey she suffered a jolt when she was singled out for enthusiastic praise by her coach, causing the other players, her buddies, to resent her and turn against her. The experience had a profound effect on the sensitive tomboy, and she gradually withdrew into dancing.

She escaped from Vermont at age sixteen, moving to New York and trying to audition for dance companies. Turned down repeatedly for a lack of experience, she wound up lying about her age to get jobs as a go-go dancer. She also worked as a waitress and a barmaid before temporarily giving up on New York and heading for California, where she was hired as a dancer for *The Andy Williams Show* and *The Ed Sullivan Show.* She began studying jazz dancing when it became apparent that her body was wrong for ballet.

She didn't like California and returned to New York where she discovered that, despite her conservative upbringing, she was considered very attractive to men. She even danced topless for a time at the Peppermint Lounge in Newark, shaking what someday would be the most famous tits and ass on Broadway. Not knowing how to handle male attention, she fell into a series of unhappy romances, and got involved with a pimp, who plied her with drugs and tried to lure her into becoming a hooker. When she called the police on him, he threatened her life.

"Whenever I don't seem to be getting anywhere in this business," she said, "I try to remember that I was almost a hooker and that I've come a long way."

Though the stormy love life continued, things began to look up, professionally. The years of dance lessons and practice began to pay off, and she finally made her Broadway debut as a replacement in *Promises, Promises,* which introduced her to Michael Bennett's choreography.

Her talent as a dancer and her erotic *je ne sais quoi* got her roles in the short-lived musical *Wild and Wonderful,* and as a replacement in Bennett's *Seesaw.* Blair's major credit, however, was understudying the lead in the Jule Styne musical *Sugar.* In the summer of 1974 she auditioned successfully for the first workshop of *A Chorus Line.*

SAMMY WILLIAMS***

Born in Trenton, New Jersey, on November 13, 1948, Samuel Joseph Williams was introduced to dance while sitting on the sidelines, watching as his sister took dance class. As children do, he mimicked her and one day the dance teacher coaxed Sammy to get up and perform along with the class. "When I realized that I could dance," he said, "I fell in love with it. It was something I belonged to, that belonged to me."

Soon, Williams was enrolled in a dance class of his own. His first teacher was John Tucci, whom Williams recalls as a father figure. However, he suffered constant teasing about being a sissy. "I danced to escape," he said. "I was afraid of bullies, but in dance class I was accepted."

Though Trenton is not far from New York, Williams grew up knowing little about Broadway. His primary exposure to dance was on the weekly *Ed Sullivan Show*. Though his brother played accordion, the Williams family wasn't a musical one. Among the family-oriented activities was a trip to the New Jersey shore each summer, where his sister danced on the Steel Pier in Atlantic City.

Williams got his first paid dancing job when he was eight. His family had taken him to see *Finian's Rainbow* at a nearby tent theater and a few weeks later when the producer was looking for two children to play brother and sister in *South Pacific,* he hired Williams and his sister. They sang the opening and closing number "Dites-moi."

Williams didn't get another chance to be in a show until his high school's production of *The Music Man*. In the meantime he continued in dance lessons, and found he had equal skills at decorating and designing. He took special pride in designing Christmas decorations for his home and school.

When Williams was in tenth grade he auditioned for his first summer stock job, at Trenton's Theater in the Park, where he finally got to appear in *Finian's Rainbow,* along with a season full of standards, including *The King and I, South Pacific,* and others.

Williams's parents separated just as he was beginning studies at Ryder College, forcing him to get a job at the New Jersey Department of Transportation and pursue his degree in the evenings. "I would daydream about the stage," he said. Ryder was opening a new theater department, and Williams took part in its first production, *Carousel* choreographed by Tommy Tune.

When Williams was eighteen, he was appearing in *The King and I* directed by Eddy Earl, who was understudying Anthony Newley on Broadway in *The Roar of the Greasepaint—The Smell of the Crowd.* Williams chanced to see Earl one night when he was subbing for the star, and had a revelation. "I sat in the second balcony and saw my first Broadway show—and I was just wiped out," Williams said. "Eddy was standing there singing 'Who Can I Turn To' at center stage at the Shubert Theatre in a spotlight all by himself, and it was a devastating moment for me. I said to myself, 'That's where I want to be, and that's where I'm *going* to be.' "

Within weeks, Williams was dancing in a national tour of *Funny Girl*. That same season he auditioned for Michael Bennett's *A Joyful Noise* on Broadway and for a summer stock production of Bob Fosse's *Sweet Charity* and was hired for *Charity*. Just three weeks after being hired for *Charity,* Williams was snatched away to make his Broadway debut as a swing dancer understudying thirty-one roles for Gower Champion in *The Happy Time*. He followed it with a six-month bus-and-truck tour of Champion's *Hello, Dolly,!* with Yvonne DeCarlo.

His luck continued when Ron Field hired him as a dancer for *Applause*. When the show opened in New York, Williams was thrilled to see a photo of himself and star Lauren Bacall on the marquee of the Palace Theatre. "If I had a dream as a child and as a performer," he said, "it was to be a dancer in a Broadway musical. I had accomplished it and I was twenty years old."

Williams stayed with *Applause* two years in New York and six months on the road, meeting Nicholas Dante, Mitzi Hamilton, and Thommie Walsh, who was his understudy on the tour.

Williams also worked in California for a time, dancing on a TV special with Fred Astaire.

Back in New York, he got hired to dance *No, No, Nanette* at Westbury Music Fair on Long Island. At Walsh's recommendation, he went to Baayork Lee, seeking a job as a replacement in *Seesaw*. Lee told him that she only was hiring dancers who had worked with Bennett before, but she took his name. During the run of *Nanette,* Lee called him, and within a day he was back on Broadway, playing the last six weeks of the *Seesaw*'s run, then going out on the national tour. Williams's name also made it onto the list of dancers invited to the original taping session for *A Chorus Line*.

PRISCILLA LOPEZ***

Lopez was born in the Bronx February 26, 1948, the third child in her family, but the first born in New York, her older brother and sister having been born in the family's native Puerto Rico. To the sound of the radio she grew up dancing and singing with her mother, who subscribed to *Hit Parade* magazine so they could learn the words to the songs. Lopez became a fan of TV's *Star Time* talent program and, at age seven, began taking lessons at the *Star Time* dancing school in Brooklyn, where her parents moved when she was a year and a half old. She soon changed to a more exacting dance school in Brooklyn Heights where she learned tap, acrobatics, and ballet.

She started taking dance lessons in Manhattan each Saturday, pausing afterward for dinner with her mother at the Horn and Hardart cafeteria. When Lopez was eleven she saw her first Broadway show, *My Fair Lady,* though she still fantasized about being in the movies.

Her parents managed to find money for Lopez's dance lessons, which spread beyond Saturdays to Mondays, Tuesdays, and Thursdays. By the time she was in junior high school, she was taking lessons five days a week.

In hopes of turning those lessons to practical use, she had auditioned for shows as early as age eight. She got a job as an extra in the film version of *West Side Story* when she was twelve, her first professional paying job.

Shortly afterward she was accepted at the High School of the Performing Arts. Little did PA realize it was auditioning someone who would become one of its most infamous students. Her experience with the head of the drama department became the basis for the *Chorus Line* song, "Nothing," about a cruel and discouraging teacher who belittles her efforts to understand some esoteric classroom techniques.

Lopez did non-Equity summer stock during her junior year, and following her graduation she was cast as the eldest daughter in an Equity production of *The Sound of Music* at the Bucks County Playhouse in New Hope, Pennsylvania. She faced a choice that summer: college or dance. "I didn't want to go to college," she said, "I wanted to work. I'd been auditioning since I was eight years old."

Lopez got hired on her first Broadway open audition, for the musical *Breakfast at Tiffany's,* starring Mary Tyler Moore and choreographed by Michael Kidd. Unfortunately, the show was one of the notable flops of the 1960s, and Lopez had to take a job in Alexander's department store in Manhattan to pay for her lessons.

Lopez wasn't stuck there for long. She read in the trade papers that Ron Field, who had just won a Tony Award for *Cabaret,* was staging a revue in Florida. Lopez hurried to the audition and was hired immediately. It turned out to be one of Michel Stuart's maiden efforts as a producer, and among the dancers in the company was another future *ACL*er, Ron Dennis.

Breakfast at Tiffany's composer Bob Merrill next wrote *Henry, Sweet Henry,* and Lopez, unhappy to be working in Florida, flew back for the audition. Lopez met Michael Bennett at that audition, and he offered her the job of swing dancer. Bennett moved her up to a regular chorus spot when one became vacant, but the show closed after just eighty performances.

Still, Lopez now had Kidd, Field, and Bennett choreography under her belt, which made it easier for her to get hired for "The Milliken Breakfast Show," which Bennett staged that year. Having raised her profile in the business considerably in just two seasons, Lopez was ripe to move into her first leading role, in *Your Own Thing,* the 1968 off-Broadway rock musical based on Shakespeare's *Twelfth Night.* It ran for two and a half years, plus a national tour and a Mexican production for which Lopez was able to use her Spanish.

Having established a reputation as a reliable triple-threat performer, she understudied Sandy Duncan in the lead of *The Boyfriend,* and played the role herself on the national tour. She came back to Broadway in Bennett's *Company,* understudying Donna McKechnie in the featured dancer spot, and taking over the role in the show's last months.

Also at this time she met trombonist Vincent Fanuele, a Broadway pit musician. They were married in January 1972 just after *Company* closed. They struggled along in their new apartment on West Sixty-ninth Street between Central Park West and Columbus Avenue for the first few months of that year until both of them got hired at about the same time, she for "Milliken," he for the Phil Silvers revival of *A Funny Thing Happened on the Way to the Forum.*

In 1973 she got good reviews in the off-Broadway satirical revue, *What's a Nice Country Like You Doing in a State Like This?,* then went into *Pippin* in early January 1974, playing the title character's scheming stepmother. Part of the reason the taping session for *A Chorus Line* later that month was held after midnight was so that she and the other people working in shows could freshen up after their Saturday night performance.

ROBERT LUPONE**

Robert LuPone was seduced into dancing by a colored light. When he was seven he saw his younger sister Patti dancing in a PTA recital. "There was a color wheel onstage, with various gels that spun in front of a light," he said. "She was wearing a Hawaiian skirt and her skirt went from red to blue to yellow to green to red. Wow. I said to my mother I wanted to wear that skirt so that could happen to me. She said, 'The only way you can do that is to go to dance class.' And that's how I started dancing."

With Patti and his twin brother Bill, LuPone formed a dance trio that made appearances at a Jones Beach Theater talent contest, where they came in second, and on the old *Ted Mack Amateur Hour* TV show.

Presaging the serious adult, the young LuPone took the precepts of his Roman Catholic religion with solemnity. But when a priest denied him absolution for throwing spitballs in catechism, he said he made his own confession and never went back.

A lover of music from an early age, LuPone remembers cutting grass the summer of his fifteenth year so that he could buy a high-quality stereo system. "The tuner was my left arm," he said, "the phonograph was my right arm. I danced to the music." Richard

Rodgers's score for the TV series "Victory at Sea" was a favorite.

That same year LuPone won a full scholarship to the Martha Graham School of Contemporary Dance in New York. For three years he immersed himself in learning about dance during the week and played in his high school marching band at football games on weekends.

LuPone studied for a time at Adelphi University on Long Island; then, in 1965, he won another full scholarship, this time to study dance at the Juilliard School. "Juilliard forces you to work beyond your capabilities," he said. "When you walk out of there you believe you are Picasso. But that's impractical."

LuPone continued his ballet training with Antony Tudor, whom he came to regard as the paragon of an artist. After Juilliard he was faced with four choices: American Ballet Theatre, Metropolitan Opera Ballet, the Harkness Ballet, or the Alvin Ailey Dance Company. LuPone chose the Harkness, but soon found he was dissatisfied with the Harkness technique. The exuberance of Broadway dance appealed to him more. He was twenty-one when he auditioned for the Lincoln Center revival of *West Side Story,* and his theatrical career was born.

Over the years, LuPone danced in *The Pajama Game* with Liza Minnelli; *Kiss Me, Kate* with Patrice Munsel and Dan Dailey, and the revue *Arabian Nights* at the Jones Beach Theater on Long Island.

Despite injuring his leg and back, he continued to appear on Broadway and off in *The Rothschilds, Minnie's Boys, Noël Coward's Sweet Potato,* and the stage version of *Jesus Christ Superstar*. When he was hired for the film version of *Superstar* his roommate was Thommie Walsh. He also came in contact with Baayork Lee, and other members of the circle he would work with in *A Chorus Line*.

LuPone keenly felt that his training prepared him to be more than a dancer, which reflected the prevailing pre-*Chorus Line* attitude about dancing as an incomplete art. He thought of himself as an actor first, so he quit dancing for a time and took a job as a night watchman while he was studying with Harold Clurman. He took roles in the productions of the Goodman Theater in Chicago and the Arena Stage in Washington and was cultivating his acting career when he heard about Michael Bennett's workshop and chose to change the course of his career once again.

4.

Subsequent Taping Sessions (February–April 1974)

It was almost noon when the dancers descended that steep and narrow stairway and into the street. Down Third Avenue, Sunday morning church bells could be heard.

"I felt as if I had been levitating all night," Walsh said. "I think of that night in a spiritual and holy way."

For nearly twelve hours people had cried and remembered and told terrible stories. They shocked each other and broke one another's hearts. "Nerves were very raw by seven in the morning," said Bishop. "We were all a bunch of embryos practically. We couldn't take any more. We were *tired*."

With morning sun spilling over them, they performed a ritual of unity, standing in a circle and holding hands. Bishop recalls, "It was like a current running through us."

Everyone who stood in that circle reports feeling a version of the same thing. Sharing their life stories had linked them. "The experience was unique to me," Garland said. "I felt that something special had happened. Something was born that night. I couldn't sleep after that when I should have been exhausted. I was so high I couldn't do anything."

That feeling persisted in the days immediately following. The tape session had been a special revelation for Priscilla Lopez, who, along with McKechnie and Bennett, was one of the only ones there with firsthand experience in professional group therapy. Lopez had been attending one such group for a year but confessed, "I had sat there for a year and never opened my mouth. But I was so elated by this experience at the taping session that I went back to my group and told them I had just found out what group therapy was about. I couldn't shut up."

It was the first glimmer of the special camaraderie *A Chorus Line* inspired in its participants. They wouldn't always get along, but from the first tape session there was the sense of a group to be defended.

The experience had been profound for Bennett as well. To corroborate his impression, he began telephoning the session participants to gauge their reactions.

"Michael starting calling and saying, 'Wasn't it interesting,'" Walsh said. "At that time I felt very special, that he was calling me and asking me what I thought about it all. But he had done that to everybody."

The dancers networked quickly to find out who had said what to Bennett and what he had said back to them. There was a consensus that even at twelve hours, the first tape session had just begun to span the breadth of their experience. Most were willing, and by this time eager, for an encore.

The second tape session was scheduled for early February, two weeks after the first, at the same time and in the same dance studio. This time Stevens asked Wayne Cilento to lead the preliminary dance class. "I was a nervous wreck," Cilento said. "I was taking a great many classes at the time and I did a combination that would kill a horse because I was so terrified. I did it to Stevie Wonder's 'Livin' in the City.' It was a great combination but the whole place was in an uproar screaming that it was too difficult.

"I remember Michael getting up and saying, 'Okay, I gotta learn this'—I had kind of won him over. He really liked it and Michael started dancing, it was real exciting."

The dancing lasted a much shorter time than at the first session. "We were all so hot to get back into that special little room and sit down in that circle and find out more things," said Bishop.

But there was no mistaking it. Something was wrong, was missing.

"It was a disappointment," Bishop said.

"I hardly remember the second session," Garland said. "It was in no way as exciting as the first. It's like opening night versus two nights later where you may have done a better performance but there isn't that excitement and that high, that adrenaline pumping."

Part of the problem was the comparative lack of spontaneity. Everyone had been primed by the first session. They began to "act"—that is, they knew the way the sessions were conducted, and had a chance to rethink their responses, so, in the manner of performers, they would do "readings" of their autobiographies. It was potentially more entertaining, but the artifice made it seem less frank.

Also, there were new faces at the second taping session. "I felt a little invaded with the new people invited," Lopez said. "I felt we were breaking the chain of continuity because we had to go back and listen to their whole lives. They had to catch up."

The first session had focused on childhood. Part of the reason so much of *A Chorus Line* dwells on childhood memories and impressions is that the most fervent tapes are from that first session. Bennett and the writers eventually developed it as a theme—the dancers are repeatedly referred to as "kids," a term they often use to describe themselves, even today. Many artists draw on the conflicts of their childhoods. For dancers, who worship youthfulness, vigor, limberness—and the freedom of spirit to turn those attributes to artistic purposes—childhood has special significance. The show's preoccupation with childhood is therefore apropos, but came about in a completely unpremeditated way. That may be another reason the second workshop lacked the magic of the first. Bennett's questions moved past childhood into early adulthood, examining what it was like becoming a dancer, coming to New York, the pain of auditions. Bennett chose to skip over adolescence, leaving it for a planned later group tape session that never came about. Very little of the material that went into "Hello Twelve, Hello Thirteen, Hello Love" came out of the tape sessions. In fact, that period remained unexplored until just a few months before the opening, making it one of the last major components of *A Chorus Line*.

For McKechnie, the second session was even more intense than the first. "When we came back there was fervor and there was more of the same [openness] but it was in progression. That's when it got into heavier things, like sexuality. People talked about their first experiences, their embarrassment, their humiliations. Some were very open and anxious to discuss it. It made me very nervous but it was interesting."

Two of the most memorable moments in *A Chorus Line* can be traced to the second session. One of them involved Nicholas Dante, the dancer who wanted to write. Bishop remembers him talking about wanting to be a writer. "He had written an interesting little piece that he had given to me," she said. "There was a blue character and a red character—red was the passionate character, blue was probably the sad character. It was this little playlet with these emotional color-characters."

At the second session, Dante shared the story of how he was sexually abused as a child, and how he came to terms with homosexuality. In particular, he told the story of working in the Jewel Box Revue, a venerable transvestite extravaganza that had survived in various editions for decades on the tatty fringes of New York's nightlife.

In particular he told of how he hid both gayness and his profession from his parents, telling them only that he was working in theater. The night before he was scheduled to leave with a touring version of the revue, his parents surprised him by appearing backstage to bid him farewell. Ambushed in high drag, he hoped they wouldn't recognize him, but they did. He was humiliated until he heard his father tell the producer, "Take care of my son."

That simple story of recognition and affirmation resonated for this group that craved approval but maintained unorthodox enough life-styles to make many of them anathema to their families. Of all the stories told in the two tape sessions, and of all the long monologues that eventually were spun out of them, Dante's autobiographical story, sculpted and recast for the character of Paul, played by Sammy Williams, wound up in the script of *A Chorus Line* virtually unchanged.

"Nicholas was one of the most honest because he revealed himself," McKechnie said. "It was like he was in search of the truth himself, and I think it showed."

One of the show's best-remembered songs originated in the

second tape session as well, though under less somber circumstances. Dancer Mitzi Hamilton told the story of how she gradually became aware that her excellent dance technique was not getting her jobs, and she didn't know why. A peek at a casting director's evaluation sheet told her the story. She got top marks for dancing, but her appearance had been found wanting. Her solution was to head for a plastic surgeon to have her breasts and buttocks enhanced. With the scars recently healed, she was looking forward to great changes in her professional and personal life.

Thommie Walsh recalls that she was so proud of her latest developments, she took off her blouse and showed them off. As her shirt came off, "Dance: Ten; Looks: Three" was born. (It was originated in the show by Pam Blair, though Hamilton later assumed the role.)

"So we do the second session and Mitzi Hamilton bared her breasts, which in a sense we all did," Walsh said. "Once again there were the catnappers and the people who didn't smoke, and the people who ate more, and the people who danced better than other people . . . and then there was the intrigue of Mitzi Hamilton's new breasts. It was twenty-five people jammed into a studio loft creating a time capsule. It was very communal and, again, very spiritual."

That sense, that feeling, was rooted in the original Peacock-Stevens concept. "It was going to be more like what you'd call a communist society," Bishop said. "It was going to be very even and very fair. That was the intriguing thing. Everyone was going to be able to say, 'You know how you could do that step better . . . ?' Or 'I have an idea for a line for this . . .' That was my fantasy of how this project was going to come out."

As it turned out, she said, that's more or less what made this project so special for the participating dancers. Holding to that ideal enabled them to make it happen. "*I* was able to," said Bishop. "I think that Michael opened the door for that to happen. I think at times he regretted it. But that actually did happen, ultimately."

But as of the second tape session, there was no longer much talk of starting a dance company, per se.

"All of a sudden this other idea started to reveal itself," Baughman said. "We didn't even talk about forming a company that night. I remember at the second rap session, Bennett saying, did we think there was a show here? We were like a bunch of puppy dogs wagging our heads, we were all so in love with the idea."

But after the second tape session, most of the participants heard nothing for several months. A group of the future *Chorus Line* people worked together that spring in a short-lived musical titled *Music! Music!* at the City Center. Directed by Martin Charnin, later to stage and cowrite *Annie,* it was a survey of American music going back to 1895. With a narration written by Alan Jay Lerner, it featured Robert Guillaume and Larry Kert, among others. One of the other featured performers was Donna McKechnie. Renee Baughman was her understudy. As choreographer, Tony Stevens oversaw the singing and dancing ensemble, which included Michon Peacock, Trish Garland, and Thommie Walsh. Theoni Aldredge did the costumes.

Music! Music! opened April 11, 1974, a year to the week before the first preview of *A Chorus Line.* It would prove to be a busy year.

Bennett's vague idea for a dancers' musical suddenly had acquired characters, if not a plot. The tapes provided a mass of material from which to work. To fill in gaps, Bennett conducted additional tape sessions in his apartment, with a variety of New York dancers. The eventual number of dancers on those tapes totaled fifty-two, but only two of the dancers from his auxiliary private tape sessions got hired for the show: his left hand, Baayork Lee; and Pamela Blair. Bennett's continuation of the tape sessions was significant for another reason. It had begun as Stevens's and Peacock's project, but from the moment Bennett put himself in charge of the tape sessions, it became Bennett's project. He had the clout to get a show on its feet, and the dancers instinctively deferred to him.

The other dancers from the tape sessions became involved in other shows, and for the time being, "the dancer project," as it came to be known, seemed to have moved to the back burner.

"The next thing I remember," said Walsh, "I was auditioning for my own life story at the New York Shakespeare Festival."

5.

Preparations for the Workshop (Spring and Summer 1974)

In an unspoken agreement, "the dancer project" had become "Michael Bennett's dancer project" and they waited to see what he would do next, confident that it would be something wonderful.

The dancers admired Bennett and trusted him. In many ways, he was a fulfillment of their fantasies. He had started just as they had, living the gypsy life, going from show to show, including some legendary ones like *West Side Story,* and some lesser-known ones like *Subways Are for Sleeping, Here's Love,* and *Bajour.* He also had gone the next step beyond, becoming a recognized choreographer. The Buffalo-born Bennett had a talent for making contacts quickly, upward, downward, and laterally in his business. He preferred to work with the best, and once he had established a contact, he would return to the relationship again and again. He was quick to do a favor, quick to repay favors done for him—and unhesitating to call those favors in.

In the six years since he'd made his debut as a choreographer, he'd worked on several flops, including *Henry, Sweet Henry* (1967), on which he made one of his first important contacts, with his rehearsal pianist, another ambitious young man named Marvin Hamlisch. But he'd had his first hit and his first Tony Award nomination with *Promises, Promises* (1968).

Aside from demonstrating a recognizable style—particularly in *Turkey Lurkey Time,* an office Christmas party number that featured a trio of Margo Sappington, Donna McKechnie, and Baayork Lee—he showed he could work comfortably with a first-time Broadway composer, in this case pop tunesmith Burt Bacharach. Opening just a few months after *Hair, Promises* demonstrated that a rather conventionally structured Broadway musical could incorporate contemporary music and dance and not look silly. Not all rock music had to be sung or danced by hippies.

Promises, Promises also introduced Bennett to his next important contact, librettist Neil Simon. Producer-director Hal Prince invited Bennett to work on his upcoming project, *Company.* It was the first in composer Stephen Sondheim's remarkable sequence of 1970s musicals that continued with *Follies, A Little Night Music, Pacific Overtures,* and *Sweeney Todd, the Demon Barber of Fleet Street.* Opening in the first months of the new decade, *Company* was Sondheim's most pop-inflected score, utilizing a pit chorus like that in *Promises.* All these were familiar territory to Bennett. *Company* brought Bennett another Tony nomination.

That in turn led to the next Prince-Sondheim-Bennett collaboration, *Follies.* Bennett got codirecting credit and thereby shared in that year's Tony Award for best director.

Bennett had further fulfilled the dancer's fantasy by moving beyond dancing entirely. Time takes its toll on dancers harder and faster than it does on most athletes. Once established as dancers, many of them look to develop their acting ability so they can continue working onstage after their pliés begin to lose smoothness. Along with everything else that it would be, *A Chorus Line* would prove to be a bridge, helping dancers to cross into new stage careers. Bennett had already done that, directing the nondancing show *Twigs,* written by *Company* librettist George Furth. Bennett also is credited with writing the libretto of *Seesaw,* a project on which he also took over as director. Bennett was helped in his libretto work by Neil Simon, who, in addition to his remarkably successful career as a playwright was also a veteran play doctor. Bennett would direct Simon's *God's Favorite* later in 1974, and would call on Simon for help when *A Chorus Line* was in its last weeks of workshopping.

Threaded in and out of these projects were the dancers, for

whom Bennett always maintained a special deference. It wasn't a sentimental deference, it was a tough deference born of knowing how short and hard their careers were and how little respect they got for them. Dancers sensed this. Also, since *Promises,* Bennett's touch had been golden. That's what brought them all out on a snowy January midnight even though the project was a mystery. And that's what kept them waiting from the second taping session in February 1974 until that summer when the phones started ringing again.

"I stayed in touch with Michael after the [tape] sessions," McKechnie recalled. "I remember him calling and being very excited one night, telling me that Joe Papp had come up to his place. He heard the tapes—he didn't even want to hear all of them, just an hour's worth—and right away said, 'Okay, you can have anything you want in the theater.' Why would Joe give him carte blanche after listening to one hour only? He has great instinct. He knew Michael was not some kid off the street. At the time, I believe, Joe needed the connection with commercial theater. The Shakespeare Festival was having financial troubles and Michael told me he [Papp] was on the verge of losing everything. Michael wanted control, and that's what Joe gave him. Joe's whole nature was to invest in creative things. Most Broadway producers don't do that."

Joe Papp was, and is, boss of the New York Shakespeare Festival. The Festival began in a church basement in 1954 and graduated to a flatbed truck, performing the Bard's works to ghetto kids in the summer of 1956. But after establishing a home of its own at the former Astor Library in Greenwich Village in 1967, the Festival began offering productions of adventuresome new scripts by New York playwrights.

Things began to change with *Hair.* Begun in the most unprepossessing of surroundings with seemingly the least promising of composers and librettists, *Hair* managed to capture the zeitgeist of the late 1960s. Unable to meet the demand for tickets downtown, Joe Papp moved the production to Broadway's Biltmore Theatre where it was an immediate sensation, and ran more than four years.

It's one thing to go begging for foundation cash to keep things afloat each year. It's quite another—and a much nicer—thing to have a cash cow grazing on Broadway. Joe Papp used *Hair* to suckle myriad personal and resolutely noncommercial projects, encouraging minorities, women, and avant-garde writers to become involved in the creative process of theater.

By the mid 1970s the Shakespeare Festival was staging relatively little Shakespeare at the Public Theater, leaving most of that for its summer seasons at the Delacorte Theater in Central Park. Papp also had been put in charge of the Vivian Beaumont Theatre in Lincoln Center. The Festival had evolved as a showcase for emerging artists, a fountain of new theater talent. It also was the personal vision of Joe Papp. Papp reigned supreme in his Versailles on Lafayette Street. He would continue to give favored actors and playwrights work long after critics, and sometimes even audiences, had decided against them. Papp believed in them, and behold, there was work in the land.

And it wasn't so much that Papp's taste was unerring or even consistent. Much of what appeared at the Public Theater was critically savaged and instantly forgotten. But Papp had the ability to manage money. This brought support from philanthropists like LuEsther T. Mertz, charitable organizations like the Rockefeller Foundation, and public funding sources. He knew how to stroke contributors, make them feel a part of a cultural endeavor. He also was a shrewd producer who wasn't shy about transferring his successes to commercial engagements that would also generate income.

Perhaps most crucially, he knew how to take chances, to explore unfamiliar paths, to experiment. If nine out of ten experiments were failures, he knew that he'd have at least one success as long as he put on ten productions. The difference with Papp—and with the subscription audience that supported the New York Shakespeare Festival—is that they were as interested in the flops as in the hits. It was all part of a *process,* a favorite term among theater artists for the ongoing evolution of thoughts and styles.

Nevertheless, the commercial hits helped pay the bills, and Papp's two biggest meal tickets of the early 1970s, *Hair* and the musical adaptation of *Two Gentlemen of Verona,* had closed, in July of 1972 and May of 1973 respectively. Papp was as interested as ever in the process, but a new hit wouldn't have hurt either.

Both of the Shakespeare Festival's big hits helped launch a new generation of American musicals. A musical is a synthesis of all the art forms—a super art form whose concept is traceable back to opera composer Richard Wagner. Wagner envisioned what he called a *Gesamtkunstwerk,* a kind of supermusical. The idea is still very much alive. The goal of today's writers and performers is to say wonderful things with it, and to retain the joy.

There have been three well-documented generations of American musicals. The first was the transplanted generation of European-style operetta—shows by Victor Herbert, Rudolf Friml, and others. The second was the golden age of innocent, tuneful musical comedies—shows by Kern, Gershwin, Berlin, Youmans, and their brethren. The third was the age of the big razzmatazz spectacle that ran for years and set the standard for the biggest and best in live entertainment anywhere—Rodgers and Hammerstein were the first and were followed by Lerner and Loewe, Jule Styne, Jerry Herman. The fourth-generation musicals could be said to have come of age with *A Chorus Line,* but the roots were apparent as far back as 1957, with Bernstein and Sondheim's *West Side Story.* The new shows integrated music and drama in ways never dared before, developing musical theater into a sturdy form of entertainment that can tell every nuance of any story writers can conceive. No longer evoking just giggles, sighs, or roars, these pieces combine the latest in music, art, dance, drama, even video and computers, to capture inspiration, sarcasm, exhilaration, doubt, reverence, aspiration, fatalism, optimism—to create works that reflect our time.

Musicals were once a lower-middle-class entertainment. They were inexpensive, plentiful, and fairly crude—much as television was until recently. Wealthy and better-educated audiences stayed away for the most part, opting instead for opera.

The second generation of composers get credit for having bred the native American hybrid. The third generation refined it. As that refinement took place and musicals became more subtle, they became suitable entertainment for the wealthy and better educated. But these new audiences began to demand more sophisticated fare. As musicals have become more sophisticated, some have scared off Mr. and Mrs. John Q. Public.

Also, as they have become more sophisticated, they have become more expensive. The growing power of Actors Equity,

American Federation of Musicians Local 802, the Association of Theatrical Press Agents and Managers (ATPAM), the International Alliance of Theatrical Stage Employees and Moving Picture Operators of the U.S. and Canada (IATSE), and other unions has added hugely to the tab, as has the growth in the cost of insurance, taxes, and contracts that let point-of-origination casts participate in profits. All these have made a big dent in the number and nature of musicals.

Higher costs have driven up the cost of tickets, making them available only to the affluent, which in turn has accelerated the demand for sophistication, which in further turn has accelerated costs. This spiral is a wondrous thing to see. Much commented upon in every forum about theater, it is the central force determining what musicals look and sound like.

In the decade and a half since 1975, musicals have been running longer than ever before. But most of the people who write them today—the magic workers—stay in the background, unlike their predecessors of a half century ago.

What Bennett and the chorus "kids" did in *A Chorus Line* was to show that the more thoughtful fourth generation of musicals could be big hits. They popularized the form.

With all the progress musicals have made, librettos are still in the dark ages. Or rather, *back* in the dark ages. After the golden age of librettos in the 1950s and 1960s, when plot was all-important, shows now go begging for good solid stories and storytellers. The situation is reminiscent of the 1920s and 1930s when the idea of using musical theater to tell a coherent story was considered quaint at best; more likely absurd.

But this changed when Oscar Hammerstein II, Joseph Stein, Michael Stewart, Abe Burrows, and Alan Jay Lerner began writing shows that had tales to tell. Many had strong themes. *Fiddler on the Roof* was about "tradition." *Cabaret* was about fiddling while Rome (or in this case, Berlin) burned. *A Chorus Line* took things a step further. It lacks a complicated plot—dancers audition for a show and some get it—but its theme is rich. It's a show with a collective title character and a theme about dancers auditioning not just their steps, but their lives.

Bennett had wanted to do a show about dancers for a long

time. Now he had a theme—dancers auditioning for their very lives. He stuck with it. But how to turn thirty hours of raw monologues into a two-hour show?

A Chorus Line changed a lot of things. One of the most important is the way musicals are written.

In the old days, a show generally went "on the road," to cities like New Haven, Philadelphia, and Boston. Material was tested in front of a live audience. Bad material was cut; good material was expanded. The out-of-town tryout system worked well enough. But it was very expensive to pack up an entire production and move it from place to place. Not only was it nerve-wracking for the writers and actors who had to do their scribbling and memorizing in shabby provincial hotels, it became more and more expensive as stagehand-manipulated canvas drops and painted flats gave way to computer-run sliding platforms and architectural sets.

A Chorus Line was developed under quite a different system, generally considered revolutionary in 1974. Bennett decided to have his corps of dancer-actors perform the work for a limited audience of invited friends and colleagues. Advice would flow back and forth. Material would be tried without the huge expense of touring and without the heat of out-of-town critics.

Such a workshop was by no means without precedent. Distinguished Broadway conductor Lehman Engel had for a decade operated the BMI (Broadcast Music Incorporated, a music licensing company) Musical Theatre Workshop. The workshop met weekly and Engel would assign projects—like musicalizing a scene from *A Streetcar Named Desire*—and would critique the results. Still, it was largely a place to hone technique rather than a specific project, though several projects had whirled about the place for years.

Seeing an opportunity to break new ground and bring the whole "process" under one roof, Papp agreed to underwrite the project. Not only would he give Bennett rehearsal space—eventually an entire theater, the Newman, one of seven auditoriums at the Public Theater on Lafayette Street—he also agreed to pay the dancers $100 a week to participate. Rehearsals would take place mostly by day so that dancers could continue to work in other shows at night.

The "dancer project" was about to cross into uncharted territory.

Though dancer Kay Cole wasn't to join the project for several months, she described the situation best. "We were told it was a workshop," she said, "and at that time I don't think anybody knew what that meant. To explain what a workshop is, I think they called it 'a work in progress.' That makes it sound very official and very important. Now it's become a regular thing, but then it was very peculiar to a lot of people. I had done workshops before, in California, so for me it was not an unfamiliar phrase. There were all kinds of theater workshop situations there where a large and successful group of people work for no money."

If Bennett was going to do a musical, he needed one more thing: writers. Nicholas Dante urgently wanted to write and obviously knew the material, so he was engaged by Bennett as librettist. For a composer, Bennett turned to his *Henry, Sweet Henry* pianist Marvin Hamlisch, who also urgently wanted to write for the theater.

There were several reasons Hamlisch was such an exciting choice. One of the main reasons was not who he was, but who he wasn't. Marvin Hamlisch wasn't Stephen Sondheim, and didn't seem disturbed about it. Sondheim had defined the way state-of-the-art musicals were being written in the early and mid 1970s. They were cerebral, emotionally cool, and musically sophisticated. Sondheim had made himself the most imposing landmark on the musical landscape, and most composers either imitated him, or rebelled against him.

Hamlisch did neither. He didn't have to. He had already made a name for himself in Hollywood, winning Oscars for his ubiquitous arrangement of Scott Joplin's "The Entertainer" in the movie *The Sting;* and winning it again for his own composition, "The Way We Were" from the film of the same title.

But Hamlisch's heart belonged to Broadway, and Bennett saw him as a writer able to handle Broadway razzmatazz and Sondheimesque introspection with equal facility and unself-consciousness.

A lyricist was less easy to find. They turned to Ed Kleban, one of the shining stars of the BMI Workshop. He had been developing a musical there, titled *Gallery*. Bennett was impressed by what he heard of the score, and convinced Kleban to put it aside to come aboard the Bennett-Hamlisch project.

The production team was now in place. By late spring, Bennett began to reestablish contact with the dancers.

Few people who have seen *A Chorus Line* will forget the looks of exultation on the faces of the characters who ultimately pass the audition and are hired for the unnamed show-within-a-show. Equally unforgettable are the looks of despair on those who are eliminated—characters the audience has come to know personally.

The dancers who had participated in the tape sessions were veterans of the audition wars and they were about to go through it all again. This time would be somewhat different; this audition would cannibalize itself. Their joy and pain would be carefully chronicled for use in a musical that was itself a giant stylized audition. But one thing was the same about the auditions for *A Chorus Line*. Some dancers were accepted and some were rejected.

For a few, the deck was stacked. Bennett wanted them in the show and very little would dissuade him. One was Baayork Lee. "I got a call from Michael and he said, 'Baayork, I'm doing this show and you must come down and you're going to have to sing.'

"I'd always wanted to be an opera singer," Lee said, "but faced with an audition, I suddenly became paranoid. In those days, of course, the chorus dancers danced, singers sang, and actors acted. Triple threats were not a necessity yet. So I had only one song, 'I Enjoy Being a Girl,' Pat Suzuki's number from *Flower Drum Song*. But it wasn't right for what Michael wanted. He wanted me to sing 'Put On a Happy Face.' I bought the sheet music but had no one to play the accompaniment. So, I called Michael and told him I wasn't coming. He assured me everything was going to be okay, so I found myself down at the Shakespeare Festival with a room full of people. And there was Marvin Hamlisch playing the piano. So I tried to 'Put On a Happy Face' but I forgot the words. I fell all over Marvin trying to read the lyrics over his shoulder. Suddenly I wasn't Michael's Pat Suzuki. I'd forgotten the words. I came totally unprepared. I wasn't special, I wasn't perfect. I'd disappointed Michael and embarrassed myself. I left humiliated. That evening I called Michael and cried 'I can't sing! I can't sing!'

"He said, 'Baayork, stop worrying about it. If you're not in the show, you're going to assist me.'

"That was wonderful. I knew I would be involved. I was going to be working with Michael again. That's all that mattered to me."

Lee had skipped the tape sessions but Bennett and Dante clearly felt she had an interesting story to tell, being an Asian dancer and thriving in an industry where shows like *Flower Drum Song* and *The King and I* are a rarity.

Lee was working in that spring's "Milliken Breakfast Show," and remembers, "Michael came to a rehearsal at City Center on Fifty-fifth Street and said, 'Come to my apartment. We're going to talk on some tapes.'

" 'Oh no!' I thought. 'What am I going to say?' Well, Michael got me started in spite of the fact that April Nevins [a dancer] and Jeff Hamlin [who later became production stage manager for *A Chorus Line*] were there. Michael was so relaxed and coaxing. 'It's okay, Baayork, just talk.' I found myself talking about my childhood and how I wanted to grow up to be a prima ballerina. The conversation was flowing now. Then, out pops my big secret: I always wanted to be an opera singer. Everybody was shocked. It wasn't like what Thommie Walsh and Sammy Williams had told me on the phone, where they sat around all night dragging out the dregs of their lives. I went in and it was painless, absolutely painless, because I was with Michael and I trusted him."

Aside from being hired to play a character based on herself, Lee was hired as dance captain of *A Chorus Line,* a job that called upon her to assist Bennett by memorizing his choreography and making sure all the dancers learned it and executed it properly. As co-choreographer Bennett turned to Bob Avian, another fellow dancer from his earliest days in the theater.

With those crucial jobs filled, Bennett was ready to start fleshing out his chorus line. His next choice was also a natural, since he had been consulting with her since mid-May.

Priscilla Lopez said, "I remembered how Michael had told us that he didn't know whether it would be a book or a film or a play or maybe just that night. I realized that something was taking shape when he started calling me periodically and telling me about the progress he was making. At one point he called me at the theater, where I was doing *Pippin,* asking me if I wanted to accompany him to one of those Tony Award parties, cocktails I think it was.

"I couldn't believe it and said, 'Oh yes.' Even though I knew he was gay it didn't stop me from fantasizing about him. The only one I had to share these tape sessions with was Vinny [Fanuele, her husband] and he was crazed at the idea of my being out all night. He painted our entire apartment while I was gone.

"One day Michael invited me to his apartment," Lopez said. "Nicholas Dante was there typing. I read what he was writing, and it was about me, material from what I'd said at the tape session. Another day I went to his house and Ed Kleban and Marvin Hamlisch were there. I sang for them. Then I got a call to come down to the Shakespeare Festival, but Michael said not to worry, it wasn't really an audition. Just that everyone was going to be there and I'd sing something.

"I remember I was wearing white shorts, sneakers, and a green *Pippin* T-shirt. I went in and sang and left. I didn't read anything. I felt I had it all along, there was never a question in my mind."

Another sure bet was the woman Bennett had choreographed in *Promises, Promises* and *Company,* and whom he'd chosen to chaperone him to the tape sessions—the woman who would, in a move that would confuse almost everyone, become Mrs. Michael Bennett within two years.

"Can you imagine people auditioning for their own life stories?" said Donna McKechnie. "I knew I was going to be in the show. I had to show up at the audition just for appearances. I hate auditions but I wanted to audition that time. I didn't talk to too many people at the auditions except Trish [Garland], Kelly [Bishop], and Steve Boockvor. Trish was talking about her reading and shaking so much. I think I would be furious if I had to read my own dialogue in an audition. I said I wanted to sing for Marvin, and Michael said okay. I felt that if I'm going to sing, I'm going to sing something I would never do at an audition. So I came with a rose and sang 'Un Bel Dì' or something and they applauded at some point, but I wasn't finished, so I kept going."

Not everyone was so confident.

"Michael was the only reason I got the job," said Baughman. "At the audition I was a basket case. I laughed and cried through the whole thing, just as I had at the rap sessions. My trouble is that when I talk I cry. After the audition Nicholas Dante called me and said he wanted me to know that I had done a great job, 'but Ed and Marvin don't want to hire you.'

"I didn't think it was horrible because I knew I had sung so badly, but I couldn't believe that someone else was going to do my life. It was my life and I wanted to do it. Of course I couldn't know at the time that it was going to turn into a hotshot show. Because of the rap sessions I just knew that I wanted to be a part of it."

Baughman, a practicing Buddhist, dealt with the frustration in the way she knew best. "I remember doing my chanting," she said. "I knew they did have another girl they liked very much, Victoria Mallory [ingenue in the 1973 musical *A Little Night Music*]. As it turned out, Michael and Nicholas convinced Ed and Marvin that they should hire me for the first workshop and if it didn't work out, they would let me go."

Thommie Walsh read his own monologue at the audition, a memoir about his moving to Florida with his grandparents when his parents separated. As Walsh was reading the story from two typed pages, he realized that other actors were reading the same monologue, auditioning for the same part. He began to get upset. "I thought it was a joke," Walsh said. "I hated it. I thought, 'How can anybody do this better than I?' So I decided to act it to no end. I gave them Marlon Brando. And Michael said, 'Just stop it. Put that down and tell me about yourself.'

"I put down those two pages of monologue that they had condensed from my part of the tape. I was real and honest and pure and naked, totally vulnerable, appealing. He said, 'Now sing your song.' So I sang 'Forget Your Troubles.' I could see Marvin Hamlisch just freaking out about me, and Michael is kind of going 'It's all right, just cool it.' I could see the body language happening: Michael wanted me but Marvin Hamlisch did not want my ass at all.

"Afterward, Nick Dante called me up and told me all these fierce things about my singing and acting. He had me totally freaked out. Because he now has been assigned as 'author' of this play. I'm so paranoid I started going to a vocal coach.

"But I got it. Oh yeah, I did."

Both Garland sisters were called to the Shakespeare Festival audition as well. As McKechnie said, Trish was shaking visibly. "I've always hated auditions," Garland said. "Jacki and I went down to the Newman together, we had similar times. We auditioned together a lot anyway. I screamed when I found out we had to talk. We also had to sing. I sang 'Someone to Watch over Me' and Marvin stopped and said, 'I want this an up tune.' I told him I had worked so hard on this being a ballad and now you want me to do this fast? He said, 'Yes, I want to see how it works.'

"Inside of me I couldn't believe that they wanted me to completely change. I just did it. Then they asked me to read. I was beside myself with fear. I hadn't given that much information on the tape. I found out later that I was not a major contender. I read, and it turned out to be Jacki's monologue. The paper was shaking so badly that I made a crack about them using heavier paper the next time they asked me to read. They got hysterical. That broke the ice. They asked me some more questions and thanked me."

The Garlands' ordeal wasn't over yet, however. They were soon invited to a callback. Afterward, Trish was called into the Newman, put on the stage with a group of dancers, and told they had all been hired. It was a joyful moment, but it didn't last long. Missing from the group was her sister, Jacki. Trish had been hired to play the character based on her sister. "None of us could really believe it," Garland said. "I asked her which monologue she did, assuming that they were using different monologues. Jacki had done her own."

Though the part eventually changed and Trish did not play a character directly based on her sister, she said, "I think it was a most painful experience for her. Having always been first, having always been in the forefront. Having not been in the forefront really developed my character. I was able to withstand almost anything. But she didn't have that same facility because she'd never really been defeated. In different little ways perhaps, but generally not by anything, and especially not by her sister.

"At first I don't think it was as painful as it grew to be later on, when the success of the show propelled itself. But she was really good about it, trying to be happy for me. It's different when someone is effortless in their joy than when someone is happy for you but wishes that they had it, too. I can understand that. But I remember saying to her, 'Why can't you just be happy that I got something?' "

Kelly Bishop said, "For my money, Jacki was the Broadway gypsy. She was the one I'd worked with. I didn't know Trish, though I'd seen her at auditions. Suddenly Trish's in the show and Jacki isn't. Michael was brutal, that's why he made so many enemies. He was ruthless in what he went for in terms of casting. There could be any number of reasons why someone did or did not get something. I could tell you almost person by person why people did or didn't get in. Some people didn't get more to do in the show because he or she might have been . . . boring. Some because there was just a genuine dislike. 'That person just drives me crazy'—it was that personal with Michael. And there might have been a situation where he might not like someone but would hire them because they had *this* quality and could sing, too."

Bennett also had his eye on Bishop, though in the months following the tape sessions they had completely lost contact with one another. Bishop had gotten her first principal role playing Anita in a dinner theater tour of *West Side Story* and was feeling very satisfied when she returned to New York in late summer. "The day I arrived in town Michael called me to come down to the Shakespeare Festival and audition for Marvin Hamlisch. I went downtown and saw all these dancers that I knew there, and Michael handed me pages to read. I looked at the pages and it was a transcript of what I had said at the tape session. And I went, 'My God, this is exactly what I said,' for five pages. Michael came up to me after that, as I was walking out, and he did a little Michael Bennett thing: kind of grabbing your arm and leaning his head on your shoulder, and talking to you. And he said, 'You got the part.'

"And I thought, 'How clever. You got me to play me. I would have been livid if they had gotten someone else to play me.' At the time I thought, 'Big deal. So who else would be saying these words?'

"But as I went outside I saw three or four other dancers that I'd worked with who were my type who either had replaced me in shows or who I had replaced. And I realized they were up for my part. And that's when I actually got mad."

***

Nevertheless, the auditions were going well. Bennett was assembling a cast that not only reflected the spectrum of dancer "types," but offered him an equally vivid palette of dancing, singing, acting, and comedic skills.

Thommie Walsh remembers that Bennett was in a celebratory mood when he and Bishop came down to see him performing in a drag revue at the Persian Room of the Plaza Hotel. The date is easy to pick out: August 8, 1974. While the three clustered in the bar and were talking excitedly about the prospects for the workshop, the bartender tuned the television to a national speech being given by President Richard Nixon. Faced with impeachment and possible criminal prosecution, Nixon finally was resigning. The new President, Gerald Ford, declared shortly thereafter, "Our long national nightmare is over."

Walsh said, in general, the dancers were oblivious to the headlines. He recalled Nixon's resignation speech only as an annoyance, saying, "All we could talk about was the auditions."

Nevertheless, the final auditions for the first workshop of *A Chorus Line* were conducted in an air of renewal, of a fresh beginning.

Wayne Cilento had a mortgage and was planning a family, and was working in the chorus of the revival of *Irene* then running on Broadway. In fact, he continued to work in that show throughout the summer, until the first workshop began in late summer.

He answered the call to the Newman and auditioned with a monologue he had done for Bennett in *Seesaw,* though he considers his entire performance in that show to be his audition. He was hired to play Mike Costa, a character modeled on himself. But the uncertainty had bothered him. "Looking back, I realize how devastating it would have been to have someone else hired to do my story, I'm glad I never had to deal with that one."

Bennett also used his network of contacts to draw in other dancers of merit. He had dancers who could dance and sing. What he needed was more dancers who could act.

Ron Kuhlman, another veteran of "The Milliken Breakfast Show," auditioned at the Newman, but then didn't hear from

Bennett for several weeks. He was in the middle of a bicycle trip to New England when Avian contacted him and asked him to do a second audition. Rushing to a bus terminal, he nearly came to grief when his bike was sideswiped by a drunk driver near Danbury, Connecticut, and he was thrown into a ditch. Injuries were minor, so he made it back in time to read the monologue.

At that point, Kuhlman had been doing more acting and less dancing. "I could handle the monologue," he said. "It was no problem for me. I guess the dancing would be for me like reading would be for some dancers who didn't do a lot of acting. Then I had to sing for Marvin, and Marvin was against me, I know. I could see him shaking his head, 'No, no.' But in spite of it all they hired me to do the workshop. From the beginning I felt like this was a real special group. When we found we had gotten it I was standing with Trish Garland. We were very excited, hugging each other. It felt special right away."

Robert LuPone was in a similar position, careerwise, but the transition was more of a wrench for him. "In August of 'seventy-four I had just finished *Boccaccio* [at the Arena Stage] and I had made the great big jump from chorus dancer to actor and was on a roll of regional theater in principal acting roles," he said. "That's something I was very proud of because I had decided that my dancing future, although I was talented, was ultimately limited because I didn't want to be a choreographer. I made a conscious decision to study acting at twenty-three and finally at twenty-seven I was starting to get roles.

"My agent at the time said, 'This man, Michael Bennett—you should go audition for him.'

"I said, 'Why?'

" 'Because he's doing a musical about dancers.'

"My comment at the time was 'I don't dance anymore,' but my agent convinced me to go.

"I went down and I sang at Joe Papp's, in the Anspacher Theatre. Michael was sitting at the top of the bleachers about a hundred feet away from me and I was onstage and I felt that to be very odd that I was auditioning up to a man. I found that an interesting metaphor later.

"I sang 'Once in Love with Amy' for Marvin Hamlisch who

was the news to me because he had that year just won an Academy Award and he was a Juilliard graduate. I was truly impressed with auditioning for him and I knew nobody else in the room.

"I was nervous and unfocused, young, and not really wanting to be there. I wanted to be at the Goodman or the McCarter or Long Wharf or the Arena Stage doing significant acting work. I started to move side to side while singing and Michael made one brief hand gesture that immediately got to me and calmed me down. That moment of direction immediately endeared me to him because nobody in an audition has ever done that—ever been personal.

"At the end we talked, only to find out that I was going to get a callback for a dancing audition. As I was wont to do in those days, I didn't show up for the dancing audition. Because of that, I considered the job gone. But through my agent a few days later I found out that in fact Michael Bennett still wanted to see me. That was the next moment of endearment, of respect.

"The dancing audition passed and I was called back again, this time at the Newman among all those people I did not know. I read a little bit again and I sang again. I sang poorly because at that time I was petrified of singing and it was all happening very fast. There was a lot of excitement and I had no relationship to it whatsoever. But at the end of that, Michael turned around and said to everybody, 'This is the cast. Welcome to the Shakespeare Festival.'

"Suddenly I was cast in the show, and I was totally bewildered. I didn't know what to do. I didn't know if I wanted to do the show. I hadn't read a script, I didn't know anything about it. And then it was a workshop. So I said, okay, I guess, why not. I had no job, I'd give it a try. I don't know how I made that decision, I don't know why I kept to that decision. The next thing I knew, I found myself doing this show, dancing—doing exactly what it was I didn't want to do."

Rick Mason had exactly the opposite feeling when he got a phone call from Jack Hofsiss, then casting director of the New York Shakespeare Festival, inviting him to audition. "One of my goals in life when I was a kid was that I wanted to be in an original musical," Mason said, "and I wanted to do an original cast album. The name of the show didn't mean anything to me at that point. I only knew it was for Michael Bennett. I was asked to go up and sing a song, and I think I sang 'I Met a Girl' from *Bells Are Ringing*. And they all went up to the back of the house and had a conference and I stood on the stage waiting and I believe it was Michael or Bob who came down and said, 'We'd like you to do this role.' I still didn't know what role it was. I wasn't asked to read, I wasn't asked to dance, just asked to sing. I had worked with a couple of the kids, and I knew Baayork and Wayne from 'Milliken,' but I didn't know them well. They were still the pros to me and I was still the young novice coming in to make his niche in this community."

Pamela Blair's connection with *A Chorus Line* came as the result of a happy accident. "I ran into Michael on the street one day and he told me he was having some dancers up to his apartment and we were going to talk, and I agreed."

Margo Sappington and other dancers were at this mini taping session, and Blair recalled the fun she had. But, she said, "I didn't really want to do Michael's show, I just fell in love with him. I wanted to get involved with him."

For her audition, she said, "I remember first I made an idiot of myself in Michael's apartment singing something by the Beatles off-key. I sat on the piano bench next to Marvin. I hate to sing anyway. Then I remember having to go down to the Newman and having to sing onstage."

Whatever her deficiencies at the auditions, she had a quality Bennett was looking for, and she was cast. But to put Blair in the show, someone had to be cut. Dancer Mitzi Hamilton had poured out the most intimate details about her plastic surgery but Bennett decided to cast Blair as the character modeled on her.

That wasn't even the cruelest cut from the *Chorus Line* team. Although Tony Stevens was hired for the first workshop, his co-originator Michon Peacock was not. Bennett was providing all the impetus at this point. It had become his project in more ways than one.

Though Peacock, Hamilton, and Steve Anthony from the tape session did not make the workshop, several others did, including Candy Brown. Bennett hired several more new dancers, including Barry Bostwick, who had originated the role in *Grease* that later would be made famous by John Travolta, and who would make a name for himself a few years later, playing the hapless Brad in *The Rocky Horror Picture Show*.

All this left one key role to be filled. Because Nicholas Dante was going to be spending all his time writing the script, it was decided that someone else needed to be found to play his alter ego who had come to be named Paul. Paul was going to recount Dante's story of his emotional encounter with his parents backstage at the Jewel Box Revue. What they needed was an actor who clearly was a dancer, but who could convey the delicacy and sincerity of the part. Bennett had someone from the tape session in mind, but needed to know if he could act the part.

Sammy Williams recalls that there was a "presence" between Bennett and himself during the rehearsal period for the road company of *Seesaw*. "Before we left town," Williams said, "Michael said he wanted me to learn the role Tommy Tune was doing. He said he wanted me to do the role for a bus-and-truck company after Tommy left. So I did, and went on tour with that, knowing I would eventually be playing the big balloon number ["It's Not Where You Start"]. It was almost too much to believe. This man who's the best in the business wants to give me this role.

"It was in July and I was in Philadelphia when I got a phone call from Michael. It was Thursday and he asked me what I was doing for the weekend. I said I had no plans and he asked me if I would like to come into the city for the weekend, on Sunday. He said he wanted to talk to me.

"I honestly thought I was being called to discuss playing the role of David in *Seesaw,* though there was scuttlebutt about Michael's new show. At that time he was living on Fifty-fifth Street. We spent the entire day together, it ended up being my audition for *A Chorus Line*.

"We talked for a long time. Small talk at first, then he started asking me personal questions, about my family, growing up, how I felt about certain things. He talked about himself, told me a bit about his childhood, about how he got involved in the business. He wanted me to know as much about him as he wanted to know about me.

"There was no tape going. As a matter of fact, we talked a little bit, went to the ballet and saw Jerome Robbins's ballet that afternoon. We stopped and talked with Jerome Robbins after the ballet, then we went back to Michael's apartment and talked some more for about another hour.

"Finally, Michael asked me if I knew why I was there. I said I thought he wanted to talk about me replacing Tommy Tune. He said, 'That too, but I have another show coming up and there's a role I think you're right for, and I'd like you to read for it.'

"He asked me if I remembered Nicholas Dante's life story, and I said yes, I had worked with Nicky in *Applause* and I knew about him working at the Jewel Box. I remembered vaguely what he had talked about at the tape session. I remembered the feeling that I had gotten from what he had said and how I felt for him, but I didn't remember exactly what he said. Michael said he wanted me to read for that part.

"He said, 'You're more right for Nicholas's life story than you are for your own, so don't be offended that you're not reading for yourself.'

"I said okay, so he handed me the monologue. Mind you, I never had an acting lesson, had never gone to an acting class, never even bothered to want to open my mouth on the stage because I was so afraid of being called a sissy. I had this real high voice. So acting was not something I really wanted to do.

"So naturally I wasn't reading it well at all; I was reading like I was reading the telephone book. I got about three sentences out when Michael stopped me and told me to try it again. He gave me a little bit of direction. I listened to him, and started reading again. This time I got messed up on the words, I was real nervous. He stopped me again and told me to try it again but it was just the same.

"So he said he had an idea. He wanted me to reread the monologue while he was out of the room and when he came back, to tell it like a story, the way I remembered it, in my own words.

"By this time it was about three or four P.M. He came back and I started telling him the story, that 'Paul' had been raped at the age of six, et cetera. And he started talking about how the kids harassed Paul in school and how he was smart. Paul was always afraid to answer questions because there was always a mumble or remark because he was effeminate.

"Well, it suddenly dawned on me that that was what my school life was like, and I fell apart. I couldn't even carry on after that. I cried for an hour because I had never let that out before. Michael just held me and rocked me and I kept sobbing. Then he started asking me questions about school and I started telling him how I hated it, how I hated being called a sissy, hated getting up in the morning and going to face all those kids knowing they didn't like me. How I was different from everybody. He opened up Pandora's box.

"Finally he calmed me down and called Marvin Hamlisch on the phone and told him there was someone in his apartment he wanted Marvin to meet. He said, 'I think we found him.' It didn't make much sense at the time.

"We got into a cab and went over to Marvin Hamlisch's house. I had no idea who Marvin was. Michael just said, 'We are going to a friend's house to meet somebody.'

"While we were in the cab he asked me if I had ever thought of what I wanted to do with my career. I said I was twenty-five years old and didn't want to be a chorus boy at thirty. If nothing happens to me by that time I would stop dancing and do something else. He asked me if I'd ever considered acting and I told him no. He said, 'You'll act first before you give up dancing.' He didn't say another word to me for the rest of the cab ride.

"We got over to Marvin's house and he had me sing for him. The only thing I could think of was the song ["I'm Way Ahead"] that Gittel sings at the end of *Seesaw* where they break up. So I sang that for Marvin. He asked me if I could read music, and I told him no. He asked me to listen and he started playing 'The Way We Were,' and I tried singing with it. Then Michael asked me to tell Marvin the same story I told him, Nicky's story. I did, and once again I just fell apart. I got to the part about school and I broke down.

"We left Marvin's house and went back to Michael's and for about the next three hours Michael asked me more questions about my family. Michael never said anything to me about whether I had the job. He never said, 'I'll call you.' He just said, 'Thank you for the day, thank you for sharing yourself with me.' That was it.

"I went back to my apartment on cloud ten. It must have been about two or three A.M. when I finally got home. I went back to *Seesaw* in another world. People kept asking me what happened but Michael had told me not to discuss any of it with anyone.

So I didn't say anything and my close friends were real angry with me.

"A few weeks passed and the tour was in some place like Indianapolis. We were having a big opening night party and Michael arrives and takes me aside to ask if I would like to do his new show, and I said of course. He told me he would call me and let me know when I started.

"So we get to Chicago and on a Thursday night at about two A.M. the phone rings and it's Michael. He tells me, 'You're leaving the show on Saturday, make sure you have your bags packed. I'll have your trunks sent. There'll be a ticket waiting for you at the airport, et cetera. We start rehearsals August fifth, on Monday.' But he wanted me there on Sunday to sing for Marvin or something or other.

"Now, the company knows I'm leaving. Saturday matinee comes around and I'm thinking I'm on my way to be in a *Michael Bennett production*. I'm going to be a big star. So I decide that I'm going to *perform*, give them better than the best because I'm going to be a big star like Lucie Arnaz and John Gavin [stars of the *Seesaw* tour].

"We get out there in the 'Ride Out the Storm' number and I'm wearing these enormously tall platform shoes and doing this disco dance and I'm throwing my body around and all of a sudden I hear a crack. By the time I walked offstage I couldn't even bend over. Doom sets in. I had sprained my back."

6.

Beginning of the First Workshop (August–September 1974)

The workshops that preceded the production of *A Chorus Line* took place in four locations.

The dancers did most of their work at the Estelle R. Newman Theater, with 299 seats the largest of the seven performing spaces at Joe Papp's New York Shakespeare Festival in Greenwich Village. Eventually, it was the space where *A Chorus Line* would premiere seven months later, in April 1975, and have its three-month off-Broadway run.

The Newman Theater's stage was a platform at the foot of eighteen steeply raked rows of seats. From that stage, the dancers faced a tilted wall of empty seats receding toward the back row, where Bennett often sat when he addressed the group. Looking from the stage, the workshoppers, and later the audience, entered from the right. By no means is it as funky as you might expect for off-Broadway. Bright, buffed, Spartan, it might as well have been a corporate amphitheater. The difference was the smooth wooden stage.

Other significant ensemble work was done at the Dance Theater Workshop at 219 West Nineteenth Street, a complex of mirrored dance rooms with comfortable floors and other amenities for the sweaty athletes who are dancers. It was known as Jerome

Robbins's place because it was leased by Robbins's New York City Ballet as rehearsal space. Rooms not being used by the ballet were rented or loaned to other dance companies, and to musicals or plays in rehearsal.

Through his many contacts, and Papp's, Bennett arranged for Hamlisch and Kleban to work on their score in music rehearsal space at Lincoln Center. Whenever the dancers were to work on specific songs, they would shuttle to the Upper West Side and sit in an acoustic room with Marvin and Ed.

Dante sometimes worked on his libretto at his apartment, but the script was shaped at Bennett's apartment on West Fifty-fifth Street, which is where dancers were taken when they needed to do more taping or just to read.

But the writers spent a great deal of time slumped in the seats at the Newman, or observing from the doorway at Jerome Robbins's place. During the early workshops, they spent a great deal of time just watching.

"It's all a blur," said Blair. "But the first workshop was fun. We danced all the time."

"We weren't doing any kind of script stuff at first," Lopez said. "That came later. We were just dancing."

At first there was no music. Michael's longtime musical collaborator Robert Thomas (later billed as music coordinator of *A Chorus Line*) played drums, and dancers improvised Bennett's combinations to pure percussion. When Hamlisch would appear and play accompaniment, the dancers would listen eagerly, knowing they were listening to parts of the new score for their show. When working on a musical theme, Hamlisch would play it and the dancers would improvise. There was little notation at this point. Bennett and Avian moved the dancers about, calling out suggestions, then stepped back and watched. As their assistant, Tony Stevens would explain and review what Bennett and Avian had proposed; then he'd work alongside the individual dancers.

Dante and Kleban watched, too. They had the taped interviews to work from, but they also wanted to see their characters in their natural environment. They would take notes, do little interviews, disappear, reappear. Hamlisch tried themes that sometimes vanished, sometimes changed, sometimes repeated.

"It was so alien in terms of a script," LuPone said, "in terms of a beginning, middle, and end; expositions, climax, resolution of a play. Nothing was there."

Something was there, but as yet it had no form. That was confusing. Until 1974, almost no one hired dancers for a show until there was some music for them to dance to. It made no economic sense to do it otherwise. Dances might be altered, substituted, or cut as the show progressed, but there usually was a script, a song, a style the dancers could dig into. The first weeks of *A Chorus Line* were an almost blank tablet. Quite literally, they were making it up as they went along.

"I was very excited about the first days of rehearsal," McKechnie said. "It was one of the best experiences I ever had. Because we didn't get into the meat of it yet, it was just sort of the *idea* of it, of all of us being together. Finally dancers were going to be acknowledged, I loved that. I thought it was real special and I felt privileged. I knew from the way we had started that we were all going to have input. We were going to be used that way. Having the luxury to take all the wrong roads first. To experiment. The process was fantastic, but I also thought that was a very difficult thing to do."

Dancers were paid $100 a week for six days' work—that was the deal. Even in the summer of 1974, it wasn't enough to make ends meet. Or just barely. If you had a rent-controlled apartment or a roommate. If you didn't eat too much. Long-term investment or not, no one saw it as a way to get rich. "People aren't in theater because of that," Bishop said. "That's not what compels anyone to be here."

Because the dancers were some of the cream of Broadway, they had worked often in recent years. "I had worked for less wages," said Lopez. "I had just come off a show so fortunately for me it was okay." Like Lopez, several had salted cash away or were able to collect unemployment.

Some maintained jobs while appearing in the workshop. Cilento continued to appear in *Irene,* Lopez in *Pippin*. Others pursued work in industrial shows, and in those rare, surreal, lucrative gigs: commercials.

The dancers who had taken part in the tape sessions already had a bond. The newcomers spent the first few weeks trying to build one. "When I joined the workshop," Kuhlman said, "I had to tell my life story in front of everyone. That was kind of hard because now it wasn't the same atmosphere as I'm sure it was that evening they did the tapes. They were all relaxed and sitting around. So there we were in the theater in front of this group of people who were picked, and we were talking about our lives. I was trying to be totally honest in that situation. I don't think I was trying to impress Michael because I think I was constantly telling them, 'You know, I didn't dance when I was five or six or eight. I didn't start this until college and even then it was something on the side.' Actually I didn't know if I should be there.

"I didn't mind the music part of it," Kuhlman said, "but the dance part was hard. I mean, developing the dance. I felt I needed to contribute some kind of step or something. I probably worked harder than others in terms of the dance stuff because I had to be able to show them I could do it. I remember Michael saying, 'Okay Ron, go up and do a turn.' I was so nervous that of course I fell off the turn right away. I managed to get one in that was good, clean. But it was real hard and nerve-wracking and Bobby LuPone, bless him, helped me out with my turns. He and I got to be real good friends."

Sammy Williams had the unique frustration of having been at the taping sessions and having his day-long audition adventure, only to find himself unable to dance because he'd sprained his back. "That's how I started *A Chorus Line*," he said. "I was freaking out. I wasn't able to dance the entire first workshop. Michael kept telling me not to worry about it. They would work around me, they wanted me in the show, there was plenty of time, my back would heal. I was totally paranoid about not being able to stay with the show. I didn't know if I would be able to dance anymore because I had so seriously hurt my back."

Though Williams was not dancing, he was there, and the writers watched him just the way they watched the rest of the dancers. Injuries are as much a part of being a dancer as anything else. Sometimes they're an interruption in a dancer's career, sometimes they're the end of it. The sight of Williams, as injured dancer Paul, stretched out in pain was transformed into one of the most moving passages of the show. But that transformation was still in the future.

Similarly, the writers watched Stevens work patiently with

the dancers, and soon there was the part of Larry, the dance assistant.

Williams said that even though he couldn't take part physically, "it was exciting in the sense that we were working on a new show so it was that whole creative process that was beginning to happen. Nobody knew what was happening because Michael didn't know what was happening. It was all experimental. He kept saying, 'Try this, try that.' Michael was trying to find a style, a dance style for the show. In order to cope with the stress, I was doing Valium and I remember Bob Avian coming up to me and telling me that Michael didn't like anyone doing drugs during his rehearsals."

The earliest script consisted of little more than raw transcripts of the tape sessions. In some cases they were identical to the material used at the audition. Work had advanced relatively little on the libretto, though that rawness was part of the show's concept at that point. What could be more real and immediate than the dancers' direct words? Dante and Bennett pulled the most promising story threads from the tape sessions, spun these threads into makeshift characters, and assigned them names, more or less at random.

For Cilento (Mike), Lee (Connie), Lopez (Diana), Bishop (Sheila), etc., developing a character was easy because they were largely playing themselves. For Garland (Judy), Williams (Paul), and the newcomers, it was harder, because they not only had to develop a performance, they had to help define the characters as well. Dancers like Walsh (Bobby) and Baughman (Kristine) had it even harder, because their characters kept changing.

McKechnie's character, Cassie, based in part on her adult self, didn't exist in the first workshop. She played Maggie, which is based on her recollections of her childhood. A dancer named Kay Cole would inherit Maggie after Cassie was created.

"From all the tapes, Michael selected stories, certain things that were to be used, and assigned them to different characters," McKechnie said. "There was a little piece of our lives in each of the characters. Maggie was always someone who had left the chorus to try better things, then had no luck, be it in New York or Los

Angeles, and she was just coming back. The love interest didn't happen until later."

Kuhlman's "Don" monologue was based on the taped memories of dancer Andy Bew. "In the original monologue," said Kuhlman, "Don talked about his mother being a dance teacher and how he hated dancing. He told how a time came when she made him dance and he quit. He was more interested in being a kid in the backyard building a tree house. He didn't dance until twelve, when he became interested in ballroom dance. Now, when I was a kid I was into ballroom dancing, too. To this day I love to go ballroom dancing, as well as rock and roll. So many of the things in his [Andy Bew's/Don's] monologue paralleled somewhat what I did. That's why, at the actual audition, I was relating so well to this monologue. Don's mother died in Chicago and a friend of his encouraged him to get back into show business. A friend of mine told me about a show when I was in college. That was my very first paying job in theater. Don went on to say that he met a lot of girls on the tour, got laid a lot, and had a good time. When the tour was over he went home and bought a Corvette and was hot shit because he had been in this touring company. Friends told him another audition was on, and he went back to New York. The monologue ended with him saying something like, 'I was young and Mr. Cool and I still have the Corvette.' "

Kuhlman said, "The most emotional strain or frustration was that I wasn't doing more acting. The part was sort of there but the writing wasn't clear and clean at that point." Like many of the other long monologues in the first workshop, Kuhlman's was almost entirely eliminated from the final version of *A Chorus Line*.

The only vestige of the "long monologue" period that remains in the show is Paul's emotional memoir about the Jewel Box Revue. Because his character was so clearly defined, and because he had little else to do, being injured, Williams began working on characterization right away. Insecurity also had something to do with it. "I didn't know anything about acting," he said. "I went to see as many plays as I could because I didn't know how to act and I wanted to study people who did." In October, Peter Shaffer's *Equus* began previews at the Plymouth Theatre and word got around quickly that it was something remarkable. "So I got myself a ticket and I sat in the first row and watched this boy named Peter Firth play this character [of a young man obsessed, on a religious level, with horses] and I was amazed. He made it so real. I knew that I had to bring to my role what he brought to his: that power and that incredible moment. I knew that I had the material to do it with, but I didn't know how. That was always a big problem for me. I didn't know how to bring it across."

Though Williams's monologue was the only one that survived in more or less its original form, *A Chorus Line* was like a sequence of Sammy monologues, many with similar dramatic impact—but which ultimately became numbing through repetition. Different dramatic forms had to be found. To keep the characters from becoming a series of sealed vertical columns, parallel and never intersecting, they needed to interact; there needed to be dialogue among the dancer-characters.

So three sets of characters eventually were linked in romantic relationships. The roles of Cassie and Zach were not created until the second workshop. In the first workshop, the writers tried to develop two couples—one romantic, one comic—in traditional musical comedy style. In *Guys and Dolls* the romance of Sky and Sarah is contrasted with the comedy of Nathan and Adelaide. In *Hello, Dolly!* it's Cornelius-Irene contrasted with Barnaby-Minnie.

In the first draft of *A Chorus Line* it was to be Al and Kristine as the romantic married couple hoping to get a show together, versus Sheila and Don as the hot-blooded comic pair.

As for the Don-Sheila romance, Kuhlman recalls, "I not only had the monologue, we had a lot of things, Kelly and I. Sheila and Don had once had an affair, and now I was married, so there was this whole thing going on now that we were standing on this stage together. Don also talked about coming home from rehearsal, getting tap shoes—some of that was Michael Bennett's story. I assumed it was a combination of stories."

"The relationship of Sheila and Don was going much like Cassie and Zach would go, only on a different level," Kuhlman said. "But it just didn't fit in with the rest of the play. It was interesting to me to be able to have that kind of part going on and I was very upset when they cut it out totally. But I understood why they cut it, it conflicted with the Cassie and Zach story and was just extraneous."

In the first workshop Robert LuPone was cast in the role of Al, paired with Renee Baughman as Kristine—two recently wed dancers. A new actor named Don Percassi would be hired to play the part in the second workshop when LuPone took the Bennett alter-ego role of Zach. In the first workshop, Al was developed as an aggressively macho Italian dancer. In the show's logo, Al is wearing the TKTS T-shirt and holding his wife's hand. Kristine's primary characteristics were her skittishness and her inability to sing. The characters were based roughly on Denise and Steve Boockvor, who had taken part in the tape sessions but not in the workshop. The nonsinging dimension of the character, however, was drawn from Baughman.

At first, the parts were the largest in the show and long scenes were written for Al and Kristine. But gradually the writers' attention moved elsewhere. The characters were less musical than they seemed at first. Just about all that remains of their story today is the song "Sing!," which was written after the first workshop ended.

"I should never have been at that first workshop," said LuPone, who found his career as a dramatic actor abruptly sidetracked. "I was bewildered by the fact that I was there. It was totally my resistance to my destiny, I guess. I danced, but I resisted the dancer things all the way down the line. Michael never pushed me. He just let me slide and people were understanding. It was a compassionate sense of a workshop. I did have a lot of fun in the first workshop, as Al. I was very fond of Michael. Fond is not the word. I obviously felt I needed him or something in my life."

The chance to dance for Michael Bennett had drawn most of them to the project. Now his longtime collaborators had their chance to renew their artistic relationship, and the newcomers had their chance to measure Bennett against his legend.

Bennett was exploring as much as the dancers were. Baayork Lee, who had known Bennett the longest and who worked with him so closely throughout both workshops, saw very clearly what the challenges were. "Michael knew he was dealing with a lot of people who never had opened their mouths onstage," she said.

"For him, I think it was experimenting. We were all on virgin territory and that's the hardest place to be. Dancers who have replaced us in the roles had the advantage of having heard the words and knowing how to get to that point where you can cry onstage. How do you explain to a person who's never had acting classes how to do a six-page monologue and cry? Michael was a choreographer. As a result, some of his techniques as a director of actors were unfortunate. However, he got the results he needed for the show.

"I think he knew we had something and this was his time. He never doubted for a second that this was going to be a growing process for all of us. He had been so disillusioned about working with directors and designers. He wanted to work with dancers on a show that was a clean canvas: no costumes, no sets, no props. He knew dancers were smart and disciplined. They could sing, dance, and act. But many of them just didn't know they could do it all. Michael was a cheerleader for dancers, because he was one, too. It really was a dream of his. He knew the injustices that dancers were up against—no respect. He'd been there. He wanted people to sit up and take notice of dancers. He wanted dancers to know that they didn't have to be behind the star, that they didn't have to just hum in the background. That's why he was determined that *Chorus Line* be the be-all for dancers. And it *is*.

"In the first workshop I was the assistant and I played myself," Lee continued. "I did all the things an assistant would. I'd give a warmup before rehearsals. At that point there was no one playing the director in the show. We would speak to a void at the back of the audience. I would say, 'Zach, do you want the kids in now?'—stuff like that. And then I would wait a few beats, shake my head, and say, 'Okay, I'll get them.' Obviously that concept didn't work. I had a few other lines. Mostly my job was to learn the dances as fast as I could and help people when they had difficulties. I felt that my being in the show, being on that line, was totally secondary.

"I didn't feel as though I was management because Michael was there. I had watched him all these years create from nothing. Once again he was doing it. I was a soldier in his army, and I gave him my all. He didn't know what he was creating, and we didn't know either. I was one of the lucky ones because, as an assistant, I was able to sit next to him and listen to him express his inner thoughts. So I understood his point of view and why he did certain things.

"Michael talked to me a lot about respect for dancers, the dignity of dancers. I never even knew the word, couldn't even spell it. And there was Michael Bennett, feeding nineteen people and making them sing, dance, and act: 'You *can* sing. Give him another note. It's too high but he's going to do it because I want him to do it. You can't do that step? Put your foot lower. That doesn't sound right? It doesn't sound natural? Change it. What do you *feel* like saying . . . ?'

"He was finally doing what dancers had never heard before. He was asking how we felt. And we began to respond. 'Gee, Michael, I didn't really say that in the tapes. I think what I said on the tapes was a little better.'

"And he was replying, 'Fine, darling, do it if it makes you comfortable.'

"All of a sudden my eyes are wide open and I understand what my dancing teacher, Syvilla Fort, had talked about: the humanity of your art. Michael was creating artists the way they did in the old days: The first thing on the agenda is that you take care of yourself and others as *human beings*. I had reentered the temple, that St. James Theatre the first day. And now I had entered a new beginning. I was one year old."

Bishop became deeply involved in Bennett's directing. "He played these little theater games. He'd say, 'Okay, I'm going to ask character questions.' He pointed to one woman and said, 'How old are you?'

"And she said, 'Me or my character?'

"And he said, 'I'm asking character questions. How old are you?'

" 'Me or my character?'

" 'Listen to me. I'm asking character questions. How old are you?'

"So she said however old she was.

"He said, 'Is that the truth?'

"She said, 'Me or my character?'

Bishop laughed. "I felt like a little kid in first grade jumping up and down wanting to raise my hand: 'Ask me! Ask me! Every question!' I knew I had a character."

"You can't even say that he broke the rules," LuPone said. "He just didn't know what he was doing. It's that simple. He was faking it, and he had the fortune to have Joe Papp pay for a nineteen-member sandbox. In a way, I respect him for that. We all should have that. Then a lot of our shows would be a lot better.

"Michael and I played a game that I understood: cat and mouse. I was basically the mouse and Michael was the cat; or I was the cat and Michael was the mouse. The way I played him, the way he played me, was sex. I used my charm and my sex as a weapon. I heard that he was gay, so as much as I was being manipulated unconsciously or consciously I was also manipulating. During the first workshop I found him very understanding and he played me like an instrument. He got me to do what he wanted. I do believe that terror is what brought the group together. The only way the group became an ensemble was a direct result of terror and manipulation on Michael Bennett's part."

As one of the people whose job it was to carry out Bennett's instructions, Lee was aware of Bennett's strategies, and had mixed feelings about them. "I knew why it was important for him to manipulate certain people in particular ways. The most important thing at that time, during the first and second workshops, was the result. We have now seen the result. My God, he was brilliant at what he did. But how he did it was another story. I consider him brilliant in the way he structured the show. The simplicity of the dancing and singing came out of the individual monologues. Every one on that line was an individual; not one character was like another. And yet all of us had a common ground. Yes, there was a lot of pain. He knew how to press buttons on every single person. On me he knew how to press the button that made me say to myself 'soldier . . . at ease' and make me part of *it*. 'Just experience this, Baayork, experience it with us now. Come on, give, open up.' For me, this was the transformation from a little girl to a woman, which is a very big step in one's life. No matter how he did it to me, no matter how he pulled at my heartstrings, he dared me to do it. He got me through that door.

"And he did the same with every single person in the show. That in itself is an art. He knew how to get the best results from every single person on that stage. A lot of people would say, 'Oh, he could have gotten better from me.' But maybe he didn't want better. Maybe he wanted just what you gave him. And he would stop you there. He got you just to the point where it was right for the show, and then he would shut you off.

"I was lucky to be on both sides. I got to listen to the hurt egos and the mangled hearts, and then be on the other side, hear why it was done that way. He pampered some people and some he pushed into corners and frightened. But everyone allowed it. I believe we all wanted our private moment with Michael, to be touched by his genius, to work with him—yes, to be manipulated by him. We all wanted him to love us."

As a management style, it was a gamble. In most cases it paid off. Trish Garland found she could thrive in the chesslike atmosphere. "With so many directors you can tell exactly what their next move is going to be. Michael intrigued me because he didn't think the way most directors do. That always excited me about him. My respect for him as a director grew and grew, though I could never quite figure out his vision at that point. I remember wondering how this was all going to work out. How is this going to make sense?"

"He was excellent at manipulating," said Pam Blair. "To be a good director you have to know how to manipulate, it just depends on how you do it. Michael could be very nasty, but he was excellent. That's why he was so successful. He was a master at that. He could convince you that he really cared about you. I keep thinking about all those moments that he did that to me and he could see in my face that I believed him. I wonder if in any of these moments he did care. It's embarrassing to know how many times I gave him that power, relinquished that part of me."

"What did he have over us?" mused Cilento.

Blair offers a theory of Bennett's spells: "Don't you think that's what a lot of dancing is, just having that central figure, that guru that we all want to follow? We're disciplinarians and we need a leader. And we never say no. That's a mortal sin in the dance world. You just do whatever they ask you to do somehow. I love that discipline, I think that's what makes us all love dance. The first workshop for me was about Michael Bennett and dancing."

Bennett found what each of the dancers was looking for in a guru. It may have been a taskmaster, a teacher, a courtier, a lover, an apache-dance ravisher, or even a father.

"I guess I'd be a liar if I said I didn't fall in love with Michael Bennett at one time or ten times or twenty times during the course of my life," Walsh said. "And that was his greatest power over us all. We loved him."

Said Baughman, "I didn't fall in love with my director. I fell in love with Michael as a daddy. I wanted to be a good girl for him. He saw my potential and he gave me this wonderful opportunity. He nurtured me."

It was the same for Blair: "I think that I spent all those years looking for a daddy, that's why I got into so much trouble in this business. I had trouble with authority figures. I wanted so badly to please them and a lot of them can't handle it. They don't want to be needed, they don't want to be loved, they don't want the responsibility. I think it's a part of me that will never change. That's who I am deep down inside. That's why I had so much trouble with Michael Bennett. I wanted so badly for him to care about me. He did play favorites. Kelly was a favorite, and Donna definitely. That hurt a lot because *I* wanted to be a favorite. We all did. It wasn't until the gala nine years later that I realized he didn't really care about me. That hurt. What had been important to me wasn't the show, it was *him*. That was his charisma. We allowed him to put us through anything he wanted. It was our incredible need for this funny-looking little man to love us.

"But it was a role he cast himself in that he couldn't really play and come out winning," Blair continued. "Can you imagine being faced with our little faces every day just panting to be told what he wanted? Of course he did keep us all in the dark. We never knew from one moment to the next whether we were acting or doing the show, or if it was real life. And he enjoyed that. I just wished I had enjoyed it as much as he did. I could, today. That's what makes me so melancholy sometimes."

And Blair wouldn't discount the simple animal attraction that drew dancers—particularly women and gay men—to work for Bennett. "We're sexual animals," she said. "Anyone who's interested in dance is, I think. But I came out of it stronger, because I think in the end I was doing it for me. And he didn't fail all the time. He did create this incredible show and we were all a part of it."

Though Bennett became more businesslike as the project ripened, in the beginning he used the most personal kind of influence over them. It wasn't so much a job as a fellowship on a quest. "He sort of handed out emotional IOUs at the beginning," said Lopez, "but down the line when we started cashing them in it was like he didn't have enough in the bank to give us all. I fell out of love with my director. No, I fell out of *worship* for my director and then maybe I just loved him. The whole experience made me realize he was just a man with problems, he was just a person, not perfect."

Not everyone was willing to let Bennett off that easily.

"Sometimes he'd be very supportive," said Walsh. "I would do a new monologue at that evening's performance, and Michael would say in front of the whole group, 'Thommie, you were really great tonight,' or whatever. But there would be other times, in rehearsals, when he would scream, 'Don't do it like a faggot!' There definitely were extremes in his direction. Every day was a game. You could be rolling along for three days feeling good about your work and then he would throw you off and you'd be lost for days. He often would play one person against another, which I thought was really unfair. That was his biggest flaw. I was aware of this trip early on but it still didn't make it any easier. One day Wayne would have a monologue or a song and dance or something like that, and the next day I would have a little bit more. I could just feel him watching the two of us react to one another. It was a work in progress so there was a lot of time to watch the monkeys in their cages. You had to wear a lot of armor in those rehearsals. Every day was an event. They were very emotional days, but that was part of the excitement."

New material cascaded through the workshop: music, dance, monologues. Despite the novelty, the constant turbulence had its effect on Bennett as well as the dancers. Rick Mason remembers, "One day I was in the lineup and I was giving my name and saying something like 'If I get this show I'll work real hard.' So Michael yells at me, 'If you don't speak louder I'm taking it away from you.' That freaked me out because I never felt that I was given any kind of direction. For a majority of the kids he let them find their own niche and grow with their own abilities. He would give ideas but he wouldn't give readings. He'd try to make you work at it, and then if he liked it he would say do it again or expand on it. Most of us, being dancers, were still getting used to being able to verbalize feelings. I remember him giving me one direction: 'You're cute enough, don't try to be cute.'

"That was one of the few directions I got from him: He was saying, 'Take it down.' I tried it a number of different ways and I guess until he felt that I was comfortable with it or that it worked he would say, 'That's fine.' I never got 'Good job'; I always got 'That's fine.' "

During the first workshop the volatile mixture of emotions never exploded. That's partly because there was a great deal of tolerance, and partly because the dancers still feared that if they got out of line they would simply be dropped from the project. Having little clout, they felt at Bennett's mercy. Bennett did nothing to soften the hard edges of this conviction.

That was left to others, the unsung heroes who stayed in the background, but who acted as the emotional lubricant that kept Bennett and the dancers from suffering too much friction.

"Bob Avian was the bridge over troubled waters," said Lopez. He served as an ambassador between Bennett and the cast members. When Bennett's commands would hurt feelings, it was Avian who would come around and explain them in more diplomatic terms.

"He was a saint," said Walsh. "When it was real hard for me, I don't think I could have gotten through it without looking at Bobby and seeing him kind of twinkling and saying 'Breathe.' He was a kind of comforting spirit."

Avian was not simply Bennett's assistant, but was co-choreographer of *A Chorus Line*. The 1976 Tony Award for best choreography is engraved with both their names. "I don't know if you can separate Bob Avian from the success of this show," said McKechnie. "He's as much responsible for it, in my opinion, as Michael."

"His input was much more than anybody realized," Lee said,

"in terms of shaping and concepts and things like that. He's very apparent in the production."

But Lee herself proved to be another of the small cogs that kept the big wheels turning smoothly. "Baayork held us together many a time," said Garland.

"Baayork was determined to keep that show intact," Sammy Williams remembers. "She was always after us to keep rehearsing. She was always for the good of the show, which was no easy task to take on."

Lee had a tougher taskmaster than Bennett to please: Lee. "I think Baayork was trying too hard," Lee said of herself. "I also think that she had a lot of hats. She was the porter, the railroad guy who sold the tickets, the conductor who took the tickets, the passenger, and the guy who stoked the fire to move the train. She was trying to be a mediator, trying to let them know that Michael really cared and understood."

After *A Chorus Line,* Baughman went on to assist choreographers on other shows and she began to appreciate what Avian and Lee did. "I learned how hard it is, not only learning all the material and teaching it, et cetera, but dealing with the choreographer. It can be very hairy. The people I've worked with have had tremendous emotional outbreaks, there's so much pressure. Bob and Baayork were a very stabilizing influence."

There was another even more powerful force that kept the top spinning. Faced with a shared task, a potent leader, and, as it seemed at times, a common enemy, the dancers began to turn to one another. Said Cilento, "Even today, there is a love between all of us that no one can ever really explain. That Line, that Line is incredible. I mean, every one of us knows every one of our ins and outs. That's something no one can ever take away from us."

The bond that was forged in the tape sessions was annealed in the first workshop. Trish Garland said, "The workshop was total absorption, learning—and some rapture."

The dancers worked together from early morning until dinnertime. For those appearing in a show, like Cilento in *Irene* and Kuhlman in the off-off-Broadway show *It Pays to Advertise,* evenings meant more work. Those not appearing in a show would work with the writers. The rest would just go home and collapse. Or try to. Often they found themselves on the telephone with one another, analyzing the progress, trading gossip, crying on one another's shoulder.

"This workshop was not a ten-to-six like other jobs," said Williams. "You had to totally immerse yourself into it. I would take home all this pain and anxiety every night."

Sometimes the caller was Bennett. He didn't call everyone. He cultivated an informal cabinet of dancers whose feedback he would solicit periodically. Aside from Baayork Lee and Tony Stevens there was Bishop, Walsh, Baughman, and Garland. "At that time I could easily talk to Michael," Garland said. "We'd talk about the show and this and that, there was that camaraderie. Michael would sometimes call just to find out how I was getting on. Just conversation."

Bishop remembers, "Michael and I used to talk every night after rehearsal for a couple of hours. I could count on that phone call about two hours after I got home. We'd talk about what had gone down during the day. I gave him my opinions on things that I wouldn't dare say in rehearsal. He'd give me his opinions on things. He was very open with me."

Then, the dancers would call each other, or visit. Because several were trying to subsist on $100 a week, they did very little lounging in cafés. If there was an informal *Chorus Line* clubhouse, it was Dobson's, a restaurant on Columbus Avenue at Seventy-sixth Street. It was a favorite of the group of friends that included Walsh, Bishop, and Lopez. Lee and Williams were irregulars. Others joined periodically, but this group remained allied from the tape sessions right through to opening night.

Though *A Chorus Line* opened in Greenwich Village and has a Village "feeling," few of the dancers lived in the Village. With a few exceptions, like Wayne Cilento who lived with his wife in suburban Westchester County, they lived on the Upper West Side in a territory centered on Dobson's.

Though they were preparing a musical comedy, their lives were prosaic. "I didn't go out much at first," Bishop said. "I always dashed off because I had to walk the dog."

When workshop sessions started running late, Bishop began bringing her German shepherd, Venus, to the workshop sessions, where she became something of a company mascot. When they worked at the Newman Theater, Venus stayed in the Green Room. Bishop, Lopez, and Walsh took the same buses and subways to and from the workshops. When Bishop brought Venus she would take a cab, dogs being banned from New York subways. Cabs were expensive and when Bishop couldn't afford the ride, she'd simply hike home. But one night it was raining.

"Priscilla used to wear ponchos all the time," Bishop said. "So she pulled the poncho over her head, put on glasses, and acted like she was blind." Seeing-eye dogs are the exception to the subway dog ban. "I couldn't have done it but she did. We were too embarrassed to get off at Forty-second Street. Instead we rode up to the end of the BMT line on Fifty-seventh and then we all ran off the subway together."

At lunchtime they rarely went out to restaurants. Most of the time they'd bring lunches—fruit or sandwiches—and eat in the Green Room, where Venus would beg scraps. "She knew that when intermission came she'd be a very happy dog," Bishop said.

Still, living on $100 a week meant life-styles approaching the *La Bohème* level. "I found out that Priscilla was on a diet for her hypoglycemia," said Bishop, "and when she told me it only cost her three dollars a day to eat, I got on her diet. It was an apple and a banana and almonds and this and that."

Having chums gave the dancers an emotional safety net for their daily high-wire acts. Sometimes, however, it led to exclusivity. "I think Priscilla [Lopez] made me the craziest," McKechnie said. "I felt she was very unfriendly. . . . I was very hurt with Kelly because she seemed to follow suit and as it turned out, the more I got to know Kelly the more I felt she was a good friend, I really liked her. But in that situation for a time they were like Frick and Frack and that used to drive me nuts."

McKechnie had good reason to feel isolated. It was clear to all that she had a special protégée status with Bennett, and like any teacher's pet, she was treated as something of a pariah.

"Priscilla never made me crazy," Baughman said. "But I was intimidated by her. She was so strong and together about her opinions and so outspoken and spunky. I was a little afraid of Kelly and Thommie too."

Instead, Baughman became the focus of the second circle of

friends within *A Chorus Line*. She espoused Nichiren Shoshu Buddhism, a form of the religion that is surprisingly popular among performing artists. The most appealing aspect of this complicated faith is its emphasis on keeping oneself centered and serene in the midst of turmoil. Meditation and chanting are employed to promote a tranquillity and concentration that several of the dancers found valuable, if not indispensable.

"Quite a few people joined Buddhism during *ACL,*" Baughman said. Dante, Garland, and LuPone were the other stalwarts, as was Bennett for a time. One of the originators of *A Chorus Line,* Michon Peacock, had been the show's original Buddhist as well. "I loved it," Baughman said. "It helped me a great deal. I would chant before I went to rehearsals. It would sort of free me. I felt very confident. I felt that I could do almost anything. I still appreciate the philosophy. Although I don't practice within the organizations and I don't proselytize, I still do chant occasionally.

"I became aware that there was a Buddhist camp and a non-Buddhist camp in *ACL.* That was an unfortunate aspect, but I wasn't too aware of that. People used to stop off in our dressing room to pray. I was kind of glad that happened."

Baughman had a circle of friends outside show business, and after work she would spend time with them. "In the first workshop I was doing all these big scenes with Bobby [LuPone, who played her husband, Al] and Michael, so I was just having a great old time. My friends just thought it was wonderful. They were very supportive."

Rick Mason was neither a Buddhist nor a member of the Dobson's group. That, plus being one of the dancers hired after the tape sessions, meant he had to work for his place in the project's inner circles. "I felt very alienated my first day at rehearsal," he said. "Everyone knew each other. I had heard about Thommie Walsh, as he was supposedly a little bit of a terror. He was very easy with the remarks, very fast-mouthed, and I was terrified of being included in his verbalization.

"It got easier as we got to know each other, but I ate lunch alone a lot, which was my own doing. I could have jumped in there and been bolder and said, 'Hi, can I join you for lunch?' But I wanted to take it cautiously and slowly. I didn't want to become a pain in the ass because those guys were so close-knit. I didn't want to be the third or fourth wheel, this new kid always inviting himself, I wanted to be invited. There definitely were camps and I wanted to be part of all of them. I didn't pick one group specifically, I just wanted to be included. I would go home a little depressed and frustrated that during the course of rehearsals I wasn't given something that someone else got, or even a chance to see if I could do it."

Still, day after day spent in each other's company encouraged the growing sense of camaraderie.

"We were singing a song that became 'Resume' and I had some lines," Trish Garland said. "Suddenly, Michael said 'Stop!' I had no idea I wasn't singing it right. Donna [McKechnie] said, 'She'll get it, she'll get it.' Suddenly she reached out to protect me, and from then on she kept saying I would be fine."

Increasingly separated from her sister Jacki, Garland found herself forced to seek out her colleagues. "This was excruciating to me because, again, I'm basically private about my personal life. Not having ever been in therapy or not having been in a position to have to expose myself, I guess I did feel it was necessary but I guess I didn't know how to go about it, to allow myself the liberty or freedom to offer whatever was in there.

"I loved the creative part of it. We were singing and dancing every day. That to me was always joyful because I always loved Michael's work and I could always do his work. It felt easy for me. But then after lunch seemed to be the foreboding time because then we would have to speak about our lives [for the writers]. I remember just shutting off. In the beginning I didn't feel that I was, but after a while . . . I would hear people rattling on about their lives and when it got to me I just felt blocked. I would come home and I wouldn't want to talk about it to my [artist] boyfriend, George. I completely shut him out. Then somebody from the workshop would call and I would go on and on, my mouth would not stop because I guess we had a relationship. I didn't have to explain my feelings.

"But instead of being moved in two feet, I withdrew ten more feet. I was so involved in my own life, my own little area, that I had no time to enjoy anybody else's or even know what anyone else was going through. I knew everyone was going through their own thing because we'd talk on our lunch break. But actually while we were involved I didn't see anybody else in pain because I was so involved in my own pain. I don't even know why it was so painful, why it was so hard for me to expose myself. Maybe it was because all my life I had lived a fantasy and now the fantasy was no longer going to be a fantasy. I was going to have to deal with the real truth of things."

Like Mason, Kuhlman saw himself as an outsider. "In terms of people I went out with, I guess I was pretty much of a loner because I really didn't go out to lunch that much with anybody; occasionally but not a lot. I do remember groups forming. You're always aware of that going on. That happens, that's good. I just don't usually get involved in them. I don't like to dish."

But Kuhlman eventually found his ally in LuPone. "Bob became my good buddy. I do remember us getting together and talking about his wanting to do Zach" when that part was created. "When they cast Barry Bostwick [as Zach] he was angry about that. We talked about that for a while."

The only person who deliberately withdrew was Williams. "I didn't talk to friends," he said. "I tried to deal with it on my own and I didn't deal with it very well. I was never any good when I was at the theater. I was always having some problems, coping with something and I was always nasty to people, flip and ugly and sometimes unkind. But it all stemmed from problems that I had dealing with the whole experience."

"Sammy got all tangled up with his feelings about his character," said Bishop. "He began to realize that he was going to be a major portion of the show with the most profound and awesome piece of material that anyone has in the show. So he became a thing unto himself. I have a feeling that Sammy wanted a song. And yet he had the most powerful piece of material in the show."

That piece was Dante's Jewel Box monologue. It was one of his clearest pieces of writing for the show. Other people's monologues gave him more trouble.

The impression was, in Wayne Cilento's word, that Dante was a "secretary" who never got far beyond transcribing and editing the original tapes. Though the quantity of material they were given to perform got longer and more detailed, it did not acquire dramatic shape during the first workshop. There was little or no dialogue, just a series of long monologues punctuated or underlined by dance.

"Nicholas Dante is disappointing as a writer," LuPone said. "That is my personal belief. I hope that I'm wrong; I wanted very much for him to keep writing and prove me wrong. He's been crazy because of what happened to his head with *A Chorus Line*. We're talking about an ego that just shot through the roof."

Baughman took an opposing view. "Nicholas is an incredibly talented writer. His contribution to *A Chorus Line* was enormous. Not only the Paul story, but the concept for the montage was Nick's."

Dante dealt with the pressure by working as hard as he could, always taking time to meditate or chant to calm himself. "Nicholas tried to get me to be a Buddhist," Baayork Lee recalled. "I said, 'Why should I go and chant with you when I can go home and chant with my father who is a Buddhist?' Nicholas had a hard time. Having been a dancer and having danced with some of us, then trying to make this transition as an author must have been very hard for him. He was learning his craft. My favorite line he wrote for me was 'a peanut en pointe.' "

Dante's angst was especially apparent to those who had been closest to him before he turned from dance to writing. One of his closest friends had been Thommie Walsh, but Walsh noticed a gradual change. "He began to make me nuts because he liked to call me up and tell me that I was messing up and 'Get your act together' and 'Michael's going to fire you' and little torture kinds of things like that. He always insisted I'd become a fuller person if I became a Buddhist, so I didn't really relate to Nicholas writing this play as much as I relate to him bothering me or tormenting me, making me feel inferior. His vibes were unwanted most of the time."

Dante had been tossed into the deep end of the pool and he did his best to keep his head above water; keeping faith with his people, the dancers, while fulfilling Bennett's script requirements and feeling his way as a writer. For the development of *A Chorus Line,* Dante's greenness as a writer had a profound effect. A more experienced writer may have tried to lock in scenes and dialogue right away. However, although Dante floundered in the first workshop, and the script of *A Chorus Line* failed to jell, it remained fluid, which enabled Bennett and the dancers to experiment freely, to draw on their own resources, and to express more of their characters purely through dance.

"Nicholas's influence on the show in terms of contribution was more than anyone could ever appreciate," McKechnie said. "All our presences were felt and our ideas used. Nicholas's courage to stay with the show and support it and give of himself was, I think, the turning point in the show's success—if not the turning point, then the heart of the matter."

But that didn't always make life easier for the dancers putting themselves on the line each day.

"I don't think many people actually understood what was going on," said Trish Garland. "I remember coming in and having lines, creating words and shaping something, and then coming in and no longer having them, and hearing other people say my lines. I didn't understand that they were playing with different things. I immediately took that as meaning that I was bad, that something was wrong. But one day we were all talking and suddenly there was some sort of form taken. I realized then that we were actually creating as we went."

The same was true for Hamlisch and Kleban. Both had more extensive backgrounds, lyricist Kleban in the BMI Workshop and Hamlisch in Hollywood. But like Dante, both were working on their first real Broadway score. Bennett believed they could cut it. He also knew that their salary demands would be less than an established writer's—and they would be more malleable, more amenable to his wishes and visions.

As a team, Hamlisch and Kleban were a blind date. While those two never fought or even disagreed in front of the group, the dancers got a clear sense that neither were they very close personally. They didn't pal around. They had a working relationship. Hamlisch's music had always been slicker and more pop-oriented. Kleban was more closely allied to the New York musical theater continuum. Trained carefully by Lehman Engel, whose experience dated back to the Rodgers and Hart era, Kleban also was primed to the latest currents in Broadway songwriting. With *Company* in 1969, *Follies* in 1971, and *A Little Night Music* in 1973, Stephen Sondheim had established an emotionally articulate and intellectually brittle new standard for Broadway lyrics.

In 1976, Hamlisch and Kleban would beat Sondheim to a Tony Award, *A Chorus Line* bested *Pacific Overtures.* But in the first workshop during the last weeks of September and first weeks of October 1974, Kleban and Hamlisch knew that to write a credible score, they had Sondheim to compete against. Hamlisch met the challenge by playing in a field where Sondheim had never had much success—the pop tune. Hamlisch's score contains brief references to classical sources, but actually refracts generic Broadway brassiness through a pop idiom.

"Marvin was a little boy who had been given a game to play," said Lopez. "In the past he probably had sat alone somewhere writing his songs and then presenting them. Now he suddenly had to work in a whole other way, exposed to a lot of people. I was in awe of that, although as performers we are always on display, our mistakes for the world to see."

In social situations Hamlisch would assume an emcee personality, cracking jokes both verbal and musical, as he played.

"Marvin was such a character," Garland said. "I loved seeing him create on the spot. He absolutely charmed me with his creativity. I really felt that this was not an ego-gratifying show for Marvin because Marvin loves to write those singles, those hits. He didn't do that at all and that must have required immense change in him."

Williams conceded, "It's really his music that brought life to our show. Without his music, we would not have the show that we have. His influence was very, very strong. The same for Ed Kleban, his words. I think Marvin more than Ed. Ed was very quiet, he was more in the background. His words are very beautiful."

Kleban had reason to stay in the background. In writing the lyrics to *A Chorus Line,* he took on Sondheim more directly. To do so, he knew he had to get inside the dancers' heads, to listen carefully to the cadence of their speech and the precise shape and weight of their thoughts. That apparently was not an assignment he relished. He was a shy man who, like Hamlisch, preferred to work in his garret, then emerge with a finished product. Around the dancers, he worked methodically but unobtrusively.

Lee remembers, "He was there taking his little notes in the audience an awful lot."

Said Blair, "He was very shy but he seemed genuinely interested in what we had to say. He seemed capable of hearing."

As collaborators, Hamlisch and Kleban tended to go their separate ways—and therefore made two distinct impressions. "I found Ed Kleban to be a nebbish," LuPone said. "Marvin was a separate entity, a craftsman. He knew what he was doing. He may have had an ego, he may have been intelligent, he may have been ignorant, he may have been all the human things—but he was an artist and a craftsman. He didn't need Michael Bennett's manipulation to get him to produce. He was able to deal with Michael professionally and 'craftually.' What I find interesting about all those guys is that they haven't produced anything: Jimmy [Kirkwood, who joined the project in the second workshop], Ed, Nick. Marvin has, but that just goes to show that Marvin wasn't that involved with Michael."

The first song they worked on was the opening combination. "It seemed like the whole workshop was about the opening number," Bishop said, "trying to find the opening of the show. And we did do really bad stuff. It was sort of like . . ." Bishop began to sing, the rhythm sounding similar to a line Baayork Lee still sings in the show about being four foot ten: " 'Five foot five; one hundred and *elev*en; hair, brown; eyes, whatever,' " she sang. "That was the melody. It was very peculiar. The concept was right. He took the concept and made it that audition, but the music was wrong."

"Nobody liked it," Baughman agreed. "It was corny and trite," And nobody missed it when it went.

The dancers worked on the song that evolved into "I Hope I Get It" from the first weeks of the first workshop through the middle of the second workshop. It was constantly changing in form, absorbing material until it ran fifteen minutes, then being cut down to almost nothing, then growing again.

For those five weeks the dancers worked mostly on their long monologues, their extended scenes, and some dancing. Aside from the constantly evolving opening combination, they worked on three other songs: "Resume," "I Can Do That," and "At the Ballet."

"Resume" and "I Can Do That" are modular numbers that changed relatively little in form or content. Bennett tried them in

FROM THEIR POINT OF VIEW: In the last moments of the show, the dancers of *A Chorus Line* stand tensely as the director, Zach, begins the final elimination. From left: Nancy Lane, Thommie Walsh, Kelly Bishop, Donna McKechnie, Michel Stuart, Baayork Lee, Wayne Cilento, Nancy Cole, and Ron Kuhlman. PHOTO BY PAUL HERMAN

THE AUDIENCE AND THE MIRROR: The intimacy of off-Broadway's Estelle R. Newman Theater was something the dancers hated to lose when they moved to Broadway. Here the closeness of the audience can be sensed from the reflection in set designer Robin Wagner's mirrors as Bob Avian (left) and Michael Bennett (in numbered jersey, center) put the dancers through a routine. PHOTO BY BARBARA J. ROSSI

IMAGINE ME—THIS KINDERGARTEN TEACHER?: In rehearsal at the Newman Theater, Richie, played by Ron Dennis, struts through the "Gimme the Ball" sequence in "Hello Twelve, Hello Thirteen, Hello Love." PHOTO BY BARBARA J. ROSSI

THIS BOOK WOULD COVER EVERYTHING: Rehearsing "Hello Twelve," Rick Mason, as Mark, tells how, when he was a teenager, he got hold of a medical textbook and misdiagnosed his wet dreams as gonorrhea. The line embarrassed Mason, especially as many of the rest of his lines began to be trimmed. Behind him, Pamela Blair can be seen at left; Priscilla Lopez at right. PHOTO BY MARTHA SWOPE

DANCE LIKE EVERYONE ELSE: At Zach's order, Cassie (Donna McKechnie) tries to dance in unison with the rest of the Line. Left to right: Wayne Cilento, Kay Cole, Sammy Williams, Pamela Blair, Michel Stuart, Nancy Lane, Rick Mason, Renee Baughman, Ron Kuhlman, McKechnie, Thommie Walsh, Patricia Garland, Don Percassi, Kelly Bishop, Ron Dennis, and Priscilla Lopez. PHOTO BY MARTHA SWOPE

PEANUT EN POINTE: As Connie, Baayork Lee explains how she realized she'd never be ballerina Maria Tallchief, as Michel Stuart, Donna McKechnie, and Kelly Bishop listen. Lee went on to become a choreographer and to stage *A Chorus Line* in Europe, Asia, and Australia, as well as in dozens of towns across North America.

PHOTO BY MARTHA SWOPE

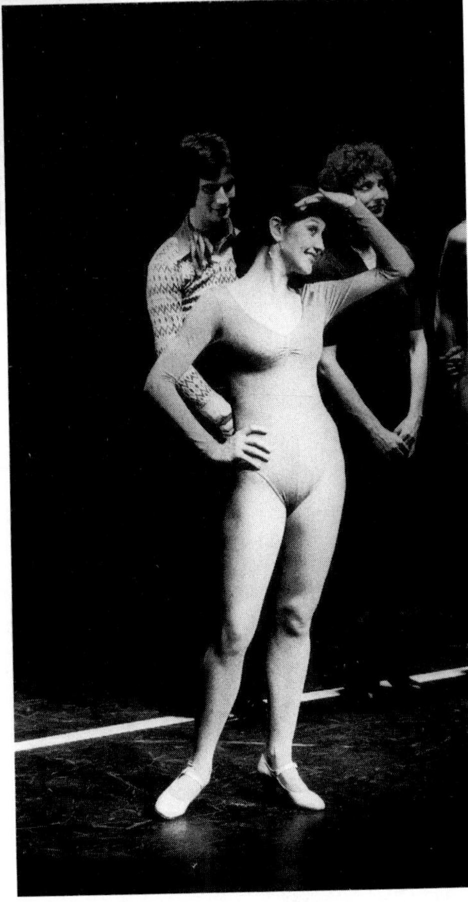

CAN THE ADULTS SMOKE?: Kelly Bishop, in her Tony Award-winning performance as Sheila, asks Zach if he could change a harsh spotlight. She's wearing the unflattering costume that she says has made fifteen years of Sheilas miserable.

PHOTO BY MARTHA SWOPE

LEARNING THE STEPS: Backstage at the Newman, dancers concentrate on a movement called "ring the bell" in "Hello Twelve, Hello Thirteen, Hello Love." From left: Sammy Williams, understudy Crissy Wilzak (Renee Baughman visible in the crook of her arm), Nancy Lane, Thommie Walsh, Wayne Cilento, Patricia Garland, and Baayork Lee.

PHOTO BY BARBARA J. ROSSI

DYNAMIC TWIN FORTY-FOURS: After seeing much of his role as Don cut, Ron Kuhlman was left with a comic monologue drawn largely from Michael Bennett's experience working in strip joints in Buffalo, New York.

PHOTO BY MARTHA SWOPE

I'M WATCHIN' SIS GO PITAPAT: Mike Costa, played by Wayne Cilento, rehearses his show-stopping routine "I Can Do That" as others look on, wondering what they'll say or do when called upon. Visible behind him are, from left, Patricia Garland, Ron Dennis, Don Percassi, Renee Baughman, Pamela Blair, and Rick Mason.

PHOTO BY MARTHA SWOPE

DOWN THE STREET FROM DOBSON'S: Members of the Dobson's group that evolved during the two workshops, from left, Kelly Bishop, Thommie Walsh, and Priscilla Lopez. With them are Bishop's German shepherd Venus (left), who became the Line's mascot, and Lopez's Chelsea. PHOTO BY VINCENT FANUELLE PHOTO

WHAT DO YOU DO WHEN YOU CAN'T DANCE ANYMORE?: Recreating the infamous knee injury scene, Sammy Williams (center) is tended by Thommie Walsh (left, as Bobby) and Robert LuPone (as Zach). Behind them are Ron Dennis, Donna McKechnie, and Rick Mason. Williams won a best featured actor Tony Award for his performance.

PHOTO BY MARTHA SWOPE

THE CHANCE TO DANCE: With her mentor (and future husband) Michael Bennett, Donna McKechnie learns the original version of "The Music and the Mirror" in which Rick Mason (at right) and three other men performed with her. That version was done for four previews off-Broadway before the four men were cut and the number was made a solo for McKechnie. She was named best actress in the 1976 Tony Awards.

PHOTO BY BARBARA J. ROSSI

I HOPE I GET IT: Director Zach (Robert LuPone) and his assistant Larry (Clive Wilson) discuss the preliminary eliminations after the opening number, "I Hope I Get It." LuPone is wearing his original costume before it was redesigned to make him look older. Donna McKechnie's face is visible at rear.

PHOTO BY MARTHA SWOPE

different spots in the show, and gave the songs to different people at different points.

The first song fully to reflect the content and structure of the tapes was "At the Ballet," which grew directly out of the taped monologues, particularly Kelly Bishop's story of her parents and Donna McKechnie's fantasy about her absent daddy.

"I never thought I was, in a private way, very special," Bishop said. "I mean, I knew I had talent, I was very professional and a good performer. But I never thought my life story had been particularly intriguing. So I was very touched that he chose me to play that particular kind of performance. I knew what he was doing. He was looking for 'the ballet dancer.' A large number of dancers start out in ballet. I'd say sixty, seventy percent started out with their mothers taking them to ballet school, and wanted to be ballerinas when they were little girls. That kind of dancer, that kind of background, he wanted to have represented among chorus people. But my story had other things in it: my father's alcoholism, the divorce—all sorts of things that gave substance."

Bishop spent most of the first workshop telling that story in a long monologue which she said was a direct transcript of what she had said on the tape. "One section of it was my saying, 'Do you remember that Doris Day song, "Que Será, Será"?'

"Everyone went 'Yeah, yeah, yeah.'

"And I said, 'Remember when the little kid says "Will I be pretty, will I be rich"? I asked my mother that and she said, "No. You'll be attractive and very different." Well, that is not what I wanted to hear! It broke my heart. I wanted to turn into this beauty and I wanted my mom to tell me that.'

"In the song ['At the Ballet'], that went to another character, but the words are still there: 'pretty . . . different . . . special.' "

A lot of Bishop's monologue was about the enchanted world that ballet represented to her when she was a child. "I was particularly thinking of Danilova," Bishop said. "I went to see Danilova when I was a child. Danilova is not a beautiful woman. Actually, she's much more glorious-looking now in her old age than she was. There are a lot of funny-looking ballerinas. But they get onstage and they're gorgeous. And the prince does fall in love with them and they do go off into the sunset. And that's what appealed to me about the ballet. I thought I was very ugly. But in *Swan Lake* or some other ballet, it didn't matter what your face looked like, it mattered how you acted, how you danced, how you projected. It created the illusion of beauty."

In her monologue, Bishop added, " 'But now I am pretty. Inside now I accept myself.' "

Though Bennett had her perform the monologue often during the first workshop, he would inform her that the piece was being adapted as a song.

"A lot of people were dying to have a song," Bishop said. "But it was my terror. I wanted to be the actress of the company. But one day Michael pulled me out of rehearsal and said, 'Go down to the Green Room, Ed wants to talk to you.'

"Ed and I just sat and talked about my childhood. I told him about my father's philandering and about his drinking. I talked to him for about two hours. He was so overwhelmed. He kept dwelling on 'How old was she?' I said she was twenty-two. And he said, 'She bought that story? She believed that no one else would ask her to marry?'

"I said, 'You have to understand where my mother came from. She was raised like a little nun. She couldn't go out on dates. God, what an insecure child. And pushed ahead in school so she was in college when she was sixteen, which didn't add to her security. So when my father told her that no one else would have her, she believed him. And so she married him.' Ed was bowled over by that. Obviously, you can tell from the way it came out in the song."

Not long afterward, Bishop was again pulled from rehearsal and sent into a separate room, where Hamlisch and Kleban were waiting with a piano. Shortly after she arrived, she remembers, they began to sing the first draft of "At the Ballet," which is substantially the way it is still sung. "I was just overwhelmed," Bishop said. "I thought it was the most beautiful piece of music I had ever heard. I heard the story, I heard the words, and I looked at Ed and I thought I can't believe this man . . . from that hour and a half or two hours I talked to him, he had plucked those things. I thought there were odd choices, too. 'Though she was twenty-two, though she was twenty-two, though she was twenty-two . . .' I thought, what a strange choice in terms of lyrics. Who knows what it could have been? But obviously that was what had caught him.

"I was, I think, in tears when I heard it.

"It's got three full melodic lines: 'Daddy always thought he had married beneath him . . .'—that one. Then there's 'Everyone was beautiful at the ballet'—the pretty one. Then 'Up a steep and very narrow . . .' So you had three where most songs have two. It's wonderful."

Though Bishop said she believes she could have handled the song as a solo, she said she had no desire to do so. "You don't understand how terrified I was to sing," she said. "They used to call me the Elaine Stritch of the company for more than one reason. I will open my mouth and say things in the most abrupt and sarcastic manner—like Elaine Stritch. She also happens to be one of my idols. She's terrified of singing, too."

Through the first workshop and into the beginning of the second, "At the Ballet," was performed by Bishop, Donna McKechnie in the role of Maggie (later assumed by Kay Cole), and by Jane Robertson in the role of Bebe (later taken by Nancy Lane).

"The song starts out with my story," Bishop said. "The Indian chief is Donna. That was left over from her spoken monologue. She was a war baby. Her parents were married young and quickly and her father went off to war. She used to see his picture and she used to kiss his picture every night. She used to have this whole fantasy about what a father was. Her fantasy father was an Indian chief and he would say, 'Donna, do you want to dance?' and she'd say, 'Daddy, I would *love* to.' And every time she told that monologue we all wept and she'd weep, too. It was the most incredible moment.

"The whole thing about 'I don't know what they were for or against, really—except each other,' was a verbatim quote from Donna. When he came to the hospital and said, 'I thought this was going to help but I guess it's not,' that was all Donna. So the song is mostly me and Donna."

McKechnie said, "Maggie was the character in the show that was specifically my life story. The first part of 'Ballet,' her speech, and *The Red Shoes*—even though that was Kelly's story, too. That was the fun part. You realize you weren't the only one who saw *The Red Shoes* and it changed your life."

Kelly Bishop's Sheila character was well defined from the beginning, but she began to get lines that had been taken from other people's monologues, or made up entirely. "There's that horrible line in the montage that I hated singing," said Bishop, "but I knew nobody could hear it: 'All you run around with is bums.' And then there's one line you can hear: 'Darling, I can tell you now, your father went through life with an open fly.' I was horrified when I heard that line. I didn't want to do it.

"Michael said, 'You have to, you have to, you have to.'

"My mother would never say anything like that. Several of the things Sheila says in the montage I knew came from someone's mouth but not from mine."

Cilento remembers two of the dancers who had important roles in the first workshop but did not stay with the project: Michael Misita and Candy Brown. "Candy had a real big part at that point," he said, "and Michael Misita was doing 'I Can Do That.' Michael [Bennett] hadn't really developed me yet. I knew that 'Gimme the Ball' (the story of a dancer who turned his back on a career path that would have made him a kindergarten teacher) was going to be my part. But at the second workshop when Michael Misita left, I got his part. *I* had been doing *his* life story and then we were talking about just juggling around real-life situations that were mine that he was taking away and I was getting other things." Bennett had paired Cilento and Walsh as well, trying to decide which story threads would be designated toward which character. "We were trying things that did work and didn't work," Cilento said, "switching parts with Thommie and me—Thommie doing monologues that I was doing, and just juggling around the situations. It made you feel really insecure, that you weren't good enough. Thommie was better than I was so Michael was giving Thommie stuff that I wasn't able to cut."

LuPone was satisfied with the role of Al, at first. "I was ultimately the guy who didn't fit in. I was ultimately the strange guy. I was ultimately the tough guy, the insensitive guy, the hardnose. I was those colors and I can play that, I was comfortable with it. It didn't matter that nobody knew me and I didn't know them. It didn't matter if I didn't dance. I wasn't going to dance and that's all there was to it. Or, if I had to dance, I would be brilliant for two seconds and then walk away."

Blair eventually was given a role based on the life of dancer Mitzi Hamilton, who had been at the tape session but had not been chosen for the workshop. But "I didn't have a part right away," she said. "I did have one monologue at one point. I told about my go-go days a little bit and the incident where my life was threatened. It was sad and Michael said he liked it very much but he was going to make me a funnier character. He thought it was too heavy. I think that's why I got the part. I had this filthy mouth and a face like an angel. I loved to shock people, that was my trip. I can't really remember which part of the role was Mitzi Hamilton's and which was mine. I know the first line was mine and the part about wanting to be a Rockette and getting on the bus in my little white outfit."

Toward the end of the first workshop Priscilla Lopez was told to go up to the Lincoln Center rehearsal room where Hamlisch and Kleban worked. "It was the first time I got to hear 'Nothing' and I guess I cried," she said. Her taped anecdote about being belittled by a teacher at the High School of the Performing Arts had been rendered nearly directly into verse. "I couldn't believe that this was going on paper in a song, something I said. I was ecstatic, and by now I'm positive that this is going to be *the* show and I'm doing what I want to do."

When it came time to stage the song, Bennett experimented with making it a chorus number, with the other dancers playing Lopez's taunting classmates. "I was very upset when Michael began to stage 'Nothing' because everyone was in the number," she said. "What were all those people doing there? I was so happy the day that he said, 'Okay everybody just go upstage and off to stage left.' That pleased me."

7.

End of the First Workshop (Late September 1974)

Toward the end of the first workshop the dancers found that many of the dances they had been performing free-style were being sculpted and combined into a single extended dance montage. "We did this major dance combination which was great," Cilento recalled. "I got real good positive feedback from Bob [Avian] and Michael. They said they loved the way I danced."

The original number, referred to informally by the dancers as "The Dance Combination," eventually was broken up, however, and bits were scattered here and there throughout the show. A new dance and song montage eventually grew in its place, bridging "At the Ballet," "Nothing," and other numbers yet to be written for the middle of the show's first half. It served to build the dancers' confidence, since it gave each of them a chance to shine, much in the way a jazz combo will improvise, each player having a chance for a solo riff. For those who were dancing for the legendary Michael Bennett for the first time, it was exhilarating but also stressful. They knew their mettle and potential as dancers were being carefully appraised for other dances and songs yet to be written. Yet it was very satisfying for the dancers. This is what Broadway dancers strive all their careers for, to create new works with the best choreographers in the business. Every step they took, they knew, was taken at the top of their profession.

During this time the show acquired one of its fundamental

visual images. The dancers would arrive each day and sit in a semicircle, just as the original dancers had done at the first tape session eight months earlier. Knowing that a potential audience would want to see everyone's face, Bennett one day offhandedly asked the dancers not to sit in circle, but to line up and face front. It was very informal at first, friends tended to stand with friends. But with a few adjustments (and substitutions in the second workshop), the chorus line had taken place. After each segment of "The Dance Combination," the dancers now would return to their starting positions on that line.

"The Dance Combination" gave Bennett and Avian a chance to try a variety of styles, to clear their throats choreographically. It had the potential to stop the show. But stopping the show meant breaking the momentum. For a show with no clear story yet, momentum was a precious commodity. So "The Dance Combination" was not continued beyond the first workshop. It was cannibalized for parts however, and one of its fragments survived in McKechnie's dance solo, "The Music and the Mirror," which had yet to be written.

Kuhlman said, "It didn't seem as if there was any definite outline of what was going to happen or how it was going to happen, except all these grandiose ideas about the [remaining] numbers. I remember Michael talking about the finale number being this big thing with grand pianos. I couldn't believe it. I guess that's what we had to go through in order to wind up with a show as great as the one we got."

Through elbow grease, tears, and a lot of sweat, the dancers were defining how a musical theater workshop worked. In the old days of Broadway the writers would knock a show more or less into shape, then get it "on its feet" with live actors and try it out in front of a paying out-of-town audience. The same thing happened in the *Chorus Line* workshops, but in different combinations. The writers were still knocking the show together, this time with their first draft "on its feet," but no paying customers. It was like movie people reviewing daily rushes of a film in progress, or athletes analyzing videotapes of their practices to pinpoint strengths and weaknesses. Like figures on a video screen, the dancers were fast-forwarded, rewound, replayed in slo-mo, then their words and movements were analyzed and edited.

People who work in nine-to-five jobs can just begin to imagine the climate of intense creativity into which these people immersed themselves, and which was maintained virtually around the clock. Increasingly during the five weeks of the workshop, performing took precedence over all other personal relationships. They were utterly occupied with their bodies, carefully toned machines that were being stretched as far as they could go in every direction. Preoccupation lingered into the night, affecting eating patterns, sleeping patterns, sometimes even sexual performance (pro and con).

Wayne Cilento said, "I was in great shape then. But mentally, it was heavy-duty. We were always on the brink of an emotional breakdown and juggling lives and playing with vulnerability. We were all so vulnerable we would have fallen apart at the drop of a hat. Emotionally, it affected us a lot."

"I tend to bring things home with me but it was definitely not a ten-to-six like most other jobs," Donna McKechnie said. "I was going with Harvey [a hairdresser friend] then and I felt it was very important. I felt relieved to have a relationship at that time because I didn't like the feeling of being absorbed by the workshop. I can get too intense and don't forget I'm still trying to fight for my own integrity. So this show to me was the answer, creatively. But I was happy to have this sweet romance. It was a nice balance."

But the balance was about to be upset. Though the dancers had been rolling along busily for five weeks earning $100 apiece, that relationship could not continue forever. "Bennett's dancer project" was acquiring mass and momentum. The Shakespeare Festival now had to decide how to deal with dancers who were more than just dancers. Since many technically had helped with the creation of the show, and since union rules governing such things are strict, they needed to get releases from the dancers, and to offer them some form of token compensation. But the Shakespeare Festival had to tread carefully. Twenty-two people getting full author's royalties would make the resulting project financially questionable to produce. Some way had to be found around the question of who owned the rights to the story.

"I was doing *Pippin* at the time," said Priscilla Lopez, "and

Nicholas Dante caught me on the way out from a matinee. He was waiting at the stage door with this paper for me to sign. I looked at it and something told me I shouldn't sign it."

Terms of the contract called for each of the participants to receive $1—a single dollar in cash in most cases—for the right to use their stories in the show and their likenesses on merchandising, plus a single percentage point of royalties to be divided among all those who had been present at the pertinent taping sessions. It worked out to a few cents apiece for every $1,000 in royalties.

Lopez considered refusing the contract. "But at the same time," she said, "I felt—and it was probably true—that Michael Bennett didn't need me in order to do this show. But I wanted to be a part of it, so I felt that if that was the price I had to pay, it was okay."

Others had similar experiences. "The contract was thrown to us on a break," Thommie Walsh said. "It was just that lackadaisical kind of way. 'Here, sign this before you go back' was the attitude. 'This is your dollar and this is the way it's done' was the tone of it. 'This is all legal, this is all ethical.'

"All along at the same time I was saying to myself, 'If I object to this, do I have this job?' "

"I remember that we were given a sheet of paper to sign," said Trish Garland, "but I don't remember it saying I was giving my life away for one dollar, or I wouldn't have signed it. We were in a break and it was passed out like they passed out the script or new music. I remember some questions being raised. But Michael or someone said, 'If you don't want to sign it, then we just won't put you on the logo.' Well we all wanted to be on that logo."

"I was being manipulated to do what management wanted me to do," said Robert LuPone. "But I liked working for the Shakespeare Festival. I felt it was a step in the right direction. Ultimately I felt my interest was in working with those writers."

As close as she was to Bennett, Donna McKechnie also felt the bite. "It was absurd that we signed our lives away for one dollar. I feel real stupid about that. But you have to recall the atmosphere at the time. Here we had a group of people who were working together on this show, and are made to feel it's designed for them. Plus it's the Shakespeare Festival and all this money is going to go back into other shows, so why shouldn't we sign it for a dollar? It's just one of those things. Someone said this was just standard procedure, I remember hearing that."

For the first time there was grumbling by the entire group. Though the implications did not dawn until the show became a hit, many of the dancers who signed the releases still feel that it represented a betrayal of their dream of a utopian "dancer project."

"That dollar means not really getting a thank-you or really being recognized," Cilento said. "It says that without Michael Bennett or Nick Dante or Ed Kleban, the show wouldn't be. Well, that's not true, because without us, without the tapes, there wouldn't have been any show. How would Ed Kleban have written those songs without our monologues? Was it fear of exposing Ed Kleban and Nick Dante? That this was really us and thirty-five hours of tapes that made the show what it is today? Would that have put us into too much power? Was he afraid we would have had too much control and it was just Michael Bennett's project? I just think we were smacked in the face.

"I don't think it was ever expressed in public the amount of time and the amount of pain and manipulation that he did to our lives to get a show that's brilliant," Cilento said. "But it was all a very personal thing to all of us. I think it was a brilliant way to come up with a successful project. Broadway needs more like it. But I don't think anyone recognizes the fact that we had a major part in putting that show together."

Thommie Walsh was even more emphatic. "Basically we were cheated out of a lot of money. We created it, we helped write that damn show. We signed away our faces, our life stories. We could be very wealthy people today. If there's any anger I have about *A Chorus Line* and anything I experienced, it's having given up the right to that money. I think Michael, the producers of *A Chorus Line* and the Shuberts, the New York Shakespeare Festival—all those people might as well have stolen it. People are living in houses in the Hamptons because of *A Chorus Line*. None of us are."

Bennett now had a basic outline, a few semisolid characters, some strains of music, plenty of dancing, and the rights to the story. Lots had been done. But without out-of-town tryouts the show was still in pieces. Much more work lay ahead, preferably in another workshop. And his seed money was at an end.

To get more, Bennett arranged a hearing that the dancers nicknamed "the Papp test." Bennett invited the Lord of the Public Theater to inspect what his research and development funds had wrought. When Papp and associate Bernard Gersten sat down in the back rows of the Newman Theater that October, they saw a four-and-a-half-hour behemoth of soul-searching with three songs and one enormous dance number. The show opened with a number that was a patchwork of resume information and motivational anxiety over needing a job. The character of the director hadn't been developed, so the dancers replied to a voice that only they could hear.

That was followed by "I Can Do That," then several long monologues that introduced Sheila, Maggie, et al., and turned into "At the Ballet," the only clearly articulated ensemble song.

Literal hours of monologues then segued into "The Dance Combination," then more monologues until the finale when the dancers vanished.

Though still rough-cut, to put it charitably, the play had something that many more-polished productions lack: It grabbed you on a gut level. The stories were alternately joyous and heartbreaking, and were recounted with the immediacy of personal anecdotes, which they mostly were. The dancing flowed naturally from the situation. Hamlisch's gift for accessible tunesmithing was in evidence.

The next step was taken by Bennett and Papp behind closed doors. It appears that Papp promised to underwrite more development time if Bennett would agree to let his name and the appealing music from the show be used to help raise funds for the Shakespeare Festival. Bennett and certain dancers would perform what amounted to auditions for would-be NYSF investors and donors. Bennett apparently agreed. He needed some time off anyway to fulfill a contract to direct Neil Simon's next comedy, *God's Favorite,* scheduled to open on Broadway in December.

But Bennett and Papp had not finished their tough-nosed negotiations. Papp wanted Bennett to do *A Chorus Line* at the Vivian Beaumont Theatre in Lincoln Center. The large thrust space had severe acoustic problems and was anything but intimate (problems that apparently were solved in subsequent remodelings). Bennett insisted on one of the smaller theaters downtown at the Public Theater. When Papp and Bennett reached a standoff, McKechnie said, Bennett went to the Shubert Organization, Broadway's largest theater-owning and -producing company, and began negotiating to do the project as a traditional commercial endeavor. Based on Bennett's track record, the Shuberts were immediately interested. It was a tactic on Bennett's part, since he knew the show was not ready for Broadway and was unlikely to become Broadway-ready in the pressurized environment of a commercial tryout. But to obtain the ideal environment he needed to go to the brink. It worked, and Papp agreed to let Bennett have the Newman, the largest of his downtown theater spaces. Not only had Bennett won his preferred venue, he also had piqued the interest of the Shuberts, which would prove invaluable to everyone once the show was looking for a Broadway transfer six months later.

The dancers were told that the workshop was over, but would be resuming sometime after Christmas when additional money was raised. Several of the dancers, Priscilla Lopez was one, were asked to perform at the money-raising auditions, with the understanding that when the workshop resumed, their place in it would be secure.

Even as the dancers were recovering from the jolt of the story-rights blitz, the stress of "the Papp test," and the letdown of the workshop coming to an end, Bennett was preparing one more surprise.

On the last day of the workshop, he was leading the group in a dance. Recovering from a high kick he seemed to lose his balance, and collapsed on top of one leg. Grimacing broadly, Bennett clutched his knee.

Kuhlman immediately suspected that Bennett hadn't really hurt himself. "He wasn't a very good actor in terms of pain," Kuhlman said. "I don't think I analyzed it too thoroughly. I must have reacted initially with horror but after a while I realized what he was doing. He was looking for a reaction, manipulating us into some kind of response."

Not everyone caught what was happening right away. Some

reached out to help him physically, some ran to call a doctor, some offered painkillers. At that moment Bennett stood up, unharmed after all. He asked them all to lock into their memories the precise emotions they were feeling in that instant, and to recall how they had acted on those feelings. He told them he wanted them to think about how they would feel if they couldn't dance anymore.

"I hated it," McKechnie said. "I got really upset. I could see what he was trying to do but that element of manipulating people's emotions is what I really didn't like. It was very effective, however. 'How would you feel if you couldn't dance anymore?' Maybe he knew that dancers don't really want to deal with that. You can't—it goes against your whole spirit. You must go into denial. So I think he tried to counter that."

"A lot of people felt like they'd been used," Blair said. "We gave him our lives; he could have given us an opportunity to display our wares a little more honestly. He didn't have to manipulate as much as he did."

Rick Mason said, "I think my first reaction after he got up and left was anger. But when he told us what the reason was, I was impressed that he would go to that extent to find out how we would react. Who would run to him, who would scream, who would say, 'I'll call a doctor.' He was playing a game with us—for his reasons, a very needed game."

And on that tumultuous chord, the first workshop came to an end.

8.

HIATUS (OCTOBER 1974–JANUARY 1975)

The dancers of the Bennett project (it still had no official name) felt that they had taken part in something special. But dancing is a risky career track, and none of them could know for sure whether anything more would come of it. Free-lancers have no steady source of income or benefits, so when one job ends—especially one that they had done for the love of it, plus $100 a week—they immediately must start hunting for a new one.

So they scattered across the city and across the country, taking jobs in regional theaters or road companies. Some went directly into Broadway choruses or returned to the audition circuit.

Bennett himself moved immediately into another project, directing for the first time a new play by Neil Simon. *God's Favorite,* which opened December 11, 1974, ran 119 performances, making it one of Simon's shortest-running plays.

One week later another "Bennett project" participant was back on Broadway. Pamela Blair made her Broadway drama debut as the nubile young wife in *Of Mice and Men* starring Kevin Conway and James Earl Jones, though the show ran only a few months. In the who's who section of the program, the entry on Blair stated, "She most recently appeared in a Michael Bennett–Marvin Hamlisch production at Joseph Papp's Public Theater."

She recalls that she invited Bennett to see the show, and he turned up the next night and commiserated with her over the reviews, Bennett having gotten a dose of the same medicine just days earlier. He may also have been compensating for having been too busy with *God's Favorite* to accept Rick Mason's urgent invitation earlier that autumn to come see him as Bobby in *The Boyfriend* at Equity Library Theatre.

During the hiatus between workshops, Joe Papp gave Baayork Lee the opportunity to choreograph two productions, the *In the Boom Boom Room* revival and an experimental musical, *Apple Pie,* at the Shakespeare Festival.

Thommie Walsh headed west to Las Vegas where he was hired as lead dancer in singer Ann-Margret's nightclub act at the Hilton Hotel. Marvin Hamlisch had written special material for the show, which was choreographed by Walter Painter. They played three or four triumphant weeks in October and November, then returned for Christmas, New Year's, and beyond.

While the first workshop was still under way, Bishop had been asked to audition for Helen McFudd, one of the speaking roles in the national touring company of *Irene.* This fit with her resolution not to take straight chorus roles any more. Getting over her initial dislike of the part and the musical (and because her bank account and unemployment insurance were running out), she took the job, though it left her with only the company of her pup, Venus, that Christmas in Denver.

Robert LuPone went back to Washington, D.C., to work at the Arena Stage, determined to get his career as a dramatic actor back on track. Donna McKechnie also did regional theater, appearing in a production of Molière's *The Imaginary Invalid.* "I really enjoyed that departure," she said.

Ron Kuhlman did a series of productions at a dinner theater in Allenberry, Pennsylvania. One of his protean duties was playing a Puerto Rican bellboy in *Cactus Flower.* For help with the accent, he called fellow workshopper Priscilla Lopez.

Afterward, with money in the bank, and assurances from Bennett that once the "dancer project" got back under way he would be a part of it, Kuhlman went on a vacation to Hawaii.

Trish Garland had suffered a strong emotional reaction to the soul-baring of the first workshop, so she also set off on a vacation. Her boyfriend George took her to his parents' house in Spain, and then on a side trip to Morocco. Though she didn't realize it at the time, the Morocco trip gave her something that would enable her to continue in the second workshop. But for the time being, she still felt withdrawn.

Sammy Williams was withdrawn as well, but not out of choice. His back was still hurting from his summertime injury in *Seesaw*. It was difficult for him to move, much less dance. "I went to Baayork's house on hiatus and now I'm really freaking out," he said. "I still didn't know if I was going to be able to do this show. Finally my neighbor came to me, one of those health food guru kind of people, and she asked me if I had ever done yoga. I said no, so she gave me three yoga exercises and she guaranteed that my back would be fine if I did them three times a day. Well, I did those exercises religiously three weeks, and I want to tell you that in three weeks I was up in Tony Stevens's dance class, dancing. I couldn't believe it."

Renee Baughman's story is closer to Bishop's, though she didn't have the satisfaction of being in a show. She had worked steadily in musicals from the time she arrived in New York, but December 1974 was a dry period, and she began working as an office temporary to make ends meet. She hit bottom working as a hostess at a teachers convention. "I remember standing and folding flyers and crying, thinking, 'Here I am, twenty-six years old, and I should be dancing on Broadway.' "

Most of them wanted to land a job in the chorus of what looked then like the biggest musical of the coming season, Bob Fosse's *Chicago*. It was a tough choice. Both *Chicago* and the "dancer project" were scheduled to go into production in spring 1975. As personally as they felt attached to Bennett's show, it was still nebulous at best, and tentatively scheduled for off-Broadway. Fosse, who had a following as devoted as Bennett's, was planning a full-scale Broadway extravaganza, his first since the enormously successful *Pippin*. Ironically, one of the first dancers he hired was Michon Peacock, one of the two originators of *A Chorus Line,* who had been eliminated by Bennett in the summer's auditions.

"Christopher Chadman, Candy Brown," and Baughman, "they all got the big show that year, *Chicago*. Everyone wanted to work for Bob Fosse." Wayne Cilento, who spent the months immediately after the workshop looking for and buying a new house, also auditioned for Fosse. "I had no idea *A Chorus Line* was going to be *A Chorus Line,*" he said. "I really wanted to go do *Chicago.* It's the best thing that ever happened to me that I didn't get it."

Then there was perhaps the most notable departure. It now was time for the other remaining *A Chorus Line* originator, Tony Stevens, to part ways with his brainchild. How could he resist? Fosse had invited him to serve as assistant choreographer.

Chicago would later compete with *A Chorus Line* for the 1976 Tony Award. And lose.

After *God's Favorite* was out of the way, Bennett returned to work with Hamlisch, Kleban, Dante—and Papp. To keep the project alive, the team played auditions that winter for potential Public Theater backers while continuing to refine the script and score.

For Lopez, the auditions also afforded an opportunity to get closer to enigmatic lyricist Ed Kleban. "He was so closed off, so serious," she said. "I thought there was a person inside of him screaming to get out. I thought he was very frightened. I couldn't make him laugh or even smile, and I could usually do that with people. It was unsettling because I want to get through to people and when I don't it upsets me. But as time went on I feel that he did finally open up to me."

Kleban may simply have been absorbed. During the hiatus between workshops many of the songs now in *A Chorus Line* were written.

Some of the dancers had hoped the second workshop would get under way immediately after *God's Favorite* or at least soon after Christmas, but the resumption date was delayed and then delayed again.

Baughman couldn't stand doing office temporary work much longer, so she telephoned Bennett on New Year's Eve, "and begged him to get me back on the stage," she said. "He told me not to worry, that it was really going to happen. And to convince me, he played a recording of Ed and Marvin doing my song."

It proved to be a revelation to her. Baughman had nearly been cut from the first workshop because she was unable to sing. Hamlisch and Kleban had opposed her hiring but Bennett had insisted. Making the best of the situation, they wrote her a simple song, titled "Sing!," about not being able to sing. It emphasized the lyric and called for wrong notes to be sung at crucial moments. "So I knew there would be a second workshop," she said, "and I knew I'd have a song in it."

With the musical score developing healthily and with the success of his fund-raising efforts, Bennett knew he had to announce a second workshop soon, to keep the rest of his carefully chosen core dancers from defecting to Fosse or elsewhere. Once Papp gave the green light, Bennett tried to assemble a second workshop as quickly as possible, to begin rehearsals the last week in January. In addition to filling the roles of the major characters, he knew he'd need a backup corps of dancers to act as swings and understudies.

There was one painful chore that needed doing immediately, however. Whatever input the dancers and other writers may have had, and whatever inspiration Bennett may have drawn from Dante's early monologues, a point came when he realized that for all Dante's good intentions, he was simply too inexperienced for the project. A co-librettist would need to come aboard, someone who could cut the mustard in the disorienting freedom of the workshop environment, but someone pliant to carry out what now was Bennett's vision exclusively. He turned to James Kirkwood, a former actor and comedian who had written several well-received novels, including the semiautobiographical *Some Painted Pony* and *P.S. Your Cat Is Dead.* The latter had been dramatized off-Broadway in a critically successful but brief run. It had acquired enough of a cult following that a revival was being prepared for Broadway. Because little rewriting was required, Kirkwood was available and feeling particularly sanguine about Broadway. Though this was his first professional libretto-writing credit, he would be billed as co-author with his name above Dante's.

Dante may have had something to do with the choice. Baughman remembers that Dante had long been a fan of Kirkwood's, and six months earlier had given her Kirkwood's books to read. Dante had championed Kirkwood to Bennett as well. Bennett, wanting to pick a collaborator who would work harmoniously with Dante, investigated Kirkwood's plays, and met him at a cocktail party to size him up. The deal was struck.

After Kirkwood agreed to join the project in late December, Bennett set about filling the new vacancies in his lineup. Like a sports coach patching his offensive team, Bennett sought dancers with personal or technical strengths that compensated for or buttressed weak spots. He looked for another strong actor, a happy-go-lucky person, a strong singer. He advertised in show business publications, put the word out through his personal network of dance contacts, and in early January he held the second round of auditions for the still-sketchy "dancer project." The workshop crowd was about to get an infusion of new blood.

"My agent at the time was driving me and his friend down Eighty-second Street," Kay Cole said, "and he was saying to me that he'd gotten a call from the Michael Bennett office and that Michael Bennett wanted me to come in and audition for this planned workshop. I found out later that Michael had seen me in a show. My agent told me it was going to be like a chorus audition, everybody would be asked to dance and sing and talk a little bit about their lives. It sounded very exciting. How could you say no to that, working with the best people in New York City? My agent said the Shakespeare Festival had a very good reputation. Obviously Michael had a very good reputation. Doing a workshop with those people, working with Marvin, Ed Kleban—it had a very good feeling especially when Jimmy Kirkwood became involved. It's like when you look down on a racing form and you see a horse named Happy Hoofer: It makes you smile and say, 'That's the one I want.'

"The day I auditioned," Cole continued, "Michael told us that the show was about dancers, a backstage story with real people and real stories from tapes. We would have input and our own stories would be incorporated. It would be a very honest account of a dancer's experience. And that's what it turned out to be.

"I went to the Newman Theater and there were a lot of people there, mostly women. We danced for a long time, then we were asked to sing. Michael asked would I sing this song that he liked that I had sung for him once before, 'I Think I Like You' from *Doctor Doolittle*. I had not remembered auditioning for him. I sang for him in the morning and then we danced, danced, danced for Marvin and Nick Dante and the whole group."

The pace picked up as the day went on and Bennett, Avian, and the writers weeded fifty dancers down to twenty. The writers took even more careful notes this time on the audition process.

"It felt electric," Cole said. "There's a kind of energy when people are at auditions. Sometimes it can be very negative because people are nervous and they're scared. But this was different, everybody seemed to want to do it. Everybody was emotional, I know, when they got eliminated. You could feel it. None of us were eliminated until after we had sung, danced, and talked. Then there was an elimination and we sang again for a larger group of people."

Nancy Lane had been dancing in the same touring company of *Seesaw* as Sammy Williams, and had watched him ascend from that production into what clearly was the Michael Bennett inner circle. "I didn't know what a workshop was all about but then I read in the trades that Michael Bennett's workshop was going to have auditions again, for a second workshop. I figured I would go down. Even if I don't get paid because it's a workshop, so what? I'll be dancing and I'll meet other people. My whole life has really been geared to adventure. I try to see the positive in every situation. I just knew he would take me.

"I was sick with a bad cold. We danced a lot, the combination was great and real fun. Then we had to sing and I met Kay Cole for the first time and I was just bowled over by that voice. I was very nervous waiting to sing and then it turned out that my real good friend, Richard Riskin, was the piano player. I had these real complicated lead sheets from *Zorba,* a real long song. I tried to sing the hell out of it. I made jokes with Michael about my usually sounding better than I did that day.

"I got a callback and lo and behold I had to dance with the singers. Of course the singers petered out one by one, they were huffing and puffing and couldn't remember the steps."

Ron Dennis also was chosen that day. A veteran of children's theater who had completed a successful stint in the Broadway musical *Don't Bother Me, I Can't Cope,* he went into the audition with some trepidation. "I had auditioned for Michael before and I had danced my butt off and could never figure out why I was never hired. I figured it was because I was small." Dennis heard about the audition through his friend, Candy Brown. When Brown left for Fosse's *Chicago,* Bennett decided he needed another man on the line and changed the gender of the role. Coincidentally, it was Brown's part that Dennis was chosen to fill.

With the departure of Tony Stevens to be a choreographer's assistant in real life, Bennett now needed someone to fill the assistant's role in *A Chorus Line*. He chose Don Percassi, who had been working as warm-up comedian for the TV game show *Money Maze*. He knew Donna McKechnie, as well as another dancer, Carolyn Kirsch, who had been asked to audition as an understudy. "I went down when I heard they were looking for understudies," he said. "It was funny because just the week before I had walked down Lafayette Street and looked at the Public Theater because I had heard about this project being put on there and I didn't know what it was. I went in and looked around. From its name I had thought it would be a place where they do street shows. The following week I got a call to come in. Carolyn Kirsch told Michael that I could sing. So I came in and sang for them, that's all I did. He knew me as a dancer. I had auditioned for him in [Bennett's 1969 show] *Coco*. I could tell then he was special. Some people have a certain look in their eyes and he had that look."

Though Percassi was auditioning just for an understudy role, "I was real excited," he said. "I knew it was a project I would like to do. I knew that if Michael was involved it had to be terrific. I wasn't that nervous because I really didn't think I had a chance to get the job."

At the conclusion of the audition, Bennett called together the group remaining on the Newman stage. He looked them over carefully, then stepped back and grinned at them. "Michael told us we had the job," said Cole. "He said it was an ensemble show and he told Crissy [Wilzak] and Donna [Drake] that they were understudies and that everybody would have input into the creation. By the end of the day I had a particular affinity with Nancy Lane so I was delighted when she got cast. Don Percassi and I had done a terrible show together and had a wonderful time. We felt very friendly, so that was another triumph. All the people I knew or even connected with just that day were kept. So the bond started to form at the audition.

"I was so tired and relieved at the day's end; yet I was really excited," Cole said. "I had an apartment on Eighth Street with a friend of mine and I think it was my turn to walk the dog. He got an extra long walk that night 'cause there was a lot of pent-up excitement. I'm sure I called my mother."

Bennett had one more face to add. Looking for a more seasoned performer, Bennett offered a job to Michel Stuart, who had danced in shows with Bennett in the earliest days of his career. Now an aspiring writer and producer, Stuart had been away from Broadway for nine years, but he knew Bennett wouldn't fetch him out of retirement unless it was for something special. "When Michael called me about *Chorus Line* I hadn't spoken to him in quite a while," Stuart said. "He said he was doing this show, that he had done a workshop of it several months before. And I said, 'Michael, we both did *West Side Story* in the fifties, we both turned down *Hair* in the sixties. I know this is going to be the show of the seventies and I will be there tomorrow morning.' "

It was now one year since the first telephone calls from Tony Stevens and Michon Peacock that set the whole project in motion. Tony and Michon were gone, as was their concept of a dance cooperative. But they had given birth to something else, completely unexpected. Like an unpredictable tropical storm, *A Chorus Line* was diffuse but powerful, and had acquired its own peculiar momentum. Even the participants weren't sure where it would hit land, or what its winds would bring.

On the eve of the second workshop the revised cast was eager to get under way. Some bank accounts had been replenished, but some had not. Some of those who needed jobs to pay bills in the short run had moved to *Chicago*. Some, like Baughman, knew that resuming the workshop at $100 a week meant several more months of lean times. But already there was a certain magic accruing to the project.

"The word was going out about the show," said Rick Mason. "From the first workshop there was starting to be a buzz around the city. We felt a pride in being involved with this potentially interesting project. But we really didn't know. I don't think any of us knew for sure until the reviews came."

That magic reached out for the four dancers who had strayed the farthest afield: Trish Garland, Thommie Walsh, Robert Lu-

Pone, and Kelly Bishop. It brought them back just in time for the commencement of the second workshop.

Garland, who had spent the holidays in Spain and Morocco, returned to New York shortly before the group reconvened. "When I got back Nicholas Dante told me that Michael was trying to get in touch with me to let me know that I could stay in the show and knowing it was a very small part—or I could leave. I reeked of fear and it was very hard to deal with," she said. Her fellow Buddhists, Dante and Baughman, rallied around her. "They said to me, 'This is when you fight harder than you've ever fought before,' " Garland said. "A part of me didn't even know if I wanted to do it or if I had the capacity to go through the pain. But when someone's going to take something away from me then I want it more than I've ever wanted it before. I'm very grateful to Nicholas and Renee for being my support system at that time. They kept insisting that I could change this, they would help me. They said that if I chanted every day and studied, that I could get anything I wanted. So I started chanting."

Walsh was still dancing in Las Vegas with Ann-Margret, but when she and her husband-manager Roger Smith heard that Walsh had a Marvin Hamlisch Broadway show in the offing, they released him from his contract.

LuPone was determined not to return for the second workshop. He even had a Broadway musical role all lined up: in *Boccaccio,* which he had done at the Arena Stage in Washington, D.C. (*Boccaccio* would arrive on Broadway in November 1975 and run one week.) "I told Michael I quit, that I can't do the second workshop," LuPone said. "But he did it again, I don't know how. He manipulated me into turning down an already existing show that was coming to New York to play at the Edison Theatre, something that I had done and also had gotten good reviews in. Two roles, Bisetto and Ferdinand. They weren't dancing roles, they were acting roles, and they were exactly what I wanted to do—and yet I turned that down for *ACL*. And I turned down another role that came my way from the McCarter Theatre. He just came after me and suddenly I was back in *ACL,* second workshop, sweating my butt off dancing, and not having a role. (LuPone was still playing the trimmed-down role of Al at that point.) I guess I believed in

Michael. I just followed that guy around like this was the greatest thing since saltwater taffy."

After the lonely Christmas in Denver, Kelly Bishop was still out on the road with *Irene*. But even at that distance, the grapevine had kept her supplied with news. "About the time we got to Houston," she said, "I started hearing that Michael Bennett is having auditions for this project he's doing. And I'm dying. I want to be there."

The feeling apparently was mutual. Once he tracked her down and found she still wanted to be involved with the "dancer project," Bennett worked out a deal with the producers of *Irene* and got Bishop out of her contract. "I got back on the plane with my dog and came back to New York," she said. "I went down to Nineteenth Street (Dance Theater Workshop) and I remember that being very gratifying too because not only was I out of *Irene,* not only did I get my wish, but I walked into rehearsals and it was like everyone was waiting for me to get there. I was so pleased. As if my ego hadn't already been pumped up enough by him buying me out of my contract. Everybody was there, in their dance clothes, but it looked like everybody had been just fooling around. But then it was like, 'Oh, she's here,' and everything suddenly got together: 'You two stand there and you . . .' It was like they were waiting for me."

9.

Beginning of the Second Workshop (January–February 1975)

"It was really rapid how soon after auditions we started rehearsals," Kay Cole remembers. "Like couple of days or the next week. I think a lot of people had a really good premonition that the show was going to be incredibly successful," Cole said. "I tried to be calm. I don't know why I decided that the way to deal with the impending success was to be calm or sort of philosophical about it. I told myself I was going to be very focused and very gentle about not getting too excited or not wanting it so badly, only to be disappointed. So we went to work."

The second workshop was different from the first. Starting the fourth week in January, most of it took place in the rehearsal rooms at Dance Theatre Workshop, "Jerome Robbins's place" on Nineteenth Street, instead of at a theater, but that's not what made it so different.

There were the new faces, too: Ron Dennis, Don Percassi, Michel Stuart, and Kay Cole for the primary cast. And there was a whole new category of dancer that had joined the proceedings, the understudies: Nancy Lane, Scott Allen, Chuck Cissel, Donna

Drake, Brandt Edwards, Carolyn Kirsch, Carole Schweid, Michael Serrecchia, Leland Schwantes, and Crissy Wilzak.

The new dancers looked up to the remaining tape session veterans, Kelly Bishop, Thommie Walsh, Wayne Cilento, Priscilla Lopez, Trish Garland, Sammy Williams, Donna McKechnie, Renee Baughman, and Jane Robertson. The arrival of the big freshman class made juniors of Baayork Lee and Pam Blair, and made sophomores of Ron Kuhlman, Robert LuPone, Rick Mason, and Barry Bostwick.

"The changes didn't bother me," Mason said. "I was just very grateful that I wasn't changed. I was now one of the old ones."

But even the entrance of the new dancers wasn't really what made the difference in the minds of the participants. The second workshop existed in its own world because it wasn't playtime anymore. The lighthearted experimentation of the first workshop gave way to the serious work of the second. The first workshop had been a game. The second workshop was a forge. In the second workshop *A Chorus Line* took its final shape, and the road to opening night was by no means a straight one.

"I remember the first day of that second workshop very well," Lopez said. "Once again we had to go around and tell our lives. It was "What I Did on My Summer Vacation"—what we had done during this break."

Garland, who had been chanting to work up her courage to resume her place on the line, said, "I inwardly groaned, wishing we could just get the script and go on with this. Michael finally calls my name. I get up and start talking. Now remember, no one had laughed at me at the first workshop. But I had a very funny experience in Morocco during the hiatus and I decided to tell it.

"I had concocted this grand scheme to sell jeans to the Moroccans. George's parents ran a clothing store and they suggested we take some jeans on our trip, thinking we could sell these hip American clothes and perhaps make some money. What none of us realized is that a woman just doesn't do that sort of thing over there. They live in the Middle Ages, the women all tiny and dark and covered from head to toe in those chadors, like you see in Iran. Picture that—and then picture me, this enormously tall, white-skinned redhead in clingy jeans and a crop-top, shlepping a huge suitcase full of jeans through the narrow streets of the medina.

And me, I'm oblivious. I was so intent on being a businesswoman, I just barreled though.

"George and I had decided to play it like two hitchhikers: I'd be the girl who gets the guy to stop. Little did I realize the kind of ride an Arab man would expect! So I get to my first customer and he doesn't know what to make of me at first. I'm showing him the jeans in the suitcase and he's checking out the jeans I've got on. So in his own Arab way he starts to come on to me. He moves right up to me, looks into my eyes and talks about caressing fine material. Real subtle. Now, I'm used to that and I know how to turn it aside. But Arab men, they're not used to being turned aside. When they tell their women 'now,' they mean *now*.

"But I'm not cognizant of this. I'm still being Trish the International Tradeswoman. It just killed his ego. He got furious. I mean, he didn't say anything—and he certainly didn't buy any jeans—but he sort of got this gleam in his eye . . .

"After that I tried here and there, all over the medina. The shopkeepers would listen to my shpiel, smiling, but . . . *nothing*. I was so frustrated! Afterward, when George and I figured out the problem, we imagined little Arab ragamuffins fanning out over the medina with the word: Don't buy from the American redhead!

"Well, I was telling this whole story at the workshop—complete with imitations of sly George and the ego-shattered Arab and prim old me—and people were *laughing*. It was like music to my ears. It had not happened for so long that it was just pure music. And I looked up at Michael and he had this huge smile on his face.

"From that moment something changed. I could have lost this opportunity with my you-can-go-to-hell attitude. I think now that I would have been very bitter had someone else done that part. I can't even imagine how horrible it would have been for me. I absolutely base my reformation on the chanting. From that time on, Michael would say, 'Trish is my rock.' I suddenly became this solid person. When the lines wouldn't work he would say 'Give them to Trish, she'll make them work.' So suddenly he found the character. She eventually became so non-sequitur because she had all the lines that didn't quite work. But I started enjoying myself, I started being a part of what was going on. Judy Turner had come to life."

The first day of the second workshop was a revelation for Sammy

Williams, too. Having found exercises that eased the pain in his injured back, he was eager finally to augment his acting work with some dancing. "That morning I was excited beyond belief," he said, "because I could get in there and get back into Michael's good graces. Michael had not put me down because of my back, but I felt that I had to prove to him that I could dance. So we get to the first day, everyone is milling around, and five minutes before rehearsal started, Baayork called me over to the side and she said, 'You had better watch your hands because Michael thinks you're too effeminate. He doesn't like that stuff so when you get in there you'd better butch it up.'

"And she walked out, leaving me standing with my mouth open. Well, I wasn't too secure when I walked through that door. And for three weeks Michael didn't look at me or associate with me. He kept telling me to put my hands in my pockets and made me feel absolutely rotten. I hated myself, him, everybody around me. I was terribly self-conscious. It was like being in school again.

"Then he said, 'Let's do a run-through and this time we're going to do your monologue.' It was the first time I had had a chance to do it. I fell apart in the middle of it, but I got through it. I walked off and stood in a corner and cried. Michael came over to me, and I demanded to know why he had done this to me. He just said, 'You were marvelous' and walked away. And that was the beginning of my rehearsals for *A Chorus Line*."

Slightly in awe of both Bennett and the veterans of the first workshop, the newcomers did their best to acclimate. "I was surrounded by so many dancers that I had known of, but never worked with," Ron Dennis said. The lone island of black in a sea of white faces, he said he later took to referring to the project as *A Group of White Dancers*.

"When I came to New York," Dennis said, "the biggest problem for black dancers was if you were too dark. They had all these variety shows on TV and they were only using light-skinned blacks. Then along came the World's Fair and suddenly that all changed around, like 'Milliken': one black person a season and usually they were light-skinned. I discussed this a lot with other black dancers. I know a lot of people felt more bitter than I did about that and

I really wasn't bitter. I just know there was more to be said about what I could do. I just felt I was given a crumb (in *A Chorus Line*) and I made it into a slice of bread. I thought it was important that I be in a show: a new face, a small face, a black, and a male in a show that's basically about white gypsy dancers at work all the time. You couldn't name one black dancer who was a gypsy who had done a lot of shows.

"But I was not bitter about racial equality in the theater, which I was only becoming aware of since that whole black movement in 'sixty-eight. There was a lot of intermingling then, black and white couples. Then the whole black movement all of a sudden decided that you had to get back to your roots. They were saying, 'Deny all that stuff.' To prove that you were black and you had to give up all your white-learned values and a culture you had been brought up in, which was predominantly white.

"Because of that upbringing, some of us really had no sense of black culture. So we went off and read books and learned about it. In the process, a lot of black people I know totally dropped their white friends and did a whole switchover. It has not changed for a great many of us since then. But I don't find that healthy for the way of the world.

"During that whole period everything was so militant that I think people were hiring blacks because they felt they had to. So a lot of black performers were hired who were not worthy of the gig, not at all. When I was back in New York in 1983 and 1984 I saw a lot of wonderful new kids that were well-rounded performers, singers, dancers, et cetera. I don't know what the next few years will bring for the talent that I've seen, but it's much better for black kids coming up now because they don't get as much of the stigma. They don't feel like they're being hired just because they're black. Things may be changing with this whole new crop. They're much more outgoing, much more ready to play and get ahead in the world of whites. You have to play where the money is.

"I had known Sammy Williams before from seeing him on the street," Dennis said. "I admired Donna from seeing her at auditions and I always thought she was so fabulous as a dancer. I also had seen Trish at auditions, but I didn't really know any of those people. I guess I have such a wonderful defense shield about going into new shows and scoping it out. I'm friendly and charming but I don't like people too close. All I know is that I was a bit reclusive for a week or so until I got to know people better. Right away Sammy and Wayne Cilento and I would talk. We had similar senses of humor and personalities but Sammy and I kind of hit it off right away. He was very free and everybody seemed to know him. I liked listening to Pam Blair because she was very funny. That's about where I stayed. The company was supportive for the most part. I didn't feel any animosity.

"I would go home thinking about how exciting this was, whatever we were working on, and how people were working for a common goal. I think that was the first new show I had ever done, from scratch. So for me to watch that whole process was so unlike anything I had ever done. I would analyze how the show was being put together, looking at just the social creative aspect of it; who was friendly with whom, that kind of stuff. I watched a lot."

As an older dancer making his return to the stage after building another successful career, Michel Stuart had a unique point of view. "I looked around at all these younger people and knew I could dance as well if not better than these people—if I had the endurance. I didn't get a script. We started dancing the first day. My body was in great shape. I had been swimming all summer. I hadn't danced in so long but my legs were fine at that point. A year later they said, 'Hey, it's time to stop,' but at the time it felt like I had never stopped dancing. I didn't even think of doing this show as 'being in the chorus' because I knew that it was going to be something other. I knew just from the conversation I'd had with Michael that whatever this was, it was not going to be like anything I had ever done before in my life. And that always interests me.

"Pam Blair had been doing the 'Gregory Gardner' part [after Christopher Chadman's departure] so she kind of blocked me into where I had to go. They welcomed me. There was a lot of love there. Everyone was so happy to be doing it. I wasn't able to afford to live on what they were paying me, but it wasn't an issue. I knew it was going to be the show of the seventies."

Stuart was happy because he had worked with some of the

dancers previously, particularly Priscilla Lopez, whom he had hired for a Miami Beach nightclub act in the late 1960s. The feeling was not mutual. "I remember one very traumatic day for me, the day Michel Stuart joined the company," Lopez said. "A few people were excited but I wasn't. I hadn't seen him since the Florida thing and he was the authority figure. Very intense. But the moment I saw him he was another person. We actually have become good buddies. But at the time I groaned. Here I had been feeling so good with everybody, there wasn't one bad vibe. It was and still is very important to me that I feel comfortable in my theater life. I was anticipating trouble."

Lopez's friends were still the members of the Dobson's group, Walsh and Bishop, with whom she continued to commute home daily on the uptown BMT.

Ron Kuhlman went into the second workshop with one of the biggest roles in *A Chorus Line:* Don, who was paired with Kelly Bishop's Sheila as the sexy comic couple.

"There were some people who didn't come back to the show after the first workshop and I felt a loss of part of the group there," he said. "People like Candy Brown, whom I stood next to. We would always joke around. She was a lot of fun, as was Tony Stevens. Already we had become part of this group and I felt sad that they were gone. Then it was like the first day for us, in terms of meeting the new people and getting to know them, that they would be fine. I was sure that Michael would pick people we would all get along with. I certainly got to know people more and liked them more and more."

For those, like Kuhlman, who remembered the comfort of having a safety net of friendships during the first workshop, it was important to find allies. The Dobson's crowd and the Buddhists were still there, but other bonds were formed as well. Garland still depended on her fellow Buddhists Dante, Baughman, and LuPone; she said she also became close with newcomers Stuart and Percassi, particularly the latter, whose easygoing manner and comedian's sense of humor endeared him to just about everyone.

"I adored Percassi," Garland said. "I remember defending him one particular day. He couldn't see and wanted contacts and they got them for him. That was a touching moment. He was the one that was picked on the most, I felt. And we all loved him."

As the heart of the Dobson's group, one of the first people asked to the tape session, one of the most proficient dancers, and quickest with sharp-edged repartee, Thommie Walsh was the favorite of some dancers, though several who felt intimidated by him steered clear.

"I would say Thommie was my best friend," Cilento said. "I really loved everybody. Renee was such a wreck she could make me cry every time she opened her mouth. Percassi made me laugh a lot."

Sammy Williams felt overwhelmed by some of the other strong personalities in the cast, especially Kelly Bishop ("She had so much attitude and I was afraid of that. But I ended up liking her a lot") and now Michel Stuart ("I didn't hate him but he scared me. Perhaps it was because they were older and had been around. They knew what they were doing and I didn't").

Pam Blair had the reputation of being the freest spirit in the cast and the most unpredictable. "Pam Blair used to make me crazy," said Trish Garland, "when she'd get hysterical and crying and she would be patted and fondled."

Ron Dennis said, "Pam and I hung out a few times and she'd drink and talk about how she beat up her men. I knew Pam liked saying things like that because she would get attention, and Pam would bait you until she got attention. She would keep after you until she got a rise out of you. The calmer you got the more hysterical she would get and until you got angry at her she didn't feel like a woman. I knew how sweet and how nice she was, but she'd go off on a tangent and keep at you."

Whether for friends or enemies, the dancers tended to turn to one another. Characteristically, McKechnie was another story, spending most of her social time with Bennett and Avian. The difference was not lost on her fellow cast members. By the second workshop her special status as "teacher's pet" began to widen the special rift between her and the rest of the dancers.

The lines were being drawn during the early weeks in February, some separating people, some enclosing people. But the one person all of them became linked to, directly or indirectly, whether they liked it or not, was the new librettist, James Kirkwood.

Baughman said, "I was concerned when they first brought him in because I figured that Michael didn't think Nicholas could do it. Nicholas had already done so much I knew he could do it. However, Nicholas had turned me on to Jimmy's books about six months before so we were big fans of Jimmy's. I felt that if they had to bring anyone in I was glad it was someone Nicholas admired so it would be easier for him. I know Jimmy didn't do as much in the show as he is given credit for, but I don't think that's his fault. He was a known writer so naturally that's going to be the assumption."

McKechnie said, "I think it was kind of crushing to Nicholas at first but then he realized it was his first thing and he could use the help. But it posed inherent problems for Jimmy Kirkwood, too. Things did shape up but I wasn't privy to those meetings after rehearsal when the writers got together.

Like Dante, Thommie Walsh had read some of Kirkwood's books, "so I had great respect for him before he had arrived on the scene," Walsh said. "Our show's book didn't seem to be getting any better and we were still faltering so I welcomed his presence when he came. My stuff became a little stronger after he was present."

At least one of Kirkwood's recurring images, finding the dead body of his mother's boyfriend, appears in both the book and play versions of *Some Painted Pony,* and in *A Chorus Line,* in a song that would be written in the second workshop, "Hello Twelve, Hello Thirteen, Hello Love."

Lopez said, "I always thought that Michael Bennett brought Jimmy Kirkwood in because he thought the show might not be any good and he didn't want to take all the blame. And James Kirkwood was riding high at that time. He was respected and he would add more credibility to the project."

Whether he had input into the choice of Kirkwood or not, it was an agonizing time for Dante, who was still feeling insecure about his status as a writer. "I remember Nicholas coming up with pages and pages and pages of things after he had spent an hour down in the Green Room," Rick Mason said. "Michael would look at the pages and say, 'No, it's wrong.' Nicholas was a very *pinched* person. The smile was never real, it was forced, it was pinched. Terrified, the man was terrified. He was doing something that he'd never really done to that level."

Yet Ron Dennis believed that the underlying feeling of the show came from Dante's "life and his being a dancer. I'm sure his input must have kept them on the right track a great deal of the time. He may have had more to say about this than he's given credit for."

Dante had transcribed the taped monologues and had spun them into generalized characters. Some of the characters had relationships with others and some had long dialogue scenes, but *A Chorus Line* was still mostly exposition. People talked about things, about how they felt, without *showing* it, without translating those feelings into drama. The material also clearly was out of control. In his watermark theater autobiography *Act One,* playwright Moss Hart writes about how elder-statesman author George S. Kaufman first showed him how to write, and then showed him the equally tricky and important art of *cutting*. Trimming, condensing, and distilling dialogue and action in Kaufman's comedies is part of what makes them so kinetic and explosive. Still working to master the art of playwriting, Dante needed help, more than anything else, in the task of play-cutting.

From Rick Mason's point of view, "When James Kirkwood came in he was just very refreshing. We noticed a distinct change in the writing when he came in. It was sharp and clean and it was crisp and inventive and clever. You could see there was some caring."

To McKechnie, who was closest to the creative team, "I always looked at Jimmy Kirkwood as a stabilizer. The sweetest, dearest person, he personified love to me. He tried to help in awkward situations, always respecting us, and always standing back and appreciating it. I don't know how he did it."

But Cilento said, "Jimmy Kirkwood? He helped Donna. I don't know what else he did."

Baughman agreed, "I believe his [Kirkwood's] contribution was the Cassie and Zach scenes. Very few of the major monologues (already written by Dante) in the show changed after Jimmy was brought on board."

For LuPone, Kirkwood's political and social skills were his greatest assets. "He had the same sensibilities that Bernie [Gersten, associate producer] had, that [Shubert Organization chairman] Gerry Schoenfeld had, that Bob Avian had. There was a sense of humor despite the terror, despite the pressures of having a commercial success or not, despite the investment of time. He was a person who was willing to take me aside and talk to me as an older actor to younger actor. Sometimes I would tell Michael 'This scene doesn't work and I gotta talk to you about it.' Then Jimmy would take me aside and explain it to me. I obviously needed that kind of support."

Kirkwood had to hit the ground running. Papp had given Bennett five more weeks, the same length of time as the first workshop, to pull his "dancer project" into shape. Bennett was convinced he could pull it off—that the experimental crucible of the workshop process would bring forth what he now saw as his personal vision. If the resulting show were a success, it would be mounted immediately that spring in a full off-Broadway production. If not, well, it would be chalked up as a worthy experiment. With a cast that had been winnowed carefully over the course of a year, and with an experienced new writer in his stable, Bennett plugged into an intense new phase of the workshopping process, in which his dancers would wring all they could from their hearts and their talent.

Kay Cole believes that working on the show was the fulfillment of an archetypal dancer's fantasy. "Anybody who acknowledges being a dancer has dreams of doing *Firebird,* or whatever. Every single person in the company had some sort of fantasy like that about dancing. So there was a camaraderie, a certain friendship innate to a dancer. And this show was about dancers. So it was like a team of huskies. You learned to pull together. I'm shy, but you just immediately became friends. Also, everybody was doing a lot of things they hadn't done before. So we were all charting new ground for ourselves in some respect. That, in and of itself, made everyone feel close. You're all alone on the iceberg together. That part was nice."

Now that there was fresh company on the iceberg, the lineup had to change as well. The dancers from the first workshop tended to keep their positions and the others filled in between them wherever it suited the action of the play. Outlining the changes, McKechnie said, "Al and his wife had to stand next to each other.

Paul and Diana [the two Hispanic characters] kind of gravitated toward one another. Kelly and me and Michel Stuart, the older ones, were a clique. "I think we felt more insecure than the others, though they didn't know it. We didn't know if we'd be cut, so we gathered for power."

Ron Kuhlman remembers earlier configurations. In the first workshop he'd stood next to Candy Brown, whose character was adapted as Ron Dennis's. He also remembers having stood next to Trish Garland, instead of half a stage away from her. "I remember," he said, "because she had on jean shorts with silver studs on them, and she has these long legs. I couldn't take my eyes off them."

Nevertheless, there was an awful lot of hard work—which is precisely what they'd all bargained for. "We'd get in at ten in the morning," Don Percassi said, "and everybody would be crying and I hadn't had my tea yet. That was the workshop. When my mother called me and asked me how everything was going I would say, 'Terrific. I go there and dance for three hours, I sing for three hours and I cry for three hours.' I told her it was getting to be an Italian melodrama or an opera. I told her I had the feeling that Marvin Hamlisch was taking his things from Puccini. I thought, 'This is too much, I'm getting a headache.' "

Despite the pressure, there was no complaint—at least not at this point—to the Actors Equity Association, the actors' union. The union was having its first major experience with its members taking part in this kind of workshop, and Bishop recalled that its objections were limited to a minor dispute over whether the performers were to get an actor contract, a so-called "white contract"—or a pink chorus dancer contract. She remembered, "Equity came in at one point and said, 'You can't be on white contracts, you have to be on pink contracts.' But there was no way I was ever going to see another pink contract in my life. You see, to chorus people, a pink contract means you're just another part of a crowd. But a white contract represents being an individual. A white contract was important to more than just me. A white contract was important to everyone because it means 'I'm an individual in an ensemble situation.' We had to put our little feet down.

"I remember Michel Stuart saying to Equity, 'You people have got to broaden your thinking. You've got to think in different terms. This is a *different thing*.'

"And the Equity people said, 'No-you-don't-understand-see-if-you're-on-pink-contracts-because-you're-backing-up-so-and-so-and-then-if-you-get-your-number-here-you-can-make-so-much-more-money-and . . .'

"And Michel was basically speaking for us very articulately when he said, 'We could care less about making more money. We care about what we're doing.'

"I've been in a couple of unprecedented situations that Equity had no way of dealing with, where they pretty much let the actors tell them what they wanted to do. So we basically told them what we wanted to do, and we always stayed on a white contract."

Stuart, who was so quick to defend the workshop process, gloried in it. "I improvised every single day," he said. "It had a real good feeling and I liked being there. I was in a structure that was very loose, it seemed for the first time, in terms of doing a show. I had never had a theater experience like that before. I was real open to it and went with it all, and I did what I was told to do. I didn't make any judgments on it because I knew it would be ever-changing. That was the nature of what I assumed a workshop was. We were given some words, we learned them, we did them, and then they were gone. So many scenes were written and thrown out. A lot of the music was not there when I joined. Marvin would take us into a room and write things that we could sing. I was one of the people who could not sing particularly well. But I was having a ball."

Though Stuart's role, Gregory Gardner, was based on tapes made by dancer Christopher Chadman, Stuart said he soon influenced the writers to help him make it his own. "My whole monologue was Michel Stuart," he said. "When I was fourteen I knew I was gay and I never had a problem with it."

He said changes in the role were "about attitude, about body language, about being older. It was about style, it was all the stuff I brought to it."

In such a high-pressure situation, friction built up quickly. "The competition came real fast with all of us," Wayne Cilento said. "Not only between us, but Michael Bennett was competing with me. It was very obvious. He would make everyone sit down while we danced. It was as if he was challenging me to outdance him.

"The insecurity happened real fast, too," Cilento said. "It was a matter of who was getting attention, who wasn't getting attention, who was getting feedback, who was dancing full out, who wasn't dancing full out. And that had nothing to do with the parts at that time. That was pure energy, ego, right from the beginning. The second workshop was concerned with the creative process so you really didn't know what was going on. Michael would go down the line and create people as he went along."

The goal of the second workshop was to consolidate the disparate monologues into a panorama of dancers' lives, and to do so in a dramatically compelling way. Looking at the mass of information, Bennett and Avian felt that the block of marble was there and the tools were in their hands—all they had to do was chip away the material that wasn't a masterpiece. The first thing they and the writers tackled was structure.

"Obviously Michael was not going to have everybody stand up and sing a song," Bishop said. "Which is the reason a lot of people didn't get a song. Consideration number one was the amount of time it would take. But number two, how do you top the last song? You have to have a better singer with a better range. You have to make it interesting and different. You can't just have one person after another sing a song or we'll all fall asleep. At that point we had a group number, a solo number, a monologue that went into 'And . . .' Now, he could have had another song and another song and another song . . . But how much more interesting to have a trio. Then you go to a duet, et cetera."

Bishop's own number, "At the Ballet," was a trio. Sung at the end of the first workshop by Bishop, McKechnie, and Jane Robertson, it underwent two personnel changes at the beginning of the second workshop. A new role was being created for McKechnie, to be named Cassie. Her original role, Maggie, was modeled largely on her early life. Maggie speaks eloquently of her childhood, but says little or nothing about her adult life. That's because Bennett and the writers had other plans for McKechnie's more recent past. They began to fashion for her the role of a dancer who had been featured early in her career, then went to California to become a star, but had had little success. This "Cassie" attends the audition because she knows her place is in the chorus.

To fill the role of Maggie, Bennett had hired Cole. To musicalize McKechnie's story about her father being an Indian chief, Hamlisch and Kleban had written one of the loveliest passages in the score of *A Chorus Line,* the theme Bishop called "the pretty one." It was written partly as a gift to McKechnie, but now that she was out of the role, Bennett had gotten the best singer he could find, but one who also could dance and who he believed displayed the temperament for the workshop atmosphere.

On the recording Cole is heard riding the theme through the climax of the number—"And he said, 'Maggie, do you want to dance?' And I said, 'Daddy, I would love to'—that had made Bishop and the others cry. At that point the music modulates and the "At the Ballet" music returns. This theme builds to a single sustained note on the open second syllable of the word "ballet." She holds it for eight beats. It doesn't cause a sensation as when Ethel Merman held a note for an entire verse of "I Got Rhythm," but the first time Cole stood up to sing the number in the second workshop, the others were thunderstruck.

Bishop said, "Kay, not having had that experience but only having the song, sang it so simply and purely that the same effect came out of the audience. I'd say ninety percent of the time I was doing 'At the Ballet' in the show, she'd get to 'Maggie, do you want to dance?' and tears would come to my eyes. There's something about Kay's voice; it's almost like a castrato's voice. The most pure, beautiful, oh, it knocks me out. I loved harmonizing with her."

Bishop said she felt no animosity because what had originated as "her" song became a showcase for Kay Cole. "I had no trouble with that at all. I get the lion's share up front, Kay gets the lion's share at the end. I was glad to have anyone singing with me."

With Cole's arrival, the song underwent some further revision. "At one point we went to one of the theater rooms over in Lincoln Center downstairs," Cole said. "I remember the basic structure of the piece, of 'Ballet,' was there. Some of the last note phrases and the harmonies and what ended up on the album weren't there, but the basic structure was. We heard Kelly's piece and that was just amazing. Ed and Marvin were trying various things in a free creative atmosphere. I had no problems with lyrics or Ed Kleban because, fortunately, I had all the great vowels, all the ones that are wide open and go-for-it."

It now was time to unveil and start rehearsing the song Priscilla Lopez had been taught at Lincoln Center during the first workshop. "When that part of the show came up and I got up and sang 'Nothing,' people were surprised that I already knew it. I felt a little strange about that, but I felt great, too. I felt that I had gotten a jump on some people and I hoped they wouldn't hold it against me. There had been a little monologue before it, but it wasn't much. I never had a long spiel like Pam Blair did. I had two pages of monologue that got totally wiped out. All that was left was the line, 'I'm so excited because I'm going to the High School of the Performing Arts.' "

In an attempt to evolve away from the song-monologue-song-monologue structure that was in danger of paralyzing the show, Hamlisch, Kleban, Kirkwood, and Dante began to expand upon the idea born in "At the Ballet." That trio told three stories that overlapped but formed a single image of escaping from unhappy childhoods into the wonderland of dance. The new number would be a choral piece for the entire cast. But instead of telling three stories, it would tell seventeen, fusing scraps of images into a patchwork portrait of life en pointe. The dancers called the new piece "The Montage," and don't bother looking for it on any list of musical numbers. Drawing on the model of film montage—the first of several times Bennett turned to cinematic effects in his staging—this sequence assembled a kaleidoscope of overlapping words, steps, and visuals. Like the big dance sequence developed in the first workshop, it changed continually. Some of its parts worked so well that they became whole songs unto themselves. Eventually it engulfed the dance sequence and filled most of the first half of *A Chorus Line,* incorporating the revised "At the Ballet"; "Sing!," the number that had given Baughman confidence back on New Year's; and Lopez's "Nothing." The sequence was not recorded in its entirety, but the number "Hello Twelve, Hello Thirteen, Hello Love" gives an idea of how "The Montage" unfolds (though "Hello Twelve" was not written until several weeks later). As they developed the number, whenever they needed a fresh bit of biography, all they would do was ask the person onstage at that moment to pull up something from their past. Many days it resembled an ongoing tape session.

"Marvin was at the Newman Theater with a piano onstage and we were all in the audience," Kay Cole said. "Michael was like a teacher, pointing at each pupil: 'Try this, Thommie sing this . . .' There's nothing like creating, especially with a large group of people. I guess in a way it's like going to church because everybody has the same reason for being there. There was a basic structure and everybody contributed, and suddenly it was like we had this bowl of wild flowers: Every color that you needed was there.

"We worked really, really hard," Cole said. "The first time we did the show it was about two hours longer than it ended up being. We were all very emotionally drained because it was the first time we got to really see the scope of what we'd been working on. The experience was monumental. Everybody was feeling so much at that time we had gotten to the point we were close enough to just let those feelings show. By the time we got to Sammy's speech every single person was crying and involved. I'll never forget that moment."

"The Montage" included a duet for Ron Dennis and Baayork Lee, titled "Confidence." Dennis's Richie character sang about the others being able to "outkick me," still he's certain "this guy is gonna pick me," because he has confidence. Lee's Connie character sings about how she "passed for Ethel Merman's girlie," and even had done a year or two "in 'Purlie,' " and with confidence like that, they're sure to get it. The song ends, however, with both of them agreeing that for a couple of confident people, they feel pretty insecure.

"Black and oriental," Dennis said. "I thought the song was just too cute. I understand that it was too early in the show and it didn't work. I wasn't even upset when it was cut. But it was cut early on and from then on Baayork and I sat like two bumps on a log. I just got more and more angry as the weeks went on because we never got an explanation. Not one word from Michael or Bob or Marvin. After that, I was never called to go and work on anything."

Though their duet was gone, the bond remained. "Baayork was my buddy," Dennis said. "Baayork saved my rear end more times than anybody has the right to save anybody's in one short negative span. If there was anybody in my corner it was Baayork. She totally looked out for me, called me 'little brother,' and I love her for it.

"But we were definitely second-class citizens. I just went home and kept practicing and thinking Aretha Franklin and trying to make something out of this song 'Gimme the Ball' [which he'd inherited from Candy Brown, who'd gotten it after Thommie Walsh and Wayne Cilento] to make it work because it was going nowhere. The show didn't make any room for minorities but that should have been touched on if it was going to be a true representation."

Instead, Dennis focused on the personal politics developing around him. "I was more involved in watching to see who in the group would have more say about the steps they wanted to do," he said. "I'm talking about choreography because that's what most of the show was about from my earliest memories. All the book stuff didn't concern me. Most of it had to do with Donna, Priscilla's song, and 'At the Ballet,' which they worked on a lot. Marvin would run out and come back with music and give it to Michael."

Cilento's song, "I Can Do That," laid the groundwork for many of the others, indeed for the entire style of the show. "He wanted it to be more conversational, to come out of thin air," Cilento said. "Michael wanted it to be a slow progression into what the style of the musical was." The original choreography consisted of some fancy footwork: a series of tap turns into a double pirouette into a fan kick, and it was nonstop, but it was not the acrobatic showboating it has since become.

Among the songs Hamlisch and Kleban had been developing during the hiatus was a second solo for Priscilla Lopez, who already was performing "Nothing."

"All along I knew that I would be singing this other song," Lopez said. "Michael would refer to it as 'You have another song, the last song in the show,' or 'Marvin is going to write this great song.' So finally I started hearing this song and it was 'What I Did for Love.' He never told me directly that this was the song I would be learning, but the clues were there. I would hear it being played around at rehearsals but no one was teaching it to me.

"One day Michael tells me to get up and do the song with

Marvin. I didn't know the song but I got up there feeling as if I'm supposed to know it. That's why I had so much trouble with some of the passages, because I had learned it on my own and I had learned it wrong."

To set up the song, Kirkwood and Dante introduced a scene that was disturbingly familiar to the dancers who had taken part in the first workshop. Michael Bennett's phony tumble and knee injury was being incorporated into the show. In the scene, Paul, who has told of the way his commitment to dancing has deepened since his Jewel Box days, falls during "The Tap Combination" and injures a knee on which he's had surgery. After he is taken away in an ambulance, the dancers are left to wonder what will happen when they can't dance anymore. Responses vary, but they agree that dancing is a career unlike any other. It's the thing they all did, not to make big money, but simply because they loved doing it. Whatever else happens in their lives, they'll always know that they performed one activity purely out of passion. That's the story of "What I Did for Love," which became the show's pop hit, recorded more than a half-dozen times in an age when show tunes are rarely recorded at all.

Another of the show's notable songs made its appearance at this time. Blair remembers the first time she heard "Tits and Ass," whose title (but not lyric) later was changed to the more demure "Dance 10, Looks 3." She said, "The whole company was there. Marvin was singing very badly, honking away. Ed Kleban was sitting there looking jolly and sweet, which he was, a little Buddha. I listened and I thought, 'Oh God—what an awful number!' It was so brash and bold. You have to understand how I am inside: I'm still upset that in kindergarten on Halloween, Mom dressed me as a witch. I thought I was a princess. That's me in a nutshell. 'Tits and Ass' was not something a princess would sing. I remember thinking that they strung Lenny Bruce up for this; here I am in pigtails and it's okay. The response, the laughs, were exhilarating. But it used to bother me, the content of the number. People thought I had had it done (silicone breast and buttock implants). Mine are all right but nothing major. 'Look at these,' I'd tell people, 'I deserve a partial refund!' "

As successful as the song eventually was, Blair felt that it typecast her as "a funny, cute, sexy person who dances." She said it took nearly ten years before she was considered for serious acting roles again.

Fear of the unknown troubled the dancers during the first weeks of the workshop. They didn't know if they'd get a song, what it would be like, whether they'd like it, whether they'd get to keep it. They were children of the generation that had grown up in the golden age of Broadway original cast recordings. They'd lip-synced to *Oklahoma!, My Fair Lady, West Side Story, The Music Man,* and *The Sound of Music,* and the pursuit of a new show in which they could do their own song on an original cast album amounted to a virtual quest for the Holy Grail.

But the pressure wasn't just on the singers. McKechnie said, "I remember Marvin Hamlisch was always trying to quit. Michael would say to him, "What do you want? Two Academy Awards and nothing after that? What about being an artist? Michael would give him the Academy Award speech and Marvin would come back every time. And I'm glad he did. The lyricism and the passion that he had, that he conveyed in his melodies, I think there's no one better. People used to make fun of his behavior. I was right there with them but I was able to know him and see him at times in a different way."

Bishop, who had one of the score's best songs, had a chance to sit with the musicians once on Broadway and listen closely to what Hamlisch had written. She said, "Marvin did some wonderful things with that show but by far the best thing he did was the underscoring. When I see the show itself I don't hear much of the underscoring. Even though I know it's there. But when you sit in the pit, it almost doesn't stop. It stops twice: It stops for Donna, it stops for Sammy. But the rest of the time is always music. And it's incredible."

By contrast, Ed Kleban made little impression one way or the other on the dancers. He never socialized with them. Their only contact was the times he would ask a dancer to come into an adjoining room with him and then would question that dancer about his or her life, hoping to elicit a word or feeling that would lead him to a lyric.

"He was a brilliant man," Stuart said. "But workwise I don't remember him much. Yet those are his words. They may have been given to him by cast members or bus drivers—you never knew where the words came from. So many of us said the same things in interviews and private moments. It's hard to pinpoint the writing of the show. But basically all the words in this piece came from the people on the line. They were structured by a group of people and edited probably by Michael Bennett totally, autonomously, at some point."

"Ed Kleban was so sensitive that I felt like I wanted to take care of him," McKechnie said. "He conveyed a kind of delicacy and I think it came through in his lyrics, his painful sensitivity."

Perhaps for that reason, plus the intense desire to introduce a new Broadway song, those who did not get lyrics of their own felt especially hurt. "I know Ron and myself and Nancy went through a lot of crazies because we weren't given a song," Mason said. "We weren't even given the opportunity to experiment. I mean, Nancy eventually got to do 'Ballet,' but she thought she had the potential to do more. Ron Kuhlman had this incredible monologue about the death of his mother [in a boating accident] that was just heart-rending. In fact, I hate to say this, but to me it was more important than Sammy's [Jewel Box monologue]. Ron did it extraordinarily. We were in tears. Ron had such warmth to his delivery. You wanted to hug him after it. He had a potential talent that was being misused.

"I felt the same way," Mason continued. "I was never given an opportunity to try a comedy line. Maybe I didn't do it well, but no one worked with me to make it well. Michael worked with other kids, with Pam Blair. Thommie Walsh got five or six different versions of his monologue. I remember Wayne getting 'Joanne' and 'I Can Do That.' I never got the opportunity to do anything in my monologue except pantomime.

"I understand that in the construction of a musical or play you're going to have certain roles, but in *A Chorus Line* they weren't evenly distributed. I think a lot of people were never given a chance. Don Percassi is a great comic and yet, God bless him, the same thing happened to him and it didn't seem to matter to him. He was an old trouper and he just went in there and did his job. But I know Don went through his crazies, too."

Despite all the work and the new songs, the show wasn't making as much progress as Bennett and the dancers expected. The more people on deck, the more cumbersome changes became. In the early weeks of February 1975, *A Chorus Line* was still an amorphous mass of plotless monologues peppered with a few interesting tunes and dances.

This situation may have served as impetus for the final two departures from the cast: Jane Robertson, who had been with the project since the tape sessions more than a year earlier; and Barry Bostwick, who had been chosen for the first workshop by Bennett to play the role of Zach, a character based on Bennett himself.

In the years since, *A Chorus Line* has been hyped as a juggernaut whose hit status was a foregone conclusion. But at this late date, less than three months before the show would begin previews, it still looked like such an iffy proposition that people were leaving it to take more promising jobs elsewhere.

Robertson left to take a featured role in the Joe Masiell musical *A Matter of Time,* which closed on opening night later that spring. Bostwick left because of mounting frustrations with Bennett over how the role of Zach should be played. McKechnie said, "Barry Bostwick had said he couldn't contain himself when he came up onstage. He wanted to find some sympathy in the character. Michael tried to tell him that you have to be very objective and very steely because that's the only way to do it, to get the work done. If you're sympathetic, your audience will hate you because then it is really you putting people through hell."

Unable to budge Bennett from this conviction, Bostwick resigned early in the second workshop.

Robertson's and Bostwick's departures caused a flurry of cast changes. Nancy Lane, who had been hired as Robertson's understudy in the role of Bebe, saw her big chance, but at first was afraid to grasp it. "I was so paranoid," she said. "I thought everyone hated me. I thought that because I was the youngest and rambunctious and eager, they hated me. Then suddenly Jane Robertson has to leave and I was so worried that I wouldn't get the part. I went up to Michael and said, 'Please let me audition for Bebe because I'm the understudy.' I was begging him and finally he said, 'Okay, okay.'

"I did it the way I wanted to do it, not the way Jane Robertson had done it, which I didn't like. But I have to tell you that my mother prays for her every night because it was her leaving that gave me a chance to do the show."

Lane thus became the only member of the original cast hired from the ranks of the understudies. She joined Kay Cole and Kelly Bishop as part of the trio that sings "At the Ballet."

"Now I'm on the Line," she said, "and I'm so intimidated by everyone because, as I said, I thought everybody hated me. Priscilla was nice enough to talk to me at lunchtime occasionally and I thought that was really neat. I really wanted to be part of that group. That was the elite, the 'in crowd.' There was Trish Garland, who was so thin and so pretty. I didn't know she was anorexic but she was thin and we all wanted to be that body. And there was Kay Cole singing her guts out—she had such a fabulous voice.

"I was intimidated by Michel Stuart and grew to hate him for a long time because I thought he was very mean and callous, cold, uncaring. I wanted to be friends with Kelly Bishop but I had nothing to say to her so I never talked to her. Bobby LuPone was okay. I thought he was a little bit of a pompous ass for a long time but he was all right. Priscilla was great, and there was dynamite Baayork. Thommie was wonderful. I really admired him because he was just so cool and he knew what he was doing and talked back to Michael Bennett. I envied that because I couldn't.

"I didn't care for Pam Blair only because she was so weird. Ron Dennis was okay but hard to get to know. Actually Donna, too, she was wonderful. Marvin Hamlisch was the sort of guy who would always date me in high school. But he was so talented, who would have thought?

"And then there was little old me, the comedienne on the Line. I was real proud to be there. But I made myself nuts more than anybody else."

Bostwick's departure from the Zach role toppled a series of dominoes. Robert LuPone traded the Al role for Zach. Don Percassi, who was playing Larry, Zach's assistant, joined the Line as Al. Bypassing the understudies, Bennett hired one more outsider, Clive Clerk (who later changed his last name to Wilson), as Larry.

But these changes did not take place as quickly or as neatly as that.

At the time Bostwick left, LuPone was still torn between his desire to be an actor and his success at being a dancer. The role of Al allowed him to do both. As the husband of Kristine (Renee Baughman), he played a tough guy, a street fighter who hated homosexuals and who didn't hesitate to resort to violence if he felt his masculinity threatened. He and Michel Stuart's character, Greg, had a climactic fight scene that provided one of the most dramatic moments in the show as it then existed.

LuPone was still resisting the dancing and he said that the fight was one of the few things that kept him interested in the project. "I was not happy with Al," he said. "I was very self-conscious because there was really no role yet, so I was basically a dancer again." LuPone became further alarmed when Bennett and the writers began whittling the role down. When the fight was cut, LuPone was distraught, remembering how he had turned down a role in the Broadway musical *Boccaccio* to stay in *A Chorus Line*.

"We had a very long show," Baughman recalls. "Bob LuPone and I had some major scenes, but they were cut. They were going to let Bobby go because he had no role left."

With dramatic timing, Bostwick left the cast, leaving open the role of Bennett's alter ego, the director Zach. Zach runs the "audition" that frames the action of *A Chorus Line*. It is for Zach that the dancers reveal their lives. Zach sits at the back of the audience, his voice booming out like the voice of God over the theater's sound system. He appears onstage several times to lead dances, including the opening, and to engage in dialogue with several of the dancers, particularly Paul (Williams) and Cassie (McKechnie). LuPone realized that by moving to that role, he could salvage his commitment to the show while enhancing his acting. "So then I heard Barry Bostwick left and that's when I really committed myself to *ACL*," LuPone said. "I said to myself, 'I can do Zach,' because that was then the acting role. Kristine and Al were, as far as I was concerned, superfluous.

"One night I was at Michael Bennett's house with Bobby Avian there, and I said to him simply, 'I can do that.'

"To his mind, I was already an actor—an 'act*uo*r,' as he called me—so we talked about it. Bobby told Michael, 'Give him a chance,' and Michael sort of looked at me."

At first Bennett was concerned that LuPone was too youthful-looking to play a veteran Broadway director, but LuPone promised that if he got the part, he would grow a beard.

"The next day I had an audition," LuPone said. "Everybody broke for lunch and then it was just me and Bobby and Michael and Marvin. I went up there and launched right into 'uh five, six, seven, eight, dada-dada-dadada-*da*-da. Okay everybody turn to . . .' Obviously I was the guy for the job. That audition I was the nice guy, full of smiles, willing to work for anybody because that's how I was in those days. I could see their eyebrows turn into a smile.

"Ultimately everybody came back from lunch, and we did it from the top of the show. I did the script and I could see I could control the group. They were responding to me. That made my commitment. It took me two workshops to really go after something in this whole project. It was Zach."

The ever-amenable and cheerful Percassi was offered the role of Al. He complied, not complaining that the part had been pared down from a central character to a supporting role. "Every time I did the part they would laugh," Percassi said. "It was too macho. Bob LuPone had been fine, but when I did it, it was silly. That's when Michael started realizing that we all had different colors. That's when things started changing. They had to make the part funnier because that's the way I am."

Aside from his easygoing temperament, the reason Percassi didn't mind a minor role is, quite simply, "I loved the creative process." He said, "They'd put us around the piano and they would tell each of us to sing something. It was actually being created on us. Michael would unleash us and if he liked it we could keep it in. You don't get that most of the time. To be free to do anything—wow!"

One of the experiments resulted in Percassi's part actually getting a little bigger. "Sing!" was the number Hamlisch and Kleban had written during the hiatus for Renee Baughman. In the song, Kristine boasts of her dancing skills, but despairs of ever learning to sing. The number began as a solo for Baughman, but though the melodic line is a simple one, Baughman, true to her character, could not carry it. The song then was redrafted for the entire chorus, but, as Baughman recalls, "I almost lost that number because it didn't work for so long. I'm sure that a lot of people wondered why I had a song when I couldn't really sing. I know it was frustrating for everybody. I remember chanting for that number whenever I got the chance."

Aside from the creative team, show business insiders often were invited to the workshops to examine the show's progress and give Bennett and Avian feedback. Many of the top directors and choreographers, including Ron Field and others, gave Bennett advice and criticism. But the piece of advice that saved "Sing!" came from an unexpected source. "It was Ed Kleban's girlfriend [Lina Klein]," Baughman said. "She was sitting in at a rehearsal, we had tried everyone helping me sing, and she suggested that my husband help me sing."

She proposed that Al and Kristine come forward and explain Kristine's problem together, since they were man and wife and it was in Al's macho nature to finish his wife's sentences for her. As the song now goes, Kristine sings the first six notes of each line, with Al popping in with the final and rhyming note—and completing each of her thoughts. Not only was it cute and funny, it also worked. The chorus still comes in at the end, but now it's a number that reveals two characters instead of just one.

Percassi said, "We tried it for Michael and I just remember him standing up and saying, 'That's the number!' When 'Sing!' was rewritten as a duet, suddenly I felt like I had something to contribute."

Percassi's step up to the role of Al left one more vacancy, perhaps the smallest regular role in the show, that of the dance captain, Larry, who appears onstage to demonstrate Zach's dance steps to the auditioners. It was mid February and Bennett was left with an opening for a dancer.

Clive Wilson had returned to New York from Los Angeles the previous June. "It was the end of a relationship and I wanted to get out of L.A.," he said. "I was at a very, very low ebb, really bottoming out, when I got to New York. I checked into classes at the Art Students League. Part of my therapy at the time was just painting, immersing myself in art.

"One night I was walking along Broadway in the sixties with a friend and this girl passed us. My friend said, 'That's Donna

McKechnie.' It had been years since I worked with her and I didn't recognize her. He then explained that she was doing a new show, and Michael's name was mentioned. But I was doing nothing with theater at that point.

"Eight or so months passed. During that time it occured to me more and more that, while I'm here, it would be fun to dance, at last, in the chorus of a Broadway show. At this point, through a friend, I went to a party being given for Jim Kirkwood. *P.S. Your Cat Is Dead* was about to open out of town in Buffalo, so this party was a send-off. I almost didn't go. However, I ended up going and I met Michael Bennett. We were remotely connected through that time back in Toronto [when they had danced together as teenagers in a CBC variety show], but he never would have remembered that. But as it turned out, he did remember, and when the subject of *A Chorus Line* came up he said something like, 'Why don't you come and be in it?' Whether he meant it or not I don't know. But he invited me to come to a rehearsal, which I was thrilled by.

"So I got down there the next day or two and sat in the bleachers. The first thing I experienced was a run-through of the opening number by the end of which I was on such a high that I could have floated out of the room. It was like going back to my roots. It was where I had lived, where I started, and that was the me I had lost. It was a very moving experience, and at that very moment I wanted to dance again so badly I could taste it.

"Still, I didn't really want to perform, to go on every night. I was interested in being involved, but as perhaps an understudy. I hadn't computed that even as an understudy I would have to go on every night in the opening number. Then Michael mentioned that the part of the director's assistant had become available because of Tony Stevens's departure, and would I be interested in playing that? Another thing that attracted me was the fact that this little show of Michael's wasn't going out of town, which meant I wouldn't have to stop my classes at the Art Students League. So everything fell into place. I thought, hey, this could be fun for a few months.

"So I called Michael and said I would love to be a part of the show, and would like to do that part. I didn't audition. He was assuming that I could still dance. I had stayed active: gym, exercise classes, and the odd dance class. It was so great to dance again. Little did I know what I had fallen into."

Wilson's arrival caused a stir. "He made me crazy, bad," Walsh said. "He was just so damn handsome and so together, and I was insanely jealous over his looks. I knew he was a child star and he just had a style that was worldly, a style that I envied."

Garland said, "I remember all the guys going 'Ooh' when Clive came in because he was so pretty. They all thought he had gotten the job because he was a close friend of Michael's. They didn't like him. I didn't know him but sort of took on that same attitude. I didn't particularly care one way or the other—but now I adore him. He became this real special person to me."

Wilson remembers, "I was nervous the first day I joined the company. Here I was in a room full of gypsies, kids who were very accomplished in the musical theater and had lots of Broadway musical credits, and who had been dancing steadily for the past six or eight or ten years. I hadn't danced since Doris Day. I worried was I going to be good enough? Are they going to laugh at me? Am I going to fall on my face? I was all at once in awe and intimidated and nervous and thrilled to be there. Thrilled beyond belief, that's the feeling that I really had after the first day of rehearsal. I remember specifically one moment sitting on the crosstown bus going home and just thinking, 'God, this is really what it's all about. I'm so glad to be alive and having this experience.'

"Baayork was a love," Wilson continued. "She came up and introduced herself and I proceeded to call her 'Miss York.' I wasn't aware either of whatever impression I made. The day I came to watch the run-through, just having come back from Mardi Gras and Key West, I had a tan in February. I had a fur coat on, I didn't know any better. I've learned. Contrary to what Mr. Walsh later said, I wasn't wearing Gucci loafers. Having come in through Michael, a friendship developed with him which I think was resented by a few people. Later on when I found out some of the things that were being said about me at this time, I could only relate it to my experiences when I was seven years old in school [in Trinidad] and I used to get beat up by black boys who resented me just for being.

"There was a group that intimidated me because they weren't as friendly as the rest. They were essentially Thommie, whom I came to love and adore, and Kelly. I didn't get as negative a feeling from Priscilla although she just didn't extend herself. Wayne was standoffish. It wasn't that he had anything to get me for, he was just such a bundle of nerves. I had been resented for being calm, although I wasn't.

"Still, there were various people who were nice. Trish was nice, Sammy was nice, Ron Dennis, Baayork. Rick Mason was very strange. I think he, too, at times felt like an outsider."

With all the hubbub of comings and goings and constant changes, the realignment of roles seemed like just another new thing to get used to. The dancers couldn't have realized that when they took their places onstage on Wilson's first day, the famous chorus line that eventually became the distinctive logo for the show had at last fallen into place. Percassi's was the last face to join the Line. Add LuPone at the back of the theater and Wilson ready in the wings as the dance assistant, and you have the original nineteen-member cast of *A Chorus Line*.

These dancers finally were seeing what they had dreamed of seeing: their hero in the throes of creation, creating dances for *them*. Their entire careers—and Bennett's—had honed them exquisitely. They were seeing, smelling, hearing, and touching each other under some of the most intimate circumstances, working side by side every day.

"In the second workshop I know that I started spending time with Michael," LuPone said, "and I felt a tremendous sense of compatibility and camaraderie, which is what I look for in an artist, something I was absolutely enthralled with. I compare Michael Bennett with Antony Tudor, the last artist I had come across that I wanted to be like. In 'seventy-five I was filled with this purpose, a sense of art and a sense of real communication and contribution that an artist could make to society and politics. Coming out of the sixties, that rang true for me."

Once overall choreographic ideas were in place, Bennett handed over much of the detail work to Bob Avian and the dancers. Everyone was encouraged to contribute ideas for steps, for lines, for lyrics. The writers relied upon that. The writers took the words and ideas then filtered them, refashioned them, and framed them. Bennett exercised unyielding final say over what went in and what came out. Bennett was raw, unreasonable, and demanding toward his dancers. And yet, the very project he was scourging them with was a homage to them and their profession.

"Michael had been a dancer himself," Kay Cole said, "and had been the workhorse of a show, which all dancers are. There's the stars, there's the second players, there are the singers and last on the totem pole are the dancers. Because he had done that himself, he had an understanding of how to make it comfortable for all of us. We were being treated in a better way than just being dancers. We were featured. We were it, stars and chorus."

The flashes of brilliance came as quickly as the flashes of temper, and both burned the dancers deeply in different ways.

"This is what was so wonderful about Michael," Bishop said. "It's why I think he was the best he's ever been in his life during that period: He was one of us, he was our leader. It was like we were a bunch of bandits or something. That kind of leader: like up in the hills. We were free to speak our minds, have our nervous breakdowns, go through whatever we wanted to go through, but he was very generous with his own life. When we sat down to talk about teenage times, he sat down to talk about teenage times, too. He was exceptionally generous and unguarded with us. It was wonderful, and I think almost the happiest he's ever been."

Despite LuPone's empathy with Bennett's views of the artistic ideal, their paths diverged when it came to Bennett's practices as a director. "To me," LuPone said, "Michael Bennett was an intellectual fraud, and as a director at that time he was nonexistent. We're talking about a neurotic, messed-up choreographer. He directed as a choreographer and put the show together on the beat as a choreographer."

Thommie Walsh observed, "The character of Zach constantly refers to the auditioners as 'boys and girls,' and that outlook clearly carried over into Bennett's attitude toward the original cast members. He created monsters and then couldn't deal with them. One minute Bennett would say, 'I am great and you are wonderful because I am making you into stars'; and the next it would be 'I hate you, you're a piece of shit.'

"In the second workshop the competition grew fiercer," Walsh said. "I felt that I was set up to compete against Wayne. That was Michael's tactic and it was hard because I loved Wayne, that dear little person. Yet there always was this shit about seeking approval from God. It happened every day."

The credits of *A Chorus Line* say the musical was "conceived, choreographed, and directed by Michael Bennett." That is not entirely accurate, but a picture of precisely what that means began to emerge in the second workshop.

Bennett did not conceive *A Chorus Line* alone; Michon Peacock and Tony Stevens had as much to do with it, in its early stages, as Bennett did. Yet Bennett did have a concept in his mind for how he wanted the project to develop, and as it took shape during January, February, and March of 1975, it began to follow the pattern of that concept. The term "concept musical" emerged after the opening of *A Chorus Line* to describe shows like *Cats, Dancin', Pacific Overtures, Bubblin' Brown Sugar, Nine,* and *Sunday in the Park with George,* which were more about a situation or an idea than a plot.

There had been others before that as well. *Fiddler on the Roof* is about the concept of "tradition" as much as it is about a Russian-Jewish milkman watching his daughters get married. Even such long-ago shows as Gershwin's *Strike Up the Band* and Irving Berlin's *As Thousands Cheer* explored themes of war and economic depression, respectively. But with *A Chorus Line* Bennett and the dancers were striving to alloy song, character, and staging in a more wholly integrated way to express both the triviality and profundity of artists' lives.

"Give Michael credit," LuPone said, "the greatest credit, for the fact that he took his concept and brought it to fruition. I think in today's theater that's a rare thing in itself."

With such a small role, Clive Wilson worked directly with Bennett relatively little, but often found himself sitting and watching Bennett work with others. Wilson said, "It was one of those alerting experiences for me. I was observing this man I admired. He was very successful in his field and I was to some degree in awe. I didn't know where he was leading but it was fascinating to watch him work. I had never been involved in the making of a Broadway show. I saw mistakes made and changes go in. The show grew and grew and got better and better."

"Because Michael couldn't communicate too well what he wanted, he had to manipulate," said Kuhlman. "Some people allow themselves to be manipulated; some people want to be manipulated without their knowing it, maybe. I never felt that if Michael said, 'Jump off the roof,' I would jump. As an actor I would try to do what he wanted me to do, within reason. I would try to do it even though I might have thought it was wrong. I would try to do it because he's the director and I'm the actor. He had a real iron hand on what he wanted and therefore he sometimes could get a better performance out of some people than if he had been more flexible. But when he really tried to manipulate people, I think he lost some of that creativity."

After the monologue about his mother's death was cut, little was left of Kuhlman's Don character. "I was disappointed and hurt that my original monologue was cut," he said. "I no longer had a role that really warranted arguing about the way a scene should be done. I felt Michael was playing favorites. That's the way he worked. He knew some people better, and knew some people were attracted to him [and he built them up]. He let that happen, I think, because he knew he could play one against the other. If it's important to you to be a favorite, then he could use you in that regard."

Sometimes Bennett was completely at a loss, and he tended to deal with his weaknesses by avoiding them.

"I was being ignored," Ron Dennis said. "Well, not so much ignored, as they didn't seem to know what to do with me. So I was put on the back shelf. I was always being told, 'We'll figure it out later.' . . . In any situation like that you always look out of the corner of your eye to see where the boss is, to see approval. I never got acknowledgment of any kind."

When things weren't working, the dancers were surprised and sometimes hurt that Bennett took out his frustration on them.

"I was becoming bitter because I desperately wanted Michael's attention and appreciation," Mason said. "I saw his manipulating, but it got to a point where I *wanted* to be manipulated because it meant I would have had some attention given to me. I would have been grateful for anything. One day I got a phone call from Michael saying I was doing a wonderful job. I was so excited! But then I got to work and found that everyone got that phone call. It was Bob Avian who told me one day that Michael said I was the best dancer in the show. I thought it was terrific, but why couldn't Michael tell me? I needed to hear it from the head honcho. He did water and nurture those few: the Pam Blairs that needed the attention, pats on the backs. But what about those of us who didn't get anything to make us stand out, but instead were pushed in the background?

"I remember a speech he gave us. We were sitting out in the audience and he was upset with us, he was saying, because we were either not doing what he wanted or we were lazy. He said, 'I'm watering you and you're not appreciating my nurturing in creating you.'

"We were all kind of shocked and dumbfounded because we thought we were putting in a little bit of ourselves, and yet he was taking full credit for it. He played the father figure. He was babysitter for many people. He had to do what he did for a lot of the kids because of their insecurities. Father figure, yeah. He became more of a tyrant, a dictator figure in many respects."

Mason wasn't the only dancer who held Bennett to those expectations. "I always loved Michael, always respected him," Cole said. "I guess that he had a tinge of father or parent figure about him and I always wanted to do the best for him. Sometimes you don't think you're doing the best, but you're trying and you just hope that they know that you're trying. I always wanted Michael to know how much I cared and how hard I was really trying. I adored him, I think he was great. He had an incredible instinct about people. He could look right through to the soul."

"In the second workshop," McKechnie said, "it was now father Michael and the kids. The relationships were very intense. At that point people called him up in the middle of the night, people were crying to him over the phone, making up, fighting, resolving it. By the time we got to the second workshop these bonds were formed."

But even more so than in the first workshop, maintaining that posture was arduous for Bennett. "I can understand what he felt," Baughman said. "He couldn't go on being a father to everybody. And why shouldn't Michael and Donna have a special relationship? They had been friends for years. You don't just turn that off. Basically I felt that Michael liked me as well as he liked anybody. I thought he brought out the best in me. I had never done a role. I was getting this great opportunity and I loved what he was bringing out in me. I romanticized the show. To me, it was all about being in the chorus, but being individuals, too. About respect and dignity."

Nevertheless, Bennett's ends sometimes came to justify his means. Pam Blair remembers, "I'd just come off *Mice and Men* where I had been told that I was incredible in the part instinctively, but because I was so frightened of failing my self-esteem was low. Kevin Conway, another actor in the show, was trying to tell me what 'making a choice' is. He said that when you know what it is that you're feeling at any particular moment and you want the audience to know, something will happen between you and the audience—and that's what 'making a choice' is. Well, I didn't want to be accused of not knowing how to make choices in *ACL* so sometimes I would overdo it.

"So I got myself into a lot of trouble. But those notes from Michael were so vicious! He chewed me out in front of the whole company one day. He'd instill real fear in us so we'd go out and play fear onstage. He did it to everybody. Once he said to Sammy Williams, 'I want to see real tears tonight. Just think of how much I hate you.' Of course he didn't mean it that way, but those were his words. Is that a good director? He almost killed some of us, the way he treated us. To me that isn't theater. I don't know what his trip was, but I don't think it's what theater should be. It's amazing because he was an incredible talent.

"I didn't feel this way when it was happening. I was too busy just trying to survive. No, I thought he was incredible and I was in love with him. But what was horrific about what he did was that he never gave us the benefit of the doubt."

With hindsight, Lopez has come to believe that "when he was doing these things he was trying to be honest at that moment. I believe it because I don't think he's that good an actor. What I think happened to him was that there was a time when he was real and open and he was reachable and touchable. I think that's how he was able to get so much out of us. Then there came a point when he stepped back and said he couldn't play with us anymore. He had to be the director now. That's when he changed and became more manipulating. But initially I think he was very real."

During the first workshop the dancers learned to appreciate co-choreographer Bob Avian's skill as a diplomat and Baayork Lee's instinct to serve as everyone's big sister. In the second workshop, with heightened tension between Bennett and the dancers, those traits became indispensable.

Wilson said that Avian "formed and shaped and pulled the show together. His emphasis might have been different on some aspects of the show; whereas Michael got into some heavy directing, Bobby was more involved with the dancing."

LuPone analyzed Baayork Lee's second workshop contribution, saying, "Her skills are such that she commands respect. Despite the politics, despite the pressures, I have never been with Baayork that she didn't give me space, and give me respect for my professionalism, who I am as a person. That's something Michael Bennett never did. She has true humility. I'm not talking about the social Baayork, I'm talking about the professional Baayork. The professional Baayork, trying to help me get a step right, would work with me and respect my contribution. I wouldn't want to do it a certain way and she would say, 'Don't do it that way, but *this* has to happen. Then she would clean it, it would have to be absolutely spot-clean, and then I'd go back and do that, but in my own way. She was wonderful."

When Bennett worked directly with the dancers, without Avian or Lee interposed, he romanced them artistically to get a particular effect, but then just as often flung them aside. The second workshop came to resemble a giant multidimensional tango, with Bennett leading.

"I was so in love with Michael that my life revolved around being around him," Blair said. "But he drove me crazy during the workshops. He'd watch us all stepping and clawing and scratching at each other. He'd try so hard to be supportive but then he'd pull the rug out from somebody's feet and he'd jab somebody else and say, '*She's* responsible' and watch us go at it. He did that all the time. He was like a cattleman standing there with his electric prod. That's what putting a show together, for him, was all about."

McKechnie said, "This show was very important to Michael because this was like re-creating family for him. And like all families the intimacy breeds love and hate. I think I glorified him as a director. I put him on a pedestal. I had a lot of respect for him and I guess I wasn't affected at that point by some of his game playing. I found myself in the position of defending him. I felt that people did not appreciate what he was doing. He was doing something very special and he was very good at it. People were being caught up in their emotions and subjective feelings because they didn't have the inner discipline as actors yet. Now my view has changed a little bit, but that's how I felt then. I felt that they just didn't know any better and they were foolish not to respect him, not to trust the situation instead of fighting for him and being competitive."

One of the people who came into conflict with Bennett, but for a unique reason, was Robert LuPone. "I took over the role of Zach and all of a sudden I was playing the Man," LuPone said. "Up to then I had had a friendly relationship with Michael. It was so warm, I thought it was honest. But in the rehearsals I did, 'Five, six, seven, eight, et cetera' and suddenly he wasn't speaking to me. He didn't direct me in any way whatsoever. He got red in the face and didn't speak to me. I found that I had become totally imprisoned by a man who personally may have been wonderful to me, but the minute I played him became horrible. All of a sudden I experienced a demon. Obviously I intimidated him in some way. I think what happened is that he wanted to be me as I was playing him."

LuPone was observing the tip of an iceberg whose bulk was hidden offstage. Ever since Bennett and McKechnie had arrived at the first tape session as a couple, their special relationship was acknowledged by the other dancers. Although Bennett talked to them openly about the trouble he'd had establishing his sexual identity, his homosexuality during the workshop period was taken for granted.

McKechnie maintains that their relationship was not sexual, and in fact was not even romantic until after *A Chorus Line* opened on Broadway. They had been very close professionally for more than a decade, and working together on this new project gave them a chance to deepen that relationship. "Michael and I in the guise of Cassie and Zach would spend a lot of friendly hours, creative hours," she said. "Those hours were the closest I believe anyone ever got, for either of us. I know it was for Michael. We opened up to each other in a way that is very difficult for both of us. To be a happy person and not be afraid of intimacy, that's a very profound relationship."

Nevertheless, in light of Bennett's subsequent proposal, McKechnie said she now can see the beginnings of Bennett's extraprofessional interest in her. During the workshops of *A Chorus Line,* McKechnie was living with a hairdresser named Harvey. "Harvey liked that I'd come home and talk to him. I was interested in what he was doing. It was a wonderful, sweet time. The first time I realized Michael was getting jealous is when he started calling Harvey 'your rehearsal boyfriend.' I would leave rehearsal and Michael would say, 'Say hello to *Harvey* for me,' one of those adolescent things."

For a while, McKechnie had a short song titled "Inner Feelings," in which her character mused about her relationship with the director: "What am I doing here?/ What game is he playing here?" The number was cut.

Bennett and McKechnie's eventual relationship had a precedent in that of choreographer Bob Fosse and his prima dancer Gwen Verdon. But in February 1975, Bennett and McKechnie were just beginning to sort out their feelings as artistic collaborators, as mentor and protégée, and employer and employee, though not yet as lovers. They took the additional risky step of exploring these feelings by creating images of themselves onstage. As the Al-Kristine and the Sheila-Don relationships declined in importance in the script of *A Chorus Line,* the spotlight gradually moved to a new central couple, Zach and the recently created role of Cassie. These were definitely fictional characters—or were they?

"When you base anything on truth," McKechnie said, "people are going to believe that everything is the truth when they see the finished product. It used to drive me nuts especially after Michael and I got married: It seemed like that character was the story of my life. But it really wasn't. It was a combination of a lot of situations with different people. At my apartment Nicholas and I would rehearse my dialogue, the business with the director. He would start reading and then we'd start improvising and we taped it. We were trying to come up organically with some lines or find clues about where I should go."

LuPone was groping for the same thing. "As you know, we're dealing with sexual realities," LuPone said. "*ACL* is a sexual, physical experience. It's a kinetic, emotional experience. It's not a cerebral experience, like a Tom Stoppard play. It draws heartstrings. The relationship between what was going down between Zach and Cassie was primarily based on immature sexual realities: jealousy, ownership, possession, things like that. There was no perspective on the part of Zach ultimately in terms of benevolence, understanding, humanism between a man and a woman. It was based in petty, insecure, immature sexual realities."

McKechnie was aware of his feelings, and friction quickly developed between the two. "There I am, the good Girl Scout defending Michael, and I'm being called Miss Goody Twoshoes by LuPone. He hated me because he got off a show where he worked with a director and director's wife and he felt he wasn't treated well. So here he thinks it's the same situation again. That was when I started feeling like a victim. I felt I had no right to fight for myself at that time. I felt that even though I wasn't guilty, Michael did seem to align himself with me, in a way. It was not sexual, but not entirely professional; he treated me as a friend he could count on.

LuPone came to feel that in order to play the part sincerely entailed forcing Bennett to see things in himself that he very likely didn't want to see. It hurt for Bennett to see this reflection of himself. The more LuPone explored the ramifications of Zach's actions, the more it rankled Bennett. As time went on, Bennett's reaction was to avoid confronting this reflection.

LuPone saw the problem first, because he was so close to it. But as the Cassie character grew, it became apparent to everyone that something fundamental was changing about the "dancer project." The show about a chorus line of equals was ever so gradually acquiring a star, or at least a leading lady.

Careful archaeology can trace the situation to a seemingly minor event back in the first workshop. Pam Blair remembers having lunch with McKechnie. "We had some wine and came back a little tipsy because I cannot drink. So Michael saw us tiptoe in about two minutes late and he proceeded to chastise me in front of everybody for not being real. He gave me a part that day [Val] because I came tiptoeing in. I had this big entrance to make. I was supposed to be late. I just ran in and said hello, which of course later ended up being Cassie's entrance. She came in with a mink coat or something, this big entrance."

The entrance embarrassed McKechnie. "We were working on Cassie, trying to find out who she is, and she comes running in late for the audition asking if anyone had change for a taxi. That almost killed me. I said to Michael, 'You cannot give me a star's entrance, they'll hate me. You're killing me with kindness.' He was trying to utilize me and my character. There was a story point that he was trying to make but I think he also was trying to be good to me, and it almost killed me.

"He always discussed this: He liked being the starmaker. He was thrilled for me, even though he gave me a hard time sometimes. But he was succeeding. I wasn't terribly aware that he was trying to make me a star. I was really slow. I was just trying to cope with doing the show. Yes, if I'm completely honest, I knew that he was doing everything he could to help me."

The big entrance was axed, but the Cassie role continued to grow. " 'The Music and the Mirror' was choreographed for me," McKechnie said, "but the reason I always felt Michael was a fabulous director for me was that we found a way of collaborating. He knew my body; our sense of movement and style are similar; we had some of the same teachers and background. I think he liked the way I danced and he felt secure enough with me that he would have an idea, visualize something of a step and I'd take off from that. It would be reciprocal, back and forth. Sometimes he would come in with an actual piece of music set."

McKechnie recalls going to Bennett's apartment with Marvin Hamlisch and music coordinator Robert Thomas, and constructing the entire "Music and the Mirror" dance in about one hour. The reason for the rush was that there were only about three weeks left in the workshop. "Time was of the essence," McKechnie said. "We just had to solve the dance number."

In the original version of "The Music and the Mirror," Mc-

Kechnie danced at center stage with four male dancers behind her. "Again, this was a situation where he was trying to make a star," McKechnie said. "It was too ambitious. There he was, killing me with love again. The ideas were right but it was just a little too much, too driving and one-dimensional."

McKechnie's resistance to Bennett's kingmaking produced stress in their relationship that spilled onto the stage. She recalled, "There was the time we were rehearsing onstage at the Newman and we were starting to work on the dance number. There was Bobby Thomas sitting up there and Bob Avian and Michael . . . and he was in a fury about something. I didn't know what and I never tried to find out but this was the one time Bob Avian came to my defense.

"We were standing in front of the Mylar [mirrors] and Michael said, 'Okay, dance.'

"I looked at Bobby and Bob and asked, 'What do you mean?'

"He said, 'Just go ahead, Donna.'

"Bobby Thomas started playing something and I started moving. Bob Avian is trying to follow me and all of a sudden I just stopped and I said, 'I don't know where you're going, what you want.'

"Michael said, 'Just do something,' and he's sitting there in a fury. It's the only time I've ever seen Bob lace into Michael.

"I don't know how I got out of that, but I know I went home in tears and was a wreck. I felt so betrayed, so abandoned, so alone. Then I got a call from Bobby who got Michael on the phone, and Michael apologized. It was the only time ever. Bobby told me later that he had told Michael, 'Don't you ever take it out on her again.' So at that point, tensions abounded."

"Obviously there was no way any of us expected Donna not to have a dance solo," Kay Cole said. "It would have been ridiculous for her not to, because she was so special, that was so obvious. We would have all thought, 'No, no, you have to give her this solo.' I never felt that about myself."

That's a more charitable assessment than many of the others later gave, but it's a reflection of an era of good feeling that arose in the middle of the second workshop.

Cole said, "I remember the day we were all sitting around after we had the three- or four-hour version of *Chorus Line* and all of us looking at each other and knowing full well that this is too long but it feels wonderful to cry like this."

The show was indeed too long. There had been plenty of cuts before: songs, monologues, and characters. But until mid February flawed or extraneous material cut from one place generally was replaced with improved new material elsewhere. The overall length of the show hadn't changed much. To use vaudeville terminology, it was all "A" material now. With just a few weeks until Joseph Papp would return for the second and final "Papp test," serious net cutting of the text was about to begin.

10.

Preparing for "The Papp Test" (February 1975)

The second half of the second workshop was like a game of musical chairs. There wasn't enough time for everyone to have a treasured "big moment," so each of the dancers did everything they could think of in order to ensure that their parts would survive the cut. Only a few were successful.

The original monologues had been stretched, intercut, musicalized, and spliced into dialogue. The separate threads had finally been woven into a play. But in the second workshop cutting, many of the threads were broken completely. To focus audience interest and sympathy, Bennett and the writers decided to follow the story lines of some dancers more closely than others. They had to decide once and for all which of the nineteen characters were the most interesting. The rest would become important supporting players in the ensemble, which would remain.

Even though Zach and Cassie clearly are the most important couple in the final script, the musical is not about them. It's still about the line. But the Zach and Cassie characters had what the dancers call a "through line." They are consistent and recognizable, and the saga of their relationship is one of several short-story plots played out in scenes cropping up periodically throughout the action.

The cuts were particularly painful for performers like Wayne Cilento, who lost most of his "through line." In the final script he is the first dancer whose story rises from prose into song. He sings "I Can Do That," the first character song in the show, and a knockout song-and-dance number. But little is heard from his character again. That wasn't always the case. Cilento briefly had another song as well, "Joanne," a more personal number about his childhood friend by that name. "Joanne was a girl that I grew up with in an apartment building in the Bronx," he said. "She went to dance school, and one day she took me with her. I got shy about it and never went back."

Cilento remembers the lyric went something like "There was a girl on the second floor/I had a crazy crush on her since I was three or four/We would watch TV/It would be cookies, Mouse-keteers, Joanne and me."

He described it as "a real Gene Kelly MGM number. I learned it one day. It was full-fledged during previews at the Newman right before we opened. But then Michael cut it. At that point it was another of those little minor nervous breakdowns. It was a great little number, very lyrical. It wasn't better than 'I Can Do That,' but it was *my* story.

"I felt really rejected and slighted on that," he said. "Every other day it was a different monologue, the spotlight monologue, the *Oklahoma!* monologue. He kept juggling the spots between Thommie and myself [and then they were cut]. I just felt cheated because I didn't have a through line. I just did my little 'I Can Do That' thing and no one knew who I was. The only thing I had to hold on to through the whole thing and made sense for me was that I knew that somewhere along the line I was one of the best dancers on that stage. I knew Michael felt that about me and that's what I held on to."

Whatever else they took from Cilento, they let him keep "I Can Do That." It is the only male solo in *A Chorus Line*.

At one time Baughman's Kristine character was one of the four major roles in the piece, but little by little Kristine was pared away. Baughman said, "If a scene got cut I didn't freak out, I didn't feel that it was because someone else was better than I was, or that Michael didn't like me. I knew that the show was too long and it had to be cut. I just didn't have those expectations. I was just happy to be there. As long as they didn't cut my number I still felt that I was part of the show."

She said she got emotional support from her stage "husband," Don Percassi. "He was always in a good mood. He was like the company mascot. I could always count on him."

Percassi remembers Bennett explaining to him, "You're not the bricks, you're the cement."

But not everybody had their frame of mind. Kuhlman said, "During the second workshop they cut my monologue and as I felt pretty bad, I didn't talk to anyone about it. I guess I just went to lunch by myself more and more. Then I started getting frustrated. I concentrated on the dance numbers, tap routines, which I like a lot."

From the carnage there emerged six clear survivors, performers whose stories can be followed clearly from the first scene to the last: Donna McKechnie (Cassie), Robert LuPone (Zach), Kelly Bishop (Sheila), Sammy Williams (Paul), Priscilla Lopez (Diana), and Pamela Blair (Val). Instead of the two traditional couples of musical comedy dominating the action of *A Chorus Line,* that concept gradually came to be replaced by the concept of a Big Six who had most of the lines and songs.

Each of the other thirteen dancers is introduced and given a chance to make an impression. But for the most part those impressions are brief, if sharp. The rest of the time they are the true chorus line.

"I had a distinct advantage in this show," Bishop said. "Number one, I had a character that stayed consistent. I also had a set piece that was so consistent that we skipped me a lot. So very often Michael would say 'Okay, from the end of Bobby [Walsh's monologue] we'll go to the end of 'At the Ballet.'

"And I'd go, 'Good.' "

But elsewhere, the cuts went on. Among those who watched their lines dwindle was Baayork Lee, whose Connie character was almost pure Lee biography. "It didn't bother me," she said, "that people were getting more lines than I, that my lines were being cut. My purpose for being in those two workshops was to serve Michael Bennett and not to be a problem to him. If he didn't want to give me lines, then I didn't get the lines. It wasn't until years later that I said to myself, 'How come I didn't get those lines? I could have done it.' Then my paranoia sets in and says, 'Well, maybe he didn't think I was talented enough. My God, and I wanted to be an opera singer and a nun and Maria Tallchief!' "

But Priscilla Lopez, who had two songs, "Nothing" and "What I Did for Love," didn't hesitate to fight for both of them. "I had never worked like this before, having little or no structure, and I loved it—until the day that 'Nothing' got cut and I decided to speak up to Michael and ask him how he could do that.

"The reason I was given [for the elimination of "Nothing"] was that in the structure of the show they were trying to proceed in one line from our early childhood to school days to when you get to New York and meet Pam and Donna, et cetera. They said that for us to go back and do "Nothing" is not right for the show.

"This didn't make any sense to me because Donna would get up and talk about all her life, all the way back. So I called him on it. I called him up and asked him if the song was being cut because it wasn't in chronological order, why would Donna get up after me and go all the way back? He got so defensive about it, he refused to talk to me about it. I would have to take it up with Bobby Avian. I brought him up short by questioning his decisions. When you get something you want to keep all of it."

She didn't quite completely succeed at that. Bennett did trim a verse partly in Spanish from "Nothing." An additional verse of Baughman and Percassi's "Sing!" also was cut at this time.

Though Sammy Williams had no song, he still had the most powerful piece of material in the show, the Jewel Box monologue. It's rare for a musical to reach such an emotional high point without turning to song. But Nicholas Dante had written it before virtually anything else, and it remained in the show, almost untouched, from the first rehearsal. "The only thing that got cut out of the monologue was the first paragraph," Williams said, "telling about a rape that occurred at the age of six. They felt it was too startling.

"I said, 'The monologue works, there's no reason for you to cut it out.' I didn't get a song, that was another hard thing. Marvin Hamlisch kept promising me a song through the whole workshop period. Every time he saw me he said, 'I'm working on it.' Finally they wrote me a song and they had me sing it one day after rehearsal at the Shakespeare Festival. I never sang it in a performance. It went, 'I remember you, mama,' or 'I loved you, mama,' something like that." It was a dancer's tribute to his parents, and it didn't have nearly the impact of Williams's monologue. "I sang this little ditty Marvin had written and they said no and that was the end of my song," Williams said.

None of the Big Six came from among the freshmen. They tend to get philosophical about it. "Coming into a situation with a lot of new people, I didn't feel like going in on my white charger and making demands," Kay Cole said. "I never expected to get anything, and I got more than I expected. I figured it was a work in progress so there's always a chance for change, either in a positive way, say somebody getting twelve songs, or in a negative way by getting only one."

Bennett and Papp had agreed that Papp would stay out of the Dance Theater Workshop studio throughout the second workshop, and Papp continued to be barred while these cuts were being made. Having the producer watching over their shoulders would have been nerve-wracking. As a result, Papp was a shadowy figure throughout the second workshop.

"It's hard to know all the facts, where the buttons were pushed," McKechnie said, "but we couldn't have done it without Joseph Papp. He gave us that theater and Michael wouldn't even let him in it! It was a mutual agreement, but that's a fabulous thing to have."

Michel Stuart remembers, "I used to call Joseph Papp 'the man on the bus'; every few weeks this man would stick his head in the door and look at us and I would say, 'What bus did that man get off of?' "

But for the most part Papp kept his part of the bargain and never went out front to interfere with Bennett.

"I think that's the sign of a good producer," Baayork Lee said, "that he allows his artist to create and then comes in at the end, which he did, and gave his critique. We never saw David Merrick in *Promises, Promises*. But by George, when we had that first run-through for him, we knew what would stay and what would go."

To maintain that sort of pipeline, as he had in the first workshop, Papp dispatched as his "clerk of the works," assistant producer Bernard Gersten. In 1985 Gersten became executive producer of Lincoln Center's Vivian Beaumont Theatre. In 1975 he was Joe Papp's eyes on the progress of *A Chorus Line.*

Gersten's personality belied his mission. Mason said, "The one who reached out to us more than anyone [from the Shakespeare Festival] was Bernie Gersten, who always had a nice, kind, pleasant word, a smile. He was more human, he sort of touched us more. Joe kept himself at a distance."

But by the end of February, that was about to change.

More than a year of work and two grueling, exhilarating workshops had gone into the project, which still had no firm title. Bennett had poured heart and soul into his vision, and the dancers had drained their hearts and their bank accounts to take part in the great experiment. The second "Papp test," then, was like an opening night on Broadway. Like Broadway, the Newman was filled with the usual friends and supporters, plus the movers and shakers of show business, as Kelly Bishop remembers. But instead of facing aisles of critics, the "dancer project" faced one crucial reviewer: Joseph Papp of the New York Shakespeare Festival Public Theater. Its long-running meal tickets, *Hair* and *Two Gentlemen of Verona,* were long closed and none of the current season's plays had been hits. Several heavy hitters had done plays at the Public so far that season—David Rabe of *Sticks and Bones* had done a revival of *The Boom Boom Room* (retitled *In the Boom Boom Room,* which didn't help much); Michael Weller of *Moonchildren* had done *Fishing;* Thomas Babe had done *Kid Champion*—and none had landed with the expected ring indicating gold.

So everything was on the line. Including *A Chorus Line,* which, despite all the cuts, wound up entertaining Papp for a neat five and a half hours. "People cried for three hours," LuPone said, "including me because I'm *acting*. Right? Of course, right!"

Afterward, Papp came backstage and made a short speech about how wonderful they all were. The next day, Bennett assembled the nineteen cast members and the creative staff. They knew the show still needed work, but it had had that profound effect on the audience. They wanted to see how deep the cuts Papp would demand and how much more time he would give to finish them. Instead, Bishop recalls, Bennett said, " 'Papp doesn't want to give us any more money.' "

That was it. Thumbs down. In late February of 1975, Papp

made a decision not to allocate any more of the Public Theatre's straitened resources to Michael Bennett's "dancer project."

"I don't blame him as a producer," Bishop said. "It would have been a very bad investment. He didn't know who Michael Bennett was. I mean, he knew *who* he was; he didn't know *what* he was. And you have to know what he was in order to be able to believe in him."

"As a spectator," Priscilla Lopez said, "Joseph Papp was one of *A Chorus Line*'s great fans. As an artist, he was willing to see something through. As a businessman, he became cautious and couldn't see something through financially."

But it wasn't quite curtains yet.

Bennett and the other creators had an idea. Why not find a commercial producer and bring the show to the stage that way? Perhaps the Shuberts, who had indicated interest when Bennett and Papp had their confrontation over the Vivian Beaumont Theatre. The same magic that had lured dancers might also lure angels. Bennett knew that courting traditional backers and taking the show private was a big risk. Would a new producer want to pay Joe Papp a share of profits? A whole new contract would have to be negotiated with Actors Equity, and who would pay the dancers in the interim? If they weren't paid, how would they live? More would flee to other projects. More auditions would have to be held for replacements.

It's a testament to the level of commitment that when Bennett told the dancers " 'I'm going to have to scrounge around and see if I can get us some more money,' " as Bishop recalls, they immediately presumed that they would stay with the show wherever it went, as long as they were financially able to. "We all were rolling our eyeballs," Bishop said. "Wondering. Everyone was kind of calculating, I'm sure—we're all survivors—how much savings was left and when the rent was due."

Having lost everything concrete but still pinning their hopes on a vision, the dancers now were planning how to avoid starvation. And in this moment the heavens opened and an angel appeared.

Her name was LuEsther Mertz, powerful chairwoman of the New York Shakespeare Festival's Board of Directors, technically Papp's boss. A deeply committed philanthropist whose fortune and time had been lavished on the Shakespeare Festival, she had attended the "Papp test" and was familiar with Bennett's work. She told Papp that she, too, believed in the project and was willing to put her money where her mouth was. Mertz asked Bennett how long he thought it would take to do the show right. Bennett said seven weeks. Mertz asked Papp how much it would cost to stretch the workshop another seven weeks. Papp told her. Mertz wrote a check for that amount, knowing that the money was a donation, for which she would receive no quid pro quo but satisfaction. For years, the Playbill of *A Chorus Line* has contained a line describing the show as having been "made possible by a contribution from LuEsther Mertz," adding that "all income from this production is used to help support the Festival's work at the Public Theater," etc.

McKechnie said she believes that, in his heart of hearts, Joe Papp never really liked *A Chorus Line*. "He's a champion of the show now," she said, "but it's not his cup of tea. He does admire it. It did so much for the Public Theater. It doesn't help him now to keep it open but he's a dedicated passionate person, and he's determined. The show got rereviewed by Mel Gussow (in April 1989), and *Chorus Line* fared better than most of the more recent shows. That's Joe Papp's care."

But Bishop said, "Every time Joe Papp dons a *Chorus Line* outfit and takes all the credit, I sit there and remember the day it was LuEsther Mertz that got the show on. And so we had another seven weeks. You're talking double the time factor here. And it was those seven weeks that did it."

11.

Seven Weeks That Saved the Show (February–April 1975)

In the seven weeks that saved the show, all the effort that had been expended before now had to be redoubled. Having spent most of the time working on dances and characters, Bennett now had to go out and kill his biggest dragon: the fact that he had little experience as a director bringing home an original show that broke so much significant new ground. He and his "tribe" now had to solve advanced structural and thematic challenges, the weakest area for a writing staff that had never done a big musical before. They were learning the rules as they were rewriting them. The same was true for the dancers, who were constantly squeezed for fresh personal revelations.

"Most times," Kay Cole said, "you can perform up to, say, ninety-five percent; you save five percent in a secret part of you. But the nineteen people on that stage were definitely giving all of who they were at any given moment. Looking back on it, I say, 'Gosh, is that where I was? Is that who I am?' It's amazing. I consider myself a better person because of it. When you're in that kind of cathartic situation, you cannot help but discover who you are, who you are not, and who you want to be."

Seven more weeks of workshop meant seven more weeks of subsisting on only $100 a week for many of the dancers. To help keep the wolf from the door, several of the dancers got jobs in that spring's "Milliken Breakfast Show," which rehearsed and performed in the morning, as the title suggests.

Rick Mason said, "I remember when we were doing 'Milliken' and Michael's resentment to us. We went from eight-thirty or nine each morning until one, then got in a cab and went downtown, did rehearsals until dinner break at six, had an hour off, then went back and did the show, had notes until eleven or twelve—we were still changing at that time—then started all over the next morning. We did that for something like a month. I have bittersweet memories of it all, but I'm glad I did it. I felt fantastic being in a hit show. But I also felt we busted ass to make the show a hit."

More cutting was necessary, that was obvious. But there were lacks as well. The finale needed to be sharpened. The production had lots of "attitude," and the acid sort of humor that arises from attitude, but it needed more straight-out laughs. Other gaps needed to be filled, too.

In order to keep up the energy of the show and in order not to rupture the illusion of being at an actual audition, Bennett decided not to have an intermission and to run the show straight through from beginning to end. Nevertheless, the dancers thought of the part of the show up until Sammy Williams's Jewel Box speech as the first act. Though Act I was largely complete, the big montage needed a point of focus. But most of the remaining work was on Act II: the development of the Cassie-Zach confrontation, the knee injury scene, the resulting soul-searching by the dancers leading to the announcement of who gets the job and the finale.

When it came time to compose the knee injury scene, the dancers sat down with the writers and described what they had felt back on the last day of the first workshop when Bennett had feigned the injury and forced them to confront their own reactions. "We were given the actual situation and we remembered how we felt," Kuhlman said, "and that gave us a clear clue in terms of actors what we would feel at the moment. So much of what's in that [scene] was *us,* if not everything."

To focus the Act I dance montage, there was yet another gathering of the dancers, the final group interview session of *A Chorus Line*. The show explored the dancers' often traumatic childhoods and it occupied much of the remaining time dramatizing the struggles of adult life. What was needed was a bridge, a close look at the pains of adolescence for a dancer, a time of life when their *Red Shoes* fantasy is either played out or quelled completely.

Much as they had in the first tape session fourteen months earlier, the dancers, now as a finalized group, sat in a semicircle and told what it was like to go through puberty, focusing on ages twelve to fifteen.

"That's when everybody started freaking out, personally," Donna McKechnie said. "People started having nervous breakdowns because they would get up and it would be one story after another."

There was a peculiar intensity to this last rap session. Everyone had watched material come and go, and they had a good idea of what would work and what would be used. Unfortunately, it called for them to delve into some of the deepest places in their memories, and to find the keys to some securely padlocked memories. In an effort to add some humor to the show, some of the more embarrassing moments were elicited, usually of a sexual nature. Worrying about when breasts would grow, getting erections on various forms of public transportation, trying to figure out what a diaphragm is, a girl practicing kisses with her girlfriend so she'd do it right when the time came, a boy realizing he's homosexual as he's in the midst of feeling a girl's breasts.

And there were the usual high school social disaster stories: pimples, braces, being asked to the prom by the ugliest boy in school. They talked about idolizing movie stars, getting their first car, landing their first job, falling in love for the first bittersweet time—and most to the point, watching dance emerge as the most important thing of all.

As much as the show's concept of putting oneself "on the line" is universal, this last-minute addition to the score evokes some of the strongest audience identification. No matter what walk of life an audience member comes from, they cannot help but see a little of themselves in the song that emerged from this talk, "Hello Twelve, Hello Thirteen, Hello Love."

"All that background was fabulous for the show," McKechnie said. "That's why the original cast could never really be replaced. Not just because of us individuals but because sharing all of that background enriched our performances."

Nancy Lane said the choreography in "Hello Twelve" was her favorite in the show. "It was fun dancing," she said. "That opening combination, we did that more than Carter has pills. It was a wonderful break-out free dance time. We called it the Monster Montage. It was wonderful to watch Michael and Baayork teach it to us."

Lane's voice can be heard on the recording answering Percassi, who sings "Changes, oh . . ." Lane sings "Down below," and Lopez sings "Up above." She also calls out, "Robert Goulet, Robert Goulet, my God, Robert Goulet" and "Bob Goulet out, Steve McQueen in." She said that after the show opened, Goulet made a point of visiting her backstage.

Kay Cole said that Ed Kleban told her a portion of the song was inspired directly by something she had mentioned to him in passing. "I was told by Ed Kleban that a small Irish ditty came into his head when I told him my mother was half Irish. He thought I should sing it."

The solo consists of Cole's Maggie character crooning a song of filial love from "across the blue sea" while the rest of the dancers voice memories of their own parents.

In these final months, the dancers' regimen became intense. The show's problems were arrayed before them like targets in a shooting gallery. Once they'd shot one down, they'd quickly take aim at the next.

A workable finale had to be found. The original idea had been a Busby Berkeley vision with grand pianos. Having junked that as too campy, Bennett and the writers began groping for a more conceptual finale for the show. Several were tried and discarded.

Lopez recalls that at one point "we were going to get someone from the audience and make her a star. Michael was going to show how it was really the chorus people, killing themselves behind the star, that make the star. He was going to have us bring up old ladies from the audience and have us all be wonderful in back of her, making her look like a million dollars. At that point that was supposed to be how the show would end. I remember putting a lot of work into that."

The show still contains the material that was to be the original finale of *A Chorus Line*. It is the song "One," which now also serves quite a different dramatic purpose.

McKechnie said the first part of the song they heard was the famous *Chorus Line* vamp, which was introduced at an orchestra read-through in the library of the Public Theater. "The vamp said everything," McKechnie said. "It's Las Vegas, but dissonant, not quite major or minor. It hits you in the solar plexus. It's a little jaded or dissonant, melancholy. The device of that being played at the back [of the action] was very powerful for Michael."

That vamp would lead to "One," in which the chorus would transform an audience member, chosen at random each night, into a star. "This was an interesting idea," McKechnie said, "but in commercial theater, he knew this couldn't hold up. The show was so precise, we needed the preciseness to communicate the message. Also, we found that we didn't need to make Everyman the One. Every person on that line was the One."

In addition to backing curtain calls, the song is introduced earlier, as a peek inside the heads of the dancers, to reveal their intense concentration while dancing. For the song, Bennett and Avian contrived some of the most demanding choreography of the show.

Nancy Lane said, "They were really very strict about us being in line and us mimicking each other so that Cassie would stand out when we first do 'One.' Boy, that was a pain! We hated that number. It was like being in boarding school. 'You vill shtep on ze line togezer!' It's not the kind of number that's easy to keep doing."

She remembers sitting with Hamlisch and Kleban in an effort to coordinate the impressionistic lyrics with the complex steps. "The dreamy part was a bitch," she said. "A lot of these people were just dancers. They didn't have any idea of madrigal singing or round singing, which was what it was. Kay Cole, the people with musical background, they got the hang of it. For the rest it was difficult to get the words and the rhythm and then to get to dance it—oy oy oy, that was another five hours."

Once "One" acquired a life of its own, gradually there emerged the finale as it's now played. It evolved from the idea that the show starts as an audition and ought to end as one. The dancers go into their final lineup and Zach announces which of the dancers got the job. To maintain tension and keep his dancers on their toes, Bennett arranged things so Zach would pick different dancers each night. At a given run-through, the dancers never knew for sure which of them would be picked that night. Did it have something to do with how well they had performed that night? Many of them suspected so, and were constantly pumping themselves for that little extra bit that would put them over the top. Which was the way Bennett wanted it.

"There was no finale [with the dancers reappearing in gold costumes for bows] either," Bishop said. "What you'd get after that was the last slow fade-out on 'Rehearsals start September 22nd . . .' and people's reactions, and the house would go to black. The house lights would come up and there would be an empty stage with a white line on it. It was the most incredibly magical, overwhelming experience. It was like, 'They weren't there when I walked into the theater, and they're not there now.' I innately knew the reaction was—'Gasp!'—it was like we disappeared."

Watching the changes fall into place authoritatively, Percassi said, "I had only good feelings about it because all the people involved were so good. How could this show miss? I tend to be a bit of a Pollyanna so you really can't take that as truth. It's hard to think of the bad things now, which I'm sure were there. I just remember being scared all the time. It was very exciting. We were rehearsing an awful lot."

Despite the boot camp schedule and the constant changes to be memorized, Wayne Cilento said, "I was really cool all the way up until around three or four weeks before we opened when Michael started juggling me around. That's when I had the breakdowns because I was very set and then right before we opened I was still rehearsing numbers, doing numbers, getting numbers cut, switching monologues, that's when I fell apart."

The show was still short on laughs, and in those days as in these, when your show is feeling queasy just before opening, you need to fetch what's known as a "show doctor." And by virtue of his work on *Promises, Promises* and *God's Favorite,* Bennett had a pipeline to Broadway's chief surgeon, Neil "Doc" Simon.

Simon spent the next several weeks ducking in and out of rehearsals. When the cast members got notes for script changes, they tended to be gags in a vein familiar to anyone who has seen a Simon play, from *The Odd Couple* through *Brighton Beach Memoirs* to *Rumors.*

Simon's arrival signified a change in the atmosphere. Things suddenly were jelling, becoming concrete. Rumors passed through the company that a production was now firmly planned, that public performances might start as soon as a couple of weeks. It took away some of the pressure, the uncertainty pressure. But added new, more traditional pressures, getting it all to fall together correctly. From here on, the dancers started referring to the workshop sessions as "rehearsals."

Thommie Walsh recalls, "It seemed we spent weeks doing things where the expression 'Don't judge the material' came about. That was thrown at us all the time. We were very close to finishing the show and now we had to make it better. It was a very difficult time. We were so close. Michael, of course, felt our commitment or lack of commitment every day. We were exhausted. He felt every goose pimple on us; our temperature rising and falling."

Genuine creative acts are rare. When one comes along, it's usually born in protracted and painful labor. The dancers and writers of *A Chorus Line* had now reached that agony of creation. The contractions were coming faster.

"I was so tired and busy trying to remember the new things that were being thrown at us every day, the changes," Nancy Lane said. "I had no time to think of anything else. When I got home at night I would just eat dinner and go to sleep. I had no idea, it's like you can't see the forest for the trees when you're in something. You're so involved you can't really see the power of it. It wasn't until we were on Broadway I think that I finally realized that this was what I had worked for. It was great then, it took me that long. When we were downtown I thought we had a fun show . . . but nothing so earth-shattering."

Clive Wilson said, "It was somewhat like being in a snake pit when . . . they were rehearsing us too much. But at that point I would have rehearsed twenty-five hours a day. There wasn't anything to take home to study but I took the excitement, the emotion of it, home. It became very much a part of my life. In fact so much so that it became all-consuming and I had to stop painting, stop going to classes. My life definitely was enormously enhanced by the fact that this was happening."

They entered what might be described as a heightened state of reality. For the Buddhists, it was one of their pure moments when they were just *acting* on a situation instead of analyzing it. Normal attachments seemed to fade temporarily. "I had no personal life," Ron Dennis said, "just dates here and there. You'd do the show, go out and have dinner, meet some people, and go home. But there were no romances. It went twenty-four hours."

Bank accounts were depleted, muscles were sore, and nerves were frayed. "I wanted to strangle Baayork at times but I loved her, too," Lopez said. "She used to drive me crazy with her emergency rehearsal calls. As Equity deputy I would explain she couldn't call rehearsals except in emergencies and everything was turning into an emergency."

Lopez recalls getting a little clenched herself. "Things straightened out until almost preview time," she said. "I have 'What I Did for Love' on preview tapes and I was still singing it wrong. One day we're at rehearsal and Ed Kleban says to me, 'Priscilla, you have to get those notes right,' and I said I was really trying.

"He said that if I was a real professional I would just do it.

"I told him that I *was* a professional and that I wasn't doing it wrong deliberately. No one had ever taught me the song. I listened to it on the P.A. system and whatever I learned I learned on my own the wrong way and now it's hard to do it the right way.

"He said that Marvin's mother knew every note he had ever written and she was going to be very upset when she heard me singing these wrong notes.

"So I told him to get Marvin's mother to sing the damn song. After that he wouldn't talk to me anymore. And then I had that breakdown for one day. I couldn't get the song right and I left the stage crying. People kept asking me if I was all right and to come back onstage and I went back. I forget who told me but Marvin said, 'The rock has fallen.' "

The incident helped cement a growing friendship between Lopez and Bishop. "Neither one of us had a lot of girlfriends," Bishop said. "So for the two of us to find another female to relate to . . . I remember doing something on one of her nervous breakdown days that I had never done with another woman that I had always wanted to do but which I was too repressed to do. I remember she had this freak-out moment downtown over 'What I Did for Love.' She just got very upset, she was having trouble with a note, everybody was very aware of it, and she just went, 'Oh no,' and started to cry. And the whole group kind of moved towards her. I put my arm around her and just took her off in a corner. We all went off in the corner together. We would do things like that. We would stop rehearsal. If someone had a problem, rehearsal would stop. There was a point where he couldn't control us anymore."

Although Bennett had a rule against drugs, it was the 1970s. It was too important to be balanced and coordinated on a minute-by-minute basis for anyone to abuse anything seriously. They wouldn't have been able to do their jobs. Bennett was not above drinking martinis at lunch, and some of the other dancers were not above celebrating their impending hit with a *hit*. Cocaine still hadn't become the tidal wave it was in the early 1980s, and if anything, the dancers were pumped up enough. Quaaludes and, as the script attests, Valium, were the drugs of choice, if any.

"All this dope stuff was happening under my nose and I didn't know any of it was going on," Nancy Lane said. "I was so into performing and doing this show and being good and being accepted that I had no idea. And to find out years later that just about everybody was taking something [to give them the stamina] to do the show! They were so tired from rehearsing during the day and performing at night. I was just floored."

An early draft of the script contains a scene in which Greg [Stuart] passes around a joint, but that disappeared about the same time the fight scene was cut.

There are no supermarket tabloid stories to report here. No one overdosed, no one became incapacitated. And not all their escapes were sinister or illegal.

Garland found the outlet for emotions in chanting or the catharsis of tears. "I don't know that I did a lot of crying on my own," she said. "I think I fought that. I thought it was a weakness. I'm sure I did but I think I cried more secretly than I did in front of everybody. I know I was not funny. I did have the facility to bring humor into a conversation but I know I was not one bit funny during that workshop. I think that my part was small because I didn't contribute. I didn't resent it, not at the time, because I almost didn't have it."

For her tension-easer, Baayork Lee said, "Wayne and I kept a bottle of peach brandy in our dressing room. He would shake so and I would give him a slug and then I would take a slug to keep calm. I told Wayne that we would become a couple of lushes. We'd be so scared, we'd hold each other's hand to keep from shaking. He'd be so nervous, we didn't even know what we had done onstage. The innocence of it all, the purity and the innocence of it all, that's what made this show."

Though her Connie role had been substantially diminished, Lee still had to deliver a performance while executing dance captain duties. It was all she could do to develop a performance and keep up with the technical demands of both jobs. "I would have Wayne Cilento hum my note five minutes before the note came," Lee said, "so that I could get the note because I could not hear it. Marvin would say, 'Now Rick sings hmmmmm,' you know like two minutes into his monologue [which precedes her singing] and so he had ten minutes to go and I have Wayne next to me humming the note."

Just as the dancers were making their maximum sacrifices, baring innermost selves, Bennett, too, found himself going through some painful self-realization. The fictional relationship of Cassie and Zach was the last major section of text to be written for *A Chorus Line*. Bennett held off work on it as long as possible.

For LuPone, who had to embody this projection of Bennett's self, "the experience of *ACL* I've had to live with and suffer for years was not an enlightening experience for me. Not a benevolent, wonderful, humanistic, exciting, thrilling experience—none of that.

"Anybody who was on the Line cannot understand my point of view because the show was about the Line, ultimately. I wanted to be part of something, and when I got Zach, all of a sudden I was sitting in the back of the house and he [Bennett] sat between me and the group onstage. From that moment on I was no longer a part of something. I was divorced from the kinetic energy, the camaraderie being created in terms of an ensemble."

Barry Bostwick had resigned over Zach's lack of sympathy. LuPone now found that he had inherited that problem along with the role.

"I remember only two rehearsals of the Zach-Cassie scene. That's as much acting work as we did. I really learned how to play the show on its feet. I didn't learn it in rehearsals and I didn't learn it in previews.

"We rehearsed Zach-Cassie only when there was nobody else around. I think he was frightened to direct, and also, as it proved ultimately, to put his own life on the line. But that's what the play is about and what makes it so dramatic and so exciting.

"But I didn't realize at the time what was going on. I would say things like, 'You know, this guy Zach must be stupid. For him to do this is ridiculous. This guy's an asshole. No man in his right mind would do this to a woman.'

"And of course Michael would shut up and Donna would go 'flub-flub flub-flub,' and I'd sit there looking at these two numb-nuts thinking, 'What's going on here? Let's work this play.' And I never realized they were hooked into each other. I never got it. I was too absorbed in this man, Zach. Under no circumstance did it occur to me that Zach *was* Michael Bennett. He'd get angry with me and I never understood why."

Recalling the same conflict, McKechnie said, "This may have been the most unhappy part for me. As the show evolved, I was having a hard time finding my character. I was tired all the time. It was a miserable time. We were still fixing and changing the show and performing long days and my character hadn't arrived yet."

McKechnie said that the Cassie character was largely Kirkwood's creation, working with both her and with Bennett. "Cassie was the hardest and most fictionalized character," McKechnie said. "She served as a catalyst to say things Michael wanted to say in the play. He did not know this when he first set out. 'We've got to find a way to get Zach involved. We've got to find a number for Donna.' "

Cassie originally had a long monologue based on something that had happened in McKechnie's own life, when she was in California and her career seemed to have hit the doldrums. She was vacuuming her apartment one day with the television on, and heard her name mentioned as the answer to a question on a game show. It was a funny monologue, but it did not sufficiently dramatize the Cassie-Zach situation. For weeks, the character stubbornly refused to come alive. "He never gave up on me," McKechnie said of Bennett. "A weaker director would have eliminated me. But because he was so strongly identified with Zach, he was determined to fix it. Though Kirkwood wrote long dramatic dialogues and monologues for Cassie, ultimately Bennett decided to cut most of them. "He went back to what was most important," she said, "which was that line."

Nevertheless, she said, "I started feeling the tensions mount and the sibling rivalry and the competitive nature. I'm not saying that I did anything to help it. It was very painful for me to feel part of a special group like that and yet not part of it. There was a group of people that I thought would be more chummy because we had similar backgrounds. But the people I ended up feeling friendly toward were the new people, people I didn't know.

"The thing with LuPone . . . there was a lot of improvisational work done on it where Michael would sit with LuPone and I would banter back and forth and then Nicholas would come in with some dialogue and then we'd start with that dialogue and maybe color it."

Thommie Walsh remembers the conflict less placidly. "Zach and Cassie would be screaming at one another," Walsh said, "and we'd be rehearsing the 'One' dance step, going 'bounce and-a bounce and-a bounce . . .' We would be doing that for five hours. Of course, I didn't understand their problems at that time."

"Michael and I almost came to blows on it," LuPone said. "I'd say, 'All right what do you want?' and I gave him that. It got to a point where he was yelling at me all the time. I said to myself, 'If this is the way the man directs, I don't want to be here.' So I quit. Quit twice. And again, I was manipulated back. He filled me with talk of my artistic mission and there I was, back on the stage again. Against my better judgment. Against what was becoming a horrific, horrific experience for me as an artist, as a man and ultimately as an actor-dancer.

"Then it would be the end of rehearsal and Donna, Bob, and

Michael would go have a drink. We'd talk about politics, sex, women, men . . . nothing that ever had to do with the scene and everything that had to do with the scene."

LuPone had made friends with Ron Kuhlman, the two of them sharing an interest in sports. Kuhlman recalls, "LuPone made me crazy sometimes once we got to know each other. He would hurt from different experiences with Michael and Donna, so we'd talk. I'd have to throw him around a little bit and beat him at handball and stuff like that."

As far as most of the other dancers were concerned, LuPone, McKechnie, and the rest of the Big Six had nothing to complain about. The other thirteen felt they were just as talented, but in the final show they would be written off, so to speak, and left with minor supporting roles.

"I started alienating myself from a lot of the kids because I was upset," Rick Mason said. "I was pissed at them for getting songs and lines. They were happy and having a great time because they were getting good recognition. I was pissed at Wayne, I was pissed at Thommie, I was pissed at Kelly. I remember a party we had for LuEsther Mertz at the St. Moritz. She gave us that dinner and there was dancing on the floor, just free dancing. I was doing some really fun stuff with some black lady who was there. We were dancing sort of hot. All of a sudden Michael gets up and literally we became challenging, like we were trying to outdo each other. I don't think we realized it at the time but subconsciously I think I was trying to show Michael what I could do without his direction, and what he may have missed. I think Michael was determined not to let this young kid outdance him."

But despite the feeling that he was being shortchanged for his talent, Mason said, "I was determined to become a better person for it. I wasn't going to let the bad taste stay in my mouth. I was doing it for Michael because he was giving me an opportunity to create a show, which I would not ordinarily have had. I was doing it for myself and my family, the people I knew cared for me and gave me support. I wanted to be in a Broadway show that I helped create. I wanted to be in an original cast. As minor as it was, I was creating a role. I was going to do the best I could. You don't want to rock the boat, but we are ego people, we live off ego in many ways, and this was affecting my ego. But I had to stay there and bite my tongue—yet it was eating me up."

Thommie Walsh said, "Just before I went on one night, Bob Avian grabbed me and dragged me to the men's room and screamed, 'Do you all think you're Katharine Hepburns? What's going on with all of you? Have you all lost your minds?' Cheering me up and everything."

"During rehearsals," Kuhlman recalled, "things were getting tense and one day Wayne Cilento comes up and says, 'I gotta get something off my chest.'

"Everybody is very tense by this time and we all inwardly groaned. Everybody was flying off the handle, there's arguments about this and that, dumb arguments.

"And then Wayne announced, 'Cathy and I are going to have a baby!'

"And everyone just kind of exploded with joy and suddenly it was like a little friendly gathering. I knew then that we were all tied together in this bond."

Throughout March as the really deep cuts were made, the dancers got to see what their characters would look like in more or less their final form. The dancers with larger roles tried to explore their characters and find out as much about them as possible. For the dancers with only a fragment of a character left, they tried to invest that fragment with as much humanity as possible to help make it live on the stage.

"I always wanted more while the roles were being created," Nancy Lane said telling the story of Bebe being an ugly duckling in "At the Ballet" and then becoming part of the ensemble. "I wanted to prove that I could do more. I never had the chance to do that in that company. But I never felt cheated."

Michel Stuart found comfort in the fact that "I felt I was part of this palette of colors. Some needed to be brighter and fuller, and they used more of that color to establish what needed to be done to make a theatrical event possible. Being homosexual for starters is one whole broad color. Now, Sammy's character said a lot about that, but not enough certainly. The colors I could have added to that could have been fun and could have been interesting and could have possibly been equally inspiring as what he did.

"But the balance of it might not have been correct either unless there had been something between Sammy and myself that we wanted to say together. No one thought of developing that area in the piece any further than the very bold stroke of Sammy's monologue and who he was. They were difficult choices to make because we didn't play many scenes with one another, so in order to say things, to contribute things, they either had to be in a monologue or you had to be speaking to Zach. Had it been a different kind of a book show I think my character could have been used within the context of that piece.

"I don't feel cheated by the show's structure or how big or little the role of Gregory Gardner was," Stuart said. "Had my part been enlarged or had I had something more, a relevant song, it would have been a different show. I don't think it would have been necessary to the show that was being made. If I had in fact been a producer at that time and had two or three or even one Broadway show and had gone back there to get a job in the chorus, if that had been my story that would have been interesting. But what we did there was life onstage exaggerated to make it theatrical and not even exaggerated too much."

Aside from singing "Gimme the Ball," which finally wound up as part of "Hello Twelve, Hello Thirteen, Hello Love" in the Act I montage, Ron Dennis's only other big moment comes in the opening sequence when his character, Richie, gets overly excited and begins executing higher and higher leaps until finally he springs straight into Zach's arms.

"I approached the show as an acting challenge," Dennis said, "not as a singing/dancing job about gypsies. I don't think I ever thought about wanting more. I wish the number had been better. It was more or less like an audition piece for me, if that makes any sense. On the other hand, meeting people made me realize how inconsequential the part was. I've met so many people who say they saw the original company and ask me what part I did. I used to get so furious at that. I would get nasty and ask them if they remembered 'Gimme the Ball' and they were so surprised to find out it was me. I was shocked that people were so unobservant.

"It happened to other members of the show, too. The subsidiary characters were not being delved into enough for people to get a sense about Baayork as a very short Oriental or me as a black. They got that Priscilla was Puerto Rican, that Sammy was gay, that Donna was a soon-to-be star making a comeback, Sheila was a bitch—and Richie was a nonentity. He was there, but what character was he, was he black? Now I laugh at it, but I used to get infuriated. Invariably it was someone white; never a black person. Black people knew."

Cilento said he believes more of the Mike Costa role would have been kept if Bennett had worked with him more. "I didn't know what I was doing as a professional," Cilento said. "I was doing what I do, then going back and not having it work the second time around. A spotlight joke worked once, but I couldn't re-create it. So Michael gave me line readings to try and get it. But I didn't want to do it the way he said it. I wanted to do it the way *I* said it, the way I *meant* it. I think that's what started me feeling insecure and made me feel like I wasn't getting a fair shot."

In the end, Cilento said, "I think Mike Costa is Wayne Cilento and I think that the relationship is Wayne and Michael. That arrogant little guy giving the director lip all the time was truly me and that was truly our relationship."

Though the actors with the smaller roles felt that attention was being lavished on the Big Six, Lopez, who had two solos, reports, "most of the time I felt that Michael left me on my own while creating Morales. The best thing he ever said to me during the whole run—it was after we had been open for a while—was that we had done this whole project in a *now* frame of reference and we were used to working what we felt at that moment. But now we've done the show and Priscilla is still doing what she feels at that moment. Michael said to me, 'You know, you're growing as a human being and you're changing a lot. But remember that Diana Morales *cannot change*.'

"It was the first time that I realized Diana Morales and I were two different things. Up until then, we were one. So the show got harder to do because it wasn't about *now*."

With the first preview on the horizon, now scheduled for mid April, LuPone became more frustrated because Bennett's laissez-faire attitude was leaving him vulnerable. "I tried to create a reality for Zach," he said. "It was always by insinuation, by implication, never by words, never by action—outside of maybe yelling, screaming, ownership, power, control—all the things that Michael represented. Then there was the one moment of compassion when I came up and touched Sammy. But it was the only time Zach was in a sense a human being or a being with more dimensions beyond his own specific need to get the show on."

It was even harder for Thommie Walsh to crystallize the role of Robert Charles Joseph Henry Mills III, a.k.a. Bobby. "My material was integrated with Connie's story and Richie's story and Judy's story and Val's story," he said. But Walsh, too, had a consolation: "I was eternally grateful for that wonderful position with two women playing on either side of me. It was a very powerful position he blessed me with. I had Donna and Kelly on one side of me and I had Nancy and Trish on the other side of me, just one off center.

"I was sometimes terribly jealous and burnt that Wayne was singing and dancing and my thing was a monologue. Once I started feeling my oats and knew my lines, then it became like that first night at the tape sessions. I had a middle and an end in my character and I made that happen. So I was basically happy with my moment."

Nevertheless, he said, "I think that all the men got cheated in that show. The leading man was in a black hole all night and the second character was a transvestite. The other men had about two lines and the girls had the show-stopping numbers. Michael's directing talents leaned toward women; he does that so beautifully."

Both the women and the men were consulted about the final major decision on the show: what to call it. The title had been delayed long enough, and now it was time to start advertising. A lot of titles had been suggested throughout the workshop: *Dancers, Dancing, Backstage, Step by Step,* and others. But for most of the second workshop, the title most often discussed was the succinct, minimalist *Chorus Line.*

Bishop recalls, "I remember when Michael said, 'It's going to be called . . . A *Chorus Line.*'

"We all liked the *Chorus Line* concept. But we said, 'Not A *Chorus Line,* just *Chorus Line.*' We thought it was stronger, and it *is* stronger.

"He went, 'No, no, no. A *Chorus Line.* I'll tell you why—'

"But everyone's going, 'Ugh! No, no, no!' This group was

pretty rowdy by then, I mean we were pretty full of ourselves. We said, 'Why A *Chorus Line*?'

"He said, '*Chorus Line* is better but A *Chorus Line* will be the first in the ABCs' [theatrical slang for the alphabetical directories of shows in New York daily newspapers containing ticket information; so named for the outsized first letter of each show]! One of the papers, *New York* magazine or something, listed it under C. But he was right about *The New York Times*—it was first in the ABCs and that's what he wanted."

The last-minute nature of the show's falling together is reflected in the fact that there was very little press about the show before it opened. The first advertisement did not appear in *The New York Times* until April 6, ten days before the first preview.

With the title, advertising, and other components falling into place, the full scope of the production finally began to dawn on the dancers, who had seen it only in its raw, stripped-down form.

"I thought this show would be just a local jive," Percassi said. "I told my friends in the theater to come and see it just to see what is done at the [Public] theater because so many of them didn't know about it. Well, I knew something was cooking when we had a nineteen-piece orchestra setting up in the lumber room. That's the first time I realized they actually were going to mount this thing as best as they could. I had seen Tharon and Robin and Theoni around, but it didn't hit me until I saw all those musicians. I knew then that it was going to be a big deal."

The three people Percassi names are the rest of the show's technical creative team: lighting designer Tharon Musser, set designer Robin Wagner, and costume designer Theoni V. Aldredge.

It was with the last named that the dancers now became closely involved. Born in Greece, Aldredge had been principal designer of the New York Shakespeare Festival for fifteen years. She had won Drama Desk, Variety Drama Critics, and Maharam awards for her costumes, and had won an Oscar for *The Great Gatsby*. In *A Chorus Line* she was being asked to do for costumes what the writers had done for a libretto: draw upon the dancers.

For the dancers these were simply work clothes. The costumes they wore in Broadway shows usually were far glitzier and more gaudily ornamented. Their work clothes—tights, leotards, trunks, clingy T-shirts—allowed them free movement, but also flattered their healthy, muscular bodies. After the show opened, this would not escape the notice of clothing designers. As the dancers were being measured and fitted, there was no way they could know they were launching one of the biggest clothing fads of the late 1970s and 1980s. The success of *A Chorus Line* would generate and ride a wave of dance mania. Coinciding with the explosion of interest in health food, jogging, and aerobic exercise, the body-hugging form-fitting *Chorus Line* costumes can be credited with helping inspire the next decade of fitness wear.

"Theoni sat in for about a week or two to see how we were dressed when we came in," Lopez said. "Michael had given us this big speech about how he wanted these costumes to come out of us, that Theoni would be doing them and she wanted to see how we dressed. Then we could talk to her if we had any particular desires. When I got around to talking to Theoni, I said I have to have a turtleneck and a shirt over the turtleneck and pants and sneakers and socks. I never mentioned colors. I was very into Katharine Hepburn at the time and that was the kind of thing she wears. I originally started out wearing my pants. I wore them for about two performances and then Michael said, 'No pants. I want to see legs, legs, legs.' And after that I didn't wear pants anymore."

From Renee Baughman, Aldredge created perhaps the show's cleanest, simplest women's look, a simple burgundy leotard and tights. The same is true for Dennis, tight dance pants and a tank top muscle shirt, though he said he hated the pea-green color and was angry that a simple change could not be made to accommodate him.

For Patricia Garland, Aldredge resurrected square-neck leotards, which had been discontinued. Donna McKechnie liked the color red and liked the way she looked in dance skirts, so Aldredge combined those two points into a costume. Cilento's classically simple ensemble of boots, dance pants, and collared short-sleeved shirt translated into his costume virtually without change.

Williams, who had been stung by Bennett's admonition that he was too effeminate, had taken Lee's advice to butch up his image. "I would wear army fatigues because I figured it would make me look more masculine," he said. "And I get cold real fast so I always had a jacket with me. One day I was asked what I wanted to wear for the show and I said, 'What I've got on, this is it.' I had on fatigues, polo shirt, and jacket, plus my bag and sneaks. It was comfortable."

Thommie Walsh's costume was a statement of personal style. "I was always wearing my little sweaters and my scarves," he said. "I was wearing scarves during this show called *Music! Music!* [for which Aldredge had done costumes] and Theoni had picked up on [the fact that] a scarf and sweater was definitely a signature of mine. I felt comfortable because I didn't feel skinny. I wasn't wearing just a leotard and tights; I had a little bit of armor. It had a lot do do with my character, that costume did. It was a good costume."

Clive Wilson found numerological significance in his outfit. "Theoni picked up on what we were wearing to rehearsal. There was a particular shirt that I wore more than any other, a green tank top athletic shirt with white piping, and it had a number on it. The costume she came up with has the number seventeen on it, which is my birthdate. At the time I was living on the seventeenth floor, and other things since then have had to do with that number. When I bought my house in L.A., the address was eight five three one and I thought, 'Hmmm, those numbers add up to seventeen.' At the time, I thought it was just another reason why I should be there, there was a rightness about it."

Not everyone was that happy. Besides Dennis's objection to the color of his costume, Blair was unhappy that simply because she sometimes wore sneakers to rehearsal, her character had to dance in the arch-crushing shoes forever.

Kelly Bishop made the mistake of wearing a too-small leotard to the workshop one day when all her better ones were in the laundry. She hated this particular leotard because it was so revealing and because she believed it put ten pounds on her. Bennett caught sight of it and told her he wanted her to wear it as her costume. Bishop protested, thinking it was because Bennett wanted Sheila to look as brazen as possible. But Bennett explained to her that in the "At the Ballet" sequence, it made her look like a naked, vulnerable child. After that explanation, Bishop capitulated, though she said every Sheila after her has hated the costume just as much.

Nancy Lane objected the loudest to Bennett's no-pants rule for women. "I'm bowlegged," she said. "They put me in tights and heels which was awful because I had a real bad back, so standing in heels for two hours did not appeal to me. She claimed that they wanted costumes that we would feel comfortable dancing in. But I hated my costume and every time I tried to tell somebody they'd tell me how fantastic my costume was. What's so great about a T-shirt and briefs and tights? So I just stayed in it and—who cared? I was working in a fabulous show. After a while it didn't bother me."

Bennett enforced the no-pants rule for all the women but Baayork Lee. Lee felt more comfortable in dance pants, and out of deference to their long friendship, Bennett relented in her case. Eight years later, when Bennett threw a gala to mark the show's achieving the longest run for a Broadway musical, the New York Shakespeare Festival published a scroll-like poster six feet tall showing the twenty-six chorus lines that had performed the show in that time. With rare exception, every Connie after Lee wore tights instead of pants.

As the off-Broadway opening loomed, the contractual status of the dancers had to change, in accordance with union rules. They had signed contracts calling for each to get a raise to $150 per week, and they were told that the terms were being drawn up in accordance with a principle of "favored nations," meaning that none would be given more than any other. It allowed that since all of them were in an ensemble show, all would be listed alphabetically in the program, there would be no individual dressing rooms, and most important, all would earn the same amount of money. It was a provision that would come back to haunt them as the show progressed.

"I have since come to learn that 'favored nations' is a lot of baloney," Priscilla Lopez said. "The truth is that, yes, you sign a favored nations contract and you get that salary, but it doesn't mean they can't give you more on top of it. But at the time of the dispute I was still in loveland with Michael Bennett." Responsibility for looking after the dancers' union rights had been shouldered by Lopez when she agreed to serve as the company's union deputy. "I was at a point in my therapy where I thought it was time for me to learn to assert myself in the world," she said, "and I thought this was a wonderful opportunity to try it out. What could go wrong, how heavy could it get? So now I'm wearing my Equity deputy badge and we had to sign those contracts.

"All of a sudden there was some kind of rift going on in the dressing room with Pam Blair throwing things and cursing. She was running on about her agent telling her that Donna was getting a lot more than the rest of us."

On her way to ask Bennett if the charge was true, Lopez ran into associate producer Bernard Gersten. "Bernie walks in and we hit him with it: 'Bernie, is it true that Donna's going to be making more money than the rest of us?' And he tells us that it was true. Well, that was all we had to hear! Everyone had something else to say about trust and love projects and favored nations and trust me, trust me!

"I said I wanted to talk to Michael about it. I was sooo brave as the Equity deputy. Michael stayed in his room for about three hours because he didn't want to face us. Finally, the King comes out and it's my job to talk.

"Michael said he heard there seemed to be some problem.

"I said, 'Yes there is, because when we started this project it was a project of love and trust and honesty and equality. That's why we're doing it and that's what you had led us to believe.' I told him we'd all been working in good faith and had been told that we had 'favored nations' contracts and now we learned it was not so. Donna was making more money than the rest of us. And if it was true how could we all go on knowing it wasn't really a project of honesty and one for all?

"Silence! Michael got up and walked back into his room and closed the door. Now I was terrified. It was very weird how I felt. Part of me was doing the Equity deputy role and I was fearless at that. I was doing exactly what I had taken the job for, so I could get the courage to do this kind of thing, speak up when you need to speak up. As the deputy I could do that. Priscilla couldn't.

"But then he called me into his room and told me that he just wanted me to know that he understood why I was saying these things to him. That it was my job as deputy and that's okay. That surprised me. I didn't expect that. I expected to be punished for it, to be shunned."

From McKechnie's point of view, the other dancers were not

giving her her due. "I felt a tension when the favored nations dispute happened because at this point I was Michael's friend and it wasn't what it appeared to be, it really wasn't. The times we spent together were about the show and how to solve the problems and I was very supportive. I think he felt very comfortable with me. He needed the support. It was difficult for people to take, but I couldn't help it. I had felt the tension before so it was no shock about how these people felt divided. Michael came to me and said, 'It's not fair that you get what everybody else is getting because it wasn't our arrangement and your contribution, what you've done with the show and what you've done in the past, has been greater.' The one thing I felt that people overlooked was the fact that I had already established myself to some degree and I had a certain credibility."

Thommie Walsh said, "It brought us all back to knowing that this was a job, this was show business. This was not a fantasy world where we were creating something special that would be untouched by human hands and would live on forever. That made it different then. We knew that it was different."

Ron Dennis agreed. "That was the beginning of the total disintegration of the team spirit as far as I was concerned. You realized that along the line somebody wasn't leveling. The money never got settled. I think it was dirty business practice even if they were trying to build up the confidence of whomever they were trying to make into stars."

Michel Stuart felt differently. "None of that affected me very much," he said. "I was doing this show because I believed that we were going to make something wonderful. Led by Michael Bennett we were going to be doing something that was worthwhile and hot and fabulous and beautiful. Not too many people understood it because they were into the nuts and bolts of a career, I was looking at something much larger than that. I didn't want to be involved in those vibrations and I wasn't."

"My perspective on the favored nations dispute and all of that was just so different," Clive Wilson said. "I was so grateful to be there that I would have paid them."

There was nothing to be done. The dancers had the option of walking away from the project, which they were unwilling to do after they had expended so much effort. Concerted action was considered, but no one could be sure if the line would hold firm, arms linked. It was a capitulation many of them would come to regret.

Finances brought discord in another way as well. Despite the experiences of those in the first workshop, the new dancers in the second workshop also signed contracts surrendering the rights to material used in the show for the sum of one dollar. There was a difference, outlined by Ron Dennis. Because they were not at the original tape sessions, they got to share a fraction of Bennett's own royalties only as long as they stayed with the show.

"We believed that if we didn't sign it, we wouldn't be in the show," Dennis said. "We were dumb enough to think our jobs were in jeopardy. We should have dared them to fire all of us. But when you have a job and you're new, you think you won't have this job or get another one. At that point I had put in all my hard work. I thought, 'Let's not be petty about it, let's go ahead and sign the paper. They are, after all, giving us one half of one percent to divide among us and that's more than anybody's ever gotten as a dancer. We should all be so grateful.' Little did I know I was stupid, as were the other five people [Lane, Percassi, Cole, Stuart, and Wilson] who signed our total lives away as far as residuals go. We didn't realize that two years down the line we wouldn't be in the show, and no more money would be coming to us. Everyone thinks I'm raking in millions today.

"It was only when I got out of the show and Sammy would call and say that he got a check that I started getting angrier and angrier," Dennis continued. "Nancy Lane and Kay were talking about it with me. There were people who had never done the show who, just because they had their life story written about in the show, were getting money that I should have been getting. I know I had a choice and because of my business ignorance I signed it away. If there's anything about the show I'm bitter about, it's that.

"I didn't have any idea of seeing a lawyer. Lawyers were something you needed when you had *made it*. Had I known what I know now about getting a lawyer when you're being asked to sign a piece of paper that important, I would have gone to Marvin Mitchelson. As you get older you learn that if something's not right, you leave or get fired or whatever."

The acrimonious favored nations dispute, coming on top of many months with slight pay, split the ranks of the dancers into two groups, which began thinking of themselves in terms of "soldiers" or "rebels." Like Wilson and Stuart, the "soldiers" were ever eager to march to Bennett's drumbeat no matter what. Like Dennis and Walsh, the "rebels" felt that the management had put them through some tough battles and now was refusing combat pay. In the hurly-burly last fine-tuning rehearsal sessions in the first two weeks of April, everyone was too keyed up to act on their feelings.

Whether soldiers or rebels, their battle was about to be joined. "Before we opened I thought we would never open," Ron Kuhlman said. "We still didn't have an end to the show two days before the opening. I kept going back to Marsha at home and saying, 'There is no book, nothing happens at the end,' and 'Oh nuts.' I'd complain to her and all my friends. I would say, 'This show is crazy, it doesn't end, it doesn't hold together well,' and on and on."

And from the haze of all the other emotions, one finally arose above the rest, an emotion that will be clear to anyone who performs: "I went through a period toward the end of rehearsals that I needed an audience," Bishop said. "I was ready for the audience."

And they learned that on Wednesday, April 16, 1975, *A Chorus Line* finally would get one.

12.

Final Rehearsals and Previews (April–May 1975)

At the same time that *A Chorus Line* was opening off-Broadway, the show business trade papers were debating and bemoaning the fact that the Tony Award nominees that year looked like an unusually sad lot.

In this context, word spread fast that something special was happening down at the Public Theater. Aside from the curiosity factor—What would an established Broadway bright light like Michael Bennett be doing off-Broadway? And with an Oscar-winning composer like Marvin Hamlisch?—the grapevine was aquiver. The New York theater community is a close-knit village; everybody finds out what everybody else is doing. Tickets went on sale in early April (Shakespeare Festival subscribers had been holding tickets to an unspecified show since autumn) and began moving fast.

Some of the same energy flowing out into the theatrical community flowed back into the Newman Theater where *A Chorus Line* was now on its feet, in costumes, in front of a set, and running through its last weeks of tech rehearsals to make sure sound and light cues were synchronized with what was happening on the stage. *A Chorus Line* had more tech rehearsals than usual because it was one of the first shows to use a computerized lighting board, which reportedly cost the Public Theater $160,000. The technology was made necessary by the 280 light cues designed by Musser.

"I felt the power down at rehearsals," Sammy Williams said, "the intensity of what we were doing. I didn't know what we were doing but I felt the intensity."

Clive Wilson said, "I think there was a growing realization throughout rehearsals that the show was coming together. But you get so unobjective at a certain point that who knows? Not even Michael knew." "By the time we got to performing it," Renee Baughman said, "we were all so ready. Everybody was wondering if it was just going to be an insider kind of show, but I wasn't worried about it. I'll admit I didn't know it was going to be as hip as it turned out to be."

Garland said, "We had never had an opportunity to view it. We were never able to be objective. We never saw how it really meshed, how things really worked."

But even at this late date, there still were some important loose ends dangling. When Bennett tried to change the opening dance sequence, moving Michel Stuart from the front to the back, he knew he was losing his last chance to build a character from the lines and steps that had survived the cuts. "I told him, 'that isn't going to work for me. I'm not asking for a song or a dance, but I've devoted a lot of time to this show and to establishing this character. If you don't change this now, this minute, I'll be leaving.' He said, 'I won't.' He didn't get it."

Stuart then walked out of the rehearsal and on the back of his sheet music for "What I Did for Love," scribbled his two weeks' notice. When he turned up for that evening's rehearsal, however, Bennett had moved him back to the front. A small triumph. "After that," Stuart said, "everything was fine because when we were all up there, we were *all* up there."

Other problems were not solved so neatly. "We go into rehearsals after the second workshop," LuPone said, "and Zach-Cassie still isn't written, not included, not involved. We're doing 'One,' we're doing the dance numbers, we're doing the strengths of Michael Bennett, which was the choreography. He was putting the show together choreographically and adding the words later. However, for Zach he had to work from his weaknesses. We were rehearsing in the dark, empty Newman by ourselves with nobody there.

"He was playing my role, which is what he wanted to do, and then he'd turn to me and say, 'Now you do it,' as if to say, 'Do it like I just did it.' He'd say, 'Five, six, seven, eight' and I would go, 'Five . . . six . . . seven . . . eight,' so I became a dolt.

"I didn't have the balls to say, 'You're an asshole'—well, I wouldn't put it that way, exactly. I'd talk to him on his terms, 'craftsurally' and 'texturally' and then say it was not being fulfilled. Either fulfill it or get another actor. I say that today but I couldn't do it then. I had a great belief that I needed him for my career, for my growth, for my art.

"When it got to be crazy and I got furious, Bobby Avian was always there. Without a doubt, Bobby Avian saved me and my investment in *ACL*. If it weren't for him I wouldn't have cared that the show became a hit. I could care less about the money. What means something to me is the integrity of the artist, the humanity of the artist, the contribution to society.

"That ultimately was my frustration, because ultimately that's what *ACL* is about, too. To me at that time, Bobby Avian lived the humanity, the integrity, and the aesthetic realism, the art that I was interested in. Michael talked it, but he didn't live it. Not at that time.

"Donna became a nemesis to me. I was dealing with someone who said she was an actress, who told me she studied acting, and I was expecting the acting courtesies, if you will, that actors share consciously or unconsciously with each other. Instead, I found the woman was showboating. In our scenes I was playing to her and she was playing out front."

On top of that, the last cuts in the show were made in the Zach-Cassie scene. Yet the scenes were not eliminated entirely, as both McKechnie and LuPone feared. "Michael and Jimmy were very diligent," McKechnie said. "A lesser director would have given up on me. In the end he said, 'What's important? We don't need to hear all the information about them [Cassie and Zach]; let the audience fill it in. The fears strike a note in people that's common: fear of intimacy, workaholism. We can touch on that but let's not make the show about that. What's really important is people on the Line."

And with the cutting of the extensive Zach-Cassie scenes the long process of writing *A Chorus Line* was finally at an end. But lost in more personal anxieties, several of the cast members still didn't clearly see the whole that their fragments of a show finally had become. "We did it alone for so long that I couldn't tell what it was," Priscilla Lopez said. "Sometimes I thought it was the greatest thing that ever was; other times I thought it was the biggest piece of crap and wondered how I could get out." Acting on her uncertainty, Lopez took time off from the last rehearsals of *A Chorus Line* to audition for *The Red Devil Battery Sign,* one of Tennessee Williams's last plays, later a flop. After all, most New York Shakespeare productions were limited runs lasting only four to eight weeks.

Lopez recalled, "My agent is telling me I should leave *Chorus Line* for Tennessee Williams right away. I was still feeling that my part in *Chorus Line* was worthless and I always wanted to be an actress and I had a chance to do a Tennessee Williams play. But *deep, deep down in my soul* I knew I wasn't going to leave because I believed in Michael so much. Then, too, much of my time and effort had been invested in *Chorus Line* and it was finally going to happen."

As might be expected in the last week before such an important test, everyone came down with a bug. Sore throats and stuffed noses ran rampant. "Michael had abandoned us or he was sick himself," Thommie Walsh remembers, "and Marvin Hamlisch all of a sudden became the daddy of the company." It was one of the first times the dancers can recall that the composer tried relating to the dancers on a personal level. "It was about the last week before we previewed," Walsh said. "He got us to a doctor for our throats because no one could talk. Everyone had some kind of goop. And I remember him dropping off a humidifier at my house because I was pretty congested. He was like a Jewish mother with chicken soup. I think he grew a lot from that experience."

Most cast members saw relatively little of Bennett that week because, unbeknownst to most of them, Michael Bennett and Joseph Papp were involved in an eleventh-hour skirmish that came closed to aborting the project once again.

When the tall mirrors that distinguish the number "The Music and the Mirror" arrived, they were inexpensive distorting mirrors instead of the high-quality flat ones set designer Robin Wagner had ordered. Unable to get help from the Shakespeare Festival, Bennett had to take time from polishing the show in order to raise money for the necessary changes, and to track down a glazier who would execute the mirror job properly.

Bennett's increasing participation in what normally are considered a producer's responsibilities caused him to negotiate an unusual deal with the Shakespeare Festival. To this day, the show is billed as being produced by the Shakespeare Festival "in association with Plum Productions."

Plum Productions is Michael Bennett, who pumped some of his own money into the show at this point, earning him billing as a coproducer, and enabling him to participate more in any profits that might arise. Bennett clearly had developed enough confidence in the long-range prospects of *A Chorus Line* to get himself a piece of it.

"I was rooting for Michael when I was Al, and when I thought Joe had nixed the show," LuPone said. "Then, when I became Zach, I wished Joe had won. But then we got those mirrors, those tacky Mylar mirrors, and there was a big fight one day and the whole show was in jeopardy . . . and then Michael got real mirrors. I interpreted Joe as losing that battle. On the other hand, I think Joe deserves credit for taking a chance on this show and taking a chance on Michael."

The score of *A Chorus Line* consists of songs that take you inside the hearts and heads of dancers auditioning for an unnamed musical. The audience learns very little about that musical, and hears only one of its songs: "One." It was Avian's idea that instead of the thoughtful downward feeling of the show's existing ending—in which the dancers simply disappeared into darkness and never were seen again—the audience be propelled into the curtain calls for that never-named musical. In this fantasy finale, the dancers appear in sparkling gold satin costumes and top hats and perform a dance combination as they take their bows. In keeping with the fantasy theme, everyone who had been eliminated in the final round returns to take part in that finale, to the reprised tune of "One." Though the moment did some violence to the logical progression of the story and theme, it proved to be immensely satisfying for the audience. Just as the eliminations were symbolic deaths, the finale was a symbolic resurrection.

The collaborative effort of Bob Avian, Baayork Lee, and Donna McKechnie, it was the part of *A Chorus Line* in which Bennett had the least hand.

Though she says she found performing the finale "boring," Pam Blair acknowledged, "That 'Rockette' number made the statement of the show . . . it was the culmination of everything we'd been saying all night long. It was as essential as *A Chorus Line* itself." The finale was the last big piece of *A Chorus Line* to fall into place.

Final tech rehearsals were held the weekend of April 11 to 13, and even the following week Bennett and Avian were still rehearsing the cast. When they broke for a rest and dinner at three o'clock the afternoon of April 16, 1975, the long gestation of *A Chorus Line* was finally complete. Four hours later the lights went down on the first paying audience. And the show began its life.

"I guess I sensed the power of *A Chorus Line* at the first preview when they totally went out of their minds," Thommie Walsh remembers. "They went crazy, crazy. We did those kicks at the end of the finale, and they were still applauding when we were putting on our street clothes. It was staggering."

Kay Cole, who is nearsighted, had gotten contact lenses for *A Chorus Line* so she could see the marks on the stage clearly. But it was the other things she saw that impressed her the most. "I actually for the first time in my life could see faces in the audience and you could feel their reactions, they were so intense. I remember a lot of applause and intense crying, because the Newman [stage] is fairly close [to the audience]. That's what amazed me. My roommate came backstage and said, 'Oh my God, it's magic.' And I kept saying, 'Really? You really like it?' "

Renee Baughman said, "It was the best experience of my life. I had friends there, everybody in awe. I had one friend who didn't even come backstage to see me, he was so overwhelmed by the show."

Like Cole, Percassi was suspicious at first that the enthusiasm was meant as encouragement from others in show business. When he realized that their enthusiasm was genuine, he worried that it was a show that would appeal *only* to people in show business. "But then people not involved in the business came backstage and told me it was the most wonderful thing they had ever seen in their lives," he said. "And these were ordinary people."

Lots of shows get cheers, tears, and bouquets. What were these first audiences experiencing that set this show apart? After all, how profound can you get in the commercial theater? "I didn't really think the show was a powerful statement in terms of society," LuPone said. "I still don't. I think *Nicholas Nickleby* was a far greater statement."

But Williams ventured a rebuttal: "Everyone related to it, in all walks of life," he said. "It's so simple, and the dancing is just a catalyst, the costume that it wears. It could be a story about office workers, doctors, lawyers. Everybody has their story to tell you, and people relate to the emotion involved. What succeeded was the honesty, the simplicity, the magic it creates, the places it takes you."

McKechnie said, "When you talk to people about their first kiss, their first feelings of sexual persuasion—all those darling, innocent feelings—you're talking about the pain of growing up. No one on this planet earth escapes the pain of living. This show says, 'You're not alone, we're all the same.' There's something for everyone. It's very powerful. And then in the finale, we're all in hats and kicking. It's a fantastic metaphor. It touches people beyond the rational, beyond the intellect. It hits people in their gut and they knew they're hearing something that is a connection with their spiritual side. But meanwhile it's a brilliantly artistic, palatable theatrical event, so you can tolerate the things it communicates to you. It reverberates, reverberates, and you have to see it again."

Perhaps because of that, the week after the show opened was like no other experience the dancers had ever had in their careers. Accolades, when they came, usually went to the star of whatever show they were in.

And these were only preview audiences. The official "opening night" when critics would come and write their reviews was not scheduled until May 21. Therefore, the people attending these early performances lacked the benefit of a review suggesting how they should react. Their responses were spontaneous, from the heart.

"My favorite thing about when we began at the Public," Michel Stuart said, "was that people would come backstage after the show and they would look at us and say, 'Thank you' with so much love and so much sincerity. I had never experienced that before. That was the greatest rush for me. We filled them with love and light and beauty and the affirmation to go for your dreams. To really go for it. They saw that we had done something that no one had ever done before. Someone had taken a group of dancers and made a literate theater piece out of it. I was very proud of Michael and all the other people for being brave enough to do that."

For Lopez, the show's success and the audience's reaction to it provided relief and validation for her decision to forgo the Tennessee Williams play. "I began to realize I was important to the show," she said.

Ron Dennis had always been popular and had a warm circle of friends, but suddenly he found he had become a *celebrity*. "I would run into my peers and they had heard about the show and would go on and on. Wherever you went, somebody knew I was in the show. It was a powerful vehicle. It was brilliantly wonderful for what it touched, but looking back on it, it seems there was an awful lot of stuff it didn't touch that it should have."

Dennis continued, "My friend came to see it and she was furious because there wasn't more than one black in the show. She's a lady who is furious about a lot of things. But she was so incensed that she couldn't even acknowledge what I had done. I wasn't fishing for a compliment but she was so angry that it never dawned on her to say anything about my performance. And I realize now, it was just plain old jealousy. Had they been the ones in the part, it would have been less of an impact. I'm sure that none of these people realized that they were envious that I was involved with something as monumentally successful as that show was. This was still off-Broadway but the word was out and you just knew it. Riding in the train, people would look at you with such envy. It was the most bizarre situation I've ever experienced and probably never will again."

Still deeply unhappy with his role and his relationship with Bennett and McKechnie, LuPone acknowledged, "When we were down at the Public Theater and all the hoopla about *A Chorus Line* was going on, I just didn't get it. I remember the excitement of the audience—and I still didn't get it. I got it when I looked out while I was in the back of the audience one night on a break or something. I looked outside and I saw in front of the Public Theater the longest line of limos I have seen in my entire life. Remember, limos were not the industry then that they are now. It was a convoy of limos, doubled, not even in a single line. It just blew my mind, and I finally thought, 'This must be big.' "

Walsh said, "To me it really didn't matter if it was a hit or not because I felt it was a wonderful experiment and we had grown so much. It didn't have anything to do with the outside world—it was about us. Soon I realized it did touch other people—at times the audience couldn't even get out of their seats they were so devastated—then I knew it was special to everyone. In five days Jackie Onassis was sitting on the stairs along with Lauren Bacall and it was impossible to get a ticket."

McKechnie said, "I didn't realize how impressive it was until some of the people started flying in from California. Then I realized it wasn't just your average word of mouth. I started getting letters before we were really performing that much: like a shoe salesman and a football player who said they broke down and cried. When I realized how it was reaching the average person I really knew it was a total artistic success, a big success, and I felt it would have a life."

In the five weeks until the press opening, Bennett and Avian still had a chance to make changes. The dancers were still rehearsing each afternoon, getting notes from Bennett and performing in the evening, so small changes went in every day. For one, the song "Tits and Ass" almost was cut because it wasn't getting the expected laughs. Someone suggested that the song's title in the program was telegraphing its shock-laugh and blunting its impact. When the title was changed in the program to the more enigmatic "Dance 10, Looks 3," the song started getting the kind of reaction it deserved.

There were two major changes in the show, however, and they went in quickly. Only the people who came the first week got to see the show in its raw original form.

Most noticeably, "The Music and the Mirror" became a solo dance for McKechnie. Until the middle of the first week Mc-

Kechnie was the lead dancer, but she was backed by four of the men: Mason, Walsh, Cilento, and Stuart.

Wilson remembers the number in its original form. "A few of us had to wheel on the mirrors," he said. "There was always something thrilling about being onstage in the middle of that number, hidden from view, with Donna out front doing all the work, knowing she was knocking 'em dead. It was a time to relieve some of the tension. I remember the four of us were wearing black gloves because we had to grab the mirrors by the edges. The feeling of being back there was akin to church giggles—but of course we couldn't laugh. We could hear the music and see the lights, and the audience was just a few feet away. There was a safety and a sense of camaraderie about it. We were in the number without being 'on the Line.' We could totally relax and enjoy the experience."

"Everything in the show was working except me," McKechnie said. "Michael called me after the show one night and said, 'Why aren't you dancing?' I said, 'Michael it's very inhibiting up there. I have to find certain marks and I'm just finding my way.'

"He said, 'You're not dancing because you're not finding your marks, is that why?'

"I said, 'Yes, Wayne is on three, I have to be on four. When we do this other section I have to be on one. That's not easy to do so that was it.'

"The next day the boys were out. I know that Rick Mason didn't want to speak to me ever after this because he thought I called Michael and told him I didn't want the boys in my number."

Mason said, "I blamed Donna for us being taken out of the number ["The Music and the Mirror"]. One day Michael said to her, 'How do you feel about the boys dancing behind you?' And she said, 'I love it, I love the security.' But one day after we were taken out of it, she made a comment, 'Oh God, it's so nice to be out there dancing all by myself.' So I found her to be two-faced. That bothered me.

"I didn't talk to Donna for about three weeks, but then I said to myself, 'You're being an asshole.' So I asked her to come into the bathroom down at the Public and I said, 'I want to apologize for the way I'm acting. I've taken things a little more personally than I really have the right to, but I reacted to feelings.'

"She kind of threw it off. I didn't get the idea from her that she really cared that I was apologizing. Donna was going through her own problems and when you're going through those problems you don't see another person's problems. I felt that number was my only time to shine. I could dance the hell out of that number—I could do it better than Donna. I was getting hotter and hotter in it. It was the best dancing I've ever done. All of a sudden one day I come to rehearsal and we were cut. My one thing was gone and it hurt tremendously. Do you know how stupid it was to say, for two years, 'Gonorrhea' [in the song "Hello Twelve, Hello Thirteen, Hello Love"]? Maybe Baayork got the same frustration with "Four foot ten." I felt I had something I could have said about my existence and my growth and pain at wanting to dance in the theater—something that would have been meaningful and memorable—other than one wet dream! And it wasn't even my wet dream! From my whole monologue I didn't get to say one thing of my own except that I was from Tempe, Arizona. 'Mark Phillip Lawrence Tabori' was Steve Anthony. That was him, he did the original tape. As for the rest of my lines, it was Michael's wet dream, it was Michael's problem with the priest, Michael finding the books—just Michael, Michael Michael."

McKechnie said she worried that "the way things appeared I could understand why people might make something out of it. But I'm angry at the fact that people were never really dealt with [by Bennett] and things really explained. At that time I didn't feel it was my job to go around and discuss it. Every once in a while that would come up in discussion with Clive or someone—'Rick's still mad at you.' I felt so inhibited about just going to individuals and getting things out in the open."

For those not embroiled in a dispute, days suddenly were magical. "I loved rehearsing during the day and performing," Nancy Lane said. "I had hated the Nineteenth Street studio when we were there, it was oppressive. But loved going to the Newman. I loved going downtown every day to work."

Bishop recalled, "I had so many wonderful experiences after performances with audience members because of that show. People pour out stories to you. They wait for you to come out of the stage door and after they get your autograph they grab you and say, 'I've *got* to tell you that my father . . .' Or, 'I've *got* to tell you, I always wanted to be a dancer.' It's like, they *had* to do it. That's the kind of reaction people were having, initially, to that show."

For LuPone, however, the unconnectedness of his character continued to trouble him. Sometimes it was as simple as the fact that he was sitting amid audience members and had to contend with them. Drunks were the worst, he said. "They'd talk to me or hit me or slap me on the back. There was a tender moment where a little girl in front of me would turn around and peep her head up and make a face at me, and then I'd have to yell to the stage, 'Who do you think you are? Get back in line.' The audience would either hiss me on the way up, or I would literally get from the audience, 'Give her the job, why don't you just give her the job?' They were that involved. There was so much I had to deal with, and I was unprotected.

"One night," LuPone said, "someone at the Newman tripped me, on cement. I didn't make it to the curtain call because they were furious that I didn't give some people the job, or didn't give Cassie the job, or whatever. I was sent to the hospital because I hurt my knees. I was a good actor doing the role and suffering not to have the recognition for what I was setting up. If only the audience could be made to understand my point of view. Or at least to have enough of an understanding to make the ambiguities far more important.

"I was the Darth Vader of *A Chorus Line,*" LuPone said. "Without a doubt it was necessary and it works in that sense. Michael was always trying to convince me that I was part of the experience with the Line, but he was absolutely wrong. I was never a part of the experience of *A Chorus Line*. I was never on that stage, and the curtain call for me every night was a humiliation. Because I had to lie to myself. I had to go out there and sell something with regard to 'One.' I never felt 'One' because I was always in the back of the house. So I covered it in Buddhism. I covered it in trying to be a human being, to be bigger than what I felt I was at that point."

***

The other major change in the show during previews was suggested by Marsha Mason, the actress who was married at that time to the show's "doctor," Neil Simon.

To keep his dancers on edge, Bennett had continued the practice of announcing a different list of eight audition "winners" each night. Sometimes the slender Garland got it, sometimes not. Sometimes the soulful Lopez or the graceful Cilento got it, sometimes they walked. Bennett would play with the choices on Percassi and Baughman. As man and wife they sometimes got the show together, sometimes stayed unemployed together, sometimes were split up.

"I never was picked," Lane said. "I always was let go. Actually I was really positive in my life at that time. I'll make the most of it, I told myself. It was fine. Michael would sit in the middle of the rehearsal hall, in the seats of the house with Bob Avian, and he would just say, 'Okay now, let's try this one, this one and this one, and the other ones, you won't get the job.' It was very hit-and-miss. They had to look like they went together, four boys and four girls, like they were partners in some respect."

"They kept playing with it," Cole said. Having built up suspense about the Zach-Cassie relationship, Bennett now found that the audience was reacting—in addition to their other individual favorites—to whether Cassie got the job or not. "It was Marsha Mason who came to see the show and said, 'You simply cannot do that. It might be more truthful, but you can't just kill off people's hope.' "

So after the first week Bennett made his final choice. From then on, unless a Zach ad-libbed, the ones chosen for the unnamed show were Cassie (McKechnie), Bobby (Walsh), Judy (Garland), Richie (Dennis), Val (Blair), Mark (Mason), Diana (Lopez), and Mike (Cilento).

Lauren Bacall and Jacqueline Onassis were only the first of the celebrities to visit the Newman Theater. For nineteen star-struck kids, it was like a visit to Olympus—no, it was more like the gods were coming down to pay homage to *them.*

Among others who attended the show off-Broadway and still glow in the dancers' memories were Shelley Winters, Ingrid Bergman, Raquel Welch, Diana Ross, Dick Cavett, Larry Blyden, Katharine Hepburn, Ali McGraw, Richard Burton, Burt Lancaster

Gregory Peck, Ann-Margret, Paul Newman, and Joanne Woodward. Not to mention some of their dance idols, Ruby Keeler, Margot Fonteyn, Ginger Rogers, and Mikhail Baryshnikov.

Blair invited actor Tony Roberts's parents to see the show on her house seats, only to have them plucked away at the last minute. "Then I discovered that those poor people were in their sixties and had to sit on the steps because Groucho Marx came and they didn't have a seat for him so they gave him mine," she said.

Kuhlman remembers Groucho Marx's visit as well. "We were all waiting backstage for him, dying to meet him. Baayork asked where he was and someone said he was meeting us in the men's room. So Baayork runs into the men's room and there he is at the *urinal*. It was great.

"Groucho gave us a cake with a mannequin leg and a hammer, meaning 'break a leg.' I remember he talked to one of the actors, Bob LuPone maybe, and he said, 'That's quite a role you have there.'

"Bob said, 'Thank you.'

"Then Groucho said, 'I had a roll this morning, I think it was a kaiser.'

Other visitors were on their way as well, celebrities of a different kind.

"My family saw the show downtown," Cilento said. "I think it was a little different from what they expected because it was so raw and so real. It wasn't showbiz and I had been in showbiz shows until then. I think they liked the fact that I had my own number."

As for Mason: "What did my family think about the show? Are you kidding? *Time* magazine, my father took it and showed everyone at work. My mother owned a beauty salon and clients sometimes would mention that they had been unable to obtain tickets to *A Chorus Line* when they were in New York City. Mom would 'modestly' suggest that in the future they should check with her and she might be able to help. So there was great pride."

A Chorus Line was the first time Thommie Walsh didn't invite his parents down from upstate to one of his openings. "This was something from the gut. In the show I talk about my father's drinking and my mother's kind of Auntie Mame mentality of raising children. And I knew I had to get through opening night before I could get over them not accepting it or freaking out.

"And when they finally came, they did kind of freak out. I think my mother saw the show a second time before my father did. She came with some of her friends and she fell in love with the show and my part and has since seen the show a dozen times. My father saw it a few months after that with some of his friends. His friends loved the show and he kind of got behind it—still making comments, however, about how foolish I was for giving away my life story for a dollar. Ninety million dollars later I feel foolish, too."

Lee recalls, "My mother came to see the show and the first thing she said is, 'You gotta take singing lessons!'

"And I said, 'Ma, did you see me acting?'

"And she said, 'Yes, but that . . . *well* . . .'

"I tried to explain to her about those terrible notes Marvin had given me to sing. Those awful notes with no melody. She was my biggest fan, but my toughest critic. After that I asked around for a good singing teacher. My mother talked a lot about everyone else and how talented they were. Ma—what about *me*?

"My father never saw the show. It didn't bother me at the time because I figured he'd get to see it sooner or later. Unfortunately he passed away and never got to see the show."

Lane's family wasn't nearly as reticent. "My family saw it downtown many times," she said. "The ushers knew them and would let them in for free. They were immensely proud of me but they still didn't believe this was going to be my life's work. Finally, when we got to Broadway they became convinced. They accepted the fact that I wasn't going back to college."

Blair was worried that her relatively conservative parents would object to her standing at center stage and boasting about her "tits and ass." "My mother was supposed to prepare my grandmother for the fact that I said 'fuck' but obviously she didn't," Blair said. "I guess she couldn't even bring herself to spell the word. She gasped when she heard it, but when the audience was laughing hysterically she informed everyone around her that I was her granddaughter. I think my sister was a little envious."

Blair said the only time she felt a little uncomfortable herself was on matinee days when the theater would be full of children.

After the first few dancers went through this with their parents, the remaining dancers would grill them anxiously about the experience. "There had been some tension about our parents' reaction," Lopez said, "so whenever a parent came to see it, we would all quiz that person about how they felt. My mother and father saw it downtown. My mother didn't respond to it at all. Maybe they didn't know what to say. After it was over she never mentioned it, like she had never seen it. I was embarrassed and didn't know what to tell the others. But then, I wasn't about to ask her, either. It was a battle of wills really. Whenever she came to see me perform I had to drag opinions out of her. But I was so proud of what I did in *A Chorus Line* I didn't feel that I had to do that and I kept waiting for her to say something, but nothing. My father had nothing to say, also."

Michel Stuart's parents were no longer alive at that time, but his sister Sylvia identified completely with one of the parts. "My sister was at the first public performance," he said. "She loved it and cried a lot. When Wayne told his story [about following his sister to dance class] she thought he was talking about her. It was the highest moment in the theater she'd ever had. It was like reading her autobiography."

The McKechnie family found it difficult to communicate after they saw the show together. "My father was very touched and moved by it, my brother told me. But after they saw the show I was eager to hear it from them and they never said one thing to me. We went to a restaurant afterward and I kept up the banter and kept it very superficial and everybody was very uncomfortable and I was in extreme pain.

"That was the last time I saw my father [who died a few months afterward]. It was so unfinished. It's always more difficult when a parent dies if you have unresolved feeling, something was left unsaid; it's hard. My mother was in conflict about it. I think she liked the idea of the show, but she doesn't know how to have her own opinions with me. I think it upset her that I had revealed something about my childhood that she picked up on, and I don't think I prepared her enough for it. So she was kind of quiet."

Patricia Garland had a special stumbling block to overcome, since her sister Jacki had been a part of the taping sessions too, but had not passed the audition. "I think it was hard for my sister

Jacki. You're real happy for someone but there's a lot of pain there. She didn't say anything but she sent flowers and made it a very beautiful experience for me. Jacki and I have never performed together except when we were little and I had flashes and thought about how nice it would be if we had been working side by side."

Williams's famous Paul monologue tells the story of a transvestite dancer whose parents come to accept his profession and his homosexuality. Williams's encounter with his own parents was no less fraught with anxiety.

"My family came to see the show in stages," he said. "My mother was the first, down at the Newman Theater, and she was devastated. The first thing she said to me after the show, the only thing she said immediately afterward, was, 'Boy, I'm sure glad someone brought you a glass of water.' She was referring to the accident scene. I thought that was the cutest thing because she was really into it.

"But she didn't say anything about the monologue or anything else. We walked from the Newman to a restaurant and she never said a word. We ordered and ate and finally she said to me, 'What's the family going to say? How could you get up there and say those things? It's so embarrassing.'

"I was devastated. I had just poured my guts out, worked over six months, and she worried about what the family was going to say. I didn't say anything for the rest of dinner. She was staying overnight in my apartment and we didn't speak. I had a very small apartment. We went to bed and got up the next morning without speaking.

"When we were in the cab on the way to the station, I said, 'I don't care what the family thinks. I worked very hard on this project and I'm real proud of what I'm doing and I'm in a hit show and that's all that matters. If you and the family cannot deal with it, that is your problem. I will never come home again.' And I sent her on her way.

"Three days later she called to tell me she thought I was wonderful and she was really proud of me.

"My father came after we opened on Broadway. My father had left home when I was sixteen years old and up to this point I had very little contact with him. No phone calls, no meetings, perhaps a card once in a while. But I did call him and invite him to New

York to see the show. I was scared to death because I was out there every night telling people I was a fag. It was humiliating for me to tell people I was a homosexual because it was for real, it wasn't just a monologue. So I was telling my father this was real and I didn't know how I was going to handle it. A long time before that, when I told my mother I was gay, she said, 'Don't ever tell your father that, he'll kill you.' So I lived all those years with a black cloud over my head.

"So here I was, inviting my father to see the show. I gave a performance that night that was one of my best, at the time. My father never called me 'son,' either. That night my father came backstage, and walked into my dressing room. He had these big tears in his eyes. I had never seen my father cry. He didn't say anything. He just held me and said he was very proud of me. Took me out to dinner, it was amazing. I think that was the beginning of a relationship with my father.

"My brother and sister came to see the show in California. They were just so impressed, they loved it, they were very proud. And my relatives came to see the show too, they were all very proud, but no one said anything. It was that doomed picture my mother had painted for me that made me so paranoid."

Having faced their families and survived, the dancers now felt ready to face the critics. After everything that had happened in the previous year, and especially considering the unofficial cult hit status the show had attained during the five weeks of previews, opening night off-Broadway was not so much a trial as a coronation. The Newman Theater was packed with the cream of show business insiders, all clutching the black-and-white New York Shakespeare Festival programs that would become valuable collector's items. Backstage, all the rivalries were put aside for one night.

13.

Opening Night and the Off-Broadway Run (May–July 1975)

A Chorus Line has no overture. The first music is the sound of a rehearsal piano playing the timeless showbiz intro, "Ya-dum da-dum-dum-*dum* . . ." Lights come up on a stage full of dancers facing away from the audience and toward mirrored panels that cover the rear wall of the stage. The twenty-six dancers (the ones who will become "the Line," plus all the understudies) observe intently and follow along as Zach (LuPone) demonstrates a series of kicks, turns, and dance steps. During his directions the only music is the piano accompaniment, but when he commands the dancers to repeat the combination themselves, full orchestration floods in.

With that musical transition, the audience is clued that the show has risen from the level of realism into that of impressionism.

As Zach assigns the dancers numbers and arranges them in groups of four, the audience suddenly finds that it can hear the dancers' thoughts. They're singing what amounts to a dancers' prayer, telling God how badly they need to pass the audition and land the job. "I Hope I Get It" is an example of one of the "internal" songs of *A Chorus Line*—which the dancers deliver as sung or spoken asides that only the audience can hear. The dancers also will sing many "external" songs—songs directed to Zach or to each other.

In groups of four the dancers perform the combination Zach has just taught them. It's easy to see that some are substantially better than others, and it's also possible to pick out dancers from the mass by their personality quirks. This one is shy, that one is overeager, another one is sexy, yet another is classy and coolly professional.

Zach asks various dancers whether they've done any previous Broadway shows, and if they've studied ballet. When one dancer admits to not having any ballet experience, Zach cuts him immediately. The elimination process is already under way.

Sheila (Bishop) sets herself apart from the crowd by sassing Zach, which gets the show's first real laugh. Richie (Dennis) gets so overwrought in his dancing that he jumps into Zach's arms, getting the second laugh.

They continue dancing to the "external" music while voicing their prayers and insecurities to the "internal" music.

When all have danced in their groups of four, Zach calls off sixteen numbers—beckoning Cassie (McKechnie) by name—and dismisses the others. While Zach and his assistant Larry (Wilson) confer, the seventeen finalists finish singing "I Hope I Get It" and rummage through their dance bags fetching their resume photos.

Then, as a percussive note pulses, they step forward holding their resume photos like masks, obscuring their faces. The surreal effect continues as they march forward to a white line that runs the width of the stage and they freeze. This moment, when we first see them assemble in their places as the eponymous chorus line, invariably gets the show's first hand.

Starting with Diana Morales (Lopez) on the far right, Larry walks down the line gathering the resume photos for Zach. Paul San Marco (Williams) sings "Resume," a short "internal" song in which he wonders aloud to the audience whether the career information printed on the back of his resume photo reflects the sum of his existence. But perhaps as important, will it get him the job?

When all the photos are collected, the seventeen dancers stand in the poses made famous by the show's logo. They will return to these positions again and again throughout the show.

The show's introduction completed, the main action now begins. Having ascended to a seat at the rear of the theater, Zach now addresses the dancers over the theater's public address system. In what sounds like the voice of God, Zach asks the dancers essentially the same questions Bennett asked the original dancers at the first tape session: what are their stage names, their real names if different, where they were born, and when.

At the left end of the Line, Don Kerr (Kuhlman) goes first, barking out the basic information before being shooed back into line by Zach. When Connie (Lee) speaks she cracks a joke to break the tension. When it's Cassie's turn, she asks Zach for a private conversation but he refuses and moves quickly on to Sheila, who flirts with him.

Zach continues in this fashion straight through the Line, extracting names and quick flashes of character. As Morales finishes her introduction, Zach changes the rules on her. He asks her to continue. She says she doesn't understand. As music creeps in under her voice, she tells Zach that all her information is on the resume. But Zach says he wants to probe beyond her resume. He wants to know about her self.

This is the moment where the show veers into fiction, but by now the audience is hooked. We already sympathize with these talented, vulnerable individuals and are ready to learn more about them.

Zach explains to the dancers that the script calls for some small speaking parts and he'll need to know more about the auditioners in order to cast them properly. On this tenuous premise Zach gains entry into their private lives.

Shyly, Morales pleads not to be forced to go first, so Zach asks Mike Cost (Cilento) to tell about his family life. In answer, Mike sings "I Can Do That," an "external" song in which he describes how he was introduced to dancing by watching his sister take dance class. The number is an opportunity for Cilento to perform a repertoire of virtuoso whirls and kicks.

Next up is Robert Charles Joseph Henry Mills III (Walsh), a.k.a. Bobby. His autobiography takes the form of a comedy routine about what it was like to grow up "strange" in the suburbs of Buffalo. As he recounts his punch-lined anecdotes, the show does a cinematic fade to an "internal" song titled "And . . ." in which Richie ponders what he will say when called upon, trying to figure out what sort of answer will land him the job. As Richie sings, Bobby continues moving his mouth and miming, but now we can only guess what he's saying. At the end of each verse we're able to hear Bobby's jokes once again. After each punch line, he says "and . . ." and the focus cuts back to another dancer who frets aloud about what she'll say when it's her turn.

At the conclusion of the song, Bobby delivers his final punch line, recounting how he was once so depressed that he felt like committing suicide, but stopped when he realized that "to commit suicide in Buffalo is redundant." As the audience applauds, Bobby curtsies and returns to the Line.

To a soft burlesque bump from the percussion, the sultry Sheila next steps forward. After giving Zach a deliberate come-on and suffering a rebuff, she lets down her hair literally and figuratively and begins talking about her unhappy childhood with a mother who was constantly humiliated by her father. She tells how she found her only escape in ballet classes, where everyone and everything seemed beautiful and perfect. This segues into "At the Ballet." As she begins singing, the chorus line retreats upstage into darkness, leaving Sheila alone in front of the white line singing her "external" song to Zach and the audience. For the second verse she is joined in two-part harmony by Bebe (Lane), who believes she is homely, and who fled into ballet because it was a place where every ugly ducking could be a swan. The song swells to three-part harmony for the third verse when Maggie Winslow (Cole) joins them and sings about dancing to bewitch an absent and therefore imaginary and idealized father.

And as the song progresses, lights come up dimly on the rest of the dancers who are far upstage, their legs swinging like metronomes at first. Then, moving in impressionistic ballet combinations, they become glamorous shadows, ghosts of three little girls' imaginations. It's the most *Follies*-like moment in the show.

At the end of the song the three women back up to the white line and the rest of the dancers move forward to fuse with them and re-form the chorus line, which is becoming etched in the audience's mind as an icon. We now know enough about each of them that their relative positions on the Line are important and significant. As with the first time they stepped into place, the moment gets a big hand.

Kristine DeLuca (Baughman) goes next, offering some comic relief in the wake of the somber "At the Ballet." Hyperkinetic in her nervousness, Kristine tells how she got hooked on show business when she was a child. Her husband Al (Percassi) reacts in exasperation to her twittering and tries to calm her down while making excuses to Zach for her jitters. Kristine calms down barely enough to tell how she dreamed of growing up to be Doris Day. Her only problem has been that she can't sing. And with that, she's already into the song "Sing!," in which she gets so flustered that she forgets the last word of each line, leaving Al to step in and supply it. He becomes so zealous in this task that she has to calm *him* down and make him stop answering for her. Her attempts at warbling emerge as dissonant squeaks, but the entire rest of the chorus line helps her to the end of the song with a big choral finale.

Next, Mark (Mason) steps forward to tell his teenage horror story of studying a medical textbook and incorrectly self-diagnosing his first wet dream as a case of gonorrhea. As he does so, the song "Hello Twelve, Hello Thirteen, Hello Love" begins. The entire company takes part in this music and dance montage, which eventually embraces several other songs. Only parts of "Hello Twelve" appear on the record album.

This cinematic kaleidoscope of adolescence is structured much like the earlier "And . . ."; Mark tells his story to a certain point, then mimes the rest as the dancers sing about their first social and sexual stirrings in high school.

Using the jump-cut technique of one dancer finishing another's sentence, the sequence moves from Mark to Connie, who tells about the frustration of watching all the other kids keep growing after she stops at "Four-Foot-Ten." This is followed by a collage of lines about collisions with parents, disasters on dates, and other cataclysms of puberty. The story returns briefly to Connie, who tells about making her debut as one of Yul Brynner's "children" in the original *The King and I* and about idolizing dancer Maria Tallchief. The action then jump-cuts to Morales, who tells about being a Puerto Rican going to Manhattan's High School of the Performing Arts. The other dancers again fade away upstage, leaving Morales alone downstage to sing "Nothing," her story of being humiliated by a supercilious teacher with a pretentious teaching style.

At the conclusion of the number the rest of the dancers return in another series of jump-cuts, first to Don Kerr, who recalls falsifying his age so he could get a job dancing in a strip joint, where he befriended a flamboyant stripper. The anecdote dissolves into a collage of teenage angst about not being able to grow breasts, about poring over *Peyton Place* in a locked bathroom, first kisses, etc. The cascade of images resolves into a sweet little chantey in waltz time for Maggie, who croons about loving and missing her mother from a great distance. Afterward, in yet another series of jump-cuts, Judy Turner (Garland) tells Kirkwood's story about finding a dead body, and Gregory Gardner (Stuart) tells about having an erection that seemed to last forever, and how he came to realize he was gay.

This disclosure leads to an eruption of exuberant dancing, music, and contrapuntal song lines that build to a climax. The lyric changes as they all reach age seventeen, a time when things begin to change in their lives. At the high point of the song's energy, Richie takes center stage and sings "Gimme the Ball," the story of an overly enthusiastic young man who suddenly discovered himself on a life track (to being a kindergarten teacher) in which he had no interest. So he derailed his carefully planned life and struck out to become a dancer. This epiphany prompts a call-and-answer response from the other dancers who became his backup singers in a rhythm and blues finale that draws the dancers back into place on the Line, and gets another big hand.

Childhood now behind, the show moves into its coming-to-New-York stage. Val tells her story about coming from a small town, hoping to win a place in the Rockettes, Radio City Music Hall's precision dance team. She recounts how she decided to stack the deck, so to speak, by getting her breasts and buttocks "done" by a plastic surgeon. Singing "Dance 10, Looks 3" (an allusion to the ratings she got from casting directors before her silicone treatments) a number invariably called by its original title, "Tits and Ass," she struts around the stage inviting people to feast their eyes on her prime assets. Val becomes so energized by the attention at the conclusion of the number that she reaches over to Mark, who stands next to her on line, and pinches his bottom.

After the applause, Zach asks Paul for his story, but unlike the others, Paul is unwilling to open up. Zach then tells everyone to take a break, inviting only Cassie to stay behind. As they speak, it becomes clear that their relationship is one of long standing, and that there is tension between them. Irritably he asks her why she's at the audition. She explains that she desperately needs a job. After early successes dancing in Broadway musicals she went to Hollywood with high hopes, but soon found herself shuffled into small meaningless roles and commercials. The harsh truth is that she can dance, but she can't act. As a result, she has little to show for her California sojourn but a tan. In her song, "The Music and the Mirror," she implores Zach to hire her for the chorus, telling him that a chance to dance is all she wants. The song starts as an "external" number, a sales pitch addressed to Zach, but soon goes "internal" and she executes a spectacular dance solo. Through theatrical white magic, a semicircle of mirrors descends around her. She reveals that her innermost soul contains multiple images of herself dancing, not acting.

If Zach is impressed, he shows no evidence of it at the end of the song. He nearly dismisses her on the spot, but he's interrupted by Larry asking if the break is over and if the auditioners should return. Zach tells Larry to teach the dancers one of the lyrics from the unnamed show for which they are auditioning. When Cassie implores again, Zach tells her to go with Larry and the other dancers and learn the lyric. She runs off happily. Zach tells Larry to send the recalcitrant Paul back to him.

After a little prodding from Zach, Paul finally opens up and tells the story of having been fondled by strangers at Forty-second Street movie theaters when he was a teenager. Accepting himself as homosexual, he dropped out of Catholic high school and went to work in the Jewel Box Revue, a transvestite variety show. Paul then recites Dante's monologue about searching for self-respect and acceptance in this bizarre "asshole" of show business. The monologue is remarkable for several reasons. Aside from the fact that it survived virtually intact from the original tape session, and that it is an unusually long and profound moment in a musical not to have been turned into a song, it was ground-breaking in its frankness in dealing with the *soul* of a homosexual character, rather than the mechanics of lovemaking or other sensationalistic details. By the time he finishes the monologue, Paul is in tears. For the first time since the opening number, Zach descends from his perch in the back of the theater and comes onstage to put his arm around Paul and comfort him. They have a private conversation inaudible to the audience.

Afterward, Zach tells Larry to bring back all the dancers. As they enter, the audience hears the strains of the distinctive "One" vamp for the first time. In a vocal and terpsichorean chaos reminiscent of an orchestra tuning up, the dancers array themselves around the stage, various hats in hand, practicing the lyrics and dance steps they've just been taught. Zach tells the dancers precisely the style he wishes to see, then steps back and watches them sing and dance "One," the only song the audience gets to hear from the unknown show for which the dancers have been auditioning. It is a typical Jerry Herman-type song extolling the virtues of the leading lady. The dancers sing one verse "externally" to the audience and Zach, then, in a remarkable shift, the music changes key and the audience is invited "inside" their heads to hear them counting off steps, muttering mental notes, and repeating Zach's directions in a lyric worthy of James Joyce.

Then, in a sequence not included on the record, Zach and Cassie have a confrontation. Zach begins it by being hypercritical of Cassie's dancing in the number. He tells her she sticks out too much; that she is no longer able to meld with people who are her inferiors. She absorbs his criticism without argument, which causes him to explode. He demands to know if she is ready to settle for *this*—gesturing to the chorus, which now is moving in coordination, whispering its lyrics. Cassie watches them for a moment, kicking and singing as one, then tells Zach she'd be proud to be a part of the chorus line. She rejoins the line and dances in flawless union with them.

Zach attempts to draw Cassie out one more time. In a scene that gauges the depth of the Cassie-Zach relationship, he demands to know why she left him. In a scene that would become increasingly autobiographical for Bennett and McKechnie as years would go by, Cassie accuses the director of being obsessed by his career, wanting to do everything—musicals, plays, movies—at the expense of his human contacts. She tells him that there was no room for her in his life, so she left.

Larry interrupts, asking Zach what he wants to do with the dancers. Zach says they should keep dancing.

The show now goes back inside the dancers' heads where they are moaning about being tired, headachy, and emotionally drained. Nevertheless, Zach orders them to perform ever more strenuous dances, a sequence listed in the program as "The Tap Combination." The strain snaps when Paul executes a spin and he collapses on his knee with a shriek of pain. The dancers rush to his aid. He'd had a knee operation, and this fresh injury could spell the end of his dancing career. Paul is borne away to a waiting ambulance.

Sobered, Zach asks the dancers what they would do if they had to give up dancing. They reply variously, acknowledging that a dancer's all-too-brief career is fraught with danger and disappointment, but remains something special, something uniquely magical that no one can take from them.

In song, Morales explains that she will always consider her dancing career to have been "What I Did for Love." Assenting, the dancers all join her for the final verse and the big Broadway finale.

The song brings the show to its emotional and thematic climax. Only one thing is left. As the *Chorus Line* vamp plays, the dancers move slowly, dramatically, back into their talismanic positions for the last time. When they're in place, Zach thanks them all for their participation and asks Don, Greg, Al, Kristine, Bebe, Sheila, Connie, and Maggie to step forward. Curtly, he thanks the front line and dismisses them.

There is a moment when no one moves and no one says a word. The vamp continues playing. It takes that long for the realization to sink in that those remaining onstage—Mike, Cassie, Bobby, Judy, Richie, Val, Mark, and Morales—have gotten the job. They don't move.

Matter-of-factly, Zach begins telling them when rehearsals will begin, how long the out-of-town tryout will last, the approximate date of the Broadway opening, what sort of contracts they'll be signing . . .

And as he speaks, the dancers begin to react. They go limp, or rub their legs, or grin at one another. As Zach continues, Judy raises her hands to the Leko light falling over her, as a child might reach up to sunlight. And on that image, with the vamp still playing, the stage fades to dark.

As the applause begins, the full orchestra picks up the vamp, which turns into "One." And through the time machine of theater we are projected into the future, to a fantasy opening night where all the dancers gave gotten the show and where all are attired, not in their sweaty rehearsal clothes, but in glittering bugle-beaded gold satin with matching top hats. And they each get a separate bow. The final glimmers of *A Chorus Line* are the last stray sparkles from their costumes as the lights withdraw into the black . . .

"Opening night—that big, important night—everybody was on their feet and applauding and I was applauding with them," Ron Kuhlman said. "That kind of experience you can't get anyplace else. You'll never get it in film and TV; that kind of catharsis just doesn't happen."

Sammy Williams said, "The opening downtown was great. I remember standing off in the wings right before I went on for the monologue and said to myself, 'This is the beginning of it.' "

The reviews were a press agent's dream. Just as the show tries to capture a quintessential Broadwayness, the rave reviews for *A Chorus Line* were classics of their kind. In *The New York Times,* Clive Barnes wrote, "The conservative word for 'A Chorus Line' might be tremendous, or perhaps terrific. . . . the conception was so shattering that it is surprising, if by the time you read this, the New York Shakespeare Festival has got a Newman Theater still standing."

Douglas Watt of the *New York Daily News* called it "the hottest new thing in town," and perhaps realizing that wasn't enough, added that the show "firmly establishes itself as the most exciting Broadway musical in several seasons."

That took care of the quote ads. The weekly magazine critics took more time to analyze what made the show tick so gaudily. Ted Kalem of *Time* magazine seemed taken with the idea of giving chorus dancers personal identities. "Behind the facelessness there is a face," he found.

Jack Kroll of *Newsweek* sang the praises of what he called "this thin motley line of leotarded, sweat-socked bacchantes," whom he described as "a family linked by blood, sweat, laughter and tears."

Kroll was unequivocal in awarding credit for the entire conception to Bennett, but he went on to say, "The true spirit of the work is Carole Bishop . . . [who] personifies the power and pathos of the dancers' vocation."

Barnes, too, unhesitatingly declared, "It is stamped indelibly as Mr. Bennett's show."

Perceptively, the *New York Post's* Martin Gottfried wrote that "Bennett capitalized on his recent direction of straight plays to handle actors, a particular problem in this case since the actors are primarily dancers."

Though Gottfried hailed the show as "a pyrotechnical exercise in theater choreography," it is significant that most of the critics reviewed *A Chorus Line* as a drama as much as a musical. Their reviews dwelled on content and theme rather than on the dancing, singing, etc.

Like several of the other critics, Barnes seemed to waver as he wrote his notice. Critics sometimes hesitate to offer unreserved praise for shows as clearly commercial as this one was. At one point he truly raved that the show "glows like a beacon heavenward" and stated, "In no way could it have been better done." Barnes then pulled his punch, writing, " 'Oklahoma!' it isn't, but no one with strength to get to the box office should willingly miss it. You will talk about it for weeks."

Barnes, Kroll, and *The Wall Street Journal's* Edwin Wilson faulted the show for sentimentality. The closest thing to a poor notice the show received was Watt's observation that "Hamlisch has provided a supple and nicely varied score which, though notably lacking in the least melodic or harmonic originality, borrows tastefully and is, happily the obvious work of a genuine musician."

Many of the reviewers pressed some of the dancers' hot buttons. Though the show was supposed to be about nineteen equal dancers, Kalem found that "McKechnie is an uncrowned star." He also pointed to the essential cruelty of the play's structure, alluding to "the Spanish Inquisition of the theater." Kroll observed that Zach "can sound like a show-biz Gestapo." In *Women's Wear Daily,* Christopher Sharp termed the process "Darwinian."

But the critics' quips buried their quibbles. The consensus was reflected in Gottfried's description of the show as "purely and simply magnificent, capturing the very soul of our musical theater."

In his June 1 Sunday *New York Times* Arts and Leisure section,

Walter Kerr called the show "a hit that was made by the public," and went on to say:

> Long before any reviewers, who must normally function as huff-and-puff artists blowing laggard theatergoers stagewards, were permitted to come near the entertainment, word had got about: something was brewing in one of Joseph Papp's downtown houses, the previews going on were as exciting as any opening night could hope to be, ticket buyers were lining up at the Lafayette Street box office terrified that they might not be able to see the show before they were told to. "A Chorus Line" was selling out before any sales pitch had been made by anybody, a theatrical event had gained momentum on word of mouth alone.

Even those dancers who had been convinced of the show's hitworthiness from the beginning were impressed by the critics' reaction. Rick Mason recalled, "We did opening night downtown and we got the reviews and they were all raves. The fever, the energy was so strong—as was the relief. We were so relieved all this was paying off. We were working as such a tight unit. I think it was probably our best performance. We had gone through all this agony and finally I could see that we had something incredible. I was crying, laughing, everything. . . . I knew then that we had something . . . and all the crap was worth it."

When the dancers arrived for work at the Newman for the Wednesday, May 22, matinee, the ticket line stretched out the door of the Public Theater and around the block toward Astor Place. "The word was out," Wilson said. "It was really an overnight sensation kind of thing and I realized that this was bigger than we thought."

But just because the show was a hit, that didn't mean that the dancers' lives abruptly became a gay whirl of parties or that they all lived happily ever after. The show itself was a lot of hard work, and although its content was now "frozen," meaning the script could no longer be changed, Bennett continued to hold afternoon rehearsals to burnish the performances.

"That was another groaner," Ron Kuhlman recalled. " 'Oh no,

THE LOGO: This is one of the photos used to design the show's logo for posters, record sleeves, even towels. From left: Ron Kuhlman, Kay Cole, Wayne Cilento, Baayork Lee, Michel Stuart, Donna McKechnie, Kelly Bishop, Thommie Walsh, Nancy Lane, Patricia Garland, Ron Dennis, Don Percassi, Renee Baughman, Pamela Blair, Rick Mason, Sammy Williams, and Priscilla Lopez.

PHOTO BY MARTHA SWOPE

HOW IT'S DONE: Arms upraised, Michael Bennett steps in for Don Percassi's role as Al in the number "Sing!" at an off-Broadway dress rehearsal. Watching him are (visible over his arm) Renee Baughman and, to her right, Baayork Lee, Michel Stuart, Donna McKechnie, Thommie Walsh, Nancy Lane, Patricia Garland, and Ron Dennis.

PHOTO BY MARTHA SWOPE

HOW MANY PEOPLE DO YOU WANT?: Patricia Garland's role, Judy Turner, was patched together from lines that weren't working elsewhere. Garland used humor to blend them into a single character.

PHOTO BY BARBARA J. ROSSI

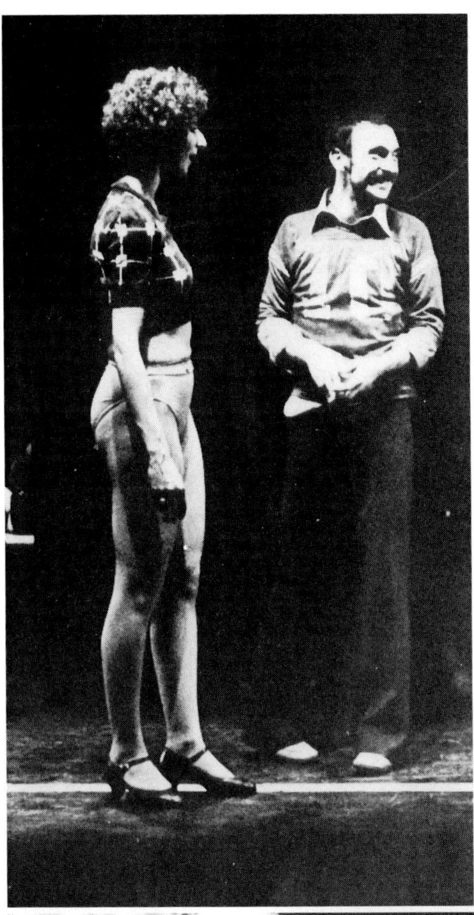

"PRETTY" IS WHAT IT'S ABOUT: Nancy Lane (in high-heel costume that took her a while to get used to) and Michael Bennett at Newman Theater rehearsals for "At the Ballet."

PHOTO BY BARBARA J. ROSSI

SEVEN WEEKS THAT SAVED THE SHOW: Michael Bennett and the original cast are captured during the endless hours of changes and finessing that characterized the final weeks of workshops before the off-Broadway opening.

PHOTO BY BARBARA J. ROSSI

DRESSING ROOM DISPUTES: Priscilla Lopez poses triumphantly in the hallway outside the Shubert Theatre dressing room on Broadway where she and Kelly Bishop persuaded the Shubert Organization to knock down a wall so they could be roommates.
PHOTO BY VINCENT FANUELLE

OPENING NIGHT: Michael Bennett and Bob Avian do an impromptu version of "One" with sterling-silver top hats that bear the engraved signatures of the original cast members. The hats were a gift from the cast to the choreographers to celebrate opening night on Broadway.
PHOTO COURTESY OF RICK MASON

PHOTO BY MARTHA SWOPE

SINGULAR SENSATION: After experimenting with several finales, Bennett followed his instinct to end with high kicks and glittering golden costumes.

PHOTO BY MARTHA SWOPE

GONE WEST: After leaving five Originals behind, the cast moved to the West Coast, hoping to spread "the word" and to take a crack at Hollywood. Much relaxed after a year's run in New York, the cast is shown rehearsing in Los Angeles. From left: Ron Dennis, Don Percassi, Renee Baughman, Pamela Blair, Sammy Williams, and Priscilla Lopez.

REPRISING "SING!": Playing a husband and wife in the show, Renee Baughman and Don Percassi had become close buddies. Here they're rehearsing "Sing!" in Los Angeles.

PHOTO BY VINCENT FANUELLE

ONE MORE TIME: In the ladies' dressing room of the 1988 AIDS benefit at the Dorothy Chandler Pavilion in Los Angeles. It was the last time most of the original cast performed the show together. Michael Bennett had died of AIDS less than a year before and was memorialized at the benefit. From left: Nancy Lane, Kay Cole, Patricia Garland, Renee Baughman, Priscilla Lopez, Asha Hanada-Rogers (who was performing Baayork Lee's role), Kelly Bishop, Donna McKechnie, and Pamela Blair.

PHOTO COURTESY OF NANCY LANE-FISHER

ALL TOGETHER NOW: One of the few pictures of the entire nineteen-member cast. Here they rehearse the finale at the Newman Theater. PHOTO BY MARTHA SWOPE

ON THE LINE: The white line demarcating where the dancers will stand cuts through the center of this photo, taken during the second workshop at the Newman Theater. In the foreground, Michael Bennett gestures while Patricia Garland, Rick Mason, Clive Wilson, Kay Cole, and Sammy Williams take a break beside him.

PHOTO BY BARBARA J. ROSSI

not more! Please!' But there was more work and more changes, more subtle changes."

It was many weeks before some of the dancers fully realized the magnitude of the show's success. They could see that it was a hit and they were pleased about that. Many of them had worked long and hard on shows that had closed in just a few weeks. Or days. But some of the dancers didn't yet understand that *A Chorus Line* would become a landmark. Some of the blame for that can be laid to simple tunnel vision. They had been so close to the project, and so much to the exclusion of everything else, that it was hard to get perspective.

But mostly they were pooped. The dancers' main memory about this period is fatigue. They recall performances slipping by in a kind of weary golden dream. "We were all very tired after those four weeks of previews," Kuhlman said. "Working all day is very tiring physically, and then to have to go on in the evening and give a performance and get emotionally involved, it was exhausting. Thank God we were young."

In some ways, time seemed to stretch out languidly, a season of amorphic acclaim. In other ways, however, it whizzed by. The off-Broadway run lasted 101 performances, just under three months.

Kuhlman said he noticed no change in the audience after the reviews were published. "I felt audiences all reacting the same, all involved, as we were involved. We loved them loving it. I remember my breath being taken away at the finale when everybody would stand and applaud. I was so emotionally involved, the tears falling."

Even after the show moved to Broadway, playgoers would come up to Kuhlman and proudly proclaim that they had seen it off-Broadway. "People would say, 'Oh, I saw that show at the Newman' just the way they might say, 'Oh yeah, I was there when the space shuttle landed!' It's the same kind of reaction, like being part of an important moment in history. To know that you're part of that is a very exciting thing."

Because this kind of success and stability often is fleeting in a dancer's life, the dancers expressed a nearly universal desire not only to enjoy it, but to be intensely conscious of their enjoyment, to step back and savor it. But that wasn't easy to do. Their schedule was so intense that they barely had time to celebrate their success.

Sammy Williams said, "After we opened I became more rebellious. I was under a lot of pressure and I was nasty to everyone. I couldn't cope with the monologue every night because I still didn't know what I was doing. The pressures of sustaining it and the new experience were hard for me.

"I remember one time in New York going over to Priscilla's and depressing her. I asked her if, when she was acting onstage, she was the character or was the character her. She said, 'You're different from the character.' And I said, 'I feel like I'm losing myself in the character. I feel like I am the character.' I think that was the beginning of my being lost because I couldn't separate the two. I would spend my days beating myself up so that I could get in there at night and cry. Michael said he wanted real tears every night and I didn't know how to produce them any other way."

On June 3, the entire cast was called in to work on its free Monday so that the original cast album could be recorded for Columbia. "We had questions about that," Kuhlman recalls, "and they said we'd be paid five hundred dollars for a recording session. We asked about what would happen if we went into overtime and they said there is no overtime. So again we asked what happens if we go past eight hours. And Michael said it would count as two recording sessions instead of one. We began at eight A.M. and it went on all day long. There was a break but we were in and out of there until two A.M. Then when it came time to pay us, they paid us five hundred dollars and we said wait a minute, you said there was no overtime and there would be two recording sessions and they refused to pay us that. Then we had to do the performance for them and we refused to do it because they weren't going to pay us. Finally we were sticking together on something. I don't think everyone was in agreement but we did stick together and refuse to do the performance. They were taking advantage of us, saying one thing and doing another. It wasn't on paper but they said, 'Don't worry about it.' You can never not worry about it."

They got the two checks.

Kuhlman said the recording session was conducted in a Columbia Records studio on Manhattan's East Side. The acoustically tiled room had a glass window on one side so that the engineers in the control booth could communicate with and see the performers inside. In front of the window was a raised platform where Marvin Hamlisch oversaw the musicians. The dancers were arrayed in groups of three or four at microphones for the chorus numbers. There were folding chairs on the periphery where they sat out the solos.

"Marvin Hamlisch was in heaven," Kuhlman said. "He had a smile from ear to ear because he was there with the guy from Columbia [original-cast recording maestro Goddard Lieberson]; it was obvious that for him to be doing a record for this man from Columbia was like a sixteen-year-old kid dancing for Michael Bennett."

It was Kuhlman's first recording session and he watched the process curiously. "I was always impressed with Kay Cole's voice," he said. "I was amazed at how much sound came out of that little body."

Although Kuhlman's own voice can be heard on "Hello Twelve, Hello Thirteen, Hello Love" on stray lines like "playing doctor with Evelyn" and "swear to God and hope to die," he, like most of the dancers not among the Big Six, had no solo. As a result, he said, he wasn't nervous. "I didn't have that much pressure. It wasn't like a film where you can do a scene and if you're not happy with what's in the camera you walk around making yourself nuts, thinking, 'I could have . . . I should have . . .' I can see where the people who had more to do [on the *Chorus Line* album] would have that feeling. For me, I was a little disappointed they didn't use anything of my monologue on the recording."

Don Percassi's most vivid memory of the cast album recording session was Michael Bennett donning tap shoes to help "sweeten" the dance segments.

They were scheduled to start early in the morning and finish before dinner with one break. Kuhlman said he remembers walking home on the break. He also remembers calling dinner guests and telling them he would be somewhat late. "I didn't show up until, what? Midnight, two A.M.," he said. "It was hard work but I had a great time. Looking back now, it was a wonderful experience."

Kuhlman's daughter Greta was born in 1986 and Kuhlman

said the *Chorus Line* album was some of the first music she heard. "She loves to sing and dance to it," he said. "You can't compare the two things, but I'd say that Greta's birth and the birth of *A Chorus Line* were the most exciting experiences of my life."

The cast album overtime pay dispute turned out to be just a preface for the next confrontation. The sight of the seventeen dancers lined up onstage left such a powerful impression that it was chosen as the logo of the show, in keeping with both the theme of the show and its overall minimalist design. Besides the poster, the logo would be used on T-shirts, the record album cover, the Playbill cover, and certain other merchandising items, the dancers were told. But when they sought a share of the profits, Bishop recalls, "Michael said, 'I don't want you standing outside of the Public Theater selling T-shirts.' "

After *A Chorus Line* became a hit, the dancers were inundated with press people wanting to interview them about their experience. "I think all of us made some terrible faux pas at times," Bishop said, "got hurt, got misquoted at times."

Confirming some of the cast members' worst fears, most of the interview requests were for the so-called Big Six: McKechnie, LuPone, Williams, Bishop, Blair, and Lopez. "Do you know what it was like," LuPone said, "hearing the bitching about the Big Six and me not even feeling a part of the nineteen, or six or anything? Okay, I certainly must have been because I got the Tony nomination, so I have to look at myself on that. But I didn't believe it was a reality that served any purpose but hype."

The dancers felt that much of the hype was orchestrated by Bennett, also the subject of numerous interviews, including one in Playbill in which he told the interviewer that he had been spoiled by the low-keyed creative pace of off-Broadway. "I loathed his giving people the impression that we were all one big happy family because it wasn't true," said Blair. "And nobody printed anything that any of us ever said. They were just interested in what Michael had to say. Later I realized that was his power. He decided what should and should not be printed.

"The other thing I resented was his leading people to believe we had made an incredible amount of money from the show. I would go to commercial auditions and the other actors wanted to know what I was doing there since I was rolling in money. Everybody thought we'd gotten a real piece of the show. At capacity we made two thousand dollars [in royalties] every three months if we were lucky. It's fallen off a lot but that's better than nothing. In the nine years time we made maybe thirty-six thousand dollars."

The 1989 *Guinness Book of World Records* reports that *A Chorus Line* has grossed $260 million.

"I wish we'd been smarter back then," Blair said, "because we really did write that show. My goodness, couldn't he have given us one half of one percent for real instead of one half of one percent divided into fifty-two shares [the dancers at the group tape sessions, plus the ones invited to his house, plus the ones at the first workshop whose life stories were used]? This lawyer later told me he thought it was one half of one percent of the writers' share. We thought they were talking about one half of one percent of one hundred percent. He said he doesn't know what the writers' share is because that's an agreement between all of them, whoever got a piece of that action.

"And I believe that they would never have missed it. He's a rich boy, and those people don't *know*. They wouldn't have experienced what we did because they had lucky upbringings and were coddled and always had money. I resent that he's never come forward and said anything on our behalf."

As they had in the past, the dancers faced this dispute by turning to one another. After the second month, off-Broadway afternoon rehearsals were called less frequently and they found they had a little more time to socialize.

"My buddies on that show were Thommie Walsh, Priscilla Lopez, and Kelly Bishop," Michel Stuart said. "During the workshop, not so. But after we began performing, the four of us used to congregate after the show every night. We would come down together, so to speak, after the show. We knew each other pretty well by that time."

Onstage they began to relax with one another as well. Rick Mason, who stood next to Pam Blair and got his rear pinched by her nightly at the conclusion of "Dance 10, Looks 3," had some less apparent encounters with her as well. "We had a blackout before we walked down just before her number," he said. "One night she says to me, 'Hold this, honey,' and put in my hand a wad of gum that she had been chewing during the previous number to get saliva going for her number. She did it more than once, sometimes gum, sometimes a sticky lozenge. I got many a lozenge in my hand, and never did she have the consideration to ask, 'Rick, do you mind holding my gum in your hand?' or even to tell me, 'I'm gonna give this to you tonight.' I never knew what to expect night to night—which in a way was good. I guess it's all part of the live performance syndrome."

Blair's unpredictable personality entertained more than one of the cast members. "She made me crazy but I thought she was a hoot," Sammy Williams said. "She was constantly worried about her voice and her performance and we were constantly telling her she was okay. One night we went out to dinner and I turned around to Pam and told her she would have to stop being crazy on that stage, it's affecting your performance. And she said to me in her haughty voice, 'My dear, when I walk out on that stage, I am an *actress.*' I slipped quietly into my dressing room and never said a word to her about it after that."

LuPone tried to reestablish the comrade-in-arts relationship he'd had with Bennett before he stepped into the role of Zach, but LuPone recalls, "I saw Michael very clearly one night" when he and Bob Avian were visiting Bennett in his apartment. "When Michael got angry about something he'd talk in this deep, guttural voice," LuPone said. "This demon would pop out. So he was angry about something someone had done to him and suddenly he says, 'I gave America *A Chorus Line,*' in this voice. All of a sudden I saw Napoleon. It stunned me."

A Chorus Line opened just over a week before the official end of the theatrical season—just under the wire for several of the season's major awards.

The New York Drama Critics Circle lost no time in naming the off-Broadway *A Chorus Line* best musical of the season, beating all the shows that had opened on Broadway proper during the previous twelve months, and (with sixteen votes) far outdistancing the two runners-up, *Shenandoah* and *The Wiz* (two votes each).

Otis L. Guernsey, Jr., named it one of the 1974–75 season's ten best plays in *The Burns Mantle Yearbook.*

Robin Wagner's scenery won one of the year's Joseph Maharam Foundation Awards.

Owing to different deadlines for other awards, many other laurels were reserved for the following calendar year. Among them were Obie Awards, given by *The Village Voice* for off-Broadway excellence, which went to Bennett, Hamlisch, Kleban, Dante, Kirkwood, Lopez, and Williams.

In later months the show would win a mantelpiece full of Tony Awards, plus the Pulitzer Prize for drama.

The awards merely confirmed what had been suggested in many of the reviews, and what was being regarded in the show business trade journals as a done deal: that *A Chorus Line* belonged on Broadway.

Though the practice is commonplace today, it was still fairly unusual in 1975 for an off-Broadway show to transfer "uptown." Off-Broadway shows generally were more iconoclastic than Broadway ones. Having originated, by contractual definition, in theaters with 499 seats or less, they also usually were too intimate to be transplanted to the wide open spaces of most Broadway theaters, particularly the musical houses.

Such a move was not unprecedented, however. Papp, in fact, was one of the leading practitioners, having sent north *Sticks and Bones, Much Ado About Nothing, Two Gentlemen of Verona,* and most notably, *Hair*. Bennett had been talking with the Shubert Organization since the Vivian Beaumont Theatre confrontation the previous autumn, and with the untimely closing of Edward Albee's Pulitzer-winning drama *Seascape,* the Organization's flagship, the Sam S. Shubert Theatre on Forty-fourth Street at Shubert Alley, was available.

"We were all pretty certain that something was going to happen," Kuhlman said. "I didn't know right away that we were going to go uptown, I just knew I was in a good show, having a great time. I didn't really care whether we went uptown or not. But the houses were packed every night. I guess I cared about the one hundred fifty dollars. It wasn't easy to live on that and the money [from a higher Broadway salary] would help. I did live right on Forty-fifth Street, Forty-fifth and Ninth Avenue in one of those old tenement houses. It was a fifth-story walkup, not the most comfortable apartment. I didn't give it up, though. I figured you're only a star as long as the show runs. But I was excited, because it was my first Broadway show."

For Papp, *A Chorus Line* had cost more than a year of hothousing; watering Bennett with creative freedom and fertilizing the whole enterprise with Shakespeare Festival endowment money. With the word on the street saying that this was certainly another *Two Gentlemen of Verona* and possibly even another *Hair,* Papp knew the time had come to harvest his American beauty.

14.

TRANSFERRING TO BROADWAY (JULY–OCTOBER 1975)

A Chorus Line played its final off-Broadway performance on July 13, 1975. After a short layover, it began previews July 25 on Broadway.

"We had been doing back-to-back shows on the weekends," Patricia Garland remembers, "five shows, which was a killer. Then we had a week off, which wasn't enough. I went to the Bahamas and just as I started to get relaxed we had to come back. I had loved the closeness of the Newman Theater. Any small intimate surrounding creates a different ambiance. But at the Shubert it became larger than life. Suddenly, for me, it became 'successful.' Not that it wasn't downtown, but it took on another perspective: Broadway."

As if to underline the change, Bennett gathered the cast that first week and made a speech saying that he had been one of them during the workshop and the off-Broadway run, but now that the show had moved from the 299-seat nonprofit Newman Theater to the 1,472-seat Shubert Theatre, one of the largest on Broadway, he would have to step away and start treating the show as less of a club and more of a business.

And there was the theater itself. Instead of eighteen reassuring rows, the Shubert's orchestra seemed to fan out into the distance. Plus, they now had to direct their performances to the two balconies rising into the darkness above them.

With their curved walls, raked floors and acoustic ceilings, theaters can be considered giant megaphones or the biggest musical instruments of all. By that measure, if the Newman was a kazoo the Shubert was a Wurlitzer.

"The Newman Theater was so intimate everyone in the audience could see themselves in those mirrors," Thommie Walsh said. "The audience was on such an upgrade. It went from a ten-degree angle to almost a ninety-degree angle. Also, now there truly was an orchestra. At the Newman the orchestra was in the wings in the upstage left area. Now we had an orchestra pit that had to be covered to disguise that there was an orchestra pit there. That covers about twelve feet, so you're that much removed from the audience. I don't think that anyone would notice a difference in our performance unless they were one of the players or one of the previous audiences [at the Newman]. But after two or three weeks we adjusted to that environment and made the space ours."

And there were compensations. For the dancers, the Shubert stage was hallowed ground.

Rodgers and Hart had done three of their shows there in the 1930s and 1940s, including their timeless let's-get-a-barn-and-put-on-a-show musical, *Babes in Arms.* On its stage Alfred Lunt and Lynn Fontanne had done the Pulitzer-winning *Idiot's Delight,* Paul Robeson and Uta Hagen had played *Othello,* and Katharine Hepburn had introduced *The Philadelphia Story.*

Listing only a few of its musicals, the Shubert had hosted the original runs of Lerner and Loewe's *Paint Your Wagon,* Rodgers and Hammerstein's *Pipe Dream,* Burt Bacharach's *Promises, Promises,* Cole Porter's *Kiss Me, Kate* and *Can-Can,* and Stephen Sondheim's *A Little Night Music.*

In light of this history, it was a little scary for the dancers to see the entire street-level exterior of the Shubert being made over for the show. The theater's marquee and showcases were done over in mirrors, with the show's title done in gold foil. The quasi-art deco look using gold and mirrors was an extension of the stage design. To top it off, a huge flashing sign was erected over the Shubert Theatre entrance at the corner of Shubert Alley and Forty-fourth Street, angled to face Times Square. *A Chorus Line* not only occupied the Shubert; it pervaded the Shubert.

"I didn't know if it would go because they'd have to change

it," Don Percassi said, "not because it didn't work, but because there would be a different kind of audience. In all the shows I've ever done they've always had to be adjusted for every theater you were in. I thought *Chorus Line* would need a lot of changing, it would never be a commercial success. We've all seen shows that got wonderful artistic reviews, but then moved and didn't work for some reason. It was scary worrying if the show was going to work in a big house. But when we did our first performance at the Shubert, it went so smoothly that it put all my worries and fears to rest. I had no doubt after that. Yet, it felt different to me."

Nancy Lane was emphatic: "I wish we'd stayed at the Newman forever. It was perfect for what we were doing. It was really gritty, real New York. I know it's glitzy on Broadway, but they really fucked it up. We lost the proximity. We were right in their laps at the Newman, they were looking up our nostrils, they could see what we had for breakfast. They got us new costumes for the finale, the lighting changed, it got more dramatic. All of a sudden we had a full orchestra. They just made things bigger. We couldn't be as intimate, as personal about our performances. It was kind of a drag. We loved the money, of course."

Baayork Lee dealt with the bigger audience by broadening her performance and playing directly to elicit laughter and other reactions from the audience. "I remember Michael saying, 'Don't play the house, play the same show we did downtown and it'll be fine.' And I remember concentrating and almost squinting so that I could block out the balcony. I wanted to play that intimate house again. We had to face the fact that we were beginning to *act A Chorus Line* instead of *being A Chorus Line*."

Robert LuPone now was stationed at the back of the auditorium next to the computerized lighting and sound control board, and directly in front of the standing-room audience. He recalls, "It was easier for me to believe that I was a big-time director on Broadway than off-Broadway. The kinetic energy carried so I had the same show, essentially. All of a sudden I had to play a little bigger, which only enhanced my belief in Zach."

He also quickly made friends with the sound technician, Otts Munderloh. "We had a whole different world going, Clive Wilson, myself, and Otts," LuPone said. "Otts was sitting one step away from me, as opposed to down at the end of the aisle. If I was working, Otts let me alone. If I was willing to talk then he would talk. He would never transgress, he was very receptive."

When the Broadway previews began, it was just over two months since the show had gotten its rave reviews off Broadway. The run had sold out quickly and there had been no tickets available. The move to the Shubert changed that to some degree, and suddenly it wasn't just the theater community insiders who were able to get their hands on tickets. Newspapers and magazines kept up a steady supply of gossip, profiles, and behind-the-scenes stories on the city's latest phenomenon. That, plus the cachet of being on the Main Stem itself, turned the dancers from cult figures into full-blown celebrities.

Rick Mason recalls his pleasure when his friends began to hit him up for tickets. "I loved doing that," he said. "My friends were terrific, very supportive. There was a lot of 'Aren't you glad you stuck with it' reaction. I grew tremendously. It changed my ability to accept a lot of things about the business and about myself."

Even Michel Stuart, who had seen just about everything in show business, was enjoying riding the unprecedented wave. "I had parties, dinner parties, I was as social as I had always been before that show; the only thing that changed was that everyone was real happy that I was doing this incredible piece of theater. It made me believe once again that all things are possible."

Lane said, "I got very sick when we got to Broadway. I had just separated from a longtime relationship and got my own apartment. I was very unhappy because I didn't know how to live alone. I got a touch of colitis. I was very anemic. The only thing I would do during the day if we didn't have a matinee was sleep, watch TV, and eat junk. So I got sick and was feeling very depressed because I wasn't friends with anybody and I really wanted to be involved and I wasn't. I hope I never have to say that again."

Aside from that, the most serious problem on the horizon arose over the allotment of dressing rooms. This may not seem like a subject to lose sleep over, but think how intensely office workers jockey for a corner office or an office with a window, and you'll have an idea of what ensued. For instance, who would get the dressing room on the first floor closest to the stage—typically considered the "star" dressing room? Also, with a cast the size of *A*

Chorus Line's, dancers had to share rooms with two or three dancers crammed into each. Who would wind up as whose roommate?

Dressing rooms hadn't been a problem downtown, where there had been only three rooms, two for the women and one for the men. All three rooms were in the basement of the Newman Theater and all opened onto a single Green Room and a stairway that led up to the stage. By contrast, the Shubert had a half-dozen dressing rooms distributed on three floors on the right side of the stage (closest to the stage door), plus a single large dressing room on the left side of the stage, and a pair of larger "chorus" dressing rooms in the basement. The basement rooms went to the eight understudies: Allen, Cissel, Edwards, Serrecchia, and John Mineo (who joined the company as a swing during late previews) in the men's dressing room; Drake, Kirsch, Schweid, and Wilzak in the women's.

Bennett seized the assignment of other dressing rooms as an opportunity to engage in a little social engineering. Lopez said, "Mr. Michael Bennett decided that he knew us so well he was going to decide whom we would room with so that we could have a good influence on each other. I understood it but I didn't like it. I feel that your backstage life is important and that you should feel as comfortable as you can. And I felt I wasn't going to be comfortable with that arrangement. Thinking about that all these years later, I decided it was good, in a way, because the cliques could have gotten cliquier. Michael's arrangement sort of neutralized things a bit."

Bishop called Bennett's assignments "bizarre. It was like he was trying to ruin the company. This company became so strong, we became an entity unto ourselves. We became 'the Blob.' You couldn't mess with us. We were tough. I think what happened with Michael was that, subconsciously, he tried to break us up. Divide and conquer."

On the theater's right side (the side closest to the stage door) Rick Mason shared a top-floor dressing room with Don Percassi. Also on the top floor was the room Wayne Cilento shared with Michel Stuart. On the middle floor, Sammy Williams went with Ron Dennis, Nancy Lane was put with Kay Cole, and Thommie Walsh shared with Clive Wilson.

"The dressing rooms divided us," Ron Dennis said. "It set up camps immediately: who was on what floor, the lower the floor the more importance, the larger the dressing room, the more importance. Still, you could paint your room or jazz it up with a phone or fridge or whatever. You could make yourself feel just as important as you had downtown. At least at the Newman when the stars came downstairs they had to see everybody because everybody was on the same floor and they couldn't miss you. But at the Shubert, if they went to see Donna or whoever and you weren't on that floor or in that dressing room, you didn't see those people. There wasn't that sense of acknowledgment as a group anymore."

Bennett made some diplomatic moves as well. He eliminated the first-floor "star" dressing room entirely, turning it into a Green Room, also used as the stage manager's office.

The first large dressing room on the second floor had been divided in two with Lopez and Blair on one side; Bishop and Baughman on the other. The arrangement might have looked good on paper, but it caused trouble from the start. Lopez and Bishop had become close friends and did not want to be separated. On top of that, neither of them liked their assigned roommates.

"Pam was driving me crazy," Lopez said, "continually asking me if her performance was good and me continually telling her she had been great. It wasn't that I disliked her; I did like her and she made me laugh. But it was draining to play shrink all the time."

Bishop said, "I'd been in the Shubert Theatre many times: *Golden Rainbow, Promises.* It was the theater I was most comfortable with, I knew every nook and cranny of that theater. The dressing room I was assigned to was my favorite: one flight up from walking in, the second floor. I remembered all the people who had been in that dressing room. They were not the stars, but the first principals. Great. I get in, and they put me with Renee Baughman, the one person I didn't want to be with, and the one person, I'm sure, who did not want to be with me. I think I'm a lot better now that I'm older, but I was very unsympathetic to what I considered weak people. I wanted to slap them rather than help them out. I wanted to say, 'Get out of my way. Stop being weak.' If anyone was terrified of anyone in the company, Renee was scared to death of me. So Michael made her life miserable and made my life miserable.

But I think he did that all over. He took Pam, with her personality, and put her with Priscilla, who has a very easygoing supportive personality. Pam was very volatile, very changeable. Wayne was a very frenetic personality, so he put him with Mr. Cool, Michel Stuart; the Aquarian with the Virgo. Subtle hint. He put Thommie Walsh with Clive, the two handsome ones, and they couldn't get along at all. Anyway, it was a mess. The theater could have blown up with the emotions. And he wouldn't change.

"So Priscilla and I decided that we'd get the wall knocked down, the wall separating our dressing rooms. Gerry Schoenfeld liked me a lot and adored Priscilla. So I said, 'Okay Priscilla, it's your job. You go to Gerry and then I will back you up.' She did, and wow! The wall came down. It's the most wonderful dressing room now. It's got this beautiful arch in it. It could accommodate six, I suppose, on a bad day. And it was amazing. I don't think Michael said a word about it."

Blair said, "When Priscilla asked me if I minded, I said yes but obviously my opinion didn't matter because they did knock the wall down. It was like what my friends had done to me in high school. I didn't know I had done anything wrong, they just turned on me. I remember being shut out of the conversations between Kelly and Priscilla. I was sitting between them but I didn't seem to exist."

When McKechnie and Garland moved to a dressing room on the other side of the theater, Blair took their room for herself.

A similar conflict began to occur when Thommie Walsh and Clive Wilson were put in the same quarters. Cilento and Walsh had hoped to room together. "I was devastated when Thommie was downstairs with Clive and I was upstairs with Michel," Cilento said, "I'm sure we all dealt with that, the initial shock of who we were supposed to be with, who we were not supposed to be with."

"My biggest fear when we moved to the Shubert was that Clive was going to be my roommate," Walsh said. "So of course Michael made Clive my roommate. But in two or three weeks' time I fell in love with Clive. He was a real regular decent person."

"I never felt I had a problem with Thommie," Wilson said. "I'm a great admirer of his. To this day I love his mind, but he would have nothing to do with me. I was a thorn in his side. I was very apprehensive. My first thought was, 'I can deal with this, but oh my God, when Thommie finds out he's gonna shit.' And he did. We sat there in the dressing room like the last two people in the lifeboat; we're either going to drown or survive. But little by little, step by step, we did. It started working when I felt safe enough to take over the design of our dressing room. Bless his heart, he went along with it. I got to love him dearly. It was one of the nicest things that happened in the show, that turnaround. It all turned out so nicely. Here we were in a big show on Broadway, with a dressing room on Shubert Alley, Thommie and I were getting along, and the dream went on."

Ron Dennis recalled, "Sammy [Williams] was constantly battling with Michael about the part and I'd hear it. He would ask my opinion without really wanting to hear it. And I'm not one to give my opinion unless you asked."

Williams said, "Ron Dennis was my very best friend; we were almost like brothers and we fought a lot."

When Baayork Lee saw the initial angst over the dressing rooms, she immediately volunteered to share the basement with the understudies, and left the battles to the other eighteen dancers on the Line. She had happy memories of that basement, where she had spent three years as a chorus dancer in *Promises, Promises*. As she had before, she filled its shelves with flowerpots, rooting avocado pits and potatoes in jars of water. She spent many dinner hours there, after rehearsals, with Alyce Gilbert, the beloved wardrobe mistress of *A Chorus Line*.

Spirits were much lighter on the other side of the stage. LuPone and Kuhlman got the single large dressing room there, which they proceeded to adapt into a makeshift combination hockey/handball court, smacking a handball against the walls and using wastebaskets at either end of the room as goals.

LuPone remembers, "We decorated it with beds and lights and rugs, and then we proceeded to destroy it with handballs and tennis balls and pitching and catcher games. We threw a handball in that dressing room every night before performance. Both of us hit that stage high as kites because we had spent anywhere between a half hour to forty-five minutes working up a sweat."

Kuhlman and LuPone had to reconfigure their ball court when

Bennett decided to partition the room to create a new dressing room for McKechnie and Garland.

"It was very noisy, very rough," LuPone said. "Donna and Trish complained about the noise, but after about six months they could do nothing but laugh: 'Here we go again, that's what they do.' It became a wonderful time for us."

Garland recalled the racket, and said the wall was so thin the four of them could do warm-up vocalises together each night. "It was wonderful fun."

The dancers had another reason to feel happy—one that very few professional dancers ever get to know. Money, lots of it and coming steadily. They had subsisted on $100 a week during the workshops and $150 during the off-Broadway run. But when they moved to Broadway they began, at long last, to make a living wage.

"Our salary meant a lot," Baayork Lee said, "because at that time six hundred fifty dollars a week was a lot for a chorus person to make. I'm sure the minimum was two hundred seventy-five or three hundred."

Sammy Williams said, "No dancer on Broadway at that time got six hundred fifty dollars. We were getting stars' salaries."

Bennett wanted the cast to understand what a breakthrough the paycheck was, but his presentation wasn't especially tactful. Lopez said, "The only time I felt truly used publicly was when Michael asked me what I had made in *Pippin* [as Fastrada] in front of the entire company. I should have told him it was none of his business but I was a good soldier and told him four hundred dollars. And he said 'See? She made four hundred dollars for starring on Broadway and you're going to get six hundred fifty dollars and that's more than fair.' But aside from the embarrassment of that incident I thought it [the money] was just fine."

Though $650 doesn't seem like a princely salary today, "it seemed like a lot of money then," Ron Dennis said. "My rent was cheap. I bought all the clothing I wanted. I was living fine."

Patricia Garland found that the money brought some unexpected problems. "It was very exciting to be wealthy," she said. "But I think it made it difficult in my relationship. Suddenly now the woman was in a better position than the man. Eventually I think it split us up. He could never meet that challenge."

A Chorus Line began previews at the Shubert in late July, but didn't wind up having its official Broadway opening until October 19. Nevertheless, considering the hoopla surrounding the show during those three months, the opening was almost a formality. Garland remembers that the publicity wasn't spread evenly among the members of the company. Already sensitive that the Big Six had most of the lines and songs, the cast began to resent that the same Big Six were getting the lion's share of the publicity. This situation only exacerbated the dressing room tensions. "Some people envied that other people were getting the acclaim," Garland said, "but some people also forgot about where they came from. They didn't share the event, but rather gloated in their glory. My being [roomed] with Donna isolated me from some of the people. It wasn't that they didn't like Donna; they didn't like the fact that she was getting the queen bee treatment. . . . She started making demands and some were being met and, well, that wasn't happening elsewhere. It created bitterness especially among those who felt that they were just as important as she."

The dancers were still nursing wounded pride from when Bennett had withheld a percentage of the proceeds from merchandising. The dancers didn't say anything until that summer, when the show's logo with their likenesses started showing up on a surprising variety of merchandising items.

It was the beginning of the great towel debate. It seems that Bloomingdale's, the Manhattan department store, began selling towels that bore the title of the show and the logo. The problem was that not only were the dancers getting none of the proceeds, but, adding insult to injury, Bloomingdale's would not even issue them credit cards with which to buy the towels, which cost more than $10. The dancers were told that because actors did not have a steady source of income, they were not good credit risks. When they pointed out that the success of the show was such that their employment would be steady, they were told that their $650 weekly salaries were another barrier to getting credit.

"The logo thing makes me so angry even today," Wayne Cilento said. "I can't believe we were all that naive and stupid. We all thought Michael was just going to use our pictures as a poster and not make anything out of it. We all tried to sue Michael for doing that to us, coming out with towels and games and posters and pads and T-shirts, and us getting one dollar for that. The only way we could stand up against him was if we were all as a unit. But some people pulled out. That broke our unity and we were just defeated and had to drop the whole case."

It all came down to money, and soon the disagreements over the "favored nations" contract flared anew.

"We were all told that we'd be getting the same amount of money," Mason said. "But through Priscilla's agent she heard that Donna was getting more money. Being a little bit of the militant, she wanted to do something about it. I know that she was defiant about us doing a photo for [Richard] Avedon because we weren't given the twenty-four-hour notice."

Sammy Williams remembers how Bennett "sat us down and said everybody's getting the same, nobody's getting any different. And we believed him, that we were all being paid six hundred fifty dollars. Which was a lie. Years later when we were in Los Angeles I took a dance class from Donna. Afterward we were at this lovely little health food restaurant. Donna and I were just chit-chatting about *ACL* and she told me that when we were playing in New York she was being paid a thousand dollars and just went on with the conversation."

McKechnie said, "I felt a tension when the favored nations dispute happened because at this point I was Michael's friend, though it wasn't what it appeared to be, it really wasn't. The time we spent together was about the show and how to solve the problems. And I was very supportive. I think he felt very comfortable with me. He needed the support. It was difficult for people to take, but I couldn't help it. I had felt the tension before so it was no shock about how these people felt divided."

McKechnie recalls working hard each night at the Shubert Theatre and feeling that she was being treated unfairly by Bennett. "I remember thinking, 'This is killing me doing eight a week for six hundred fifty dollars. That was not the agreement. Michael went back on it and I allowed it to happen.' So I didn't go in. That was the first time I'd ever done that. I got sick and then I kind of stayed sick day after day after day. Bobby Avian got on the phone asking what was going on, and I told him I had the flu. He wanted to know when I was coming in and I told him, 'In a couple of days.' And as soon as I got back, my salary went up to a thousand dollars.

"Michael came to me and said it's not fair that you get what everybody else is getting because it wasn't our arrangement considering your contribution, what you've done with the show, and what you've done in the past. The one thing I felt that people overlooked was the fact that I had already established myself to some degree and I had a certain credibility. So when there was a lot of press to be covered . . . I went out for every interview. Not everybody wanted to go out and do those interviews. People really turned them down, I don't know why."

Lee said, "I was on both sides once again. Money didn't mean anything to me. I was working with Michael Bennett. I had always known that Donna was Michael's favorite. I adjusted to that in *Promises, Promises.* So by the time I got to *Chorus Line,* I just knew where it was at. Plus, I had my own job. My job was to perform Connie, to notate the dancing and to keep the show intact. But when I heard Donna was making more money, one side of me was outraged. It was saying, 'Wait a minute, I'm standing on the Line and how come she's making more?' But the other side was saying, 'We shouldn't be talking about this because she's not here to defend herself. Maybe it's not true.' But then Bernie Gersten told us it was true. Then there were people up in arms, and running back and forth, and saying this and that and taking some kind of vote."

Renee Baughman said, "I thought it was great that some people were in a fighting mood. Pam and Priscilla were hot as firecrackers. I have always admired Priscilla for her spunk. I had never made so much money in my life, so I was happy. I didn't really begin to get it until we were at the Shubert Theatre and the negotiations came up. We were just told that we were going to make six hundred fifty dollars a week and that was it."

The experience of being the featured players in a Broadway hit was surprisingly jarring for the dancers, most of whom had expected to spend their careers dancing behind a star instead of being stars themselves. Focusing on their problems was one way to avoid dealing with the intensity of the experience of triumph.

Michel Stuart got as caught up in details as any of them, but he sometimes stepped back and tried to put the show in perspective. He said, "I think had we been together longer into that experience before we got so high, so cosmic—and lots of people did lose their head and their egos—people would have learned things."

Williams acknowledged, "At the time my ego was very, very large. I wasn't afraid to meet people, I had something to talk about, I had something that I was proud of. And I had people who loved me for what I was doing. I had letters and telephone calls, flowers and presents and dinners. So it started out as acceptance and my ego became bigger and bigger until I just thought I was 'it.' I thought I was the only talented thing around, it got to that point. It got worse when the six 'principals,' of whom I was one, started getting the notices, the interviews and all that. I certainly wasn't being very friendly with the kids in the company. As my ego got bigger I withdrew from the company even more. We were all still competing with each other for the spotlight, but as far as I was concerned, the monologue was *it*."

Cilento said, "My ego was not so swelled—at least not as big as what it was in *Seesaw*. Cathy [his wife] handled my commitment to the project. I was preoccupied but we didn't grow apart. I think I changed in a major way from downtown to uptown. Downtown was real and raw. Uptown got very slick, very Broadway."

Thommie Walsh said his friends outside the show didn't handle his celebrity status well at first. "To some of them I was able to say, 'Wait until it happens to you,' and it has happened to them since. You know you're making a lot more money but you still have the same problems.

"I began to lose close contact with friends because doing eight shows a week is really difficult. You can't do as much partying and lollygagging around. It was a very demanding show, physically and mentally. So my free time started to become a little more precious. I remained in the same apartment; I had maybe one more suit. I traveled a little bit and I definitely had more confidence, because I knew I was doing something special."

Stuart said, "We were loved and adored by everyone. People would come up to me on the streets, in the subways, and 'Thank you' is just what they said. They kept thanking us for doing this mitzvah for the world. I loved going to the theater every night and warming up, which a lot of people didn't do. I used to go down to the stage and do it with a group because I enjoy that.

"I just did the show," Stuart said. "I didn't go out and sell myself and try to get other jobs and promote myself because I was in *ACL*. Looking back on it, I can see times when I was foolish. People called me for commercials and the first three commercials I auditioned for I got, but they were all to be shot on Wednesdays so I turned them down because I had a matinee. I didn't parlay it as a career move. What it did do for me was reaffirm the fact that you could do a wonderful theater piece. It also rekindled the feeling that I wanted to be a theater producer."

McKechnie, too, stopped to savor the success, however briefly. Those three months of Broadway previews, before the aftershock of the opening hit, were many people's favorites. "When we moved up to the Shubert is when I had the best time," McKechnie said. "After the initial publicity there was a period when I really did enjoy it."

But the dancers got little chance to sit back. "Even after we moved uptown I was still trying to please Michael," Mason said. "I was desperate for his attention. He gave me three notes [ordering a change in performance] one day and I tried to put all three into that night's performance rather than spreading them over three nights. That was the night I went up on my lines. It was Baayork's lead-in from me, and I went up. She jumped in and I just backed up."

Wilson said, 'My friends were totally supportive. I remember driving uptown in a cab and Tom Tryon turning to me and saying, "Do you realize what you are in?" But even those people who were envious just thought it was terrific. They got a vicarious thrill from it. They were thrilled to be able to get house seats: 'Come to New York, I know somebody in the hottest show on Broadway!' "

Happy or sad, the dancers often felt they were floating through a dream. But they didn't have to pinch themselves, they had something better to keep things in perspective: the steady parade of their lifelong idols: Gene Kelly, Richard Burton, Steve McQueen, and many others.

Of all their visitors, the one who earned the most points with

Kay Cole, Rick Mason, and others was Shirley MacLaine, not just because she was a hoofer who had fulfilled the fantasy of becoming a star, but because she wasn't too much of a star to climb to the upper floors of dressing rooms in order to say hello to everyone.

"When Michael put me on the fourth floor," Mason said, "it was another blow to my ego. I said to myself, 'Michael's punished me, he doesn't like me.' But then Shirley MacLaine walked up to every dressing room."

Mason got to see some of the stellar visitors, including then First Lady Betty Ford, actress Cher, and British actor Sir Laurence Olivier. "We all had our pictures taken with them," Mason said, "and it felt like we had died and gone to heaven."

It was less heavenly for LuPone when President Gerald Ford attended the show—accompanied by a squad of Secret Service agents. "They're following me with their guns because I'm walking back and forth," LuPone said. "I mean they had me cased because I'm walking all over the place. They were all bugged, computerized, and they were blowing the sound system. The lights were all messed up. One guy sits next to me and I can see this bulge over his heart. It's great, I'm glad Ford's here, but all I can think of is that if I make a wrong move, the guy moves his arm and I'm dead. Now *you* perform through that!"

The opening originally was scheduled for late September, but on September 18 something happened to stretch the suspense just a little bit more. Musicians union local 802 went on strike, shutting down all the musicals and many of the nonmusicals on Broadway.

"After all this," Cole said, "suddenly we weren't working. It was awful. It seemed like an eternity."

15.

The First Six Months' Run (October 1975–April 1976)

Most shows are lucky if they see one opening night, but *A Chorus Line* seemed to have another opening every few weeks. Counting first previews off-Broadway and on, and then the climactic off-Broadway opening, this was the fourth "first night." And there were more to come, with celebrity-paced benefits for the Actors Fund and other charities, and then the ceremonies surrounding various awards.

"All the openings and benefits were strange—strange/peculiar," Dennis said. "It was sort of like watching it from a vacuum. I was thrilled to be around and to be a part of it. On the other hand, there still were those certain people in the cast who got all the attention."

Everyone already knew what the critics thought. Even so, something was different. As the dancers all were waiting backstage a moment before 6:45 P.M. (early enough to allow the TV critics to scamper back to their studios, write their reviews, and have them ready in time for their usual 11:27 slot) it finally hit.

After all the crying, cheering, back-stabbing, and hand-holding, this was it. Broadway.

"The uptown opening was blind terror," Sammy Williams said, "because I didn't know what to expect. This was the real thing. It wasn't until months later, at a matinee performance, that I was standing on a stage doing the monologue, I was in the middle of a thought process and I turned my head and caught the glare of that pole up on the second balcony. And suddenly it dawned on me that I was standing center stage, at the Shubert Theatre, in effect singing 'Who Can I Turn To' all by myself in that spot. I liked it, it felt good. My dreams had come true."

"My family came the opening night at the Shubert," Wilson said. "They loved it, they thought it was thrilling. I was back in the business, I was on the boards. It was the realization of a dream of sorts for me, and for my mother."

Baughman's parents attended in the weeks following opening night. "My mother said I had never sung that badly. When I first sent her the reviews it was very funny because she wanted to know who Donna McKechnie was and 'Who is she getting all these reviews?' My mother was sure that it [the fact that she didn't get as much space in the reviews] was because I hadn't kept up my dance lessons. And my parents didn't understand why I didn't get the job at the end of the show. They took that very personally. The one thing they were thrilled about was the fact that they were sitting right in back of Red Buttons."

"To this day I don't know what that magic was because it was truly theatrical magic," Dennis said, "and it touched so many people on so many levels. I was just in the right place at the right time with the right stuff. Now, after being away from it, I realize how many people never get to Broadway: very, very few of us, even once, much less three or four times. I was there five times, most recently in *My One and Only* [in 1983]. Most people don't get that, they're still struggling to get to Broadway. With *ACL* it was even more special because it had such a magical impact on people. We were almost like little gods and goddesses on a pedestal. It never changed me, even deep down. Most of my old friends are still my old friends. It was a wonderful, wonderful time.

"I felt special, proud, and a little embarrassed being in this big hit show. People do say that show helped change their lives. I still get embarrassed signing autographs. During that period there were so many to sign, I can't figure out why someone wants your name on a piece of paper. I know all the reasons but it still doesn't make sense."

***

After the excitement of the Broadway opening there was the Actors Fund benefit on November 2 and a visit from Laurence Olivier on November 11. Lee remembers, "It was devastating the first time we had the Actors Fund benefit at the Shubert. People were running down the aisles trying to grab us. Chita Rivera was one. They just jumped out of their seats. It was an evening for gypsies. You'd come out of the stage door and everybody would want your autograph, and there was always that person there to say, 'You know, I'm short too and I could relate to you. I'm very proud.' "

LuPone was out that night, and Wilson went on as Zach, the first person since Barry Bostwick to play opposite McKechnie. "I didn't feel right for the part," he said. "It was like one more opening night."

But as winter approached, the dancers had a new phase of the *Chorus Line* experience to get used to, settling into a long Broadway run.

"The first year was like one big party," Garland said. "We were constantly partying, even though we were working very hard we were also playing very hard. Being the toast of the town all the time was delightful . . . people would stop me in the street or in restaurants. They thought they knew us because we had exposed our lives."

Kay Cole's family flew in from Tennessee and finally saw her in the show, and had the same bowled-over reaction. "It was so overwhelming to have that kind of success," Cole said. "It was just like the biggest thing in the world. People would hear you were in *Chorus Line* and they would go, '*Oh!* We've heard about that.' People's reactions were so intense, it was wonderful to be a part of it. But the same thing happened to me as I imagine happens to people when they suddenly find they're superstars after working for twenty years—you can't believe it. You keep trying to do things that you normally did and you can't do them anymore."

For one thing, Cole was able to get a real apartment, not just the usual dancer's way station. "It was the kind of place where you knew it was going to be a regular job for a long time," she said. "There was no doubt in anybody's mind that you were going to have a job and perhaps you could maybe buy that couch you always wanted. I didn't even have a roommate. I never expected the show to run fourteen years. I remember at the time we thought,

'Wow, if we run to the end of the year it'll be a great Christmas.' So Christmas was wonderful."

Once the stress of the workshops and the opening was past, Cole began to diet and exercise, celebrating her success with health. "I'm one of the few people who didn't get hurt in the show," she said. "I used to warm up every day at the theater, I would have the massage once a week. I became really committed to keeping myself in shape and not getting hurt."

Though Cole dealt with the success in a positive way, the magnitude of it threatened to overwhelm her as much as anyone. "Everybody got so involved in the story of the show, they really believed we were those people. . . . It was amazing for me. When I started working in other situations I realized how much I had been given by the experience of *A Chorus Line,* the respectability of having been a show member, the affection people felt for the original members. Each person had their favorites. It was as if every barrier was down right from the beginning because everybody had a connection to you."

Wilson has a theory to explain that kind of reaction. "It's a simple show," he said. "Everybody loves a contest. Everyone likes to root for someone, everyone wants to see who's going to win. The format of the show is almost foolproof. You put people up there, you tell people about them and people have the chance to decide for themselves who they think is going to win. . . . There's fun in that. And heartache, too. The ones who get rejected, someone in the audience wanted them to win. Some want to identify with the underdog, some with the overachiever. Then you add the show's obvious appeal as a musical. The fine dancing, the singing, the whole thing, the package. It's made ballet a stronger force as a form of entertainment in America, reaching more of the masses than it did before. Others have contributed to that, but I think this show laid the groundwork."

As dance captain, Lee wasn't able to sit back as much as the other dancers as the show settled into its run. "After we opened I had to get on to the business of maintaining," she said, "which is an art in itself. I felt a lot of people's egos had run away with them and I had to deal with that. I had cleanup rehearsals and understudy rehearsals. I feel that I always had everybody's respect. They knew what I was trying to do."

As Zach, LuPone had a unique vantage point on the show's progress during the first winter's run, 1975 to 1976. "I saw the show every night," he said. "I got so I could tell everyone about their performances, when they were on, when they were off. I knew how they hid from me, from 'Zach.' I knew when they wanted to do the show, I knew when they didn't want to do the show. I knew when anybody was 'rolling the tape' on me and wasn't willing to play in the moment. I was able to perceive when people were dancing for me and when they weren't. There was a lot of bitching going on before and after the show but when show time came I can't think of any time for a prolonged period that anybody let the show go—outside of fatigue. There were some Saturday nights, boy, you could see it in those last kicks. I'm not just talking tired, I'm talking exhaustion. But they gave it all they had. The cast did feel that it was their show, their moment in history."

The exhaustion took many forms. Where Cole found the extended run to be an opportunity to regenerate, McKechnie found it wearing. "People started feeling pressure in another way, the pressure of continuing, of sustaining and keeping the show alive. I felt a little exploited. I mean, I exploited myself but I started feeling like I was in a fishbowl. I was overworked, too involved in the show for too long. I lost a certain perspective. I felt people were making too much of it all. I felt it was something that deserved to be called a great show but it was sort of getting out of control. My tendency was to downplay it to cope with it. So I tried to counter it by not emphasizing it so much in my life."

She had another source of stress as well. Her hairdresser boyfriend, observing the *Chorus Line* fever, "approached me and said, 'I want to be the hairdresser for the show.' It was like a slap across the face," McKechnie said. She tried to explain that a hairdresser may reign supreme in his own shop, but backstage "hairdressers don't have the same stature." When her boyfriend insisted, McKechnie told him, " 'If you really want that job I'll call Michael and ask him, but that means the end of us.' He said, 'I want the job.' "

A few days later, she left him. When old flame Ken Howard tried to return to her life a short time later, she was available.

"Whatever the reasons," she said, "I had an anxiety attack one night. I had to look down to make sure my legs were still under me. Ultimately there was no breakdown where something really crashed and I went into hiding, but there was a period when I would go in and out like this."

Though she eventually moved in with Howard, she said, "the show was my life. I would get up in the morning like an eighty-year-old. If I wasn't going to therapy I was going to a chiropractor three times a week. When pain got especially bad I was getting needles. It was muscle spasm, stress, fear, rage, dealing with the complexities of being in a hit show, the demands on me all the time—and not getting enough back in a personal way.

"I had no personal life. Ken was needy then, going through rehearsals for a new Broadway show and I was kind of taking care of him and I felt for the longest time that there was no one for me. It was a very trying and lonely existence. I remember thinking to myself that someday I'm going to do this or another show and really enjoy myself. I was still sorting out what is success to me, what a career really meant to me, how much would I sacrifice for it, what kind of relationship did I want with a man, do I want to get married, what am I doing? You think that your life will be fine and peachy once you get to a certain place that you have worked hard for, but it isn't. That's what gets scary."

"Shortly after we opened," Williams said, "I asked Michael if he had known it was going to be as big a hit as it was. He said he planned it that way. 'Your life will never be the same because of this experience,' he said, and he was so right. It hasn't been. It allowed me to release things, to grow. It made me a more conscious person. It made me more sensitive to feelings. It's made me grow spiritually, personally. It's allowed me to reach out, to accept love, to give love. *A Chorus Line* was the key to all of that."

After the bitterness over the logo towels began to fade, Lee allowed herself the luxury of getting a credit card at Bloomingdale's.

"It meant a lot," she said. "Star time. Some people in my life did not handle my success well. It hurt because you want them to share in your success. You want to be able to share this incredible experience and this abundance of love that you're now getting.

But if they can't handle it, you find yourself not enjoying it because you're not sharing it. Sharing it is the most exciting part. And I'm a sharing person."

Mason said he was particularly distressed when *The New York Times* published Al Hirschfeld's caricature of the show. It was a picture of the Line, but seen as if exaggerated through a fish-eye lens. McKechnie and LuPone were the most prominent figures, with several of the others smaller but still distinct, and a few in the back merged and undifferentiated. "Do you see me in Hirschfeld?" Mason asked. "You see two or three people, they're kind of blended. It could be Ron, Wayne, and myself. So we were nondescript. But at the same time I felt that if I had something that was memorable, maybe I would have been more distinct in Hirschfeld's drawing. I felt a part of something, and yet I was detached from it. More than once my ego did rear its head and say, 'Hey, you could have been a Hirschfeld drawing.' "

The last straw came on December 1, 1975, when *Newsweek* did a cover story on the wild success of the show. But instead of the whole cast appearing in the cover photo, there was a portrait of McKechnie executing a lunge. Bennett protested that he had no control over what *Newsweek* put on its cover, but many of the dancers say they had not even been told a photo session was being scheduled. For dancers who had watched McKechnie get what they believed was preferential treatment from the first day, it seemed that her coronation was complete.

"I was in a dressing room with Trish Garland," McKechnie said, "and she was like my best girlfriend—that is, until I got on the cover of *Newsweek*. We had a rehearsal and I was walking by this stand and I saw this foot. I recognized my foot, I couldn't believe it. I knew the show was going to be on the cover but I didn't know I was. I just couldn't get over it and I took it into the theater to rehearsal. Everyone was sitting there and I couldn't show it to them, so I hid it. When I got upstairs I showed it to Trish and she said it was unflattering. I was so hurt. It brought up so many unresolved feelings about my family, being guilty about having more than my sister, about having more than someone else. That was an unjust feeling, but I started behaving like I had no right. The need to be accepted by the group all of a sudden became more important to me than my own independence and my own celebration of my own sense of triumph. It was a shame in a way because you can't have both. The most hurtful thing was that my father had died a week before."

Mason said the situation was put in perspective for him when he would come out of the stage door and no one would ask for his autograph. "That affects you, if only for the fact that it was pounded into our heads that we were the show as a group, that there were no stars," he said. "Michael lied to us about that because if he believed it he never would have allowed Joe Papp to put Donna on the cover of *Newsweek.* If we all were the stars of the show, he would have put the whole Line on it."

Spring of 1976 was a time of consolidating performances in anticipation of Tony Award nominations and a possible California company. The thrill of the show's success banked into a warm glow. Though Lee was in charge of keeping the dances sharp, Bennett maintained personal strict control over every aspect of the show. Some of his dictums seemed oppressive to the dancers. When they went so far as to adjust their hairstyles, Bennett would upbraid them in front of the entire company. He also dismissed Nancy Lane's request to try one of the other roles. She had her eye on Sheila or Cassie, but Bennett wouldn't hear of changes so soon. He had bigger plans, especially for McKechnie. And everyone noticed.

That year's Theater World Award went to the entire cast, which in the eyes of the dancers on the Line was the only way to give an award in a show whose whole point was its starlessness. But between the salaries, the size of the roles, the reviews, the Hirschfeld caricature and now the *Newsweek* cover, it became obvious that the rest of the world *did* think the show had a star. And there was one more laurel yet to come.

16.

The Tony Awards (April 1976)

The annual Tony Awards constitute a giant two-hour commercial for Broadway. The attendant hoopla recalls the annual Oscar broadcast, though the Tonys perennially exhibit better taste, offer more consistent entertainment, enjoy better reviews, and suffer lower ratings. The Pulitzer Prize traditionally carries just as much weight, but it salutes only the writers. The Tony Awards for performance are the highest accolades American theater gives to actors, and, commercial or not, they're coveted.

They're also fairly rigidly categorized, and there's no award for ensemble performance. Like it or not, if the dancers of *A Chorus Line* were going to win Tonys, they would have to be either as "best actor/actress" or "best featured actor/actress." But to set one member of the Line above another, and to presume that the performances were not interlocking components of a whole, was to fracture the group once and for all. Therefore, as nomination day rolled around on March 23, the dancers were anticipating it—and dreading it.

A Chorus Line was nominated in ten categories, and wound up winning nine of them. The show was up for best musical (Joe Papp), best book of a musical (Kirkwood and Dante), best score (Hamlisch and Kleban), best actress in a musical (McKechnie), best supporting actor (LuPone and Williams), best supporting actress (Lopez and Bishop), best director (Bennett), best costumes

(Aldredge), best lighting (Musser), and best choreographer (Bennett and Avian).

Primary competition for *A Chorus Line* at the 1976 Tony Awards were Stephen Sondheim's *Pacific Overtures* and Bob Fosse's *Chicago,* the show for which so many of the dancers from the first workshop jumped ship. Florence Klotz's costumes for *Pacific Overtures* beat Aldredge's pace-setting dancewear, the only category where *A Chorus Line* did not bury the competition. *Chicago* was an also-ran in all ten categories in which it was nominated. The revue *Bubblin' Brown Sugar* also was nominated for best musical that year.

It's perhaps significant that LuPone was nominated as supporting actor. Even the Tony nominating committee considered *A Chorus Line* to have but one star—McKechnie.

With the nominations came the preparations for the broadcast itself, which would originate, coincidentally, from the Shubert Theatre. In keeping with the Tony broadcast's big-commercial theme, each of the nominated musicals is asked to present an excerpt, usually the splashiest number in the show. These excerpts provide some of the highlights of each year's broadcast. As the opening of the 1976 broadcast, Bennett agreed to offer the entire opening sequence of *A Chorus Line* up to the moment when the Line comes forward with their resume photos in front of their faces.

"I couldn't believe we were going to be on television," Nancy Lane said. "That was the best. It was great to be dancing and doing something I didn't have to learn because I already knew it and didn't have to sweat it out."

Cilento said, "I was not nominated but I never thought I would be. I was real happy for them. I didn't have hard feelings about it. I wasn't competing with them. I think if one of those other supporting roles had been nominated and I wasn't I would have been hurt. But the people nominated were one of those six. They were the people who had through lines and the other people were just supporting lines."

Tony anxiety had begun almost a year earlier when the show was still off-Broadway but when it appeared certain that it would move uptown. Sammy Williams says he was stopped after a performance "and someone said to me, 'You're going to be nominated for a Tony, so you had better prepare yourself.' Up to that point I'd never even thought about it. That planted a seed, so it was something that I consciously or unconsciously worked for and wanted. I was smart enough to know that I had a good role, worth a nomination. And Michael kept telling me the few times I did have a conversation with him, 'Tony time, Tony time.'

"So when I got the nomination I was not surprised. But it was the beginning of the end for me because I knew that once I won the Tony there would be nothing else. I knew that people would just put me up on a pedestal and I was not going to be able to handle it.

"But I wanted it and I was determined to get it. I remember the day that they had sent the notices: We were at a rehearsal. Michael had given us a pep talk about the nomination. Some are going to be nominated, he said, some aren't, but don't let it affect your performance, et cetera. Sure enough, that afternoon they were delivered. I walked in and showed the nomination to Michael. Bob LuPone and I were both nominated and I walked up to him and suggested that we go out to lunch to talk about it.

"We went to some fast food place and I said to him I want the Tony, and he said, 'Well, you're going to win it anyway so what's the difference.'

"I said, 'Don't say that. You're just as much in the race as I am. But I'll tell you, I'll fight you tooth and nail for it. And I'm going to get it.'

"From that point we started competing in performance. Two weeks later, after beating each other up onstage and fighting for those performances to get that Tony, we looked at each other and realized we couldn't do this anymore. The nominees had already been picked, it was out of our hands. So we stopped fighting and went back to doing the show the way we were supposed to do it."

Also nominated as best featured actor in a musical were Charles Repole for *Very Good, Eddie* and Isao Sato for *Pacific Overtures*. For his part, LuPone said he couldn't imagine where his nomination came from. "Great," he said, conjuring up the anxiety of the moment. "Okay, I'll go for it. So for the next five weeks it's 'The Tony voters are coming, the Tony voters are coming, we gotta do a good show, the Tony voters are coming.' I did the best show. I did not give myself space at all, under any circumstances, to slack off and do anything other than the best one-hundred-ten-percent show that I could do. Which means I played handball for an hour and a half. I really broke my butt. And not to get the Tony: I knew I was not going to get the Tony. Maybe as a means of defense I said, 'I'm not going to get it. . . .' I used Buddhism to override my negativity, my insecurity. So I was okay, but I didn't want to say that at least I didn't try."

Bennett nearly sabotaged Williams's chance for the Tony in a power play in the last weeks of balloting. "At one point there was some sort of function going on and Michael wanted a couple of people from the show to go and perform after our show," Williams said. "He wanted me to perform too and I said no. He said, 'But I need you,' and I turned around and started walking out. He said, 'If you walk out of this rehearsal, you can keep right on walking.' So I kept on walking and went to my dressing room. Jeff Hamlin [production stage manager for the show] came up to my dressing room and asked me to come back down to the rehearsal. I asked him why he was doing this, and he said that Michael just wanted me to come back down to rehearsal and finish it out. So Jeff left and I sat there and decided to go back down.

"He was just doing the boys' combination of the ballet and I got into my group and I did it. Then I went over to stand in the wings like I always did. Michael was showing people how to do grand jetés across the stage. And he did a grands jetés right at me into the wings and threw me a kiss. I figured everything was fine, I had come back to rehearsal like he wanted. He broke us and we all went out to dinner. I was sitting in Charlie's [theater district restaurant] and either Baayork or Jeff Hamlin told me not to go back to the theater. I wouldn't be doing the performance that evening.

"I couldn't believe it. I started to throw a fit in Charlie's and Baayork said to me you gotta go on, you gotta go back to the theater, the Tony Award people are there tonight, the Tonys are this Sunday, you have to be there for this performance. So I went back to the theater and they let me perform, but I was barred from the theater the next matinee day unless I apologized to Michael. I got very violent and said some nasty things to Baayork that I don't even want to repeat and I said some nasty things to Jeff Hamlin and all Michael wanted was an apology. I didn't feel I had to apologize. Michael wanted me to do him a favor but I wouldn't do it. He thought I was being defiant, and I was. I was just as angry at him as he was at me.

"The next day I came to the theater and there's Jeff Hamlin spread-eagle at the stage door saying he can't let me in. I called Terry Marrone at Actors Equity and told her that I was being barred from the theater. She said I would have to get it worked out and if I had any more problems to let her know.

"Finally Jeff let me in. We were rehearsing at City Center for the Tonys. I wasn't about to call Michael and apologize, to bow down to him. Finally Walsh took me aside and told me that if I wanted to win that Tony on Sunday I'd better call and apologize. Well. I walked into the office and asked Jeff to dial the number; when I got on I just said, 'Michael, I'm sorry' and slammed the receiver down. What a terrible experience. How could he bar me from the theater during the week of the Tonys? Where was that man's mind? Better yet, where was mine?"

The situation was the same in the best featured actress category. Bishop and Lopez, who had torn down a wall in order to share a dressing room, now found themselves in competition for the same award. The two of them competed against Virginia Seidel for *Very Good, Eddie,* and, in an odd coincidence, Robert LuPone's sister, Patti LuPone, who was up for *The Robber Bridegroom.* She would go on to win the best actress Tony in 1980 in the title role of *Evita.*

Bennett gave the cast his Tony pep talk after a matinee, and the cast then went on dinner break. Lopez and Bishop shared an uptown bus that would take them to Dobson's for dinner. On their way out of the theater, Bishop remembers, Lopez took something out of her mailbox. "She looks at it fast, like it's something discreet, like it's something horrible," Bishop said. "She put it away and I was just quiet. I said, 'It's a nomination, isn't it?'

"She said, 'I-i-i-it's, y-y-y-yes, i-i-it's the nomination, i-i-i-it doesn't m-m-m-mean a thing.' She was, like, poor baby.

"I said, 'Well, you know, everybody expected you to get it.' She was more miserable than I was. And I was pretty miserable. I had a miserable dinner break, she had a miserable dinner break, I'm sure. We didn't ride back together. We never did. I'm one of these people that walks into a theater for an eight o'clock performance at six-thirty; and for an eight o'clock performance she's there at seven-forty-five. So we have a different way of approaching performances. So I went back to the theater—grimly. Adult. I lived through *Irene* in Denver. I'm always going, 'God has a reason.'

"But when I get back to the theater there's something in my mailbox. I open it up and it's my nomination. I was *so* happy. I went up to the dressing room and put my hot rollers in. Priscilla came in at her same late, late time, looking like she's about to cry. I sat there for a minute looking at her in the mirror. We always talked in the mirrors because she was on the other side. And I said, 'Priscilla?'

" 'Yes?'

" 'I have a nomination.'

"She started screaming, 'I'm gonna die!' and jumping up and down. 'Oh God, oh God, what am I gonna do?'

"And I said, 'Yeah, it's freaking me out too.' "

Recalling that day, Lopez said, "In terms of my fantasies, the Tonys were the icing on the cake. This was it. It was real exciting, though competing with Kelly was a drag. There was a part of me that kept saying, 'We're both going to win,' because I couldn't bear the thought of losing or Kelly losing. So to make it easy on myself I had us both winning. Then I would feel that if I lost, at least it would be Kelly."

As it turned out, in addition to sharing a dressing room and a Tony nomination, Bishop and Lopez shared a psychoanalyst who helped them through their Tony competition.

"We both had the advantage of working out, in our own personal therapy sessions, our feelings about each other," Bishop said. "I remember our shrink saying to me at one point after the awards were given, 'The reason it was all right is that you both gave each other *permission to win*. So that's why it's okay.' But of course in the interim there were lots and lots and lots of people in this business that just wanted to see this gorgeous friendship torn asunder. People said very snide things to me about her, and I'm sure to her about me. You know, to get stuff going. And we just kept taking it."

Lopez agreed. "Many people didn't believe that and were just waiting around for our friendship to fall apart."

Another reason Bishop was relatively calm about the situation is that she was certain she would lose. "The word on the street was that Priscilla was going to win," Bishop said. "And I thought, 'Well, she's the most sympathetic character in the show, next to Donna. And very vulnerable and wonderful.' I was hearing a lot of 'You *should* but she's *going* to.' Who knows what she was hearing. The night before the awards show Michael called me and said, 'How're you doing? Priscilla's going to win.'

"I said, 'So they tell me.'

"He said, 'Are you okay? Can you handle it?' Which I really loved him for. When I've told other people this story, they go, 'What a terrible thing for him to say!' And I say, 'No it's not! He called to say, this is what's going to happen. Are you all right? Can I help you?' And I said, 'Yes I can. I'm ready for it.' "

McKechnie's nomination just added to the confusion and tension she was already feeling. "It was following suit with everything else," she said. "I'd never put a lot of stock in that anyway, but the more it started hitting me the more I realized what an honor it was. . . . I never had my sights on it when I first came into theater. After the nominations I started realizing that indeed it was nice. I felt very grateful. That may have been one of my saner moments. I started realizing that I might get it.

"I was nominated along with Chita Rivera, Gwen Verdon, and Vivian Reed. I remember Baayork saying there's a lot of excitement in the air. My mother was coming, my father had died. I don't think I was really dealing with it because I couldn't yet. I remember Baayork saying, 'You've got to go with Michael. You are America's sweethearts. You have to go with him.' I was in a perplexed situation, having made other arrangements. Yet I felt Baayork was right because I think Michael was more excited and more happy for me than I was myself."

Among the so-called Big Six dancers in *A Chorus Line,* Pam Blair was the only one not nominated. "I was so envious of them," she said. "I felt like a terrible loser. It wasn't as if I hadn't been given the material. I had an incredible number in that show. It must have been hard for those people that weren't even given a stab at it.

"I remember what it was like in the dressing room at the Shubert that night. Donna was a wreck and Kelly and Priscilla were trying hard to still like one another in spite of the fact that they were pitted against one another. I looked at them and said it's so wonderful not to be a winner or a loser tonight.

"Despite all the horrible things I've said about Michael, he gave me one of the most thrilling moments on the stage. That was the night we did the opening number at the Tony Awards; I was so proud to be a dancer. I felt as if I could fly. It was probably worth all the crap to have that one moment."

Last-minute jitters struck Sammy Williams. "There was a part of me so intense about winning it, and there was another part of me that was so fearful about possibly winning it. I couldn't sleep. I would just bawl my eyes out, saying, 'I can't handle it, I can't cope with this, this is the end of my career, I'm going to be a has-been, I don't want to be called that.' A friend called up Celeste Holm and asked about her winning a Tony and asked her how she coped with it. She said the best way to cope with it is to realize that it's not the rest of your life. It's a moment in time, being awarded for a moment in time, and you must go on."

The Tony Awards show opened dramatically with the camera panning through the evening sky over Manhattan, and a voice-over describing the never-ending quest of stage-struck performers coming to New York with the dream of making it on Broadway. *A Chorus Line* served virtually as the theme of the show. The screen image lofted over Times Square and, picking out the flashing marquee on the Shubert Theatre, zoomed in on the giant letters spelling A CHORUS LINE in light. The image then faded to the stage where LuPone was calling the opening combination, "Five, six, seven, eight . . ."

That opening, plus what could be described as the choreography of the four cameras in the theater that night, were Bennett's work, designed to enhance the show's cinematic impact.

During the ensuing program, "I was this sunshine person running around," Lee said. "Us, us, little old us, we did it! We didn't bargain for that. We only bargained for the workshop and now we were getting Tony Awards. I screamed so loud as we were watching it on monitors backstage."

Rick Mason said that to him the Tony Awards ceremony was the highlight of his involvement with *A Chorus Line*. "Opening night was hot," he said, "but not as hot as the Tonys because the Tonys meant that we had really made it to an exceptional level. Michael did put me within camera range. He put me on a side, which made me think I was being punished. And yet when I was told that I was constantly in the shot it made me feel good. It was an experience that I'll never forget. I was happy—yeah, happy—for those people nominated because it was basically a reflection on the show that I was involved with."

Bishop said, "I kept saying in my mind, 'Mine's the acting part and this calls for an actress. But she's the sympathetic character, she's got two songs, she's more featured, I'm more ensemble. Look, face it. It's okay.' I was trying to keep my energy up. My job that day was to be the most gracious loser in the world."

And then they started to announce the awards. "Yes," LuPone said, "it was time for 'And the winner is . . .' And that's when I lost. I lost the battle of wanting it because that's when I wanted it. I heard 'And the winner is'—and I suddenly thought, 'God I want this fucking thing'—'Sammy Williams.' Boom, it hit me, I lost. My eyes crossed and my ears went up to the top of my head. But what a thrill."

Williams said, "The evening I won I was elated with myself. There I was standing up there with the Tony in my hand. I was very happy. All I knew was that I had gotten what I wanted."

Lopez recalls, "A part of me kept saying that I couldn't lose. I had never lost in my life. Somehow I had always gotten what I wanted, even if I had to work very hard for it. So when I lost I was devastated, it hurt so bad. But at the same time, Kelly was sitting right behind me. When the moment came and they announced 'Kelly Bishop,' I felt like I had been hit in the chest with a truck. The whole episode seemed to be happening in slow motion. I turned to my right and there was Kelly floating past me, her face was alight, she was just glowing and she bent down and gave me a kiss and floated up to the stage."

Said Bishop, "It's peculiar at this point to watch the tape of the Tony Awards. When they said, 'And the winner is Kelly Bishop,'

I was shocked. But you could see on my face an almost imperceptible nod of my head as if to say, 'That's right.' I turned to my boyfriend at the time, I give him a little kiss. I got up, I came around to Priscilla—she was in front of me because she was supposed to win. They put her on the aisle right near the stage; they put me in back. She tells me that I was floating and if you look at the picture, I *did* float. It was bizarre. Talk about walking on air. All I remember feeling was the heat, the warmth. There was a spontaneous reaction, from the balcony more than anything. There was a roar. It was more than applause; it was a physical sensation, the sound that was coming at me. Of course with the television lights and my own heightened sense of emotion, when I hit that stage there was this—whoa. And I just remember it was like standing on the hottest day on the beach with the sun coming down. And I was so happy. I couldn't do anything wrong.

"I floated down to the stage and shook Jerry Lewis's hand. They told me that he was presenting and he didn't like to be touched. So I just shook his hand and then I just started talking. I didn't know what I was saying and every once in a while people would laugh. I was trying to explain what it meant to me and I was being very inarticulate. And then I said [that the whole cast deserved it—but she would keep it at her house] and there was a laugh. And some part of me said, 'Time to get off.' And I just went, 'Thank you' and I walked off."

The best actress award was one of the last given, which left McKechnie with plenty of time to give herself pep talks. She remembers, "I said to myself, 'Donna you always have delayed your reactions, you've never been there emotionally when you were supposed to be. You always get it about two hours later—or two years later. Wouldn't it be nice if for this once, because it is such a nice thing, to celebrate it? To be there in the moment? If you don't do anything else, can you just be there, once, and take it and look at everybody and say "Thank you" and feel like you deserve it?' I think basically I did deserve it. Not specifically the Tony, or an award, but I deserved to have something for myself. So when I heard my name, all of a sudden it was the most wonderful thing in the world. I walked up there and I didn't trip. As soon as I put my feet on the ground, unlike my anxiety attack onstage, I felt every footfall. I thought, 'I am here.' The lights were on the audience and I thought to myself, 'Take a look, remember this moment, you may never have a moment like this again. These are your peers, these are people in theater, you love theater, you're being acknowledged, you're appreciated.' I was able to look at Michael and Bob and Joe Papp and Marvin and Ed, I was able to pick people out, I was really able to speak from my heart."

Mason remembers watching from the Shubert basement. "I don't know if I was happy with the speeches that were made," he said, "because again, we were separated and there wasn't that ensemble reflection. I think Kelly's the one that said something about everyone in the cast deserving this, but I'll take it home and keep it or something like that. I remember what Sammy said, but I don't remember any reference to us."

In addition to all the other awards the show won that night, Bennett had the distinction of winning *two* Tonys, one for each of his hats, director and choreographer (though he shared the latter award with Bob Avian).

Don Percassi spoke to Bennett at the gala that followed the ceremony, and he recalls, "It was a peak period. Michael said to me, 'It doesn't get any better than this.' And he was right. It can be different but it'll never be better. I'm not putting myself down, but I think I was very lucky to be a part of that."

Dennis said he shared the high of the evening because he knew he was part of a winning team.

"This is where the family united," McKechnie said. "I felt tremendous support that night. I felt that whatever bad feelings were held had been let go by people."

For LuPone and Lopez, the party was bittersweet, as might be expected. "At the party," LuPone said, "Janet Roberts, an agent, came up to me and said one of the loveliest things that at least assuaged my disappointment and made me feel good. Janet said, 'They made a great mistake.' That's all she said. And we're talking about a tough William Morris lady. I just said, 'Thank you.' "

As a close friend of both Lopez and Bishop, Thommie Walsh had a hard night. "We had spent a lot of time together, practically every night from the time we got to opening on Broadway to the Tonys. Priscilla and her husband Vinnie and Kelly and her boyfriend Paul and myself would go out every night. We became very tight friends. At the party I remember dancing fiercely with my friend Priscilla who had lost. We danced a lot."

The Tony Awards were the climax of *A Chorus Line* for the nineteen original dancers on the Line—and an ending. In the weeks just prior to the Tonys, it was announced that the first national company of *A Chorus Line* was set to open May 6 at the Curran Theatre in San Francisco. The national company would play almost two months in San Francisco before transferring to Los Angeles for an opening July 1. Bennett's plan had been to transfer the entire original cast to the West Coast. He had even taken out advertising to that effect. But that's not the way it was working out. Not everyone wanted to leave New York. That meant that when the original cast gave its final Broadway performance on April 25, it would be the last time they all performed together. After more than a year in each other's constant company—more than two years for those who had attended the first taping session—the Line was about to be broken.

17.

Los Angeles and Parting Ways (May 1976–December 1977)

On May 3, the Pulitzer Prize jury made *A Chorus Line* only the fifth musical until that time to win the award for American dramaturgy. The others were *Of Thee I Sing* in 1932, *South Pacific* in 1950, *Fiorello!* in 1960, and *How to Succeed in Business Without Really Trying* in 1962. Those others got the award for capturing the essence of some corner of the American experience, whether politics, racism, or business. *A Chorus Line* was about entertainment. It also touched on each of those other things. Perhaps even more important, it was about putting yourself on the line and striving to be your best, or put less idealistically, to beat the next guy in the name of something beautiful.

Three days later, on May 6, the first national touring company of *A Chorus Line* opened at the Curran Theatre in San Francisco. The production had been promoted as "the original company," but that wasn't entirely true—much to the sorrow of the people on the Line.

"We started hearing rumors about L.A. fairly early on," Kay Cole said. "Once a show is a hit on Broadway then they talk about other companies. Actors as a rule tend to do that. They get in one situation and then look to the left and say, 'Oh, what's happening over there?' That's because so often nothing is happening anywhere. So when they get a wealth of happenings, they want it all."

It was Baayork Lee's dream that the original company go from city to city, introducing the show to new audiences around the country and eventually around the world. "I talked to Priscilla and she said Vinny [her husband] would like to go, so then it was Priscilla and myself. Then Ron Dennis said, 'I want to go,' and then it started to snowball. It wasn't the money, it was about letting everyone see the original company. It was about spreading *the word*."

Many of the dancers shared that motivation, but many of them also simply had stars in their eyes. Having conquered Broadway, *A Chorus Line* would be their express train to the silver screen.

"My wildest fantasies growing up were playing a Hollywood movie star," Patricia Garland said. "And that was a possibility for us, that we could become movie stars. But it was painful when we found out that not everyone was going to do it."

"I wanted a TV series," Ron Dennis said. "I wanted to be a TV star, to have nationwide exposure, residuals. I just knew I was going out there to try my luck at it."

Michael Bennett warned Lee that British Equity, for one, might not allow the entire original cast to play there. Like Actors Equity in America, British Equity gets antsy about large casts of foreigners getting work on its turf. Nevertheless, Bennett and Lee agreed that the Originals *must* open the show in California. But the question was moot since several of the nineteen had no desire to leave New York.

"I did not have any trouble making the decision not to go to L.A.," Thommie Walsh said. "I made that decision instantly. It had a lot to do with the fact that this was the first big Broadway show I had done that I knew was going to have a run. I was now on Broadway in a successful show. Everything I wanted to do was happening right now at this moment and this little man was asking me to go to California. I hate being uprooted and I was just settling. Also, I didn't have these fantasies of grandeur. I think everybody went out there thinking they were going to be movie stars and I'm sure they were told they were going to be movie stars as part of their contract negotiations with Mr. Bennett. I remember having a meeting in the Shubert Theatre. I was in my little suit because I was going to a callback for the 'Milliken Show.' Michael had a meeting with all of us to tell us he wasn't going to be our daddy. Pam Blair stood up, pointed at me, and screamed, "Look at his face, he's so handsome, he could be a movie star, why isn't he going out?' Michael was chastising me in front of the whole company and treating me like a child and saying things like 'Thommie has a lot to learn. He'll come around to it someday, it takes others longer.'

"My friend Kelly wasn't going to go either and Kelly and I were pretty close. She was pretty definite, too. Rick and Clive and Wayne had mixed feelings about it, they were tossing it around a little bit more.

"I was even offered a little bit more money in the stage manager's office. 'I'll give you another fifty dollars to go,' he told me. I always felt it was a bribe."

Ultimately, Cilento, Mason, and Wilson resolved to stay behind with Walsh and Bishop. Bishop had her career in New York, and demanded more in living expenses than Bennett was willing to pay. Cilento had his wife and growing family in Westchester. "Michael was going to divide us," Cilento said. "I was real angry about that, that it could happen so quick. We couldn't just sit there and enjoy all we had all achieved. It was like another smack in the face, another separation. I felt, "Why should I go to California when I do something in New York that is really special?' I knew I wasn't going to be a movie star because I wasn't one of the Six, and I wasn't going to get the recognition that they were."

Mason had just begun a relationship that was as important to him as a career move. Wilson, who had just arrived in New York from California the previous summer, had no desire to return West. Once Wilson made that decision, Lee asked him to assume her offstage role as dance captain. The job, which mirrored his onstage role, enabled him to help choose and rehearse the newcomers. It was a keeper-of-the-flame responsibility that appealed to him.

Most of the understudies remained on Broadway as well: Allen, Cissel, Drake, Edwards, Serrecchia, Wilzak, and Mineo.

The New York and Los Angeles companies, as well as the international company, were recruited and rehearsed in New York at the City Center theater on West Fifty-fifth Street. As they were being rehearsed, a last appeal was made to the five stay-behinds.

"I tried to coax Thommie to come," Patricia Garland said. "I thought if we could get one of them to change their mind then maybe another would, too. I just didn't want to see it come to an end. Even though there was another rebirth, it was never going to be those people. The first is always the first."

"The whole run of the show was wonderful," said Percassi. "It seemed short. Going to L.A. was sad. That was the breaking up. At the final meeting they got the two companies together and asked everybody who was going to California to step back. When we stepped back there was Kelly and Thommie and the others, and it just broke my heart. I knew we were splitting permanently."

Lee's evangelistic dream was shattered. "I couldn't look at those five people," she said. "I couldn't talk to them, I couldn't deal with them, I shut them off. They ruined my plans to go forth with *the word.*"

She treated her unhappiness by plunging into work, trying to compress a year's worth of character evolution into a few weeks for the benefit of the new West Coast members of the Line: Don Correia, Roy Smith, Charlene Ryan, Scott Pearson, and Paul Charles—plus the six new understudies. "I am talking and I'm sitting and I'm doing circles and doing the same workshop process," Lee said, "and I'm trying to find the right words and trying to get things out from them, trying to make things uniform and tailored visually, but emotionally trying to bring out what that person could give. The results have to be the same in order for the show to work. I enjoyed the challenge a lot."

With the exception of McKechnie, most of the Originals going to California got the same $650 they were being paid on Broadway, plus $200 a week for living expenses. It was enough for a hotel room, though not a particularly comfortable hotel room. Kuhlman and LuPone, who had had such a good time playing dressing room handball at the Shubert in New York, solved the problem by rooming together in a three-bedroom apartment in Sausalito from the May 6 San Francisco opening until the July 1 Los Angeles opening. "It was cheaper than a hotel," Kuhlman said. "It was heaven out there."

Nancy Lane loved the West Coast. "Everyone in town was coming to see us," she said. "We were the toast of the town, which was really terrific. My only regret is that all of us didn't go. I don't know if the five people who didn't go have any regrets, but I think it would have been that much better if we had them with us. The show wasn't ever the same after that because people started doing television, people started doing movies, they started going away on vacations and other people were filling in, other people were being cast; it was always changing."

Like the other dancers, Kuhlman used the transfer to Los Angeles as a chance to go out for TV and film auditions. But he didn't get the kind of auditions he had hoped for. "They were all seeing me as a dancer and not as an actor, so I had to prove myself as an actor." He also got a West Coast agent.

Though most of the original company was still together, the two quick moves threw them off. The Curran was relatively cozy, but in Los Angeles they were playing in a much larger theater, one that several dancers compared to a football field. "In the Newman and even the Shubert, you always felt there was a communication with the director [Zach]. San Francisco was also a little theater, it had that closeness and you feel connected. But L.A. was an amazing feeling. It was good for us because it gave us a kick in the pants, it was so disconcerting. There was no way to be lazy because you felt off-balance. You had to go much farther than you thought you did. It was like a brand-new show and that made us a whole family again."

Things didn't heal that quickly for LuPone. "I didn't like that everyone didn't go to L.A. I certainly respected their decision but I had so much hope that the ensemble, which is so important to me, would be there. The people that were replaced were missed until the other people got good—and they did get good."

In Los Angeles, LuPone felt it was his responsibility to keep the dancers alert. Method techniques rising to the surface again, he felt that as long as he was playing the director, he would behave the way a real director would behave. One night when he felt the dancers were not giving him enough respect he startled them by calling their names out of sequence, jumping directly to Renee Baughman. "It almost cost me my job," LuPone said. "Renee was furious. But I saw the Line go from 'at-ease' to 'attention' in about three words. That's all that mattered, and that's why I kept my job."

Baughman remembers the incident with equal clarity. "I was livid," she said. "Everybody knew I was on low boil after that, but I finished the show and I stormed into the stage manager's office and demanded that they call Mr. LuPone for a conference. I told them they could give me notes after the show if something was wrong but they couldn't mess around with my performance. I took it totally personally. LuPone had done this because everyone was screwing up and I guess I was just the target. It was one of the few times I didn't cry. I was proud of myself."

One of the high points of the Los Angeles run was a visit from another of their gods, Fred Astaire. He came backstage and the dancers recall bits of him: the way he carried himself, his smile, the shine on his shoes, which he'd sung about.

There was another group of celebrities that the dancers got to know better as well: each other. Baughman, for example, had shared a New York dressing room with Lopez and Bishop after the latter two got the wall taken down. "Priscilla was great in the dressing room. She could only take so much of my Pollyanna routine. She would say, 'Renee, you're angry, take this pillow and hit the chair.' I would sort of tap it and she would grab the pillow away from me and say, 'Like this' and slam it down. I would say, 'Do you think I'm really that mad?' and she would say, 'Yes, you are, now go ahead and do it!' I would say, 'Yes, Priscilla.' She was great for me, she helped me get in touch with reality."

Reality was a hard thing for Sammy Williams, who was still on a dangerous high from his Tony Award. "On one hand I felt it gave me leverage, but on the other hand I was afraid of it because I didn't think I had anything to back it up. My first audition was for MTM Productions and I sat down and this guy says, 'You can put your Tony Award in the closet because it doesn't mean a thing out here. What have you done on film?' This was about seven or eight weeks after I had won. I was devastated. We had an option to leave after six months, but I was terrified to leave L.A. and go back and face New York. I felt I had nothing left, I was totally drained. They had awarded me the highest honor and I had nothing else to give. So I stayed in L.A., I made myself a very nice home—and I *hid*."

Baughman had somewhat better luck and landed commercials and bit parts in movies. She even took acting lessons to sharpen her skills. She said she had the greatest trouble seeing the new people on the Line. "It was hard for me to see Don Correia do the role [Mike, originated by Wayne Cilento]. For a long time I didn't like him—not as a person, but I was determined not to like him as a performer. It seemed like sacrilege."

Cole said, "I think it was probably easier for us to integrate the five than it was for the five on Broadway to integrate with the fourteen. I cannot imagine what that felt like."

Meanwhile, back at the Shubert, Rick Mason could have told her. "It felt strange," he said. Mason had taken a two-week vacation during the changeover, and when he returned to the new company, someone else had done his role several nights. "Body types, voice types, delivery—everything was different," he said. "I kind of got lost a couple of times because the same body wasn't where I remember seeing it. It was the same costume but it wasn't the same person. It was a little depressing after finally realizing that it was changed and that the people you fought with and were mad at for so long—and yet loved—were gone. I decided the only thing to do was grow from the experience, because I was going to have new reactions to Barbara Monte-Britton [who took over Pam Blair's role of Val and who stood next to Mason]. But after the initial shock I knew it would never be the same."

Wilson said, "It was something we had all shared, and in a tiny way I resented someone else coming in and learning this show. It was like giving your child away. But so be it. As in all experiences like that you make the adjustment after a while, and it was fine."

As dance captain Wilson found special pleasure in helping to pick and train the next bearers of his "child." He remembers, "In the basement of the City Center we'd see hundreds of hopefuls dying to be in a Broadway show. That was a glorious experience, having these kids come in and line up and do their thing. They reminded me of myself at fifteen coming to New York. The City Center was two blocks from the hotel where I had stayed. That was part of being in a Broadway show, too. I really got off on that." Among the dancers he remembers with special pride is Cynthia Onrubia, who went on to appear in *Dancin'* and *Cats,* and served as dance captain on *Jerome Robbins' Broadway.*

Walsh said it was frustrating and painful for the five Originals who stayed behind, but he said, "I began to see something I hadn't counted on: We looked like the featured players now, where we had previously been kind of second featured players. Also, they turned out to be good kids, some of them are my best friends now. I fell in love with Vicki Frederick and Sandahl Bergman and David Thome and Justin Ross and Kathrynann Wright. They became family."

All the same, as tickets continued to sell out through the summer of 1976 and into the autumn, he said, "I was embarrassed sometimes by the success of it. I had a lot of friends who weren't working, who I thought were real talented. It seems that I was always practicing humility. I seem always to have been saying, 'Thank you, thank you' and moving away, instead of pulling my shoulders back and bathing in it. I realize now that I may never have that chance again. It's a shame I didn't enjoy it at the time as much as I should have."

At least he still had his friend Kelly Bishop close to him. They were the last two of the Dobson's group still in New York, but "one day I get a call from Priscilla," Bishop said, "and she says, 'Guess which two people from *Chorus Line* are getting married?'

"I said, '*In Chorus Line*?'

"She said, '*Involved* in *Chorus Line.*'

"I said, '. . . Donna?' because Donna was always falling in love. So I said 'Donna . . . and *Michael*?'

"She said, 'You guessed!'

"And I could see it would never work. So then Thommie comes into the theater and I said, 'Thommie, guess which two people from *Chorus Line* are getting married?'

"He looks at me for a minute and says, 'Donna and Michael? You're kidding. I'm wrong. No!'

"So I guess on some level, we always knew. I have a theory. Donna and Ken Howard had one of the sweetest romances I've ever seen. And I'm convinced that Michael broke that relationship up during *Promises* by pitting her against him careerwise. Ken'd asked her to marry him and come to California. She wasn't sure she wanted to and he basically gave her an ultimatum. She was suddenly saying things like, 'After I've worked so hard in this business all these years and he comes along and wins a Tony and he's a big star and why should I . . .' And this doesn't sound like Donna. I've never heard this from her. I thought I heard Michael in what she was saying.

"Years go by and we work together in *On the Town* and then *Chorus Line* comes around. She had gone out with a couple of guys, but suddenly Ken's back. They got together and they were so in love, I mean *so in love* that I was thrilled. The romantic in me thought 'true love.' She had gotten sick for a while and was out of the show and he was cooking for her, cooking pasta for her, taking care of her . . . and she was so happy.

"And then everybody takes off for California and the next thing I hear, she's getting married to Michael. It made me sad because I thought her relationship with Ken was so healthy. Donna and Michael—I certainly understood it, and it was romantic and show biz—but I thought it was unhealthy. And I didn't think it would last. And it didn't."

McKechnie recalls wanting very much to go to California and introduce the show there, but she knew it would be the end of her relationship with Howard. She said Howard had proposed to her, but she couldn't bring herself to accept. "I remember feeling that the relationship with Ken, the pressure of it, was too much," she said. "I couldn't get married. I didn't want to and I felt this prevailing feeling of doom if I was with anyone but Michael. I'm not trying to justify my moves but I know I didn't recover from my father's death. I felt alone, frightened, and very guilty about not being able to marry Ken. It terrified me and I tried to communicate with Ken and he wouldn't hear it, so then I felt lost. We had a parting of the ways and I said, 'When I move to San Francisco I am leaving.' It was resolved but it wasn't. We were both very upset. It was very painful to both of us.

"Then Sue McNair [Bennett's assistant, later co-producer of *Ballroom*] told Michael that I was on the plane to San Francisco and if he was going to do anything he'd better get there before Ken because he's going to be on the next plane. So Michael had a conversation with me in New York before we left and said he wanted to consummate our relationship. I won't be skittish about it: I loved Michael. But I was so stunned, I told him I couldn't cope with it. 'Yes I love you but I just don't know what to say.' It just kind of consumed me.

"He said, 'We have to be together.' But I replied, 'We're too powerfully connected for anything as superficial as a love affair.' "

And right there, he proposed. It sounds so dramatic. It surprised me as much as anyone else. It had never been in my mind that we would be together, because of Michael's life style, and my own. I've been subjected to a lot of criticism [for marrying Bennett]. There was no 'reason' for me to marry Michael. He said, 'I love you and I want you,' and that was all I wanted.

"So there I was in San Francisco and there was Michael down the [theater] aisle and it's embarrassing for me to say this but all of a sudden I was in love. 'Now my life is really true, he really loves me. In the face of all obstacles our love will survive.' It was a grand time in San Francisco. It thrilled me, it felt like a game. I was letting him know that our love is valid, that it isn't just about being Miss Goody Twoshoes or special favors. We are adults and we're in love and this was meant to be. In some crazy way I was trying to get everyone's approval.

"For the first time, I felt on top of the world with the show. I got out of all the pressure of New York. I thought, 'We're a hit, we're free, we're traveling, everybody is getting along better, everyone's having fun, we're relaxing and enjoying ourselves.' I was very much in love. Michael and I knew we were going to have a lot of obstacles. But we thought that if there is a mutual desire, like the song, love can rise above it."

McKechnie and Bennett were married on December 4, 1976.

Fiddler on the Roof ends with an enduring image. Having presented the villagers of the Russian-Jewish *shtetl* Anatevka as a circle, director Jerome Robbins gathers them in that ring one last time. Then, one by one, they turn and leave, scattering to the four points of the compass. At last only Tevye, the leading character, is left onstage with the symbolic character of the play's title. Together they, too, leave the circle, which then ceases to exist.

That's more or less what happened to the Line, though it happened in slow motion, over the course of several months, and gaps in the Line have quickly been filled. A natural centrifugal force of lives and careers eroded the original chorus line face by face.

"I just felt the need to move on," said Kay Cole, one of the first to leave in Los Angeles when their contracts expired in September 1976. Lopez, LuPone, Stuart, and Kuhlman left at the same time, heading into new productions.

"I wanted to act," Kuhlman said, "and I thought that people weren't considering me for TV or movie stuff because I was involved in the show and they didn't want to worry about a time schedule. I wasn't part of the tape sessions, so I wasn't an original Original. I guess it was harder for some of the other kids to leave because they had been more an integral part of it."

Lopez said, "I had been on such a high until I lost the Tony and I dropped a little, then I left my friends in New York and I dropped a little further, and I dropped even further because of my not warming up and taking care of myself. I was just tired after two years of having this show keeping me at a gallop."

Mason left the New York cast at the same time, even though he'd been appointed assistant dance captain to Wilson. Bishop had been the first of the five to leave the New York cast, having done so in August.

McKechnie left in summer 1976 to re-create Cassie in the London company, but had such a corrosive experience with Fleet Street, for replacing the British Cassie shortly before the opening, that she fled back to the United States, abruptly ending her association with the show, for the time being.

Walsh and Cilento were the last two Originals to leave the Broadway cast. Though both moved directly into projects that would attract Tony nominations, both left in May 1977 only after some unsubtle arm-twisting by Bennett.

Cilento said, "I'll never forget when he said to me, 'We want you to take a month off, you're a dark spot.'

"I said, 'I can't take a month off, Cathy's going to have a baby in a couple of months and I can't afford it.'

"And they said to me, 'Well, we'll give you a loan.'

"I had been getting into trouble when whoever was the dance captain at the time was cleaning the kick and told me to keep my legs down, keep them waist-level and not get them higher than my head. Now, Michael is the one who had told me to keep my legs up. I said to myself, 'This is the way he created it, this is what he wants for me, he can't take that away from me. The only thing I am in this show is a dancer, a good dancer and I know how I can dance. If you calm me down and get me on the level of the other guys, then I'm nothing, I'm leaving.' It was their way of telling me to move on. I refused the loan, took the month off, and quit in two weeks."

Alone, now, of those who had started the project three and a half years earlier, Walsh also was subjected to harassment in the form of picayune criticism. "I had been threatened with firing five months before, which is maybe when I should have left," Walsh said. "I was called into the principal's office, Michael's office, and he and Bob Avian and Bobby Thomas were sitting there drinking their vodka martinis between shows, a matinee. Michael said, 'We have a lot of notes here, regarding your performance, misdemeanors.' They were things like, 'Doesn't take ballet arm corrections . . .' I'm not taking the dance captain's notes and I'm not nice to the stage manager and I don't talk to the musicians. They were jerk-off criticisms. Bobby Thomas, the dance arranger-drummer, said a few things about my performance and Michael permitted this. I found this to be ludicrous. I remember a bizarre painting of monkeys on the wall, so my closing line was something like, 'Thank you very much but don't think I'm one of your monkeys,' and I left. I was scared shitless. I really thought I was going to get fired, but no one fired me. But maybe I should have left at that time. Michael was good about knowing when it was time for people to go on. He was bad about the way he went about doing it but he had this sixth sense. I could have handled an honest conversation: 'Get out, you're burned out,' but my also being the last Original on the Line in New York probably made him crazy. By this time he was definitely tired of the Originals."

Out in Los Angeles, Patricia Garland stayed with the show until the summer of 1977 when she executed a jump ever so slightly the wrong way in the opening number and collapsed on her leg. The next day she was running and the leg gave out completely. "I had shredded my ligaments and torn my cartilage," she said. "I thought it would be a television series or a movie that would change my life. Instead, it was this injury. I find it interesting that somebody on that Line would end up the way Paul in the show loses the job because of his knee. I lived out the show."

Pam Blair had set a limit for herself that never came: "I said I'd leave when I saw 'the sea of red,' the empty red seats. Instead, I went to see *Annie Hall* and decided to go back to New York. I eventually worked my way up to twelve hundred fifty dollars but I was so disillusioned and unhappy and tired because I had gotten so thin that I wasn't even doing eight shows a week. They finally said to me, 'Either show up for eight or get out.' So I left. I felt grateful for the push because I needed it. But I felt like I had lost my best friend."

Ron Dennis and Nancy Lane stayed with the Los Angeles company until December of 1977.

Dennis explained, "Every time someone new came into the cast, another piece of the cake was sliced away, until it was just completely different. I was the last one in the California company. Finally, I decided it was time to move on."

Percassi stayed with the show for a year in California, then came back to Broadway and stayed three more months before leaving for new shows. "The excitement of being in the show doesn't last as long as you'd like it to," he said. "You can't stop it, to have it for always. It's just a fleeting moment and then you realize that everybody goes on. Almost as soon as it becomes perfect it starts to deteriorate or disintegrate into other facets. It has to because that's how life continues. It's not a personal thing; you still love everybody, everybody loves you. But you go back to the boyfriend, the agent finds other auditions for you to go to. All our lives have gone in vastly different directions. But one thing I know: If any of them ever needs me I'm here and if I ever need them, they'll be there."

18.

A Celebration (September 1983)

For the next six years the dancers dispersed across the country pursuing a variety of far-flung careers. But in mid 1983, they heard a call they couldn't resist. It came from Michael Bennett, and there were very few of the Originals who had uncomplicated feelings about their former ringleader. But his call reached into them and tugged on that common bond that will always link the nineteen of them. Fittingly, the dancers were summoned to celebrate an anniversary with special significance not only to them, but to virtually everyone who cares about American musicals.

Broadway economics are complicated, but they boil down to a simple reality. A show stays open just as long as costs cover expenses. As soon as a show stops paying its bills, it posts a closing notice.

In the days before air-conditioning, shows generally ran through the winter and closed as soon as the weather got hot. Imagine sitting in a crowded theater in the middle of July with bank after bank of 1,000-watt spotlights, and you've got the idea why the theatrical season ends May 31. After ventilator fans and then air-conditioning arrived, shows began running through the summer. Also, as the number of new productions declined, so did competition. Shows ran longer because there weren't so many other new shows around to pull audiences away. And speaking of audiences, as commuter railroads started rolling and then, in the 1940s and 1950s, superhighways were built, the audience began to expand beyond Manhattan to the five boroughs, then to the suburbs of

Nassau and Westchester counties, and then to the entire tri-state area, including New Jersey and Connecticut.

By contract, most Broadway shows play 8 performances a week, adding up to roughly 416 performances a year. Broadway's long-run champs in the 1930s ran only about a year and a half. Helped by the above-mentioned technology and demographics, *Tobacco Road* and *Life with Father* soon shattered that record, running 3,182 and 3,224 performances, respectively. They held that record for nearly thirty years until June 1972 when *Fiddler on the Roof* edged past for a new record of 3,242, reportedly boosted in its last months by producer Hal Prince.

Prince might have saved his money. In late winter 1980, *Grease* limped past that total and ran a few more months before running out of steam at 3,388 performances. Such statistics may seem technical, but theater folk follow them as closely as sports fans follow career highs and RBIs.

It therefore was with great interest that Broadway in summer of 1983 observed that *A Chorus Line* was approaching the summit—and not being boosted by a producer hoping to land his name in the record books. *A Chorus Line* still was turning a solid profit. It would whizz past the record and keep running indefinitely.

On Thursday, September 29, 1983, *A Chorus Line* would play its 3,389th performance.

"I had heard the date was coming up," Clive Wilson said, "and I thought, 'Gee, something big should be done. And knowing Michael, he probably will do something big.' So it was no great surprise when he called. It *was* surprising that he was having everybody back—three hundred or however many people coming in, that was a little astonishing. But immediately I thought it was great. What a wonderful thing to do."

It was Bennett's plan to invite not just the original cast, but anyone who had appeared in any professional company anywhere in the world. He would restage the show to accommodate the hundreds of dancers, creating, for one night only, a hyper-*Chorus Line*.

That was the good news. The bad news was that in order to accommodate ten Sammys, a dozen Als, twenty Dianas, etc., he would have to allow more than one person to share each song and speech. The crushing news was that while McKechnie would do "The Music and the Mirror" solo, the others would have to share or surrender the material they created.

"One morning I get a call around eight-fifteen and it's Michael Bennett," said Walsh, now a multiple Tony winner on his own. "Well, I'm in shock . . . I remember saying, 'This is a great idea and I would love to do it if everyone does it, then I would be interested."

Bennett explained the terms. To keep the undertaking from bankrupting the show, dancers would be paid fifty dollars apiece, with no expenses for those who already lived in New York, as Walsh did.

Walsh agreed, but virtually as soon as he hung up with Bennett, his phone began ringing again. "It's all these dear dear friends of mine saying, 'Did you get the phone call?' 'Yes I got the phone call.' 'Does this mean I'm not going to be doing my thing?' And I would say, 'Yes that is what I understand that you're not going to be doing your thing . . .' And so now I'm giving the lowdown to the people who haven't gotten the phone call yet. People were not being reasonable, people were not going to do it. It was a very difficult few weeks. Once again, all the buttons had been pushed that had been pushed eight years ago, and the manipulation started to happen all over again. Do you have control over yourself, or does he have control over you?"

Walsh found himself in the position of selling Bennett's plan to his fellow cast members, despite his reservations about Bennett's methods and his callous treatment of the people who had helped create the show. "I decided to be there because I knew it would be something I would never forget," Walsh said. "And it was. And I'm real glad that I did it. Whatever pain I went through to do it was not that much compared to what I got out of it."

It quickly became clear that while everyone was enthusiastic about marking the date with a celebration and about getting back together, there was a great deal of trepidation at the prospect of working with Bennett. Having escaped from the gravitational field around his black hole personality, many were leery of getting that close to him again. "Everybody had open wounds, so it was really important not to rub salt into those wounds," Patricia Garland said. "A part of me was very concerned with my position, my lack of working or the fact that I hadn't established myself. Would people think less of me? I didn't want them to treat me the way I was back then. I didn't want to be sucked into that little girl kind of thing and I was so afraid that I would be. Michael and Donna would be so powerful again and I would be dealt with the same way as before. If I did go, I wanted to go totally free of the past and have a whole new beginning. I didn't want to go there trying to prove anything. I wanted to enjoy the experience."

Perhaps unsure of how his ex-wife would react to his invitation, Bennett called the other dancers before he called McKechnie. She remembers getting calls from her fellow dancers preparing her to hear from Bennett. But once on the phone with him, she said, "I let him just say what he wanted. He was very nervous. As he was describing what he was calling about and how he was going to do it, I made sure I made approving sounds on the other end of the phone. He told me about what I would do and that everybody was going to do it, and I said that just sounds great. Well, as soon as he felt the acceptance, then he was just 'gush.' There was something so delightful in his way that I almost forgot who I was talking to. There was that kind of genuine excitement.

"And I thought, 'My God, it's like back when we were doing *Promises, Promises* and *Company,*' " McKechnie said. "For a split second I had to catch my breath because it was, 'Darling. I'm so happy and it's going to be so wonderful.'

"He said, 'I'm giving a party and I want you to host it with me.'

"I thought that was very nice, very classy, and I said, 'I would be honored.' It was a very warm, friendly phone call. When I hung up the phone I thought I would go right over the edge, but I didn't. I said to myself, I haven't worked this hard on myself all these years to get spun around like this."

Wilson said he agreed to go because *A Chorus Line* had been "a very high point in my professional life" and "to have all that recalled, to have someone celebrate it, to be celebrated for having been a part of it, made me feel special. Add to that the people I was going to see, the old friends, and anticipating how interesting it was going to be, how difficult it was going to be, how much fun, how much pain there might be—who knows how my emotions would be affected? I was really looking forward to it."

Pam Blair liked the general idea of the celebration, but objected to Bennett's staging concept. "When I heard that it was going to become the longest-running show on Broadway I thought, 'Wouldn't it be great if the original company came back and did the show?' But he made it another extravaganza evening for Michael Bennett. He should have had the original company either stroll in like the stars they deserved to be, or he should have had us all stand in a line, say our names, and get off the stage. But to let some people do their number while other people barely got to say their names was horrible. Sammy Williams won a Tony Award for his part. Why should he have to share that with ten other guys?"

She got no argument from Williams. "I asked myself why I was doing the monologue with ten other people, when it was *my* monologue," he said. "I wanted to do it myself. I called Michael that night and said that I didn't think it was fair, that moment is mine, I created that.

"Michael said to me, 'This event is about what has happened to *A Chorus Line* in the past nine years. *Chorus Line* has outgrown all of us and there have been a lot of people that have done it who have put a lot of time and energy into it, not just you and the original company. And I think it's only fair to share it with everyone who had ever done it. It's true that the monologue is yours and it will always belong to you. Believe me, I am going to stage this so that you are down front, center stage. You are not going to get lost behind those boys, that moment is going to be yours, trust me.'

"I said okay," Williams said. "And I had no traumas getting there. My stuff with Michael was completely clear, so the only thing I had to do was to delight. I didn't have to fight for a position or center stage or Michael's adulation. Working with Michael again was a trip. I saw, for the first time, his ego. I saw how he manipulated people. And I sat there and laughed at him. Sometimes I thought he was boring, sometimes I thought Michael was fabulous to be that outrageous. But the important thing is that I didn't feel like I was his puppet anymore because I made the choice to be there on my own. I had the power to get up and walk out if I didn't like what he was doing to me. I had power this time that I didn't have the first time."

When Baayork Lee heard that she would be doing only part of her already brief role, she and Bennett had a telephone confrontation. "Pyrotechnics," she said. "The things he said to me were just incredible. That I had not grown in seven years and how disappointed he was in me. He pushed all the buttons to hurt. Then he said I should come to his office on Monday! I said to him, 'I'm not going anywhere with you yelling at me.' I knew then that I had grown up. Then he said he needed me to help him, he needed me to put on the show. By that time the buttons had been pushed and so I didn't hear that very well that he needed me—though I did hear it."

Walsh, with whom she was making an Orange Crush commercial, convinced her to change her mind. "He made me believe that it was going to be for *us,*" she said, "and that it would be the best thing for us, for me."

Once again serving as choreographer's assistant, Lee was placed in charge of the international *Chorus Line* company. Lee recalls, "I had a Mike from Australia, Diane from Sweden, Connie and Judy from Berlin. There was a production done in Argentina and in Mexico and they appeared in this production. It was a very special moment. I remember looking out at that sea of people and saying, 'My God, look how many people we've passed this on to. And I'm having the chance to see it. They've all experienced it, and hopefully they all got it.' "

Three of the original cast—LuPone, Lane, and Blair—did not attend the celebration. None of them tossed off the decision lightly.

Nancy Lane was shooting that week on *Moscow Bureau,* the new TV series of which she was the co-star. "My heart was in New York," she said. "I really really regretted missing it. But I was so happy I was working. Thommie Walsh called me to say that Terri Klausner would be doing my part but that she wanted to hold up my picture [at the surreal conclusion of "I Hope I Get It"] and to please send one immediately Federal Express. So I was there in spirit. I was so happy that someone had thought of doing that. It was like a stab in the heart because, I thought, what a sweet thing to do but my heart was breaking because I couldn't be there."

LuPone refused on moral grounds to attend the celebration.

"It was anathema to me for the purposes of acting, politically, and because it wasn't about the original company. Ultimately, it wasn't about *A Chorus Line*. It was Barnum and Bailey. I felt very simply that it was going to be an event to celebrate a person of questionable values. I saw the manipulation for what it was and I had made a firm commitment not to do it."

A phalanx of LuPone's fellow Originals tried to persuade him to change his mind, including Walsh, Dante, Bishop, Williams, Bennett, and finally even Joe Papp. Though they all failed, he said, "one of the delights I got was in speaking to people like Thommie who had expiated a lot of stuff that they carried around circa *A Chorus Line*. Thommie felt respect for my position, but said my concepts were untrue in terms of it being an event about Michael Bennett, and my concerns about it being a spectacle as opposed to a very personal reality that we all went through. And in fact, I heard it was very well done. It was a party and everybody had a good time. That was my delight."

Pam Blair came to rehearsals, but quit when she found she would have to share "Dance 10, Looks 3" not only with Mitzi Hamilton, the dancer on whom the part originally had been based, but with another dancer as well. She consoled herself initially by telling herself, " 'All the other kids are here, Pam. Come on, some of these people aren't even going to get to do their parts, at least you're going to get to do yours.' When he told me it would be Mitzi, I thought, 'Well, that's fair because the story was really half hers.' Then I arrive and discovered we would be three girls."

Also, Blair found that Bennett had completely rechoreographed "Dance 10, Looks 3," a disorienting change on what often was a show-stopping number. After explaining this to her, Bennett left Blair in the hands of an assistant who was to teach her the new staging. Bennett then turned on his heel, leaving the rehearsal hall. "I had thought I was being selfish so I tried to put up with it," Blair said. "I was getting angrier and angrier. I finally came to the realization that I shouldn't be there. I thought he had treated me badly nine years ago and he's treating me the same way again. I didn't need him anymore and his goddam show. I just ranted like a madwoman. I didn't have anything to do with Tom Porter [then production stage manager]. He just sort of watched me crumble."

And Blair walked out. On the night of the celebration, she said, Bennett sent her what looked like a $150 flower arrangement and a card that said, 'Pam, I would sooner kill myself than to think I could ever hurt you,' and urging her to show up. But she was unswayed. "I left a message on his machine saying, 'I only wanted to do the show because of you but I know now you really don't care about me.' I knew if I gave in and walked in he would have said, 'Oh, I see Miss Blair has decided to join us' and have walked out of the room."

Several of the dancers were sad that the full quorum wasn't in attendance. Rick Mason was angry. "That just pissed me off," he said. "How dare they ruin it for everybody, how selfish. Why can't they swallow it like I did? I went through just as much hell if not more than some of these kids. Pam's inability to do the number with two other girls or Bob's problem with Michael—swallow it! I really resented that because they robbed us. I understood Nancy's problem because of her conflict, but I was upset that she couldn't be there, because she was refreshing. She always had some wonderful quip."

Ron Dennis is one of those who swallowed his pride, but it left him with a lump in his throat. "For the little bit I was seen," he said. "it would have been just as easy to watch it on TV. That madman . . . gave 'Gimmee the Ball' to someone else. I found that out about when we were all down at his studio rehearsing that section. I went to Bobby and asked who was doing 'Gimmee the Ball' and he told me someone from the bus-and-truck company. It was a total slap in the face to eliminate me. But it was either that or remove myself, or just be crazy."

"As for the celebration," Mason said, "I enjoyed it very much; I'm sorry it went by so fast. Eight years had happened. I had gone to a different level and yet there was a lot of déjà vu looking down the line and seeing these faces. It was a tremendous high, an exhilarating feeling."

The dancers began arriving in New York the weekend of September 24–25. A party was given that Sunday the twenty-fifth, and rehearsals were held throughout that week at 890 Broadway.

Kay Cole remembered, "I had gotten in from California on Saturday morning but I wasn't at the party on Sunday because I was trying to catch up on my sleep. So Monday morning it started and you had to walk through the barriers and give your name and get your tag and then you lined up. I saw all these people and suddenly it hit me: Oh my God, all these people are really going to be onstage! I can't believe it. The line just seemed to go on forever. Somebody from our company said, 'Don't wait on line, just come on up, the Originals can come on up.' So I just went in. I think the first person I saw was [wardrobe mistress] Alyce Gilbert, who is the best person in the world. She gave me my old costume. I went up to the dressing room and couldn't believe that we were going to do this. I looked at the call board and I couldn't believe how many people were going to be there. It just seemed overwhelming. Some of my favorite people were there. Michael talked, we got T-shirts and posters and all that. Everybody was applauding and happy and I was walking around trying to see all the people. It was what I imagine a large, really intense college reunion is like. Nobody looked older, everybody looked fabulous, especially the original company."

On the morning of Thursday the twenty-ninth the army of dancers, 330 to 375 strong by various estimates, moved uptown to the reinforced stage of the Shubert Theatre. The adjoining Booth Theatre at the other end of Shubert Alley was commandeered as a giant dressing room. The two theaters were outfitted with a closed-circuit television system to coordinate instructions and cues. A dress rehearsal was given that afternoon, which constituted a private "preview" for the dozens of dancers from around the world, many of whom were seeing Broadway for the first time.

"The afternoon performance was really amazing," Cole said. "When we ran out with our pictures after the first number in the blackout, we had our faces covered and all I could remember was the intensity of the sounds of the orchestra doing the *bump, bump,* and it seemed to go on forever. Suddenly there was a ripple down the Line and whisperings of 'They're standing up, they're standing up.' I asked Ron Kuhlman, 'Who's standing up?' It was the audience. There was a sign that said ORIGINAL COMPANY, and they were giving us a standing ovation. It was just so intense, and the evening performance was just as glorious. I felt so much love, so much respect, so much of the good things about theater that people can feel for each other.

McKechnie said that moment was her favorite. "Looking up

into those two balconies and seeing everybody up there, people who had just been on the road or done leads—the metaphor was too much. I thought of all the countries, all the people who'd seen it. . . . I'll never forget that."

"When the spotlight hit my face I thought I was going to be knocked over," Garland said. "I'd forgotten the power of it. I really felt off-balance, it was so shocking. I dressed with Kelly and Priscilla, two people I had never roomed with before. I saw Donna being nervous. It was a wonderful experience and I felt that I got to know them better. There was no talk of past relationships. But there didn't need to be because it was apparent that we were all different and that we'd all grown up."

Mason recalled, "Karen Joblons, as sweet as she is, said to me, 'This has been one of the most thrilling nights in my life, to be on the stage with the original cast.' She stood next to me. Terri Klausner said the same thing, and I thought, 'I couldn't think of two nicer women and more talented women that I would want to share this with.' "

Percassi said, "I think it hit me when we saw Donna do her thing at the rehearsal. It was the first time I ever saw Michael close to tears. The positive vibrations in that place were incredible. Without a doubt, I *knew* everyone felt it and we were still connected. It went through us like a megavolt and went out to every one of those people in the audience. This is the positive part of our lives, as performers: a creative force that everyone can tune into immediately. So is the evil force, unfortunately. But that creative force is there and you know it's good.

"One of the girls from California told me she was having a hard time getting through it," Percassi said, "because we were emotionally exhausted that whole week. Even if you didn't cry, it was such an emotional experience. It was not as if somebody had died, but as if somebody had been born. The celebration was the closest thing to a religious experience I've ever had in my life. Nothing has ever moved me as much as the beauty and the truth of it. It had to do with the idea of people thinking alike and a connection between everybody.

"When we actually did the show and walked forward with the pictures and the audience wouldn't stop applauding, I thought,

Why are they doing this? We haven't done anything yet. Maybe it's for Kelly or the people I always thought were brilliant. I never thought I was anything—that was one of my problems. It's still my problem and that's why I'm still in the chorus. But that's okay and I can live with it. I dealt with it years ago.

"I was just so glad to be a part of the celebration. It's like being part of a family. When we were sitting on the floor at the rehearsal I looked around and it was so wonderful: Everyone has done well. I felt that Thommie's done well, Michel is now a big producer, Kelly's done well, she's married well, Baayork has been choreographing, Wayne had choreographed a show on Broadway and he has three beautiful children. It was different with Michael. Our relationship had changed. It wasn't Michael and the children anymore, it was Michael and the grown-ups."

Working with Bennett for the first time since their divorce, McKechnie said she saw a side of Bennett she hadn't seen in years. "His humanity was coming out," she said, "and it only comes out when he's working onstage. And in particular on this show. He was able to feel it in himself. And I think it was the only thing that kept him alive, that made him feel like a person. I felt as close as I ever got to him that week. I felt free of him that week, but at the same time I had to fight not to be seduced because I felt it coming my way. I felt he owed me a certain kind of respect, a certain kind of treatment. When people had an independent spirit, it was very attractive to him. He needed to compete with it, or conquer it. He loved being with his original company. He also was very sadistic and wanted to torture us. It was total manipulation, as much as he could get away with."

As the delayed curtain time for the gala approached, Percassi was delighted to find that Gilbert had carefully maintained all the original costumes, and had brought them out of storage for the event. "I was so touched," Percassi said, "It had my name in it and it still fit.

"I loved being at the Booth Theatre during the show," Percassi said. "It was better than the regular show. All these people looking at the TV monitors, cheering. They were just screaming, it was like watching a hockey match. You could walk around and talk to anybody, it was like being in a tunnel during the London

Blitz. I'm talking about the camaraderie of the Blitz. I looked up and saw Thommie and I went and sat behind him. Then some of the kids who had done *Chorus Line,* whom I had worked with in other shows, came and sat with me.

"When I saw Donna doing 'The Music and the Mirror' and singing 'Play me the music . . .' that really wiped me out. It's such a release, like a primal scream. Donna had gone through so much, it became so real. I know what she's gone through since then. Nobody cared if she made some mistakes, it was like that for all of us. It's like saying, 'I'm here and this is what I have to do and if you don't like it, too bad.' Only Donna could do this because she had attained such a maturity now. When I saw her, the little girl was gone. I saw it when she was with Michael. You had to be dead not to be moved by it. In spite of all that chaos at the Booth Theatre when she did that song, everything stopped. There was not a sound in the theater. Three hundred people were absolutely silent. I could feel that the girl sitting next to me was affected, too.

"The celebration was a wonderful, charismatic experience and nothing else could compare with it. We had the common memories, the common things dancers go through to become dancers, the psychological things. It's a love of what you're doing, of being a part of it; it's a family unit, all the brain cells function like one brain cell. I don't think I will ever experience anything like that again."

Stuart, who spent most of the performance watching from the wings, described the feeling as "the rush of American theater once again."

The celebration earned a huge amount of press, both print and television. In various interviews the cost of the celebration event was pegged at $500,000. Papp estimated that the show at that point had been seen by 22.5 million people. Shubert Organization president Bernard Jacobs estimated that the show had earned $300 million.

Bennett gave most of the interviews, however, and often was asked why none of the cast members had become superstars. Bennett's reply was that no one on the Line had "star quality." McKechnie said, "It killed me when Michael said that. I thought, how dare he feel so left out that he has to say nobody has star quality! How foolish. I thought, here we go again, him demeaning us like it was a fluke or something."

Nevertheless, she said, she put her resentment aside for the night of the gala. "I saw how much we were a part of it," she said. "I never could appreciate that before because I was so busy doing it, like a job. But the more I thought about it, the more I saw it was important. This will be with us for the rest of our lives whether we like it or not. Given all of that, I was ready to have a party. I didn't even know how ready I was until I got there. I felt the freedom of being my own person for the first time in a long time, and I felt the freedom of feeling good about seeing everybody, about my pride in everybody. I loved our humor. I laughed, I had the best time. That week made up for all the time I didn't think I had the support of the company."

Though she didn't get to sing "Sing!," Baughman was moved by how widely the ripples of their effort had spread. "Who'd ever have thought that from those tape sessions we would be celebrating an anniversary like that? Who would have thought that when I went to that rap session kicking and screaming and ashamed for people to see me ten pounds overweight, that those incredible twelve hours would go on to do this magnificent show, that we would be the darlings of Broadway?"

"The reaction from the audience was overwhelming," Kuhlman said. "I don't think it would have mattered if we fell on our faces. Going to the party after the performance I saw all of those people and I just froze. I just wanted to be someplace quiet, maybe with just the original company to talk about it. But it was real difficult to go out to the party, then I went into the crowd and I was lost. I just walked around for an hour in a kind of daze. People would come up and say, 'Congratulations' and 'That was wonderful' and you could tell that some people were looking specifically for other people. I felt alone, lost, even though I was jammed in between everyone."

Cilento understood what was bothering Kuhlman and even the most enthusiastic of his fellow Originals: "Michael should have pulled out the nineteen of us and said, 'If it wasn't for these nineteen people there would never have been a *Chorus Line*.' I think that's all it would have taken to make me want to say thanks, thank you. Thank you for the nine months of you manipulating my life and playing on my emotions to get this show—even though you stripped me dry of everything that was the truth to me and juggled around life stories. I think it would have justified all those pains and those hurts and disappointments—if he only would have said thank you."

19.

WHAT CAME AFTER (1976–1990)

The last major gathering of original cast members was at an AIDS benefit in 1988 at the Dorothy Chandler Pavilion in Los Angeles. Everyone attended except Walsh, Lee, and Stuart.

A Chorus Line has had a fascinating history, not only for unprecedented length of its run and the hundreds of dancers whose careers it nourished, but for the ripples it continues to send out into American culture. For one thing, it helped make the world safe for dancing. It inspired a genre dubbed "dancicals" that made dance the central reason for a show's being: *Dancin', Ballroom, Cats, 42nd Street,* and *Jerome Robbins' Broadway* are only five of the shows that would have been substantially different, or not come to Broadway at all, without *A Chorus Line* to blaze the way. Each of those shows is associated with a powerful director-choreographer—Bob Fosse, Bennett, Trevor Nunn, Gower Champion, and Robbins—who towered over the world of Broadway musicals as composers had in the age of Rodgers, Gershwin, Porter, Berlin, et al.

"It gave dancers lots of jobs," Lopez said. "It certainly helped them with respect and integrity in the business. It made an art form into a way of life. After *Chorus Line* came the movies *The Turning Point, Fame,* and *Saturday Night Fever.* It brought all kinds of dancing together—it wasn't just ballet dancing and tap dancing, it was *dancing*. It made dancing a star."

Perfected for *A Chorus Line,* the workshopping process became institutionalized to a great degree. Today, those musicals that are not imports from London generally are greenhoused in one of a half-dozen workshops or regional theaters. The two music-licensing giants, BMI and ASCAP, operate the two biggest musical theater workshops. Another is connected to New York University, another operates in the Westbeth theater complex near the docks in west Greenwich Village, and yet another was launched by Michael Bennett himself at 890 Broadway.

A Chorus Line affected movies as well. *Fame* was set in the High School of the Performing Arts. The film even takes a swipe at *Chorus Line,* perhaps in revenge for *ACL*'s song "Nothing," which lambasts PA's teaching.

"Nothing" inspired a parody in Martin Charnin's 1983 revue *Upstairs at O'Neill's.* The song, titled "Something," tells the story of Morales and her insensitive teacher, Mr. Karp—but from Karp's point of view.

There was talk of a sequel to be entitled "A Chorus Line II: The Backers Audition," but a trial balloon to that effect in the trade papers led nowhere.

More urgently, there was talk of a movie version as early as 1977, and most of the original cast members expressed interest in appearing in it. "Interest" may be putting it mildly. Were Bennett the director, nearly all of them would have killed to be in it.

But the project was delayed. And delayed. It passed from studio to studio with no one able to translate its theatrical immediacy into a screenplay. As Percassi sees it, "The show was created from the lives of the people doing it. I'm not saying the concept isn't transferable, but the chemistry isn't."

Undaunted by that, in the months after the success of *Saturday Night Fever* and *Grease,* there was talk of adapting *A Chorus Line* as a vehicle for John Travolta. Then, Liza Minnelli was touted as the eventual star. Both plans evaporated.

With the project delayed into the 1980s, Fosse launched a preemptive strike, directing the autobiographical film *All That Jazz,* whose opening number—a chorus audition set to "On Broadway"—seemed awfully familiar. "He stole the opening number," said Kelly Bishop. "He took the concept—and did it brilliantly, by the way."

But Bishop is haunted by the *Chorus Line* film that might have been. "If you look at the [1976] Tony Awards show again, you'll see," she said. "Michael got one extra camera out of the network for [the opening number]. Look what he did with that. He worked out every shot. Remember, this is not movies where you can cut and edit. This is television where everything has to go boom boom *boom.* I remember walking up to Donna and saying, 'You see what Michael is doing? He's *making the movie.* He's practicing the movie right now.' He cut to *here* and said, 'Do *that* angle.' He would have made an incredible movie. He was a very cinematic director anyway."

That movie finally was released in December 1985, directed by Sir Richard Attenborough, who later won the Oscar for *Gandhi.* None of the original cast members were in it, though several auditioned.

Cilento recalls how badly he wanted to re-create the role of Mike on film. He tried out for the role he created, but Attenborough asked him to read for Larry, the director's assistant. "Larry had a really big through line in the movie," Cilento said, "so when I read it, I thought, this is great. Maybe I wasn't right for Mike, but maybe I was for Larry." But as with the rest of the Originals, Cilento never got to do a screen test.

Bishop said she remembers watching when a television interviewer asked Attenborough why he didn't use the original cast. "He said, 'Those people are all in their late thirties by now, maybe their forties. This show is about kids breaking into show business.' I almost ruined the television set! I jumped up and stomped around the living room. Breaking into show business? *Breaking into show business!* He doesn't even know what the show's about! It's not about that!"

Cilento said the original cast members were invited to the New York opening, which was held at Radio City Music Hall. "I think someone embarrassed them into giving us tickets," he said. "We all as a group tried to organize it: Priscilla, Baayork, Thommie, myself, Donna, Sammy, Ron Dennis, Pam Blair, Renee Baughman. We all met and had drinks at Thommie's house. Baayork and Thommie arranged for there to be cars and limousines that took us. Paparazzi took pictures of us at the Music Hall and we went to the party afterwards at the Waldorf, which was pretty strange.

They were the Chorus Line and we weren't at that point. A lot of people came over to us and said, 'This is where it began.' But it was their evening and they had the glory."

Cilento said the Originals were terrified that the film would be brilliant and their performances would be forgotten. As a review, Cilento said, "I thought the opening was pretty amazing, the auditioning. But by the time they had Mike swinging on ropes and rafters, I thought, 'Oh God, they lost it.' The movie was awful. They lost the heart and soul of what the play was about. It was a shame that they couldn't capture any of it, though I was afraid they would. It was their loss.

"Why?" asked Cilento. "For one thing, I think they were going for younger dancers. I also feel that the original people have a quality in us that you can't hide. We could have brought a whole other quality, a depth, to the movie. Most of the people they got were out of nowhere, except Vicki Frederick and Justin Ross who had been in the New York company. Everyone else were dancers from all over the place, mostly from California.

"The 'What I Did for Love' scene with Cassie climbing the steps? It was just so bizarre," Cilento said. "They were just doing things for effect. We were all auditioning for our lives. I don't think you ever felt that emotion in the movie. In one sense they used cinematic tricks and in another sense they didn't use movie magic at all."

Bishop said, "My husband, Lee [Leonard], said, 'It's odd: the stage version is more cinematic than the movie.' "

Leonard also had interviewed people from the movie and asked Attenborough about why he planned to jettison Bennett's award-winning choreography. Bishop said, "He said that was 1970s choreography. But the section of 'One,' that's not 1970s choreography! That's *show* choreography. Broadway show choreography. It is generic choreography. That's the point of it. The point was to show what a show looked like, not to set a date.

"They did things in that movie that we tried in rehearsals and found out didn't work. Like having Cassie come in late. We played that game for a long time. It didn't work. It was embarrassing and it was wrong, so we took it out. How 'What I Did for Love' turned into a love song, I'll never know. So when I left that film I said to my husband, 'It's amazing. Millions of people have seen this show and understood it. Blue-collar workers, people without an education, saw *A Chorus Line* and understood it. The two people who did not get it are the director and the choreographer of that film! It was the skeleton of *A Chorus Line*. There was nothing there. There was no flavor, no taste, no beauty. Just bones. They just ruined it."

But the failure of the movie may have been the salvation of the show. The movie came and went so quickly, and was so unfavorably compared with the Broadway production, that ticket sales at the Schubert remained steady. The show had stopped selling out in the late 1970s, but the decline in its business has been very gradual. In spring of 1989 the show was doing only about half of capacity, and Papp had begun advertising it more heavily to bring business up. The Shuberts have said on more than one occasion that the show might be transferred to a smaller theater where it would regain some of its off-Broadway intimacy and perhaps raise its percentage of seats sold.

Members of the original cast have returned to the show from time to time. Nancy Lane, Sammy Williams, Clive Wilson, Kelly Bishop, Robert LuPone, were back in the 1970s. Kelly Bishop did four weeks in the early 1980s. Donna McKechnie made a much-trumpeted return in 1986, and LuPone was back in the cast in the early months of 1989.

But some will never come back. Though all the original cast members are alive and well in their late thirties or forties, several members of the creative team have passed away. Lyricist Ed Kleban died in 1987 of tongue cancer. Co-librettist James Kirkwood died April 22, 1989, also of cancer.

The Green Room at the Shubert Theatre is a shrine of sorts. One whole wall is devoted to an immense photo of Michael Bennett.

After *A Chorus Line,* Michael Bennett chose his succeeding projects carefully, but continued to be the dominating force on each project. His *Ballroom* (1978) was a financial failure but won him a Tony (with Bob Avian) for best choreography, as did *Dreamgirls* (1981, with Michael Peters).

"890 Broadway" is not the name of a musical, but it may become one yet. That's the address of the rehearsal studios Bennett bought with part of his proceeds from *ACL,* where hundreds of potential musicals were tested under the workshop process Bennett had advanced. Unfortunately, Bennett's grand vision, *Scandals,* went through several workshops there without coming into enough focus for a commercial production.

Part of the reason may have been that Bennett was increasingly troubled by health problems, which Bennett told close friends, even McKechnie, was heart disease. This was believable, considering the macerating stress of putting on Broadway musicals. But in fact, Bennett by 1985 had discovered that he was suffering from acquired immune deficiency syndrome, AIDS, which forced him, in early 1986, to withdraw as director of what had promised to be one of the most exciting concept musicals in years, Tim Rice's *Chess.* Directed by Trevor Nunn, it wound up having a short Broadway run in late spring 1988.

When Bennett announced plans to sell 890 Broadway in 1986, it provoked an outcry. How could Bennett turn his back on the theater community? Where would producers find such reasonably priced tryout space? What would this mean for musicals?

What people didn't know was that Bennett's illness was terminal. On July 2, 1987, Bennett died of an AIDS-related lymphoma at a home in Tucson, Arizona, where he had retreated, hoping the healthful climate would extend his life. His master project, *A Chorus Line,* outlived him.

Among those Bennett did not tell was his ex-wife, Donna McKechnie. But at their last meeting, she remembers, the signals were there. When she made her triumphal return to *A Chorus Line* in autumn of 1986, Joe Papp gave a dinner at the Algonquin Hotel. Among those in attendance were Bob Avian—and Bennett.

"He looked great but I hadn't seen him in a long time," McKechnie said. "The dinner enabled us to share feelings under the guise of a professional relationship. Members of the cast at that time also were invited. He was very testy with people at the dinner. He was sitting on so much, the anger and resentment. He hated not being able to control what was happening to him. He seemed weird to me. The hostility came up—but to others, not to me at all. That's what I was used to. All of a sudden I was the princess again, was the adored one.

"There were tons of flowers at the theater, saying I love you,

I love you. He came backstage before half-hour like a boy in the chorus. He grabbed my hand and held on to it like we were locked together; like we were joined at the hip. I thought, 'This is nice, but why is he so scared?' I was used to him needing a hand to hold. We walked around the theater like we had three legs. There were signs along the way that he was telling me something. But what he said was, 'The only thing I feel bad about is that I might never dance again.' I tried to reassure him by saying, 'Of course you'll dance again. I know men who have triple bypasses and who can skip and run.' I have my own mixed feelings about his inability to tell me. But I've accepted that everyone has the right to decide such things for themselves. That was the last time I saw him."

McKechnie learned that Bennett had AIDS, but only through rumors. "Like the days in *Chorus Line,* I was defending him again," she said. In spring of 1987 a friend of hers bought an apartment on Central Park South and was told that the previous owner was selling everything because he had AIDS. It was Bennett's apartment. Still, McKechnie refused to believe it.

Her resistance finally broke after Bennett died and the cause of his death was made public. McKechnie was appearing in a national tour of *Sweet Charity* at the time, and got time off to attend Bennett's memorial service at the Shubert Theatre. "I didn't know what to say," she remembers. People got up to speak about Bennett the man and Bennett the director and Bennett the choreographer. "Stephen Sondheim played a song, 'Move On,' that Michael loved so much. Michael's lawyer spoke, and his agent. But it occurred to me that it was all very show business. It was like something William Goldman would write. There was no one with real personal connections with Michael's life as a *dancer*. I realized that's why I was there. When I got up to speak I said, 'Whatever everyone else said, he was a dancer first.' And enormous applause broke out. I felt not just proud, but I felt I had represented the part of him that was the dancer, and the man that kept a lot of dancers working."

Looking back on the chorus line's stormy relationship with their director who took and gave so much, Pamela Blair said, "No matter how much we hated him, we'll always love him."

20.

EPILOGUE

"I love old churches," Don Percassi said. "Have you ever been inside a real Norman cathedral by yourself? If you ever have a chance to, go in and sit there. You'll feel a kind of intensity there. There's a sense of all this wonderful history. The people who built that cathedral were artists. Dancers are artists. Some day in some book people will read that the golden age of the United States was from 1900 to 2000 and I'll be in there, perhaps in a paragraph about *A Chorus Line*. I wish everybody could have happen to them what happened to us with that show. And I wish they would take the time, as we did, to have a meeting along the way someplace, a stop, and say, "Look, *this is happening*.' "

"The truth of the matter," Robert LuPone said, "is that ultimately no one else could understand the experience—not even Michael or Joe Papp. The only people who understand it, the only people who have a right to tell it, are the people who lived it. That's the importance of this book as far as I'm concerned."

That experience reaches through time and continues to affect their lives. The 1983 celebration made them realize that they still were carrying a lot of unresolved emotions, and so they set about to uncage them by making the oral history you now hold. Baayork Lee and Thommie Walsh organized the effort, compiling a list of questions and conducting the interviews, Lee working on the West Coast and Walsh working in New York.

"The reason this book is important," Lee said, "why Thommie and I wanted to do it, is because this book will say all the things that are true. It's important that people open this book and say, 'This is what happened.' And it was important that we got this off our chests. Everybody I interviewed felt that way afterward. Ron

Don [Kuhlman] out of everyone always seemed the calmest of people, yet he was the only one that really started out kind of hostile, because he didn't want to dredge up all of this again. Yet when we got into it, it was wonderful and he felt good afterward. With as much crap as they went through during that time, everyone's come out of it really well.

"It's been wonderful compiling this book," she said. "I just feel that in my life there is more to come. I feel it in my veins that this is just preparation for whatever it is, because I see the pavement in front once again and I am struggling down it. I'm on my way. *A Chorus Line* changed and shaped and formed a lot of ideas that I will carry on in my art and in my life. It formed a lot of good things for me, high standards. Now, when I direct a company of the show somewhere I say to them, 'It's wonderful that a producer is going to pay you for what you are about to learn.' "

During his interview with Lee in Los Angeles, Ron Dennis mused, "Publishing this book is important, I hope I might learn of things that my fellow cast members felt that I never knew about or was aware of. There's so many of those things. There is a very caring bond among all of us. I think of the people all the time. That's just how knit we are: We may not see each other but we wish each other well. I think we're getting to know one another better now, because we don't have to deal with the Godfather over our shoulder. He was a big influence on everyone's lives and it affected everyone's relationships with each other. I don't think he created it exclusively; we all create our own circumstances but he was definitely a part of all our lives.

"I feel real mellow about this interview," Dennis said. "I was nervous about doing this today, but mainly about what I was going to say. I woke up exhausted today . . . but now I'm not sleepy. I feel real coherent, relaxed. And I have a whole new perspective."

Fearful of losing the rights to their life stories once again, the original cast members spent several years in negotiations over how the book royalties would be distributed and how Walsh and Lee would be remunerated for costs they'd incurred in making the tapes and transcripts.

Important issues needed to be settled. Whose story would it be? How would it be told? Would the Big Six dominate again?

Above all, would everyone have a chance to be heard? Only by reflecting the sometimes contradictory perspectives would the book express the "group star" that every *Chorus Line* cast must try to become. Paradoxically, only by writing a book that way could the solidarity of the group be preserved. Walsh said, "I feel—then, now, and forever—that this group, no matter what happens to any of us, will always be kind of like siblings, or lovers."

The original idea was to let each of the original nineteen tell their story, then publish the raw transcripts. No commercial publisher could be found who was interested in that idea. Most suggested that an author be found to weave the memoirs into a single narrative.

A vanity press was considered as the purest way to convey the story. But everything about *A Chorus Line* had been professional. Why change that?

It took time to find the right writer for the task. One was obtained through Walsh's talent agency, International Creative Management. An outline for the project was completed in 1987, William Morrow and Company bought the project in 1988, updated interviews were conducted, and the manuscript was completed in 1989.

"For the kids on the Line," Rick Mason said, "the show changed a lot of childish attitudes. That was one thing I always resented: A lot of them were never aware of anybody else. When they were into their problems they didn't have time or couldn't see it. It's important to listen to people, to observe, to care about people and realize that you're not the only one around. In retrospect, that's probably what I learned most from *ACL:* awareness of other people's feelings. I know I would have been great doing a number, but that's neither here nor there. I let myself be hurt and I had no one else to blame other than myself and my inabilities and incapabilities at that time. If only I had done more . . . if I had been a little bolder, if I had said, 'Hey, listen to me,' I might have been given a bigger part. So I don't have anyone to point a finger at except myself. But I have grown tremendously. Possibly I would never have grown had I been pampered or part of the 'in' crowd—I wouldn't have had to, it would have all been done for me. It's an interesting concept. Things happen for a reason.

"I don't want to be painting everything black, and I don't think I have. The experiences were a plus for me. I'm sure there are going to be a lot of things I wish I had said more positively. But mine is just one fraction of what happened, seen through my eyes. The others will tell their sides. That's what makes it so fascinating: There are so many different colors that are going to be up there because there were so many colors inside us. I just hope I haven't hurt anybody because I love everyone tremendously."

APPENDIX

THEIR LIVES TO DATE

The dancers of *A Chorus Line* have gone on to achieve success not only in all areas of show business, but in the fields of fashion design, interior design, art, education, cosmetics, and social activism.

Here's their who's who:

CLIVE WILSON (CLERK)

While still involved in *A Chorus Line,* Wilson began pursuing his long-standing interest in interior design. He launched a modest free-lance business in Manhattan, which he suspended in late 1977 when he traveled to California to perform in the Los Angeles company of the show for two months. It was his intention then to leave the show, but Bennett asked him to take the role of Zach in a national touring company when the contracted Zach fell ill. Wilson opened the tour in Philadelphia and quickly found that he enjoyed life on the road, which lived up to favorite scenes of his in the film *Funny Girl.* After spending Christmas 1977 and that New Year's in Boston, Wilson left *A Chorus Line* for good. It turned out to be his swan song in show business.

After a vacation in Hong Kong and Hawaii to think things over, he made the decision to return to design full time. In late winter 1978 he formally changed his name from Clive Clerk, which he'd been using professionally throughout *A Chorus Line,* to Clive

Wilson, and opened Clive Wilson Design Associates. Specializing in residential interior design, the company maintains its base in Los Angeles, with other clients in New York, Santa Fe, and Aspen. Several of his designs have been featured in photo layouts in national magazines, including *Architectural Digest*.

RON KUHLMAN

After *A Chorus Line,* Kuhlman pursued an acting career in films, television, and theater. He costarred in the 1986 film *Shadow Play* with Cloris Leachman. He played supporting roles in *Splash* with Tom Hanks, *King of the City* with Tony Curtis, Neil Simon's *The Heartbreak Kid,* and in Mel Brooks's remake of *To Be or Not to Be*.

Among his highest-visibility TV credits are his appearances in the series *The Brady Brides,* a sequel to *The Brady Bunch*. He played Phillip, husband of Jan, the middle daughter. The concept was revived for the special, "A Very Brady Christmas," one of the highest-rated TV movies of the 1988–89 season. Two more "Brady" TV movies are in the works. He also has acted extensively in commercials.

Kuhlman has appeared in *Dynasty, Alice, Knight Rider,* and *Houston Knights,* and was a regular on *The Days of Our Lives,* playing the scheming Jimmy Porterfield.

Kuhlman has made a specialty of playing villains, or characters with a dark past. He played an accidental killer in the movie *Shadow Play* and a murderer in a production of *Heat* at one of the West Coast Equity waiver theaters where he has done a great deal of work in recent years. Among more notable productions were *Anacardium, How the Other Half Loves,* and Romulus Linney's *Heathen Valley*.

More recently he guest-starred on TV's *Hunter, Heartbeat,* and *The Munsters Today,* and played the part of the menacing Cowboy in Herb Gardner's *I'm Not Rappaport* with Artie Johnson at La Mirada Civic Theatre. Kuhlman lives in Van Nuys, California, with his wife Marsha and their daughter Greta, born in 1986.

KAY COLE

Most recently playing the role of Madame Thenardier in the Los Angeles production of *Les Misérables,* Cole has appeared in feature films including *Stand and Deliver, Coma,* and *Parent Trap.*

Off-Broadway, she played Lucy in the 1982 musical *Snoopy* and in Los Angeles played Cheryl in the Nancy Ford-Gretchen Cryer musical *I'm Getting My Act Together and Taking It on the Road.*

On TV she's performed in episodes of *Knots Landing, Hunter, The Carol Burnett Show, Police Story,* and *It Takes a Thief.*

Cole returned to Broadway in *A Chorus Line,* this time taking Lopez's role as Diana Morales.

She lives in North Hollywood with her husband, photographer Michael Lamont.

WAYNE CILENTO

Cilento has pursued a dynamic career as an award-winning dancer and choreographer, being nominated for two Tony Awards. From *A Chorus Line,* Cilento went directly into Bob Fosse's *Dancin',* for which he earned his first Tony nomination as best featured actor in a musical. He danced in *The Act* with Liza Minnelli, in the Frank Loesser revue *Perfectly Frank,* and in the film of *Annie.* He served as one of the narrators of Bob Fosse's 1986 musical *Big Deal,* and top-lined as Jack Cole in an international tour of the musical *Jack.* He also danced in dozens of TV commercials.

While remaining busy dancing on stage and television, Cilento began building a career as a choreographer starting in the early 1980s. He staged concerts "Liza in London," and "Liza at Carnegie Hall," plus music videos including Billy Joel's "Keeping the Faith" and Barry Manilow's "Read 'Em and Weep." Cilento choreographed two Broadway shows, *Jerry's Girls,* a revue of Jerry Herman songs featuring Chita Rivera; and the Richard Maltby, Jr.-David Shire musical *Baby,* which earned Cilento his second Tony nomination. Off-Broadway he choreographed *Just Once* and *Angry Housewives.*

On television he has choreographed more than two dozen commercials, including six for McDonald's and five for Dr. Pepper. Two of his commercials won Clio Awards.

In August 1982 he was featured on the cover of *Dance Magazine* in a story headlined WAYNE CILENTO: THE SAGA OF A BROADWAY DANCE MAN. He lives in Mamaroneck, New York, with his wife, Cathy, and three sons, Brian, Keith, and Doug.

BAAYORK LEE

None of the *Chorus Line* dancers has maintained as close a relationship with the show as its mother superior, Baayork Lee, who has directed and choreographed productions with evangelical zeal in dozens of cities around the world. "I've continued the passion for the theater I've always had," she said, "and I want to bring it all over the world."

She has staged productions in Australia (1977), West Germany (1977), England (1977 and 1986), Sweden (1979), Japan (1985), Austria (1987), East Germany (1988), plus a European tour (1986), a world tour (1987), and a new American tour (1989) featuring Donna McKechnie.

The *Chorus Line* productions were re-creations of Bennett's steps. She stepped out on her own in the late 1970s, choreographing *Where's Charley?* in Montclair, New Jersey, then began accumulating her own credits directing and choreographing *Barnum* in Australia (1980) with Reg Livermore, and choreographing *I Can't Keep Running in Place* off-Broadway, Phyllis Newman's *Vamps and Rideouts* in Massachusetts, and *A Broadway Baby* with Sid and Marty Krofft and Thommie Walsh at Goodspeed Opera House's Norma Terris Theatre in Chester, Connecticut.

Thanks to Roman Terleckyj, director of production, Lee has

served as resident choreographer of the Washington Opera since 1985 at the Kennedy Center in Washington, D.C. Her credits there include *The Merry Widow, Eugene Onegin, Un Ballo in Maschera, Christopher Columbus,* and Giancarlo Menotti's *Goya* with Placido Domingo.

The year 1988 was a busy one for Lee. She directed early versions of Cy Coleman's *Let 'Em Rot* (later *Welcome to the Club*) and *Starmites,* plus *Tales of Tinseltown* in New Brunswick, New Jersey, *The Coconuts* at Arena Stage in Washington, D.C., *Animal Crackers* at Huntington Theatre in Boston, and Marvin Hamlisch's *In Performance at the White House.*

Staging *A Chorus Line* in Tokyo, Lee met famed Japanese conductor Morihisa Shibuya of the Shiki Theater, and the two established an instant rapport. Shibuya, who also supervises music for Tokyo Disneyland, asked Lee to serve as Disneyland's New York talent scout. With growing respect for her work, Shibuya next introduced her to Yurichiro Watahiki, executive director of the leisure division of Lotte World, a Seoul, Korea, conglomerate. Lotte World sponsored Lee's effort to open a musical theater school in Seoul, which she hopes will serve as the prototype for such schools around the world.

In 1988, Lee launched a career as a producer. She formed Global Entertainment Productions with partners Albin Konopka and Klaus Stauffer, which made its debut in June 1989 with a musical revue for Lotte World. The revue opened in Lotte World's theater in its Seoul retail and entertainment complex. Like the schools, the revue is a prototype for what Lee envisions as a series of Broadway-style entertainments produced all over the world, using American talent in collaboration with local talent to create new scripts.

In between other projects, Lee was a prime motivator for this book. She maintains a home on Manhattan's Upper West Side.

MICHEL STUART

Stuart had come out of retirement from his dancing career to do *A Chorus Line.* When his involvement with the show ended he left dancing for good, choosing instead to return to his career as a producer.

But he didn't jump in right away. Stuart designed costumes for the Broadway show *A Day in Hollywood/A Night in the Ukraine.* He also worked as a private acting coach and taught courses in auditioning for musical theater. But Stuart had bigger plans. "I wanted to learn business," he said. "Theater is not very big business. Theater is almost a cottage industry. I learned *big business.*" He went to work in one of the city's toughest businesses, the garment industry, designing a successful line of actionwear, sportswear, and dance clothes called Michel Stuart the Dancer.

Stuart's biggest credit after *A Chorus Line* was producing *Nine,* the 1982 musical based on Federico Fellini's film *8½,* which won seven Tony Awards including best musical. He also produced off-Broadway's *Cloud Nine,* which won the Outer Circle Critics Award and an Obie. His next show, *The Tap Dance Kid* (1983), won two Tonys, including best choreography (Danny Daniels).

During the run of that show he helped launch the New York City Board of Education's Early Stages program to get children involved in theater.

As of June 1989, Stuart said he was raising funds for a play, a TV movie, and a movie for theatrical release. He recently relocated to California.

DONNA McKECHNIE

After leaving *A Chorus Line* to "save" the London opening, McKechnie came back to New York without Bennett. She was physically and emotionally exhausted from the political roller-coaster ride of British Equity and said she was "feeling defeated in every way."

She also was beginning to realize that her marriage to Bennett was over. Bennett had spent the previous year retreating into his work. She felt that their communication was "no longer about friendship, it was about work." And the separations had grown longer and longer.

During their separation after London, she played in *Misalliance* at the Williamstown Theatre Festival in Massachusetts, while Bennett went into rehearsals for *Ballroom.*

In a very theatrical way, their relationship had grown into something resembling that of their *Chorus Line* roles, Zach and Cassie—Cassie accusing Zach of workaholism, and Zach rebuffing her.

The loss of his friendship was as upsetting to her as the dissolution of their marriage, she said. "I felt very abandoned. I didn't understand it. It was not about his being homosexual. That was not the issue. He was a very faithful husband. But he was very frightened to be loved by someone who was not being paid. I took it as rejection, his fear of intimacy.

"When I filed for divorce I said, 'Why did you marry me?' He said, 'At the time it was a whim; it seemed like the right thing to do.' I was in such a victim state and so hurt I believed that's what he meant—that he never really loved me. But I realize now that he couldn't tell me the truth. How do you say to someone 'I can't stand to be in this relationship because I can't stand the feelings that come up'? When I'd accuse him of never loving me, he'd say, 'I never married anybody else.' He meant that as a compliment."

After the divorce, McKechnie's career was overwhelmed by illness. Aches and pains that had seemed routine suddenly incapacitated her. The diagnosis was rheumatoid arthritis, which became so severe by 1979 that McKechnie prepared to face life as an invalid. She says now that she believes the stress and anger engendered by her unhappy marriage and the divorce exacerbated the affliction.

She credits her recovery to two years of vitamins, therapy, holistic treatments, and psychotherapy. She returned to the stage in 1981 with a Chicago production of the Nancy Ford-Gretchen Cryer musical *I'm Getting My Act Together and Taking It on the Road.* She appeared in James Lapine's *Table Settings,* did guest appearances on TV's *Fame, Cheers, Family Ties,* and several variety shows, and toured with a nightclub act.

She produced and choreographed *Let Me Sing and I'm Happy,* a revue of Berlin, Kern, and Gershwin music in Burbank, California, and starred in *Get Happy* at the Westwood Theater in Los Angeles, choreographed by Tony Stevens.

McKechnie made what amounted to a comeback in 1986 when she returned to playing Cassie for several months in *A Chorus Line* on Broadway. The return, which attracted a great deal of press attention, replenished her visibility. Bob Fosse saw her and asked her to take the title role of *Sweet Charity* on tour, his last production.

In 1987 she opened in *Annie Get Your Gun* at the Geary Theater in San Francisco, and then in Florida. In 1988 she starred in *Can-Can* at London's Strand Theater, after heading the first English-speaking *Chorus Line* in Paris at the Chatelet Theater. In 1989 she completed a record-breaking tour of *A Chorus Line,* directed by Baayork Lee, and was planning to appear again as *Sweet Charity* in 1990 at Harrahs hotels in Lake Tahoe and Atlantic City.

Currently she is designing a one-woman concert for Disney World in Tokyo and is developing a TV movie script based on her experience recovering from arthritis.

McKechnie maintains homes in Laguna Beach, California, and New York City.

KELLY (CAROLE) BISHOP

Bishop has spent the years since *A Chorus Line* working almost continuously in many media.

In movies, she played Jill Clayburgh's neurotic friend Elaine in *An Unmarried Woman,* and Jennifer Grey's mother in *Dirty Dancing,* among other credits.

She appeared as co-star in Norman Lear's TV series *A Year at the Top,* starred in Mike Nichols's ABC series *The Thorns,* co-starred with Cloris Leachman in "Advice to the Lovelorn," an NBC movie of the week, and was guest star on *Hawaii Five-O, Hart to Hart,* and *Kate and Allie.* Soap opera credits include *Ryan's Hope* and *As the World Turns.*

In theater, Bishop was chosen by Michael Bennett to take part in his workshops of his last musical, *Scandals.* She was standby for Judith Ivey in the Broadway production of *Precious Sons,* did a

1983 tour in *Pal Joey* directed by Tom O'Horgan, played the sultry Maxine in two resident theater productions of Tennessee Williams's *Night of the Iguana* at Virginia Stage Company and the McCarter Theatre in Princeton, New Jersey. She played the countess in *A Little Night Music* at the Berkshire Theatre Festival and at Philadelphia's Walnut Street Theater.

She appeared off-Broadway at the American Place Theatre in *The Blessing* in spring 1989. She lives on Manhattan's Upper West Side with her husband, Lee Leonard.

THOMMIE (THOMAS J.) WALSH

Walsh has built an award-winning career as a choreographer of theater, nightclubs, and commercials.

Almost immediately upon leaving *A Chorus Line* he served as associate choreographer to Tommy Tune on the off-Broadway musical *The Best Little Whorehouse in Texas,* which transferred to Broadway for a four-year run. That was the beginning of a successful collaboration with Tune, which continued with *A Day in Hollywood/A Night in the Ukraine* (1980), on which Walsh was billed as cochoreographer. For *Hollywood/Ukraine*, Walsh won his first Tony Award for best choreography, which he shared with Tune. Walsh was listed as artistic associate on Tune's next musical, *Nine* (1982), which won seven Tony Awards. Walsh and Tune shared equal director-choreographer billing on *My One and Only* (1983), which won Walsh his second Tony Award for best choreography, again, shared with Tune.

Walsh was solo choreographer for *The 1940s Radio Hour* in 1979 and *Do Patent Leather Shoes Really Reflect Up?* on Broadway; *Lucky Stiff* off-Broadway; *Dancin' in the Streets* at the Tropicana Hotel in Atlantic City, and *A Broadway Baby* at Goodspeed Opera House's Norma Terris Theatre in Chester, Connecticut. He's also served as show "doctor" on several Broadway musicals in the 1980s.

His extensive nightclub choreography includes acts for Mitzi Gaynor, Chita Rivera, Joel Grey, Barbara Cook, Juliet Prowse, Donna McKechnie, and Lorna Luft.

He's made nationally aired commercials for Orange Crush, Dr. Pepper, Seiko, the Mormon Church, Perdue chicken, and IBM. He has made two educational dance videos for Hoctor Records.

Walsh makes his home on Manhattan's Upper West Side in the same apartment where he lived during the making of *A Chorus Line*.

NANCY LANE

Within a month of leaving *A Chorus Line,* Lane had an agent, a publicist, and a job in television, where she has maintained a career as an actress and writer. She has appeared as guest star on a variety of shows including *Dear John, My Sister Sam, Matlock, Remington Steele, Trapper John, M.D.,* and *Who's the Boss?*

She was a star of the TV series *Moscow Bureau,* and was a regular on two MTM series, *The Duck Factory,* playing a "nice Jewish girl," Andrea Levin; and *Rhoda,* playing a "nice Italian girl," Tina Molinari. In Paramount's *Angie,* she played Sister Mary Catherine.

Her favorite script-writing credit is an episode of *Taxi,* about Elaine, a divorced cab driver with two kids, who is reunited with an old school chum. Lane also has produced a cable television show, and has worked as an acting coach. She settled in Santa Monica, California, and married Dennis Fisher in 1987. Her son, Benjamin, born in 1988, already has an agent and does national TV commercials.

"*A Chorus Line* was the perfect vehicle for me," she said of the way it helped boost her TV career. "I used to say that if I never worked in a Broadway show again it would be too soon, but I have since changed my tune, I miss it terribly."

PATRICIA GARLAND

After the knee injury that ended her tenure in *A Chorus Line,* Garland had a chance to reconsider her career. Following her Buddhist faith, she chanted to change her karma. She decided to overcome her shyness by becoming more extroverted and assertive, and by cultivating her acting career.

She played Patty Andrews in Steven Spielberg's *1941,* Major in Clint Eastwood's *Heartbreak Ridge,* and Beatrice with Burt Reynolds and Dolly Parton in the movie of *The Best Little Whorehouse in Texas. Whorehouse* was choreographed by Tony Stevens, the man who had invited her to that long-ago *Chorus Line* taping session.

On television, Garland has appeared as guest star on *The Jeffersons* and *Murder, She Wrote, The Tortellis,* and in a variety of commercials.

After two operations on her knee, Garland underwent an athlete's rehabilitation with a trainer from UCLA and launched a parallel career in choreography. She choreographed *We Open in New Haven* for Showtime, and staged dances for James Kirkwood's play *Legends* with Mary Martin and Carol Channing. She also was assistant director and choreographer for *Hollywood at the Bowl.*

Most recently she has worked as co-choreographer and assistant director for *It Came from Beyond,* a "live cinema" production aimed for Broadway.

Garland also has resumed her involvement with *A Chorus Line,* directing and staging her own versions of the show for the San Diego Civic Light Opera, the Long Beach Civic Light Opera, La Mirada Civic Light Opera, the Santa Barbara Theatre, and the San Jose Civic Light Opera.

She lives in Los Angeles.

RONALD DENNIS

Dennis quickly made contacts in West Coast television and theater and within months of leaving *A Chorus Line* made a guest-starring appearance in the series *Baretta.* Major series in which he has appeared include *Chico and the Man, Welcome Back, Kotter,* and *Lav-*

erne and Shirley. He also performed on "The People's Choice Awards."

He kept in touch with Broadway, however, creating the role of one of the New Rhythm Boys, a singing and dancing trio that narrated the 1983 musical *My One and Only.*

Dennis performed the Leading Player (the Ben Vereen role) in the second national tour of *Pippin,* appeared in the first national tour of *La Cage Aux Folles,* and danced in the national tour of Bob Fosse's *Dancin'.* In California he did *Bells Are Ringing* at the Dorothy Chandler Pavilion in Los Angeles. *The Crucifer of Blood* with Charlton Heston at the Ahmanson Theatre, and *Kiss Me, Kate* at the California Music Theater in Pasadena.

He lives in Los Angeles.

DON PERCASSI

After Percassi worked in *A Chorus Line* in New York and Los Angeles, Gower Champion offered him a principal understudy and small part in the original cast of *42nd Street.* Percassi remained with the show throughout its eight-and-a-half-year run.

Percassi said, "I was a dancer *before* I was born," but he still studies, with Roy Lozano, whom he describes as "one of the few teachers who still gives dancers a technique." Percassi also is an avid cyclist, painter, computer enthusiast, and collector of vintage radios.

RENEE BAUGHMAN

Baughman established a reputation as a talented and reliable directorial and choreographic assistant and worked extensively in theater and movies for six years after leaving *A Chorus Line.*

She served as choreographer Christopher Chadman's assistant

on the 1983 Broadway musical *Merlin,* assisted director Michael Shawn on *Al Jolson, Tonight,* assisted Tony Stevens on the movie of *The Best Little Whorehouse in Texas,* and assisted Carl Jablonski on the 1983 "Happy Birthday Bob" Bob Hope TV special. She worked on the 1980 "Milliken Breakfast Show" and on a 1981 IBM industrial show.

Other credits include dancing with Peter Allen and the Rockettes at Radio City in 1982 and at the Los Angeles Pantages Theater in 1983.

As an actress she did a sketch with actor Gavin McLeod on "The World of Disney" twenty-fifth anniversary TV show, a sketch with David Letterman for *Mary,* and appeared on the 1981 Academy Awards show and the 1981 Grammy Hall of Fame show. She then established a fertile collaboration with producer-director Michael Arceneaux, acting as his assistant on a series of fashion shows and special events for Bill Blass (1982–84), Calvin Klein (1982–84), Jaeger (1984), Geoffrey Beene (1983), Karl Lagerfeld (1983, at Radio City Music Hall) and Basco (1983, at the Red Parrot club). Internationally, she has done fashion shows for Elizabeth De Senneville/Murjani (1984) in Paris, and Ferragamo (1984) in Milan.

Baughman currently works as marketing manager for the cosmetics firm Clinique International, and lives on Manhattan's Upper East Side.

RICK MASON

Mason left *A Chorus Line* in 1976 and did a number of industrial shows, some overseas and some in the United States. He moved to Los Angeles at the end of 1976 and danced in a series of TV specials featuring the Carpenters, Cher, and Mary Tyler Moore. Moore's show became a series, in which Mason appeared for the first thirteen weeks. In 1979 he began a year-long tour with Chita Rivera and her nightclub act. It provided a neat bookend to his career. His first professional dancing job was with Rivera in the

Dallas Summer Musical Theater when he was nineteen—and the 1979–80 tour with her proved to be his last, at age thirty.

Mason had always been bothered by sore muscles, so he decided to attend a massage school and earn a masseur's license so he could help others with the same problem. He also began studying nutrition, exercise, and pressure point application, and when he opened his business in California the next year he quickly attracted a sizable clientele. Continuing his involvement in show business, he worked for a locations company, scouting sites for commercials, TV shows, and movies.

In 1983 he left his business and moved back to his hometown of Phoenix, Arizona, to reestablish ties with his family. He worked with his mother in her consignment and antique store until it was sold in 1986. In 1987 he launched a house-cleaning service.

Mason now is engaged in what he calls a "journey of spiritual quest," which has proven to be "an interesting and ongoing challenge above all others." He is deeply involved with Animal Rights work. He keeps a house ninety minutes north of Phoenix with his five dogs and there listens to the quiet. He says, "To take the time and feel the rhythm of the universe is, to me, what life is all about."

PAMELA BLAIR

Blair has shifted easily among musicals, comedy and drama, for stage, television, and film.

Her major credits are in each of those areas. She originated the role of Amber in the 1978 Broadway musical *The Best Little Whorehouse in Texas,* played hot-to-trot housewife Rita Mae Bristow in the soap opera *Loving,* danced in the chorus of the film *Annie,* played opposite Peter O'Toole in the TV movie "Svengali," and appeared as "Claire Huxtable's" hairdresser on *The Cosby Show.*

On stage, Blair appeared in the Broadway musical *King of Hearts,* in the Genevieve Bujold role and acted opposite Mark Hamill and Robert Joy in Larry Shue's comedy, *The Nerd.*

Blair's resident and off-Broadway credits include *Real Life Funnies,* the Larry Gelbart-Maury Yeston musical *12345* at Manhattan Theatre Club, *The Hit Parade* at Manhattan Punch Line, Michael Weller's *Split* at Second Stage, *Einstein and the Polar Bear* at Hartford Stage Company, and Mike Nichols's *Double Feature* at Long Wharf Theater in New Haven, Connecticut.

On TV she's done *All My Children* and *The Days and Nights of Molly Dodd* with Blair Brown.

Blair lives in northern New Jersey.

SAMMY WILLIAMS

The Tony Award was a mixed blessing for Williams. "At one time I felt that I didn't deserve it," he said. "For a very long time I couldn't look at the Tony, couldn't touch it. Then one day I up and said to myself, 'Sam, you really do deserve this award.' It was then I started to come to terms with myself and all the things that had happened in *Chorus Line*. What's happened in the intervening years is that I grew into my self and my success."

After his initial stint in *A Chorus Line,* Williams played a drug pusher in an episode of *Kojak*. He went back to performing in *A Chorus Line* four times. Life imitated art in 1984 when he fell and broke his foot during the show's opening number. But he soon was back on his feet and performed in the 1986 European tour, directed by Baayork Lee. "It got better each time I did it," he said. "The fact that I grew up and had some of my own life experience, it just added to the quality of the role. It's the way I think Michael always wanted the part to be played. I felt good."

Williams also directed a production of *A Chorus Line* in Greenville, South Carolina. His last stage appearance was in the 1987 AIDS benefit at the Pasadena Civic Auditorium, in which nearly the entire original cast took part.

"The last time I played Paul I felt I really had grown into the part," he said. "It was Sam—*my* feelings about being a human being, *my* feelings about being gay. It was an expression of me. I feel it is what Michael always wanted me to do. I didn't have that at the time—having grown up and as life presented itself. I grew into myself, I grew into the character. I could express myself much more deeply, much more honestly.

"Looking back on this experience as I've read it," Williams said, "I see how my life was full of fear, anger, and limitation. I've grown since then and have become the free, loving, caring, beautiful person I've always been meant to be. I'll forever cherish those memories of the past in my heart as I move forward to a much higher, loving place in my life. I thank *A Chorus Line* for giving me the opportunity to look at myself and to grow. I am forever grateful."

PRISCILLA LOPEZ

Lopez won the 1980 Tony Award for best featured actress for her performance as Harpo in *A Day in Hollywood/A Night in the Ukraine.* For a week she also played Liliane La Fleur, the tyrannical producer in the musical *Nine.*

Off-Broadway she starred in *Extremities, Key Exchange, Non Pasquale,* and *Buck,* and top-lined in two shows in Los Angeles, *Irma La Douce* and *Vanities.*

She had featured roles in two films, *Cheaper to Keep Her* and *Revenge of the Nerds II.*

Lopez has worked often in television, starring in the series *In the Beginning.* She appeared in four CBS movies of the week: "Command in Hell," "Jesse," "Doubletake," and "Intimate Strangers," was a regular on the TV series *Kay O'Brien,* and *A Year at the Top,* and appeared as guest star on *All in the Family, Trapper John, M.D.,* and *Family.*

Her voice may be familiar to TV watchers from her dozens of commercial voice-overs. She says she has done everything in show business, except Shakespeare.

Lopez lives on Manhattan's Upper West Side with her husband, Vincent J. Fanuele, a Broadway conductor and musician, and their two children, Alexander and Gabriella.

ROBERT LUPONE

LuPone costarred in the autumn 1989 film *High Stakes* with Sally Kirkland. His TV appearances include the characters Zach Grayson in *All My Children,* Neil Corey in *Another World,* Chester Wallace in *Ryan's Hope,* and Tom Bergman in *Search for Tomorrow.*

Since *A Chorus Line,* LuPone has been in and out of the show, appearing most recently starting in late 1988. He was featured on the cover of *The New York Times*'s April 1989 progress report on long-running shows, in which Mel Gussow hailed *ACL* and *Anything Goes* as "the best musicals on Broadway."

In addition to playing a director onstage, LuPone became one in real life. During the 1980s, LuPone has devoted most of his energy to serving as executive director with Bernard Telsey of the Manhattan Class Company, an off-off-Broadway theater "dedicated to finding and developing a new generation of playwrights and theater artists."

Headquartered at the Nat Horne Theater on West Forty-second Street's Theater Row, MCC has a core of sixty actors, directors, playwrights, and designers. LuPone and Telsey organized the theater in 1981 with a group of New York University theater students they were teaching. MCC was incorporated in 1983 and won not-for-profit status in 1985.

Under LuPone and Telsey's management MCC offers classes, workshops, and open studios, in addition to presenting a full season of one-act and full-length plays. Special projects include a summer lab, marathon play-reading weekends, and a rehabilitative theater program designed to help amputees and paralytics. Among its many productions, Alan Bowne's *Beirut* transferred to an off-Broadway run.

LuPone lives in northern New Jersey, and says his career as an artist is "just beginning."

INDEX

INDEX

ABOUT THE AUTHOR

Robert Viagas is a feature writer, critic, and editor in the arts for newspapers on Connecticut's Gold Coast. He has written for the *New Haven Register, Stamford Advocate, Fairpress, Newsday, USA Today, The Times* of London, *Playbill,* the Los Angeles Times-Washington Post News Service, and Gannett Newspapers. He has taught journalism at Fairfield University, and lives in Westchester County, New York.

BALDWIN PUBLIC
3 1115 00305 8673

28 DAYS

14
DAY